MOBILE SUIT GUNDAM THUNDERBOLT

YASUO OHTAGAKI

HAJIME YATATE • YOSHIYUKI TOMINO

3

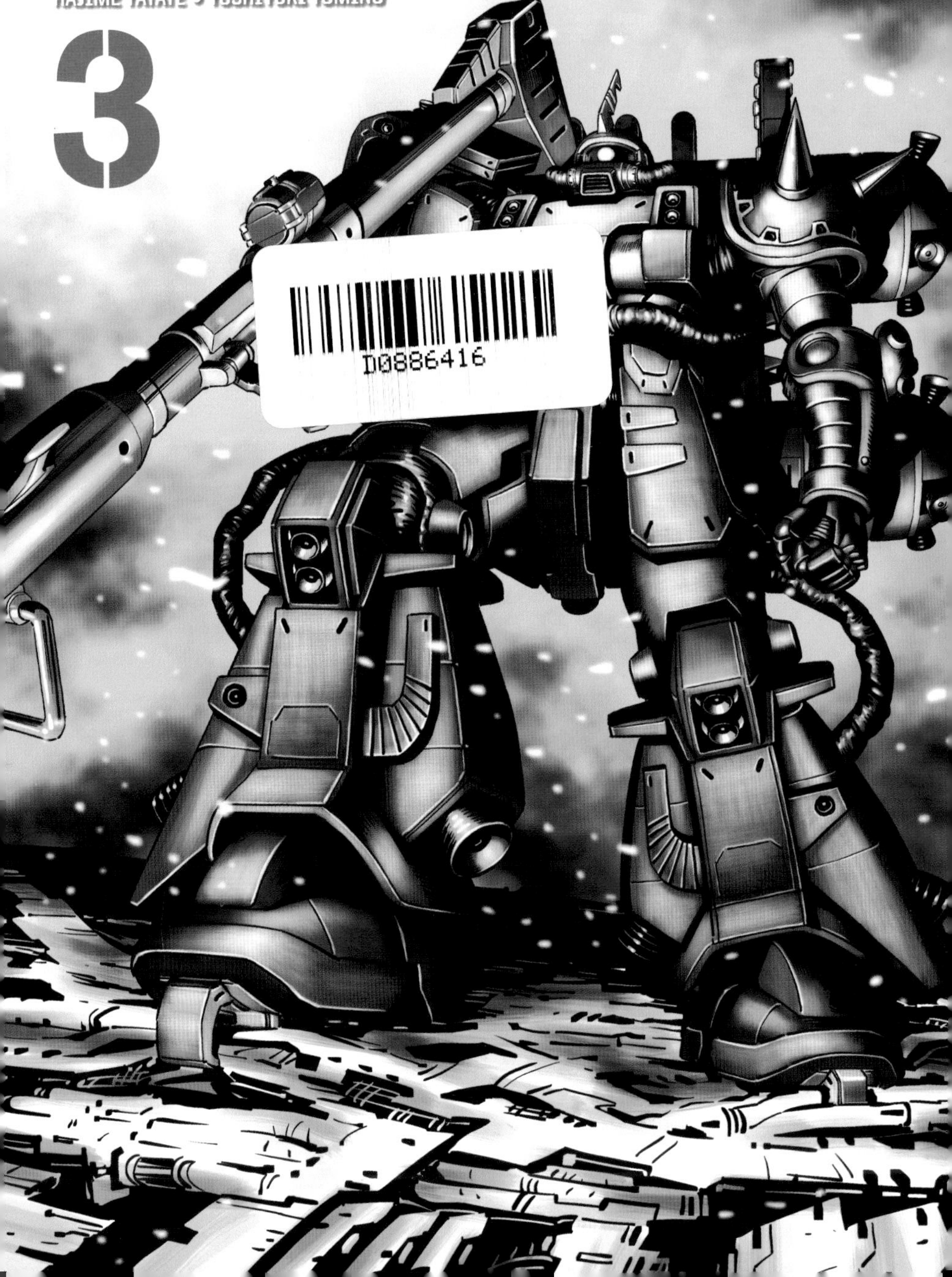

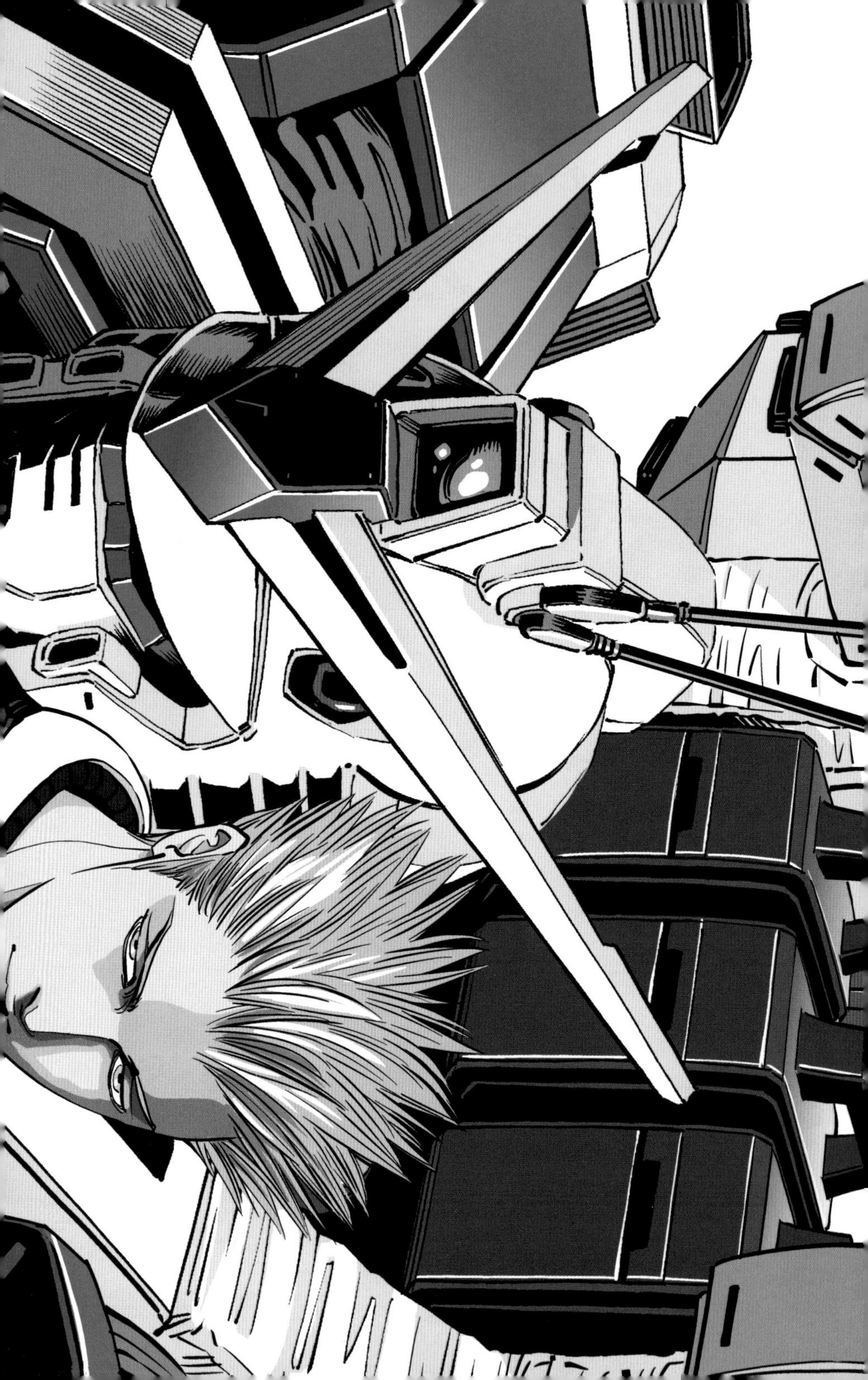

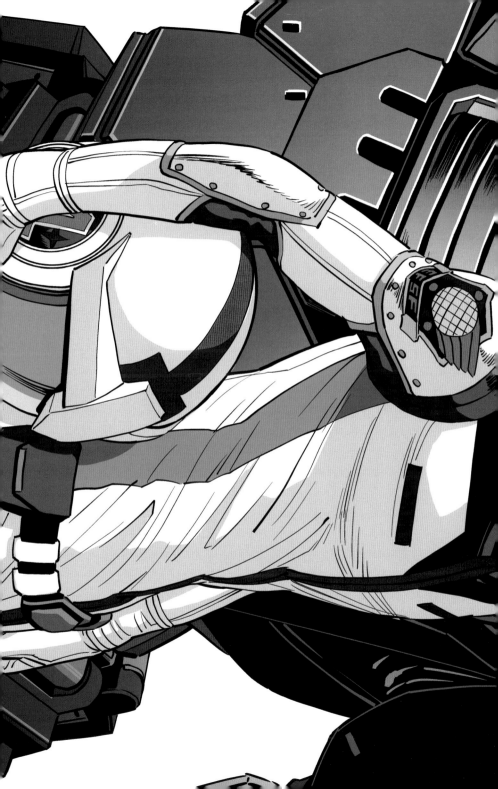

MOBILE SUIT GUNDAM
THUNDERBOLT
3

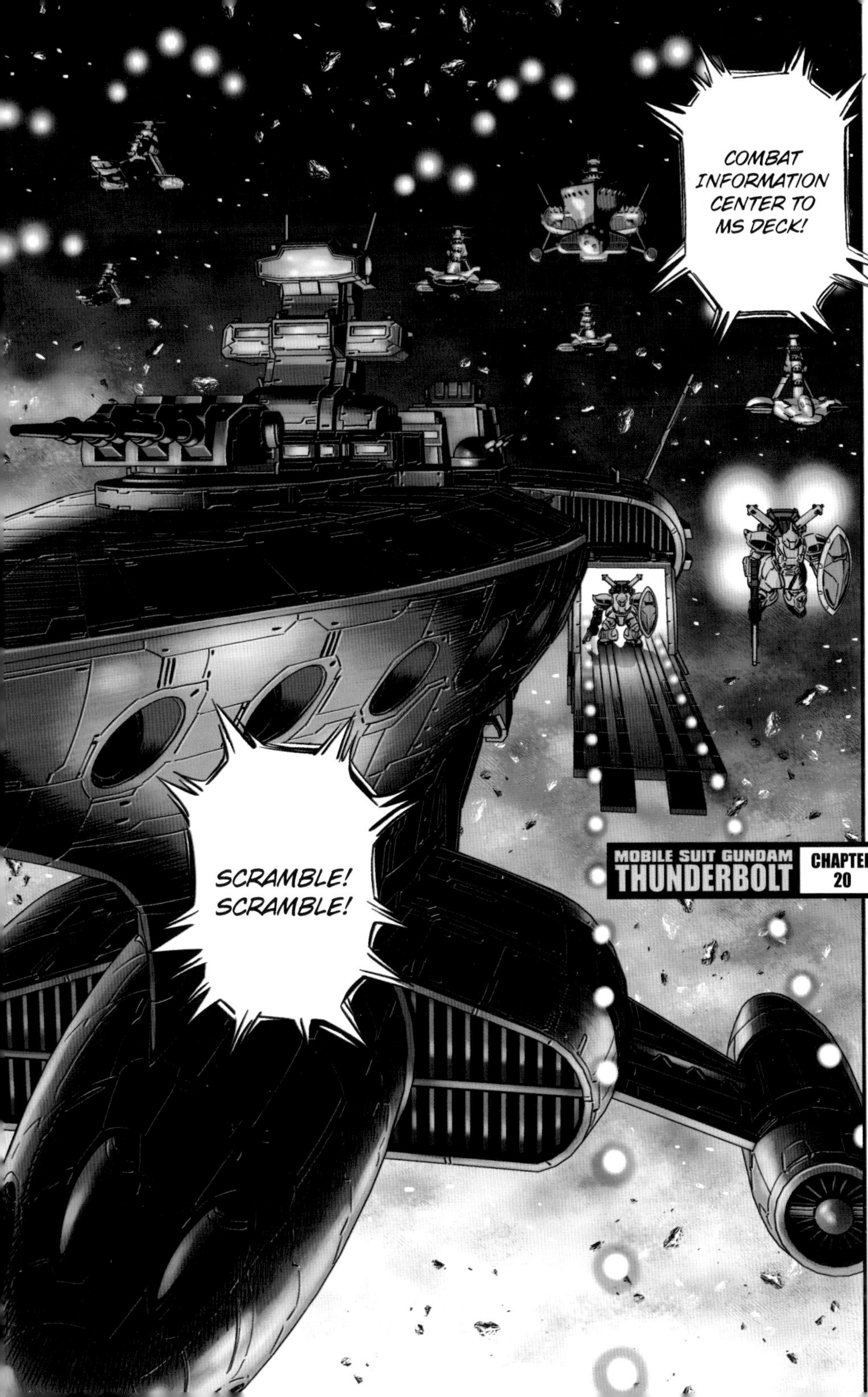
COMBAT INFORMATION CENTER TO MS DECK!
MOBILE SUIT GUNDAM THUNDERBOLT
CHAPTER 20
SCRAMBLE! SCRAMBLE!

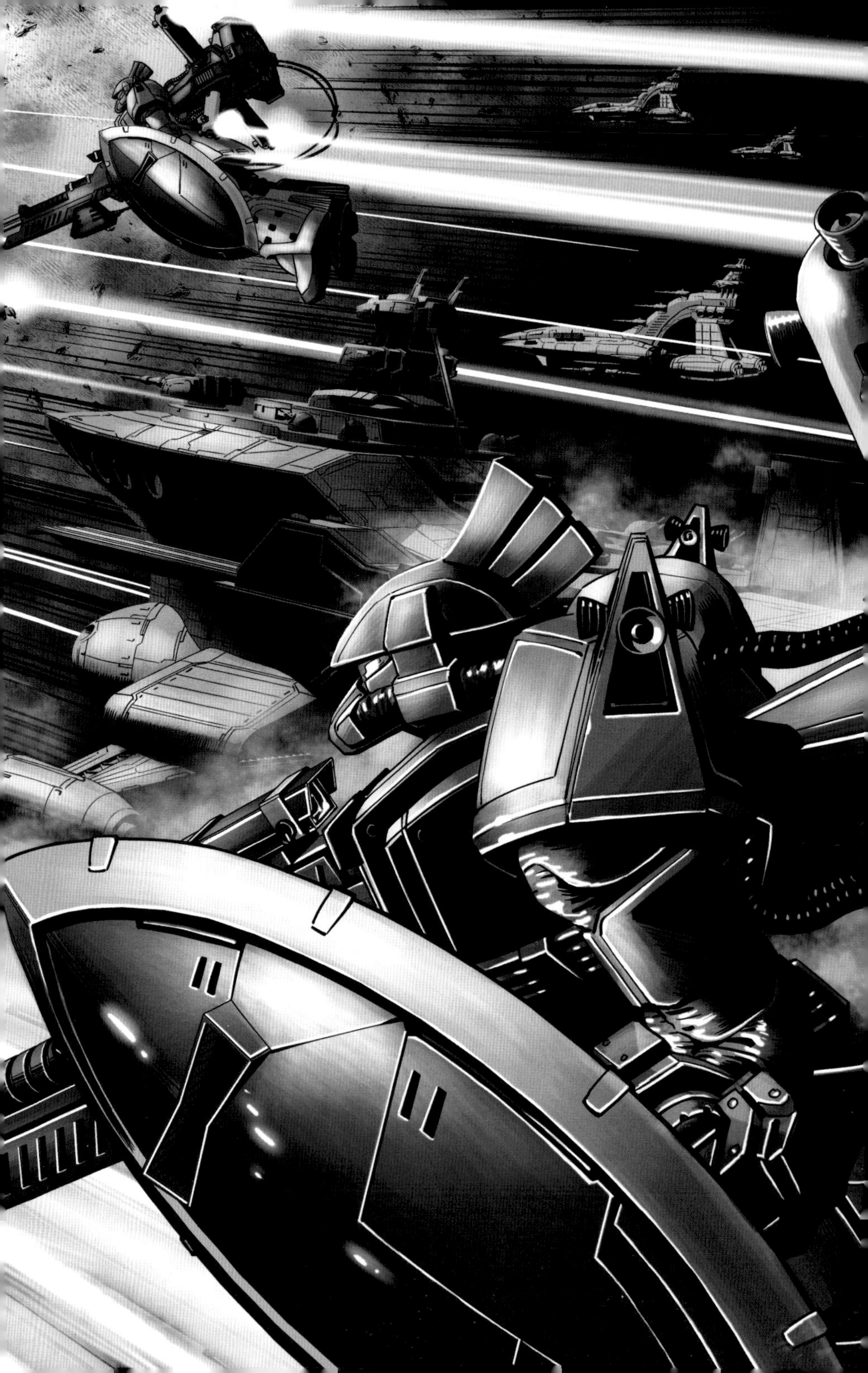

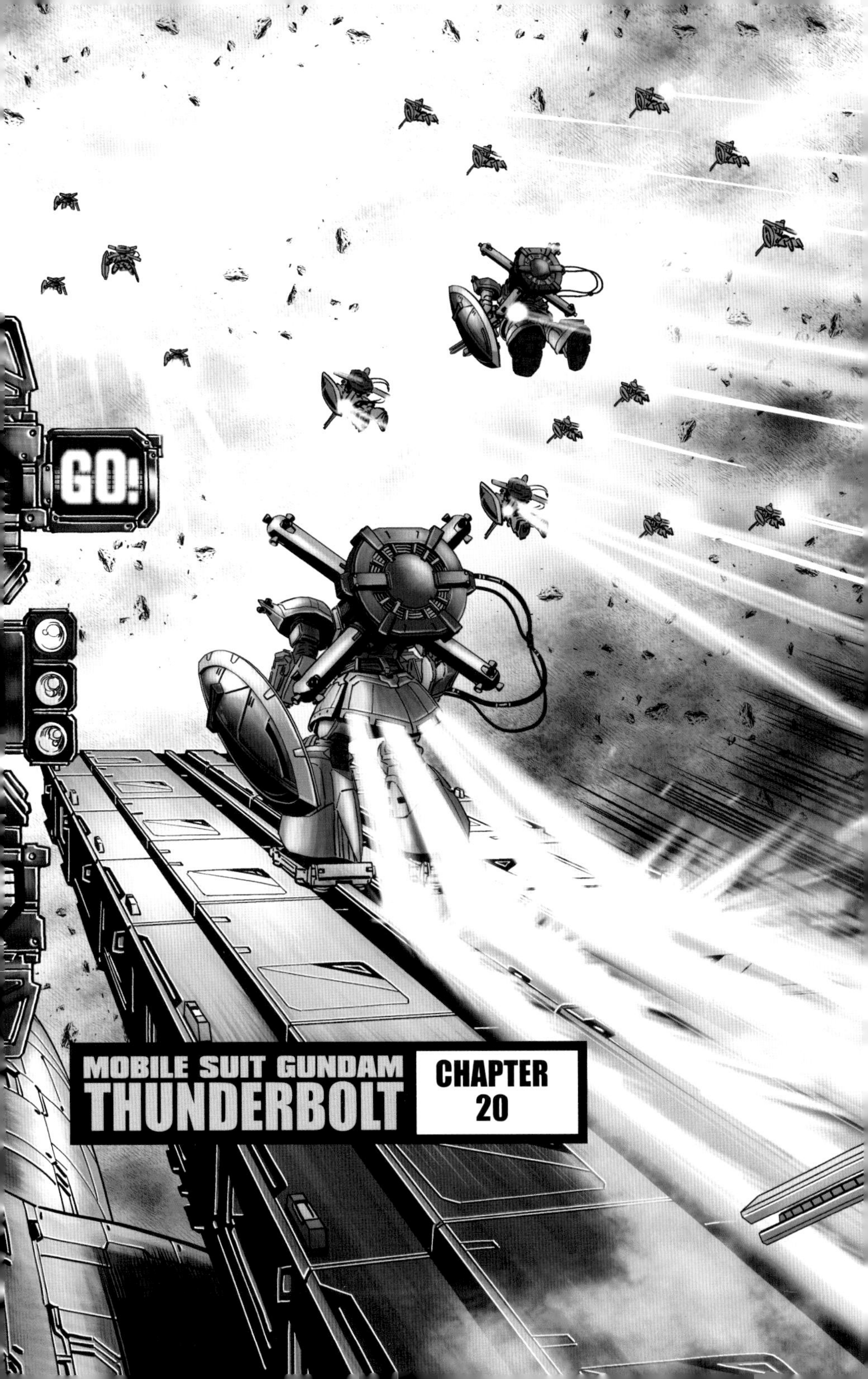
GO!
MOBILE SUIT GUNDAM
THUNDERBOLT
CHAPTER
20

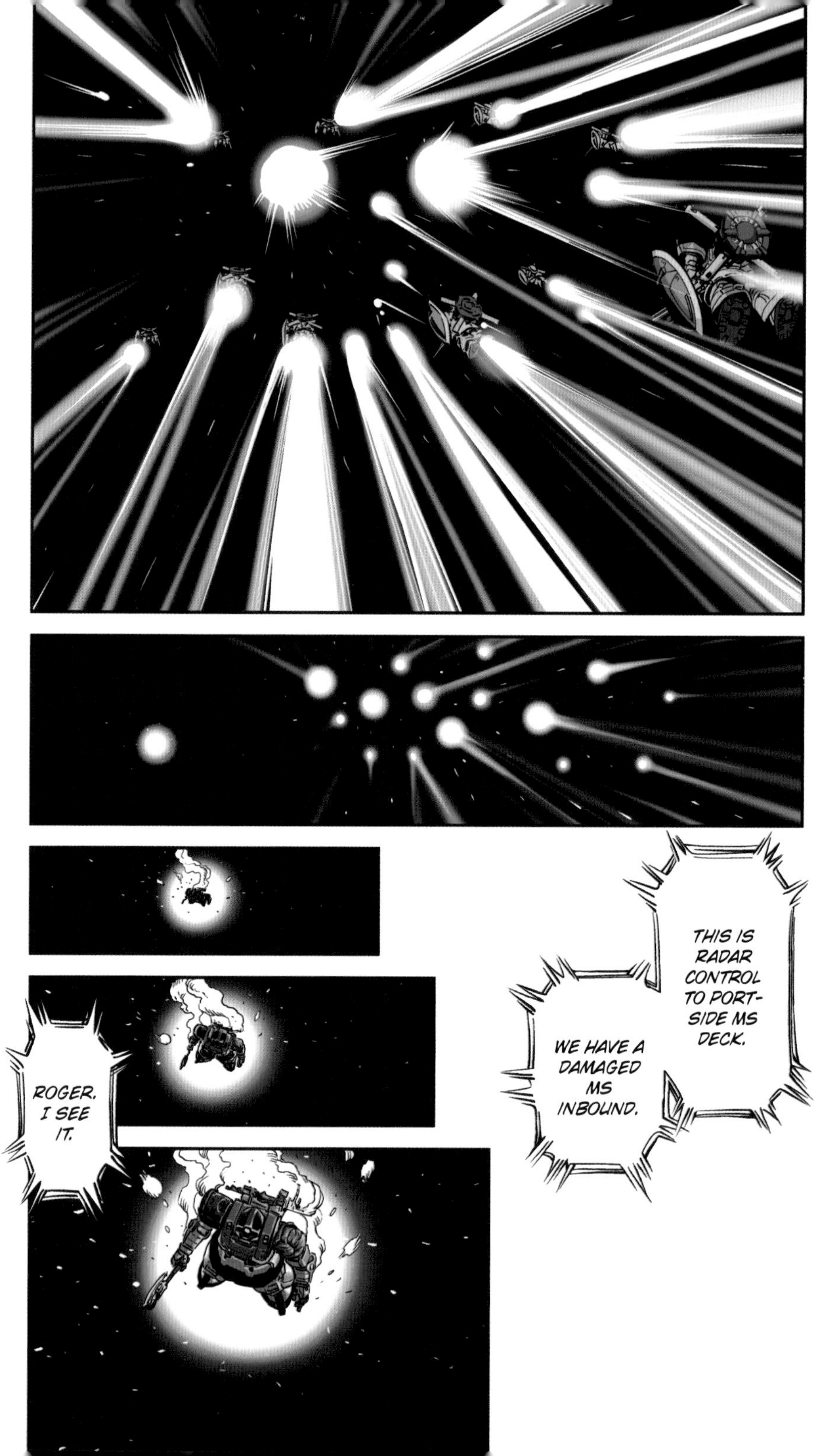
THIS IS RADAR CONTROL TO PORT-SIDE MS DECK.
WE HAVE A DAMAGED MS INBOUND.
ROGER. I SEE IT.

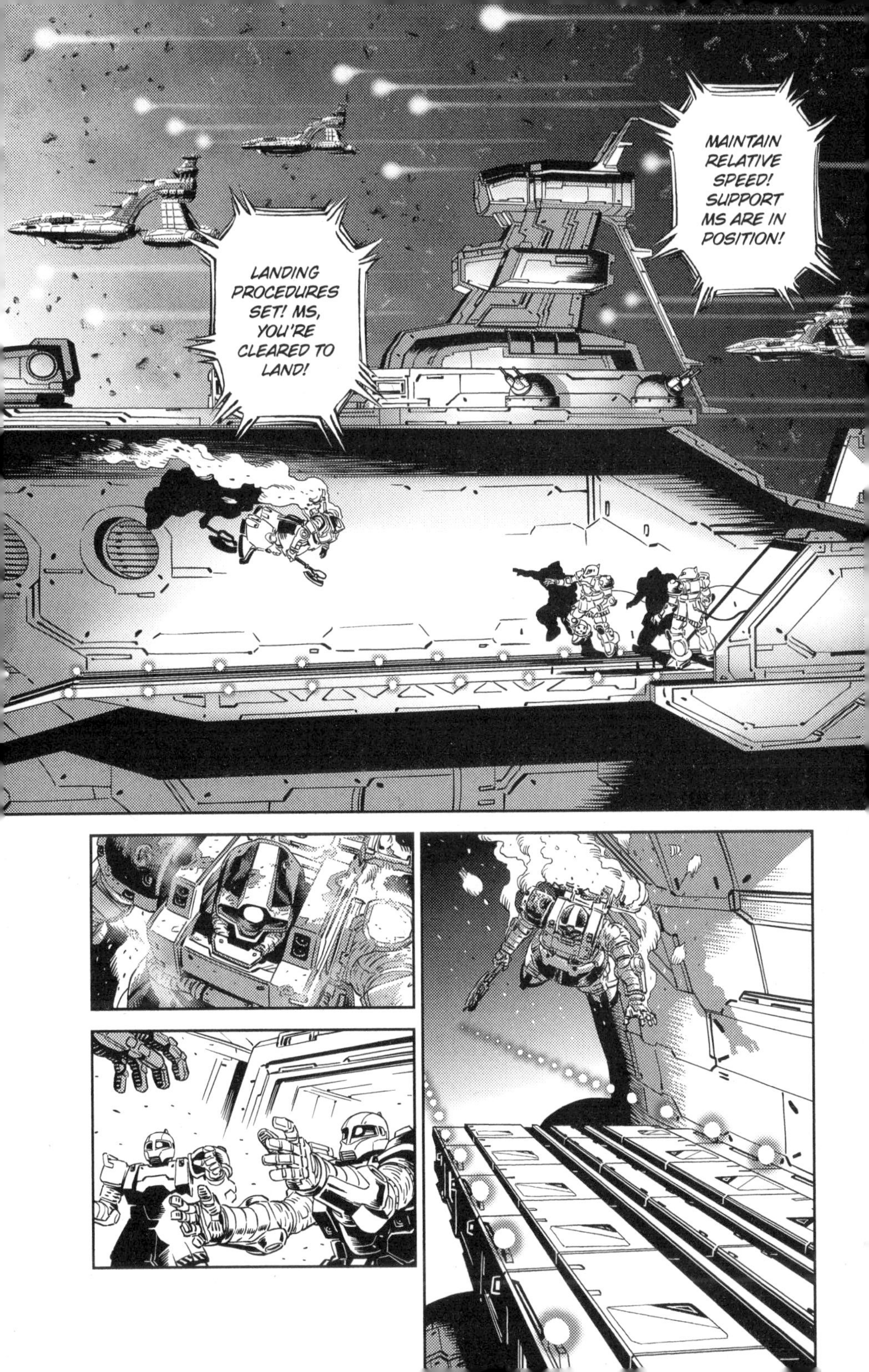
MAINTAIN RELATIVE SPEED! SUPPORT MS ARE IN POSITION!
LANDING PROCEDURES SET! MS, YOU'RE CLEARED TO LAND!

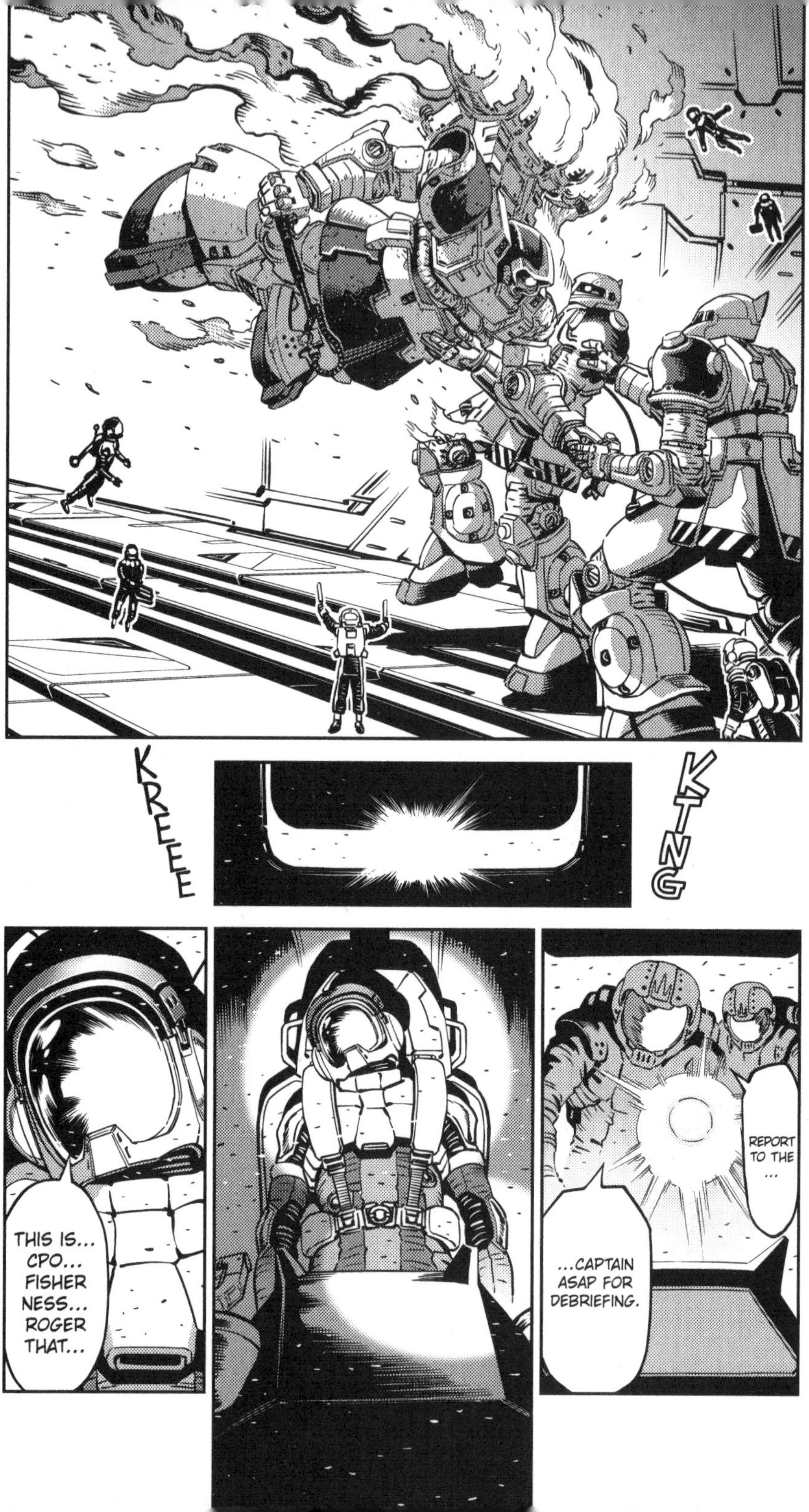
KTING
KREEE
REPORT TO THE ...
...CAPTAIN ASAP FOR DEBRIEFING.
THIS IS... CPO... FISHER NESS... ROGER THAT...

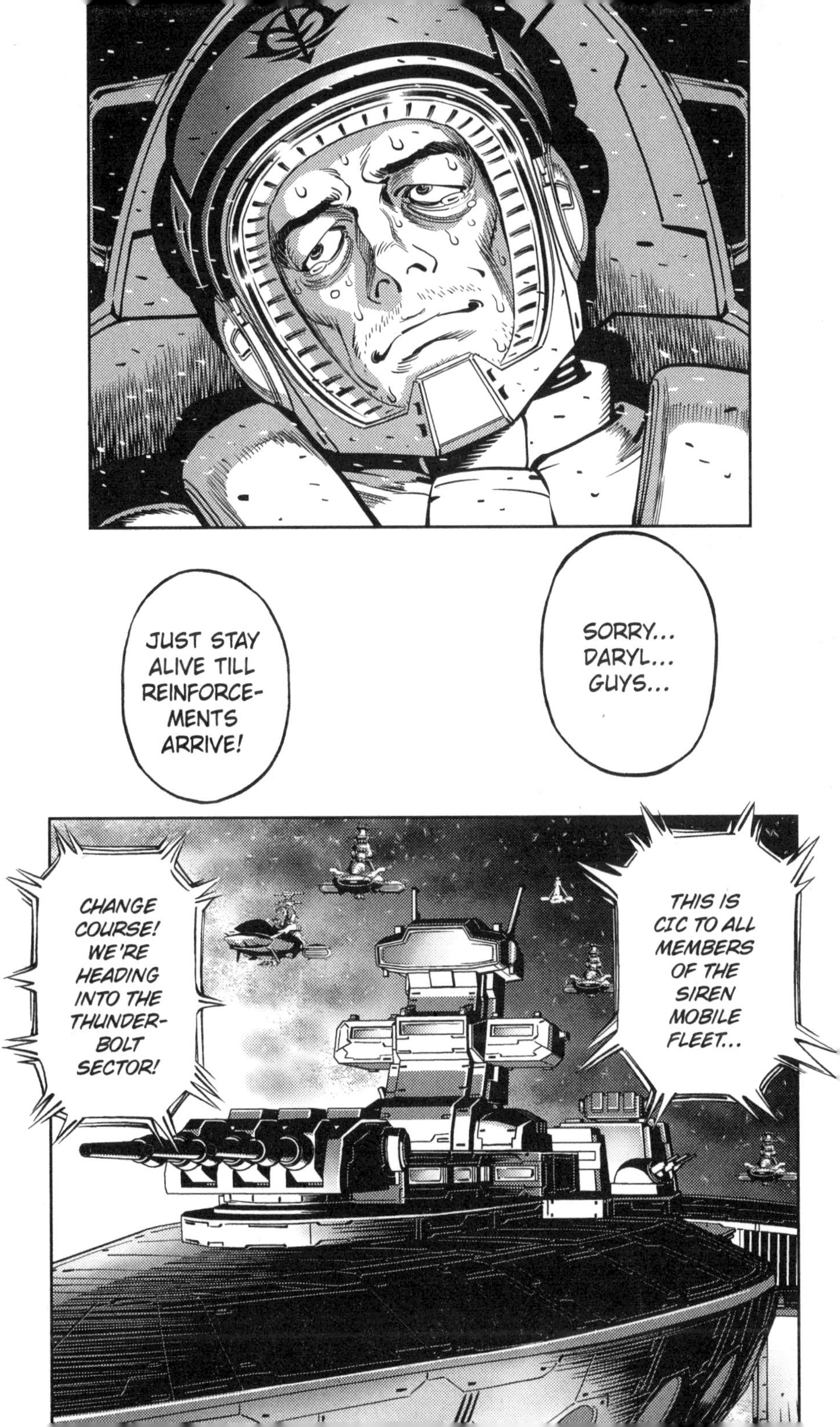
SORRY... DARYL... GUYS...
JUST STAY ALIVE TILL REINFORCEMENTS ARRIVE!
THIS IS CIC TO ALL MEMBERS OF THE SIREN MOBILE FLEET...
CHANGE COURSE! WE'RE HEADING INTO THE THUNDERBOLT SECTOR!

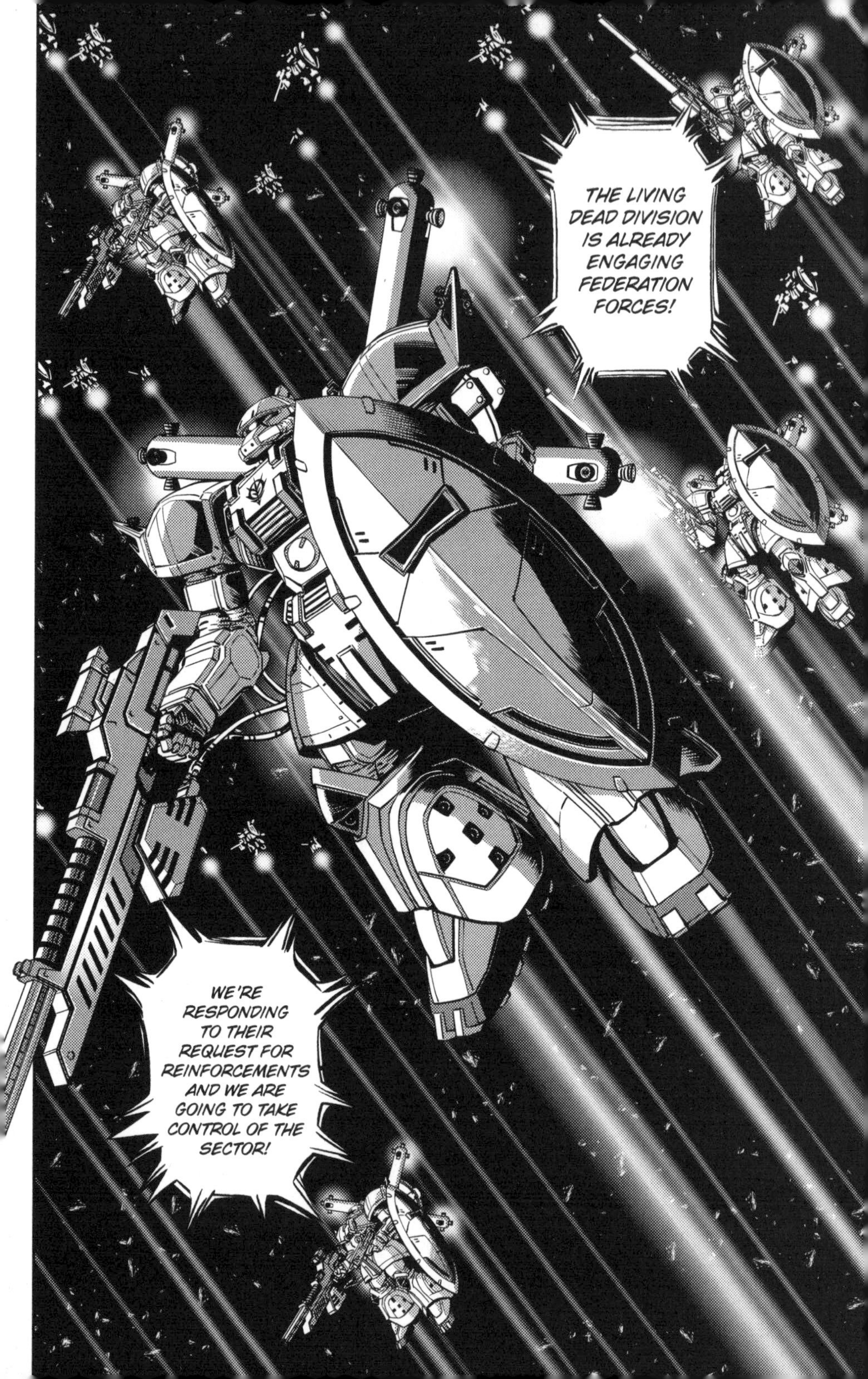
THE LIVING DEAD DIVISION IS ALREADY ENGAGING FEDERATION FORCES!
WE'RE RESPONDING TO THEIR REQUEST FOR REINFORCEMENTS AND WE ARE GOING TO TAKE CONTROL OF THE SECTOR!

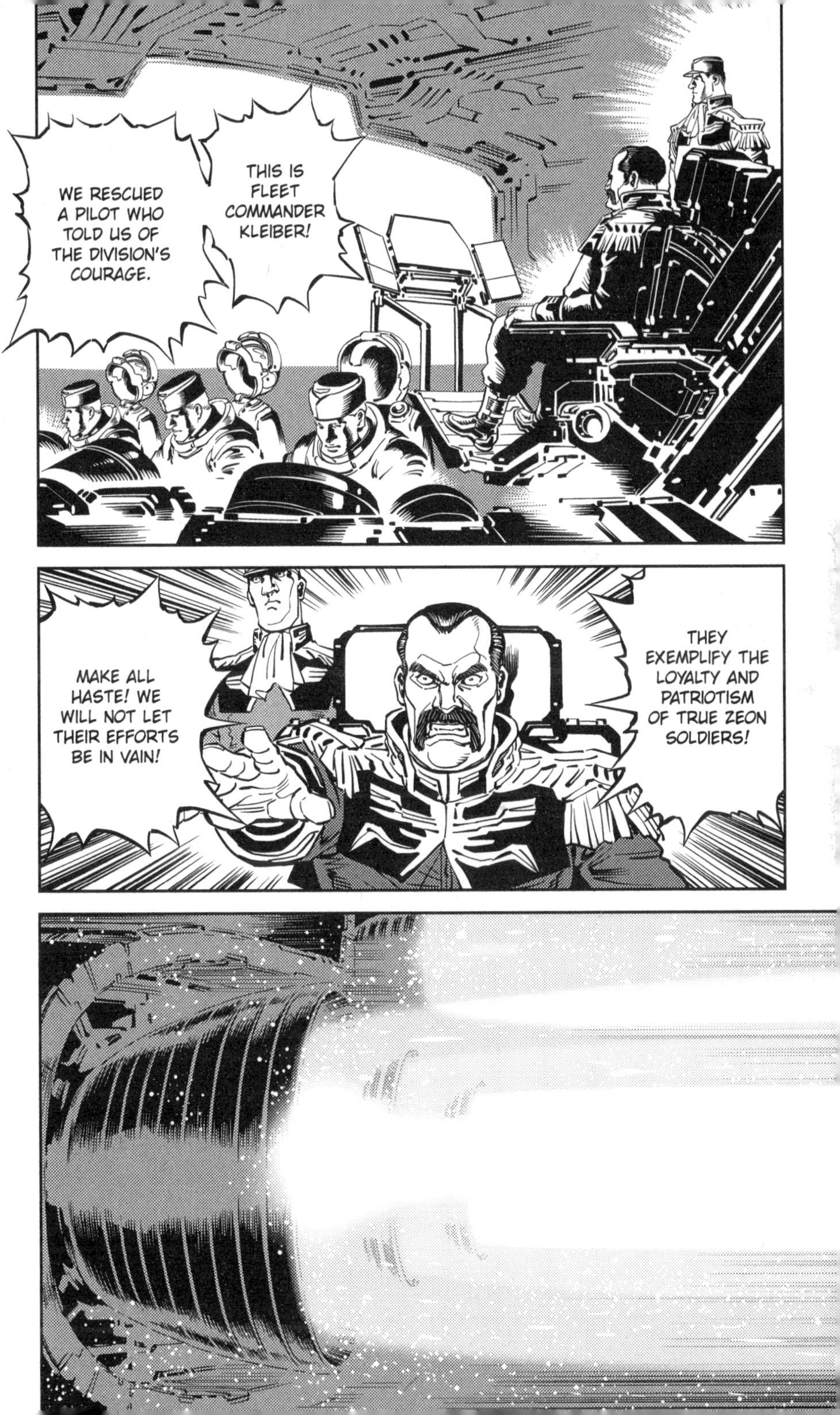
THIS IS FLEET COMMANDER KLEIBER!
WE RESCUED A PILOT WHO TOLD US OF THE DIVISION'S COURAGE.
THEY EXEMPLIFY THE LOYALTY AND PATRIOTISM OF TRUE ZEON SOLDIERS!
MAKE ALL HASTE! WE WILL NOT LET THEIR EFFORTS BE IN VAIN!

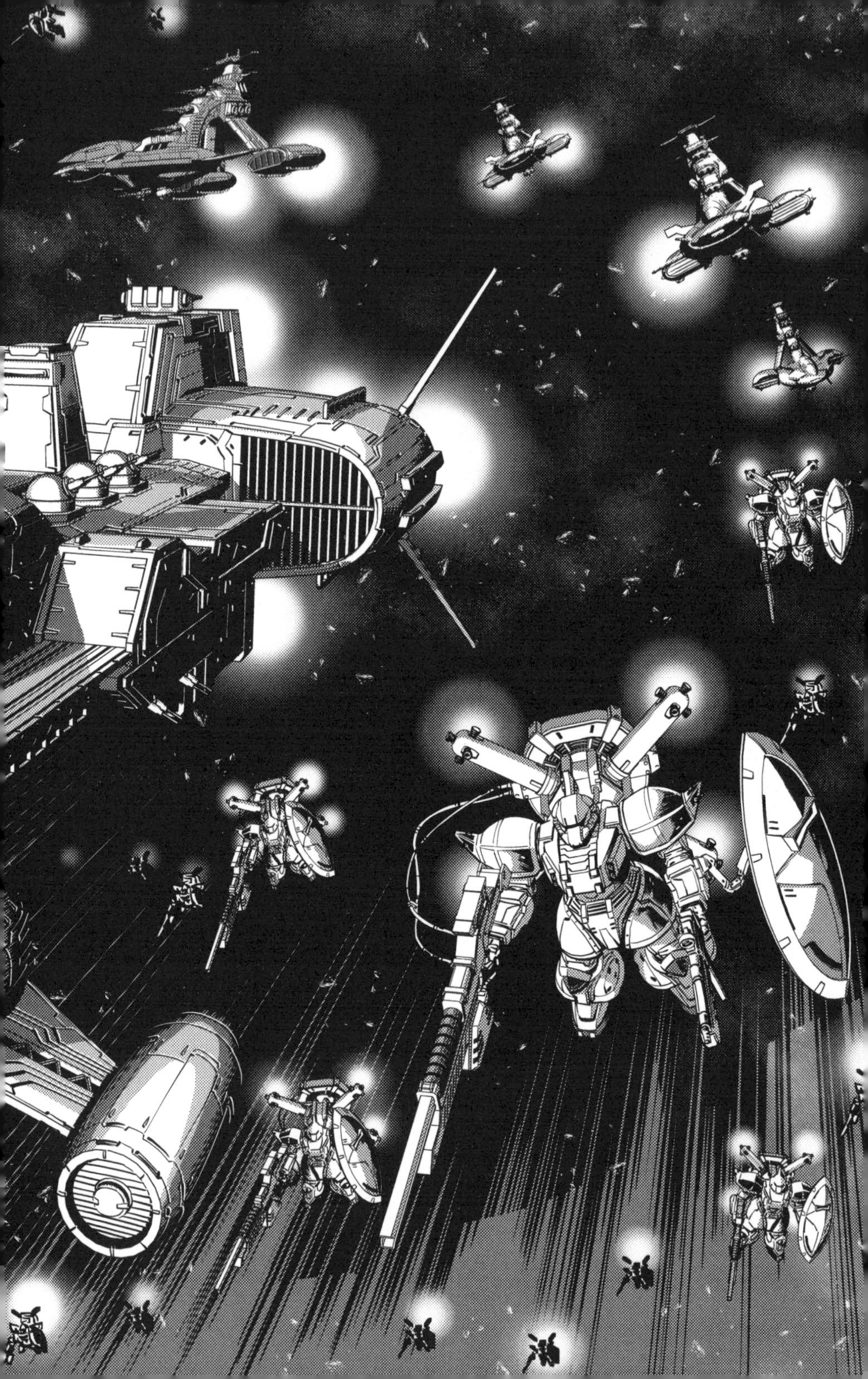

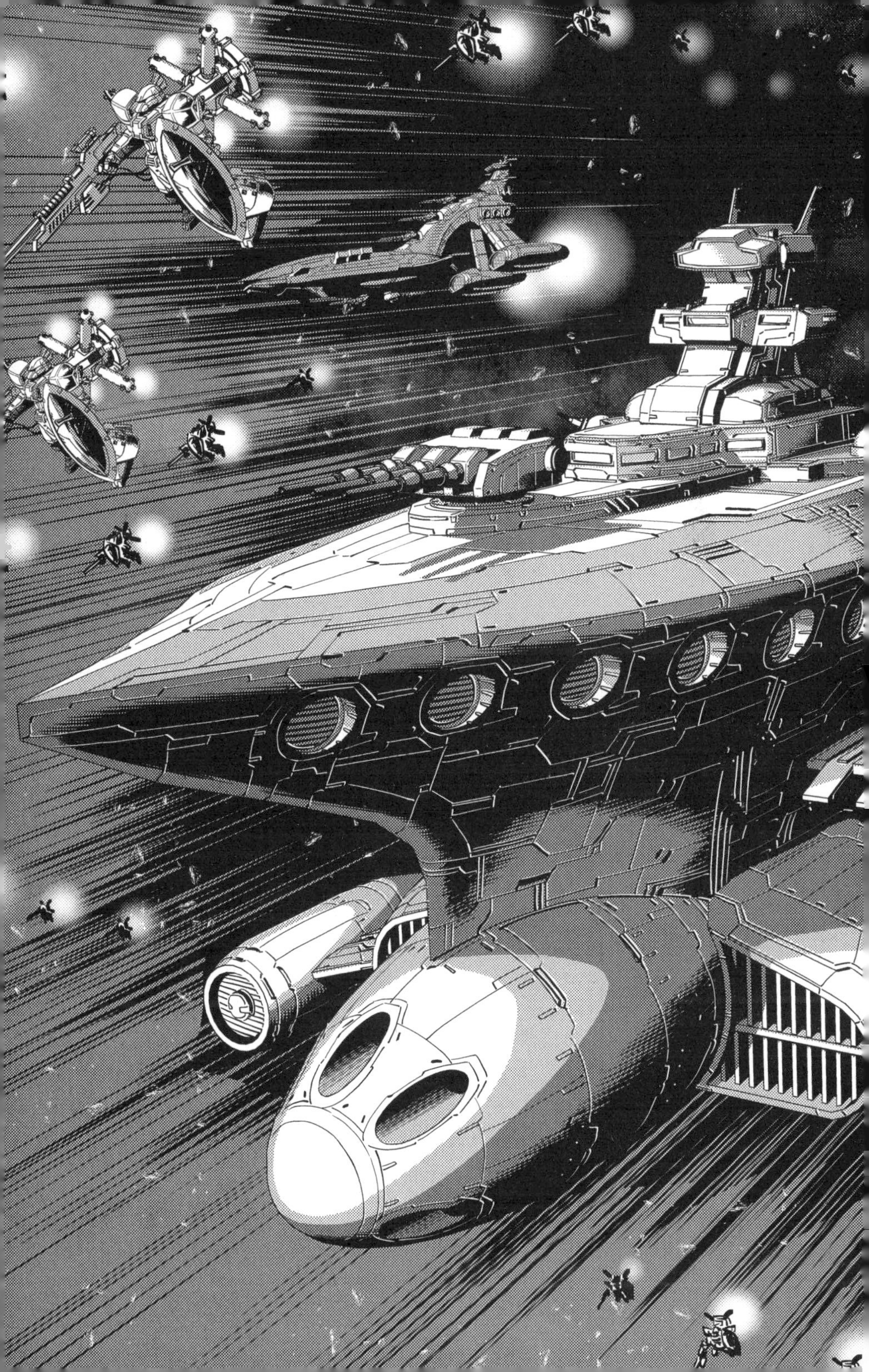

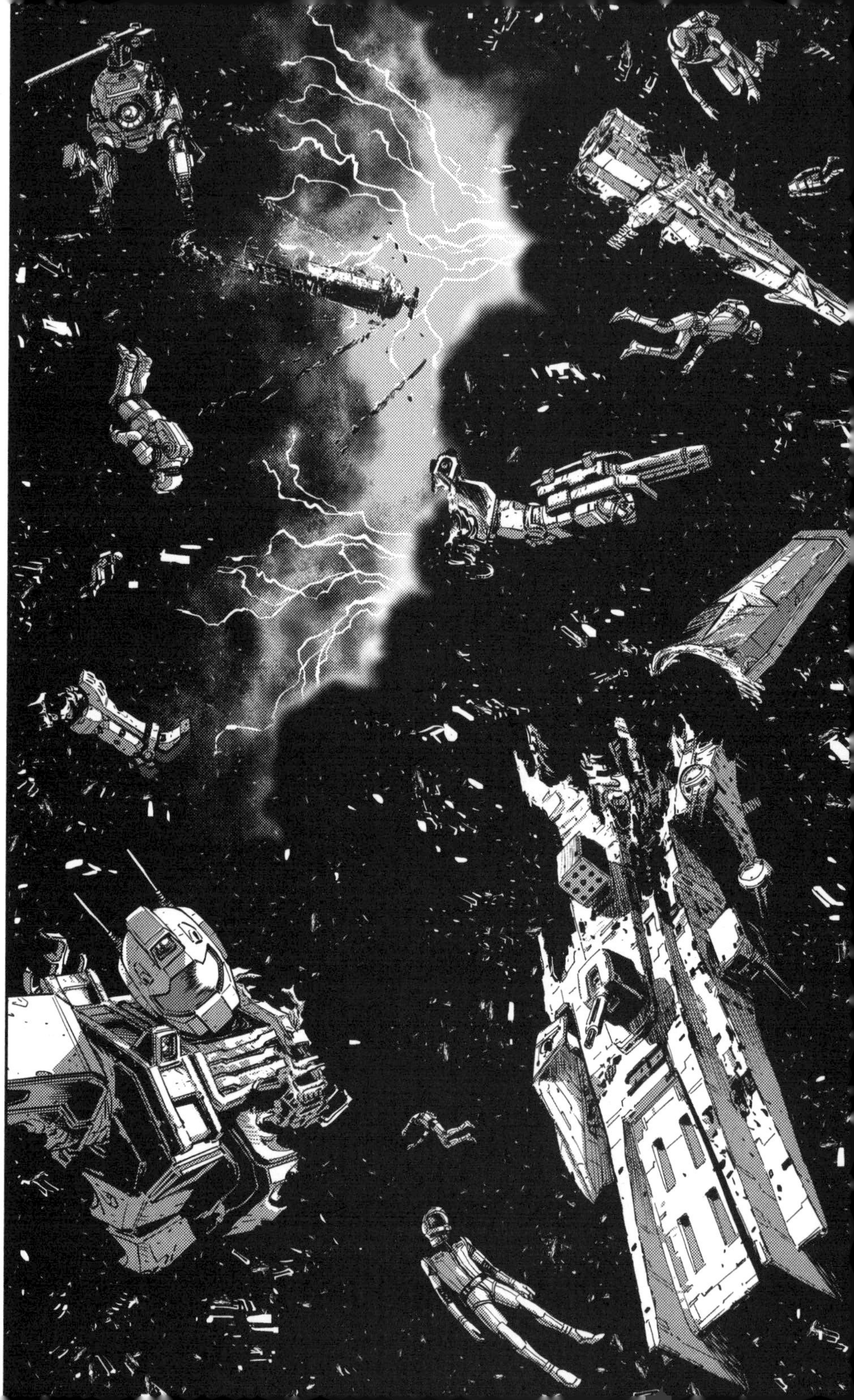

KZZT!
KSHH
THE SUMMER SUN, YOUR SMILE. ♫
KZZT
I'VE GOT YOU. NOW YOU'RE MINE. ♪
KZZT

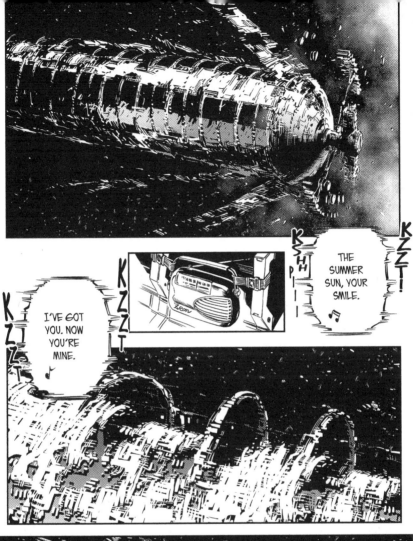

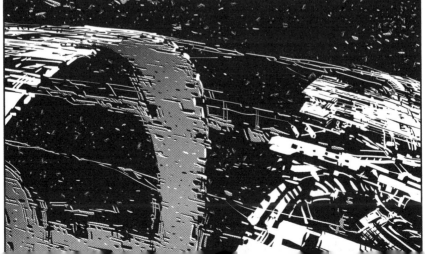

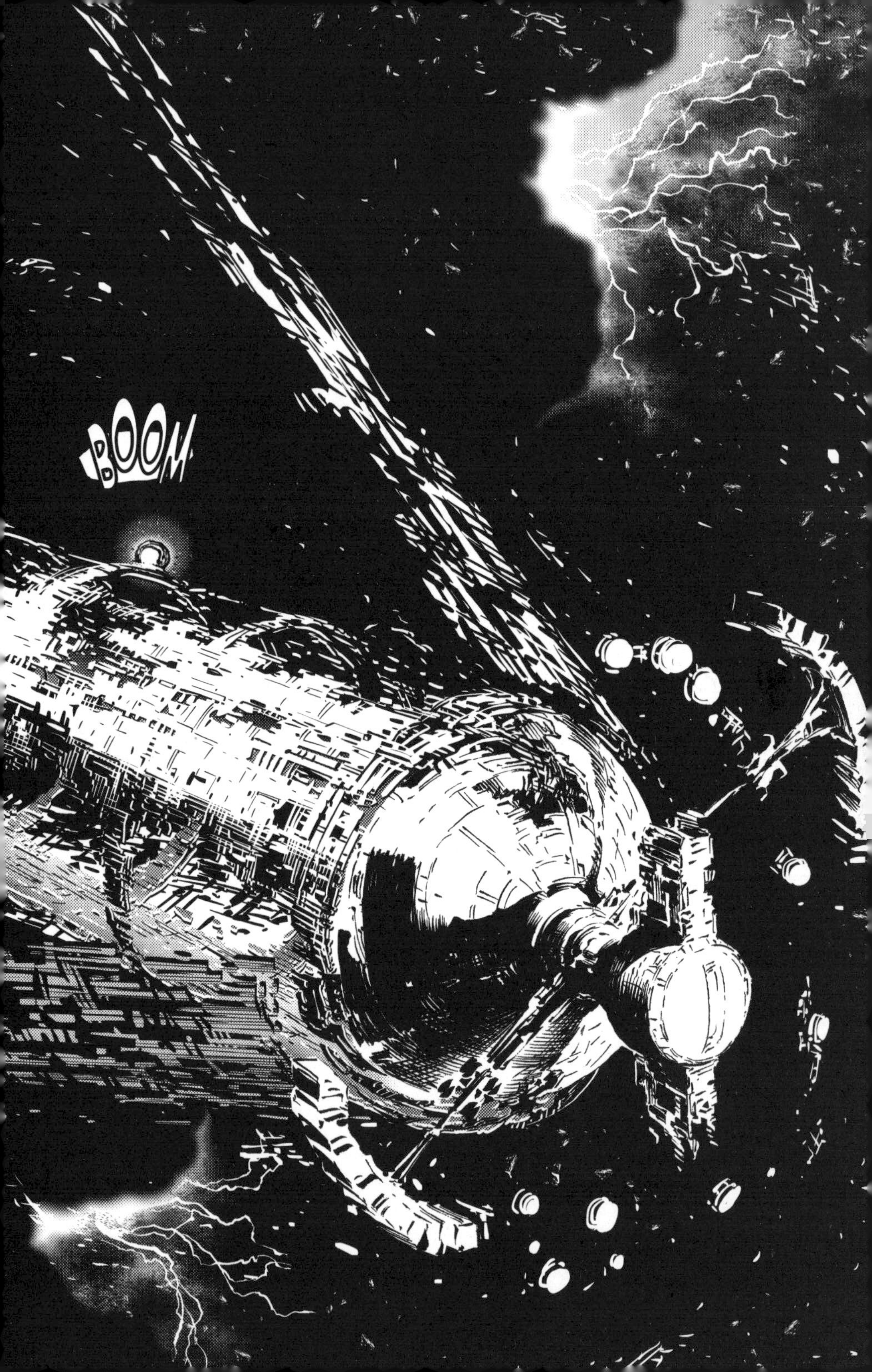
BOOOM

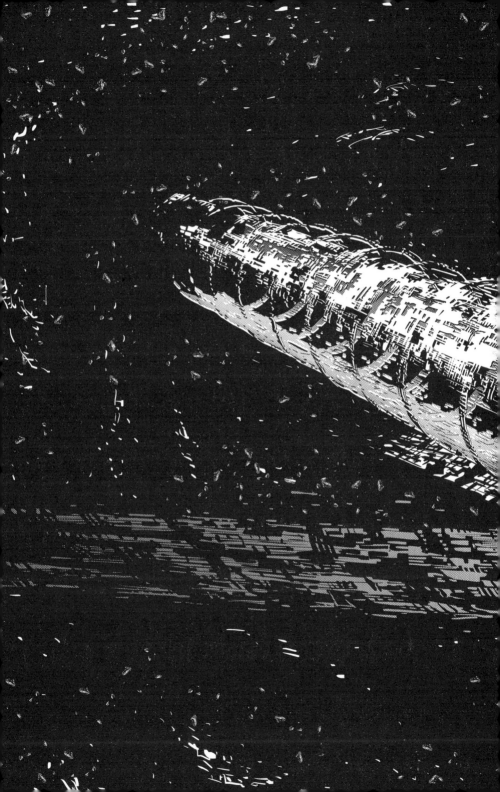

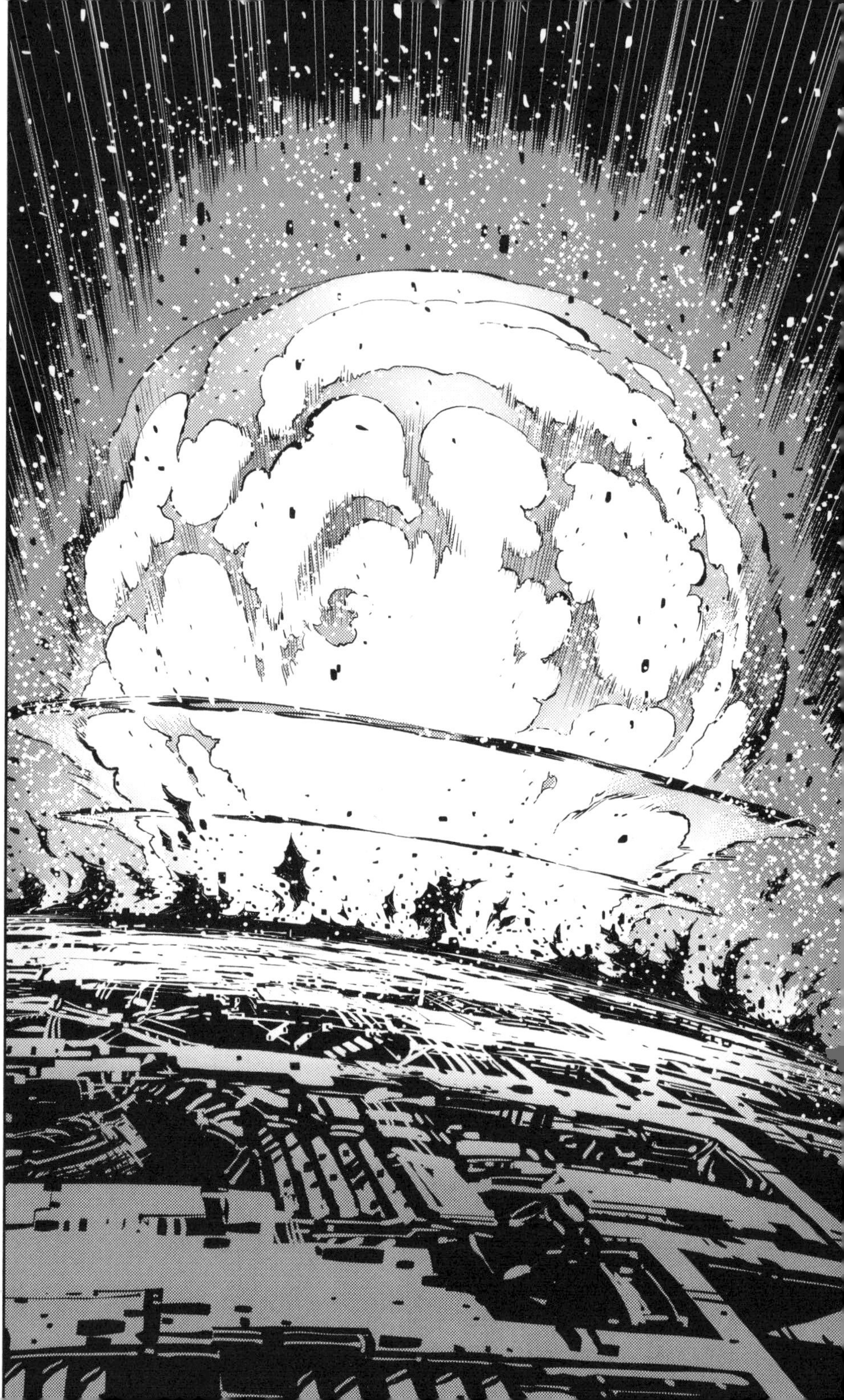

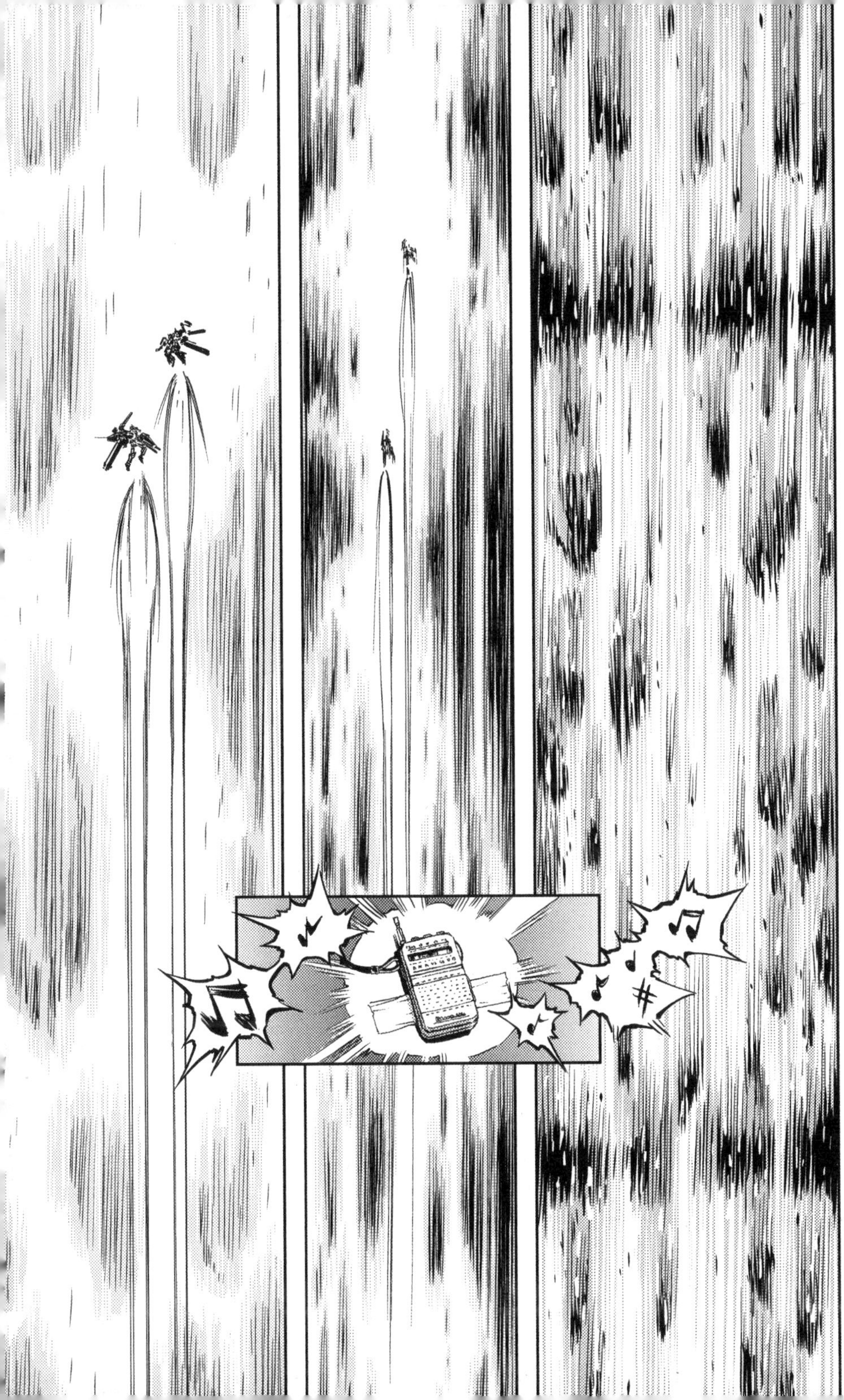

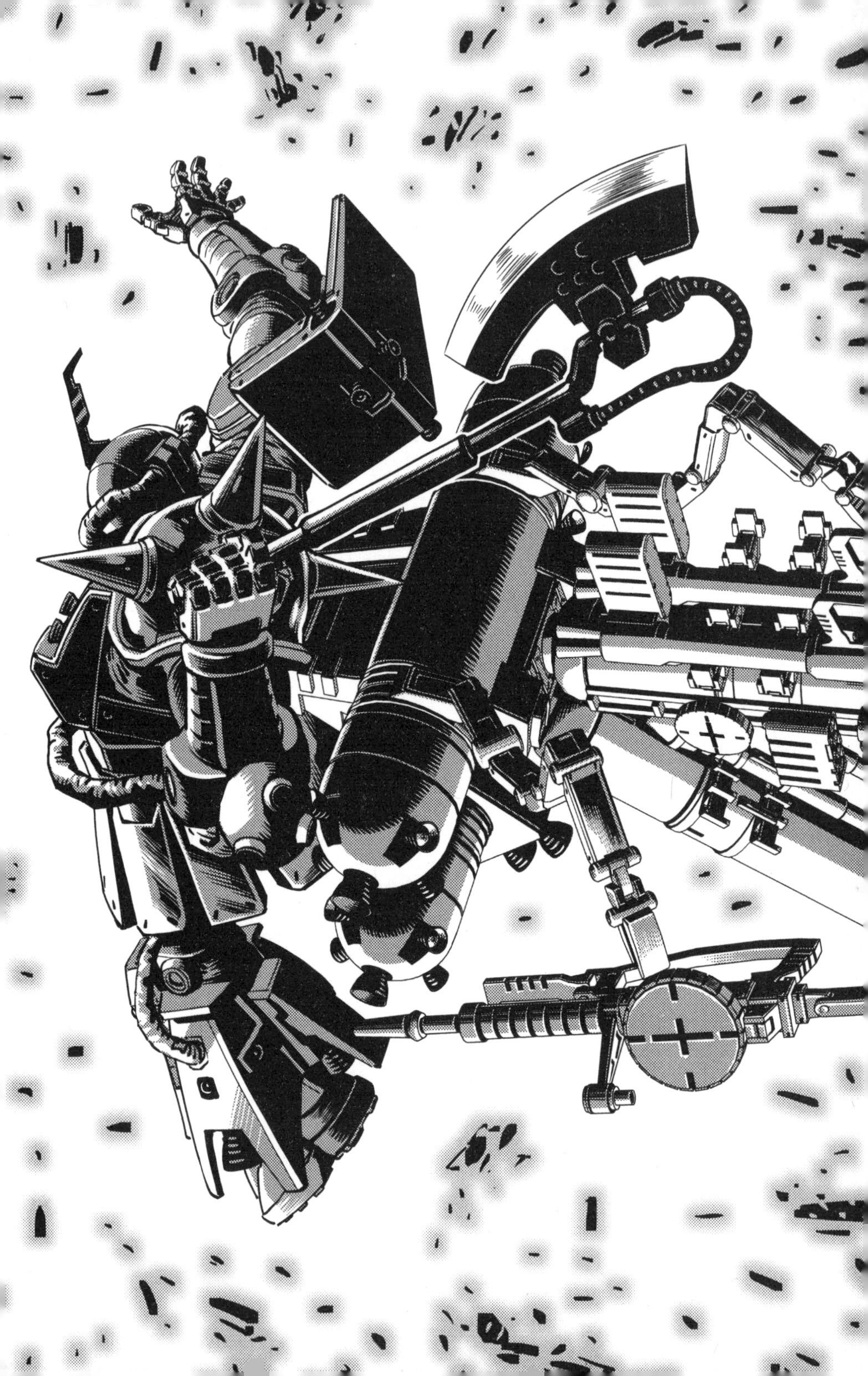

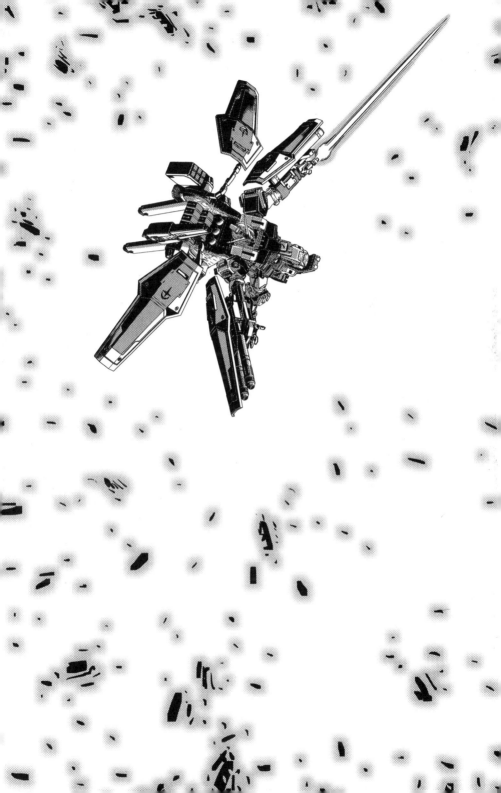

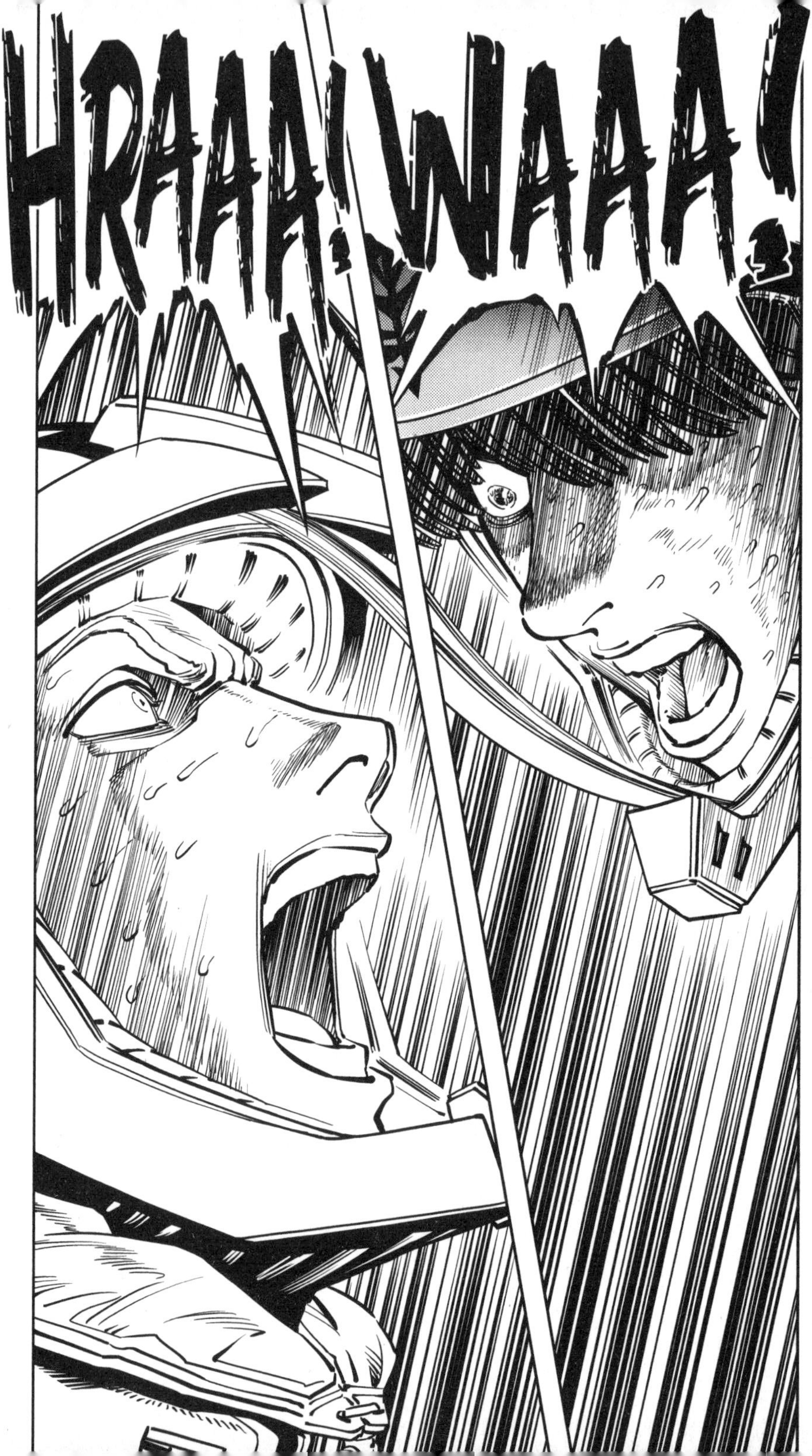
WAAA!
HRAAA!

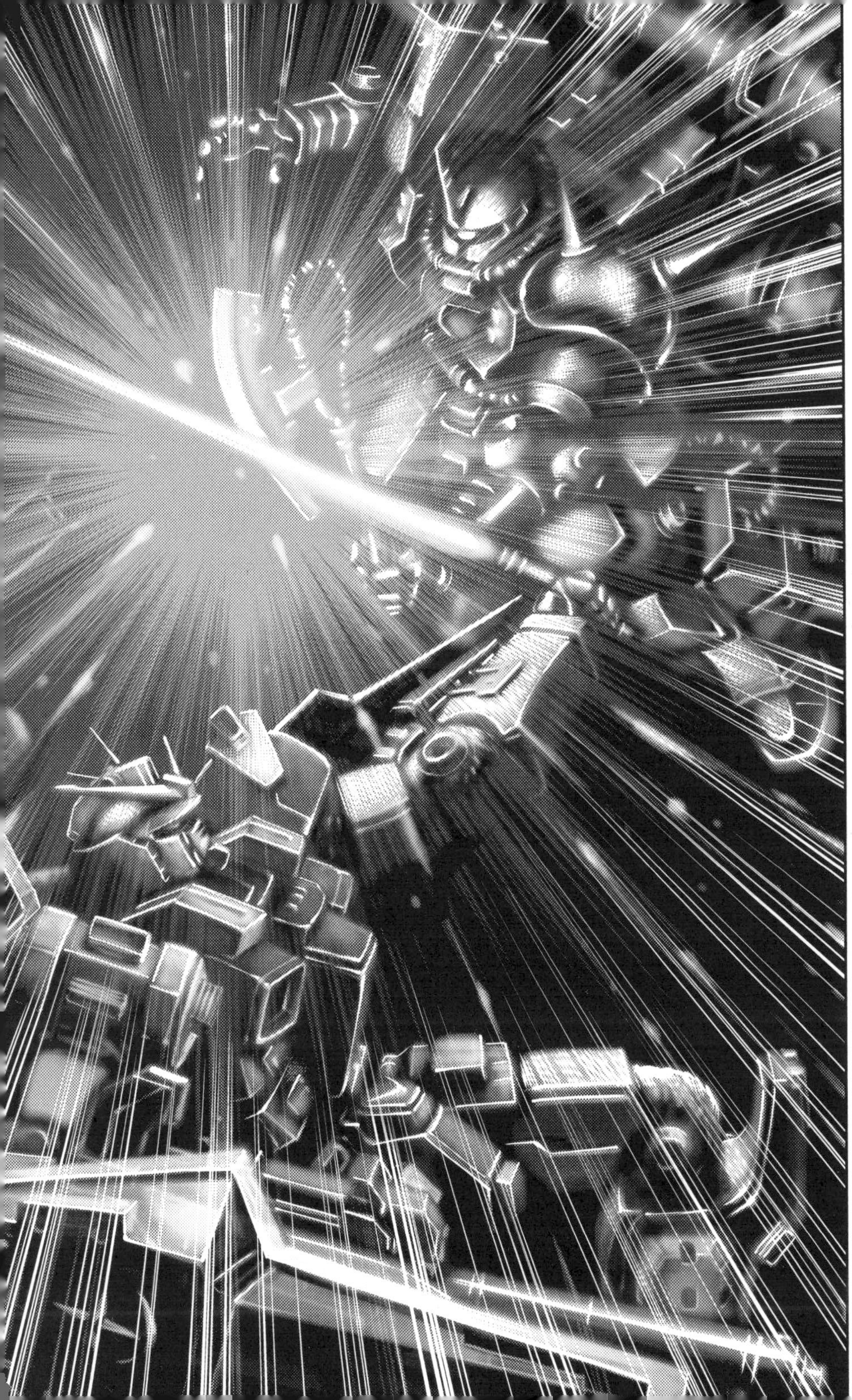

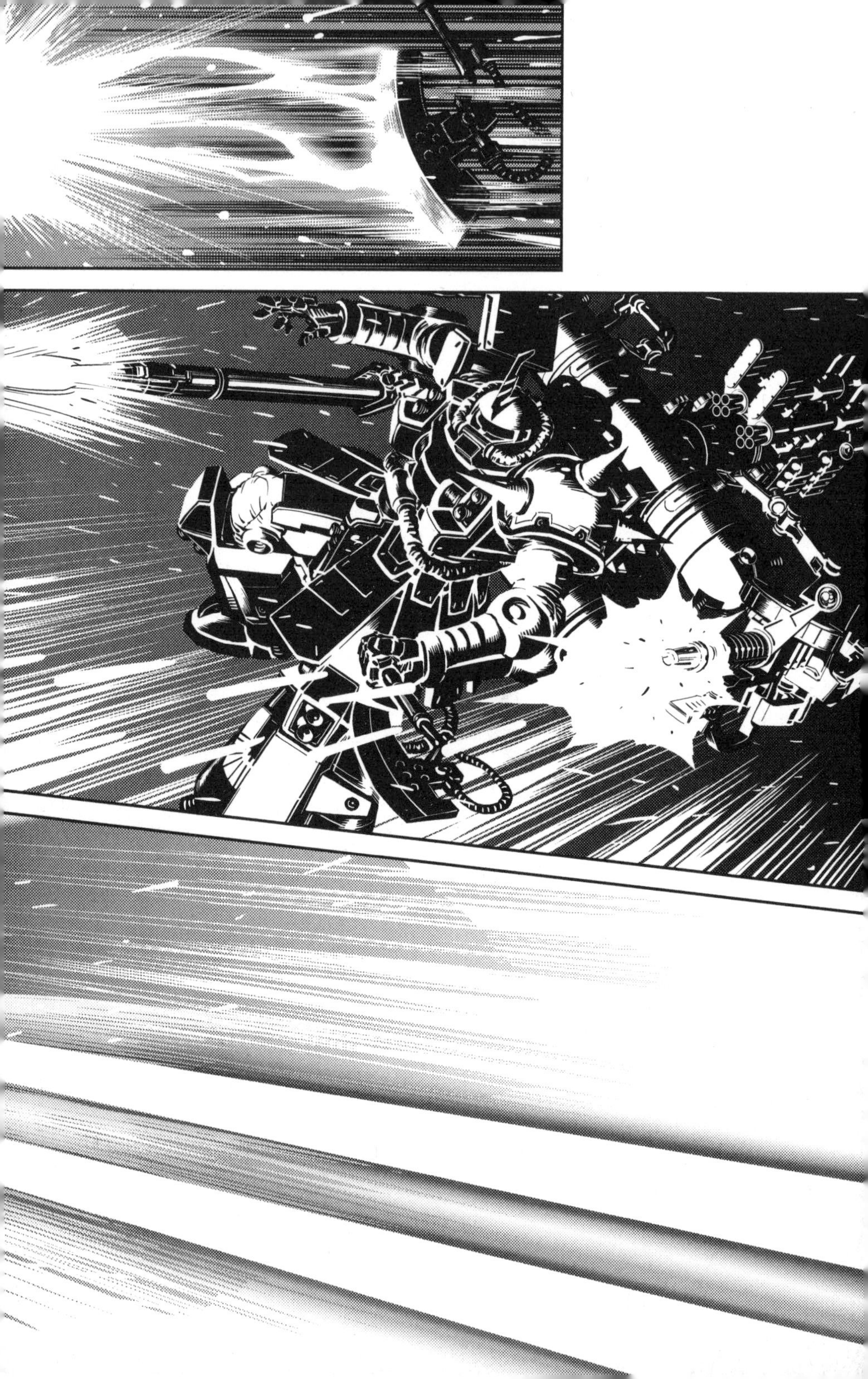

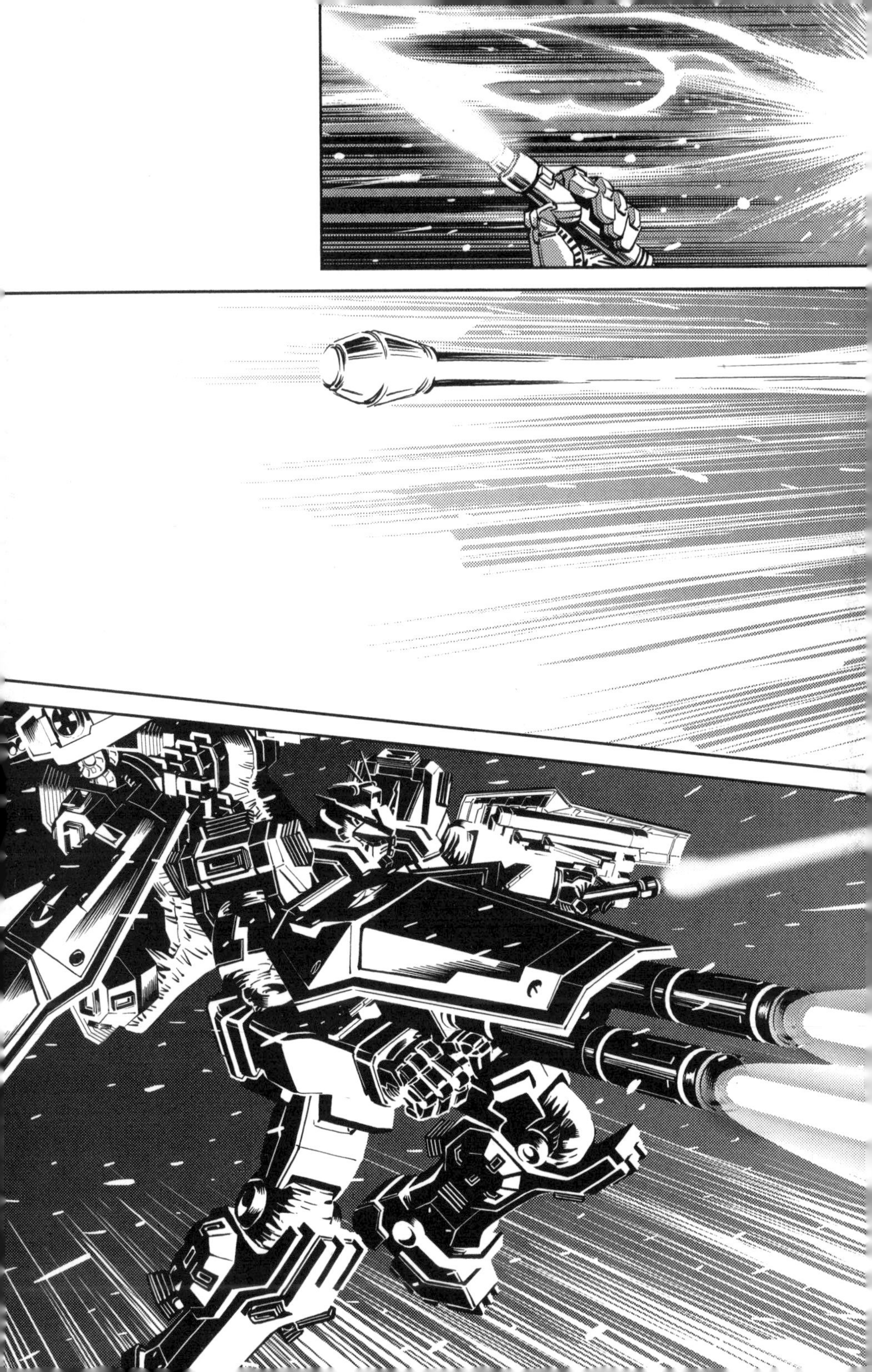

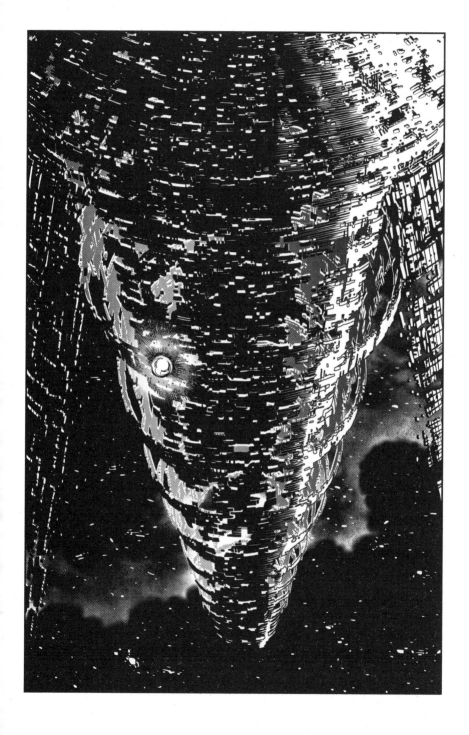

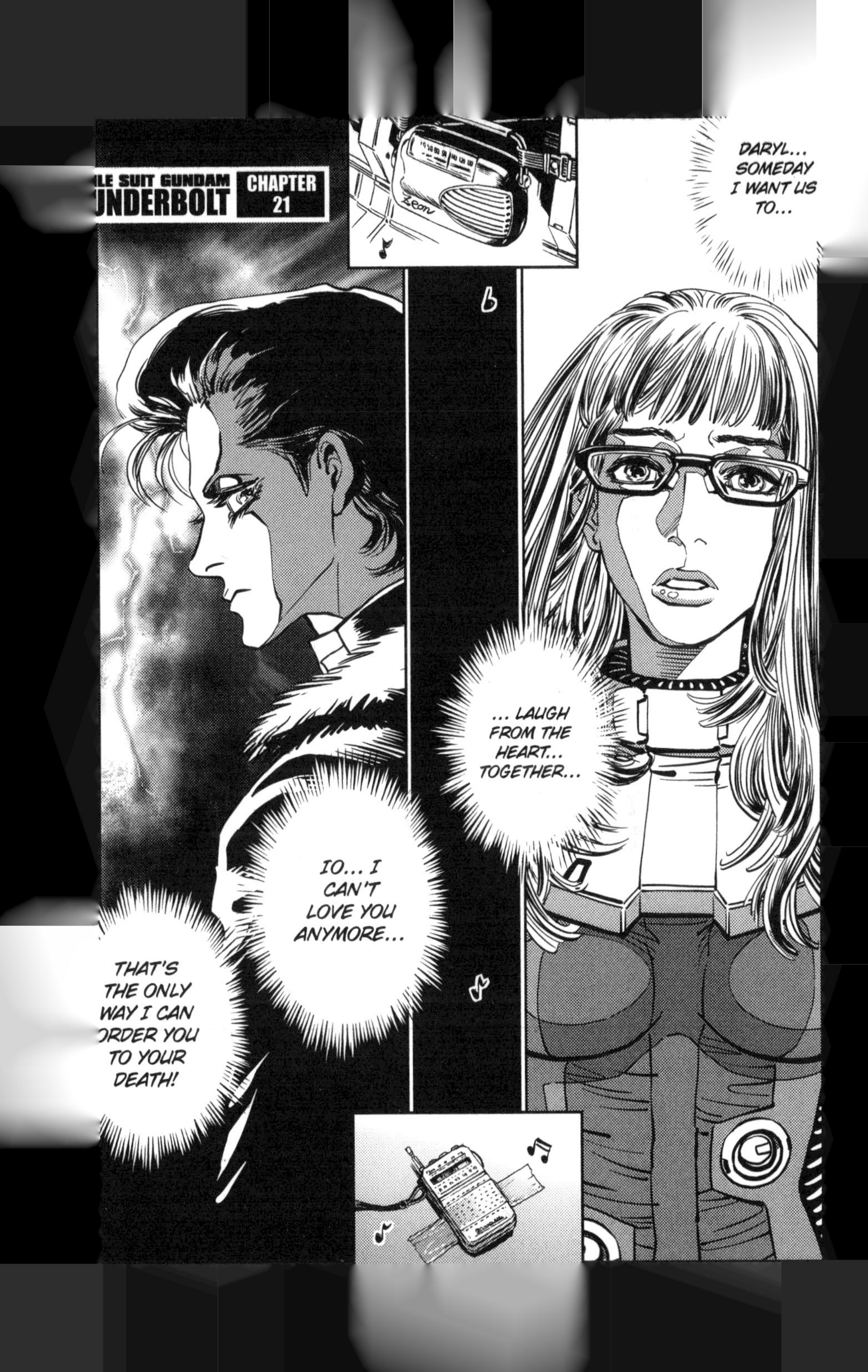
DARYL... SOMEDAY I WANT US TO...
... LAUGH FROM THE HEART... TOGETHER...
LE SUIT GUNDAM
UNDERBOLT
CHAPTER 21
IO... I CAN'T LOVE YOU ANYMORE...
THAT'S THE ONLY WAY I CAN ORDER YOU TO YOUR DEATH!

IT'S MY OWN LITTLE PROTEST...
I HATE THIS WAR...
I STILL DREAM ABOUT GOING BACK...
...TO THOSE INNOCENT DAYS.

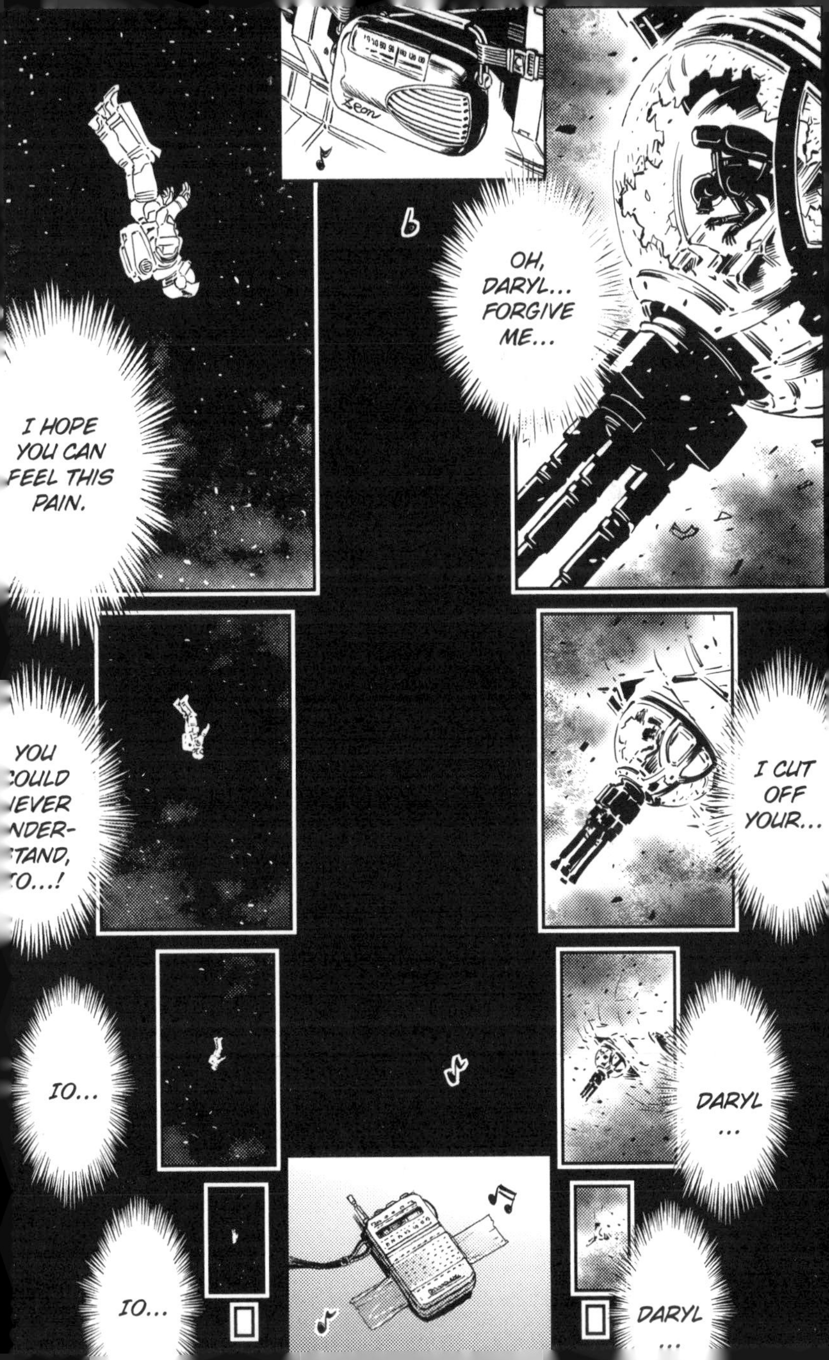
OH, DARYL... FORGIVE ME...
I HOPE YOU CAN FEEL THIS PAIN.
I CUT OFF YOUR...
YOU COULD IEVER NDER- TAND, O...!
DARYL ...
IO...
DARYL ...
IO...

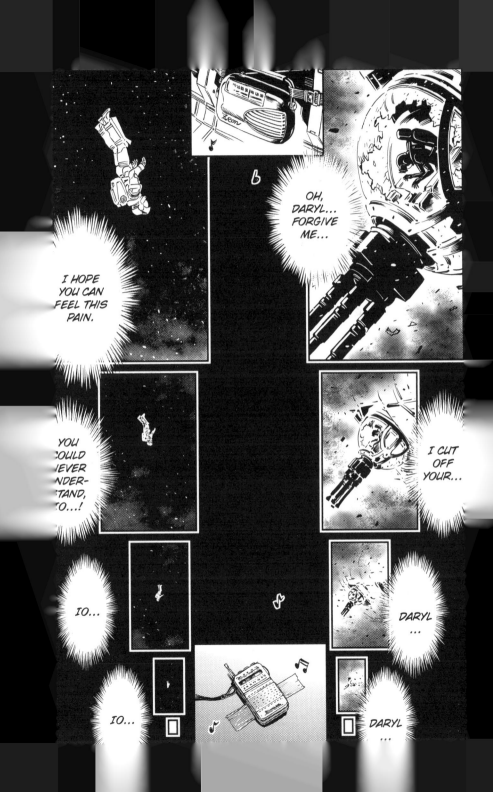

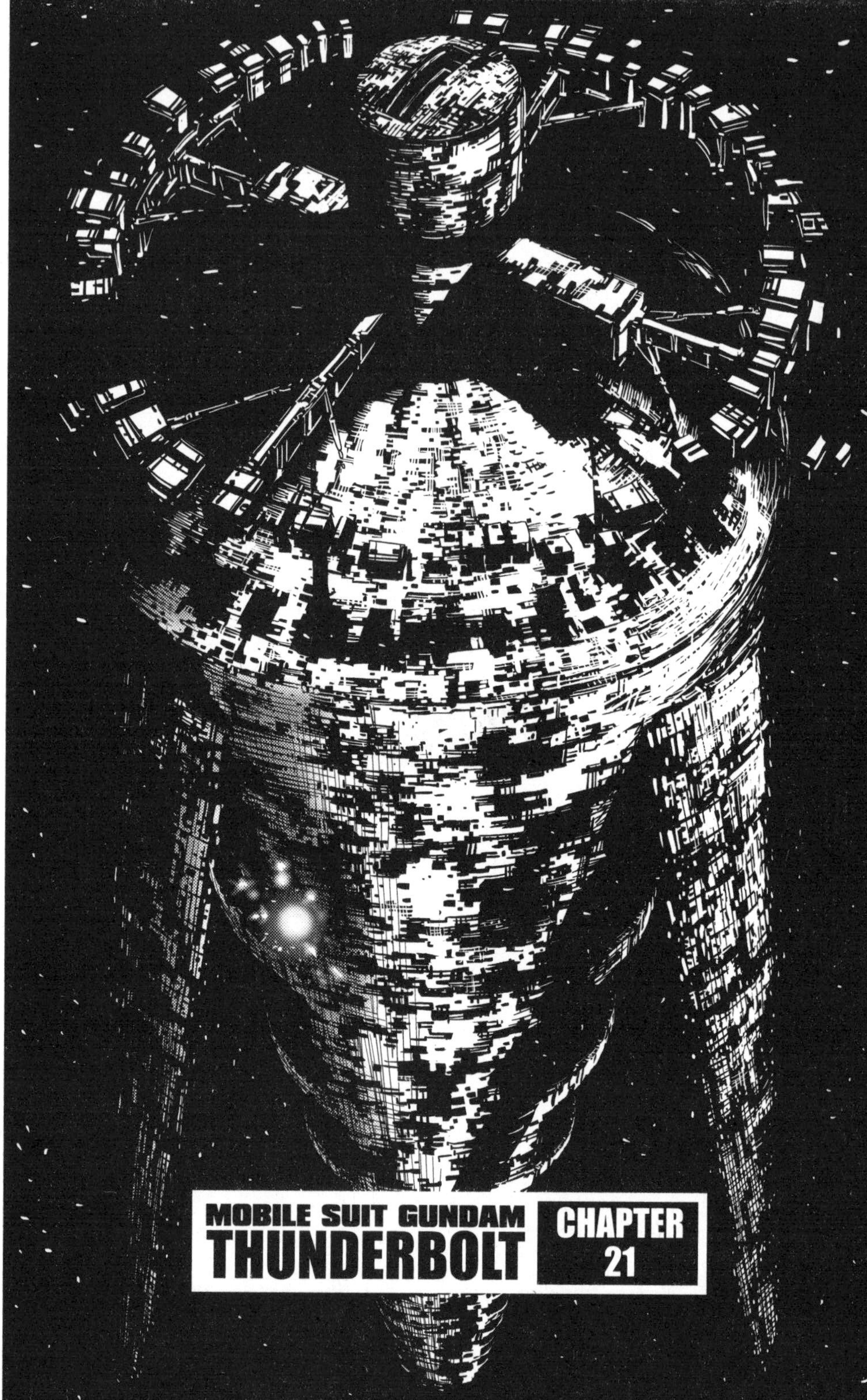
MOBILE SUIT GUNDAM
THUNDERBOLT
CHAPTER
21

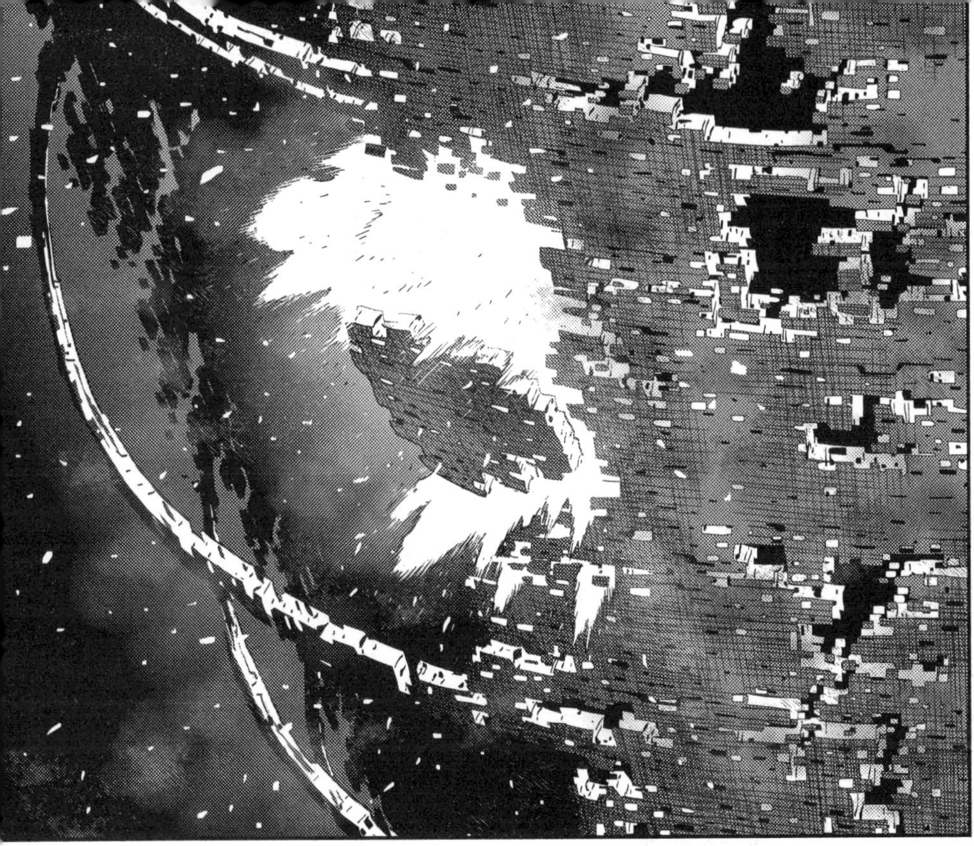
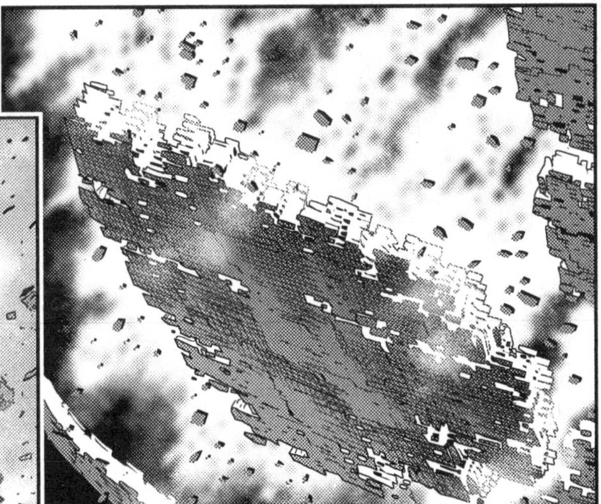
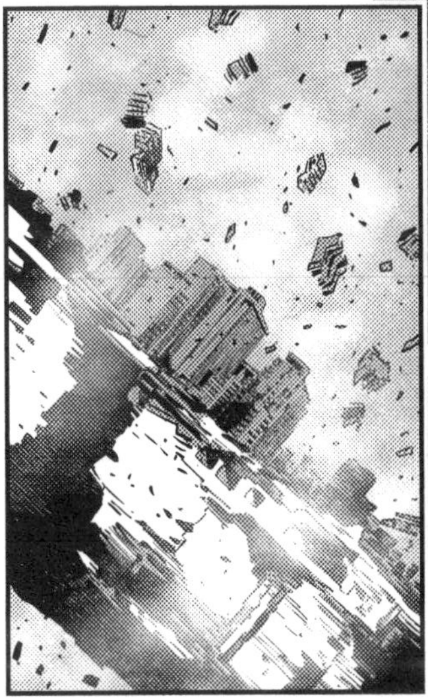

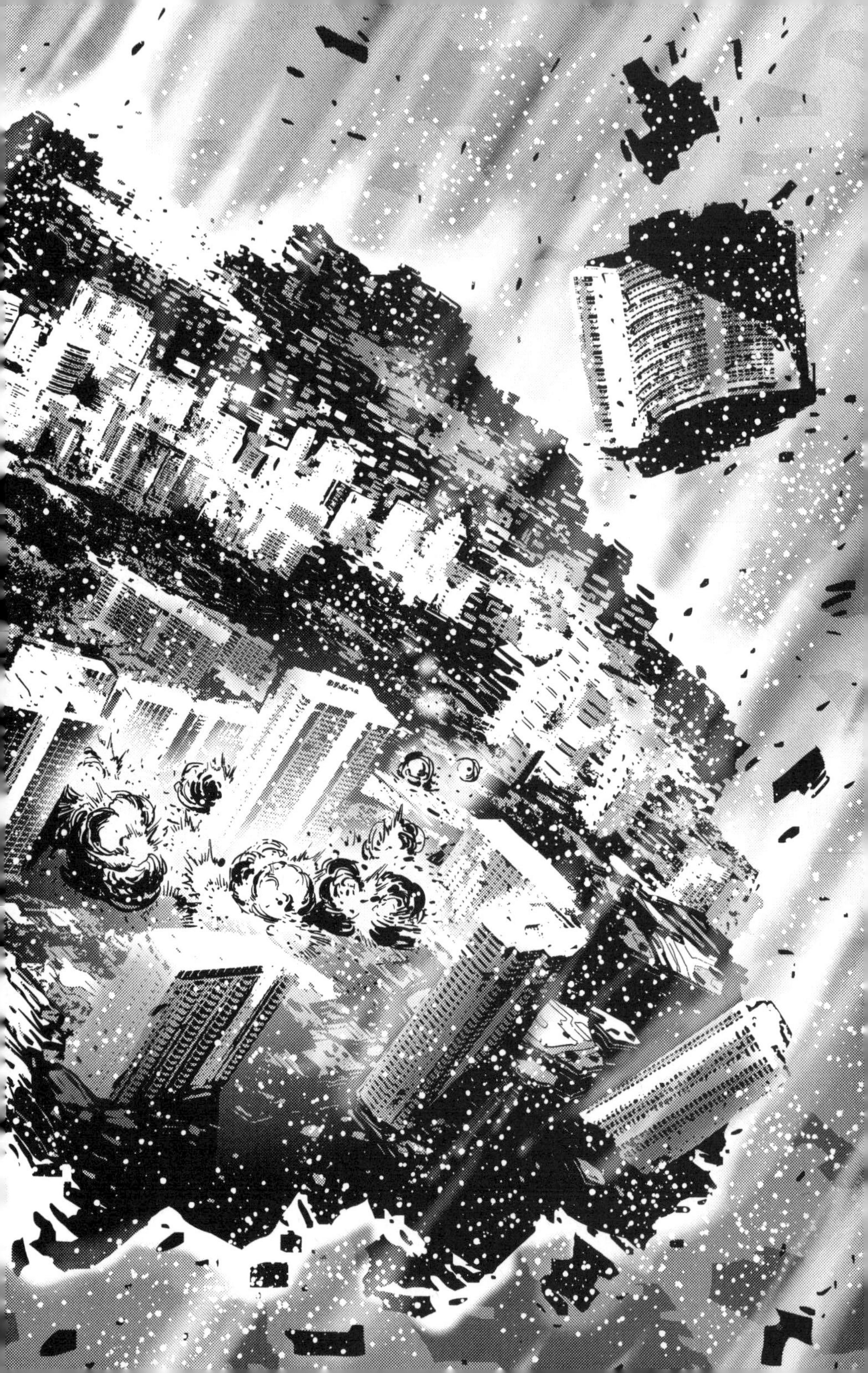

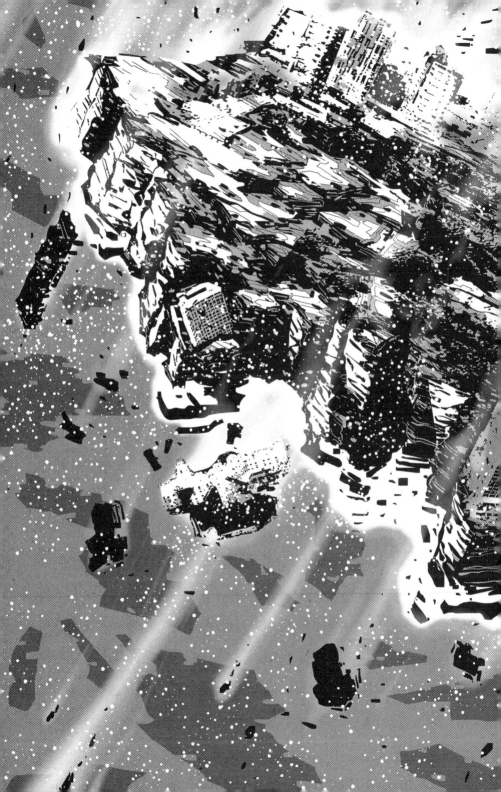

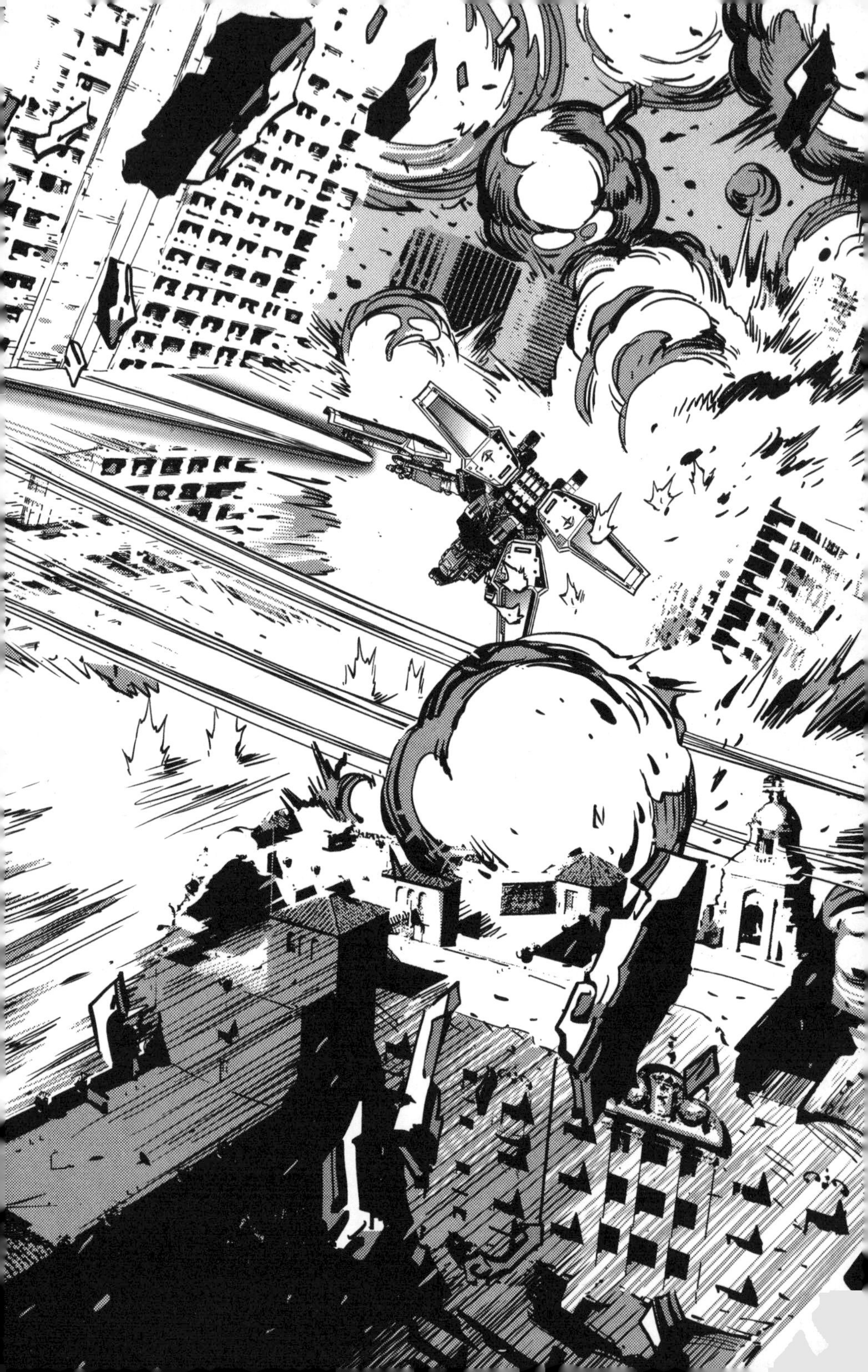

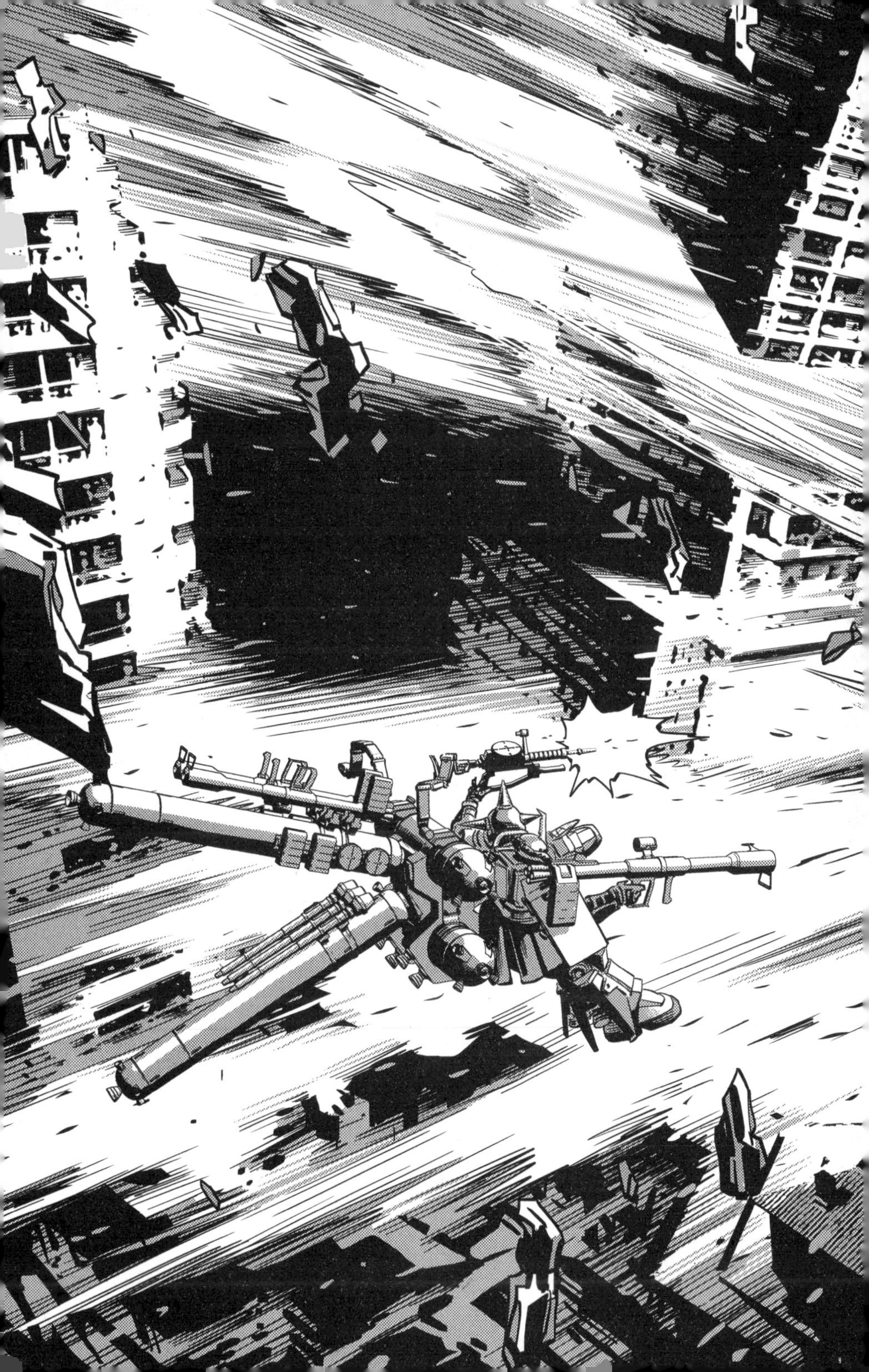

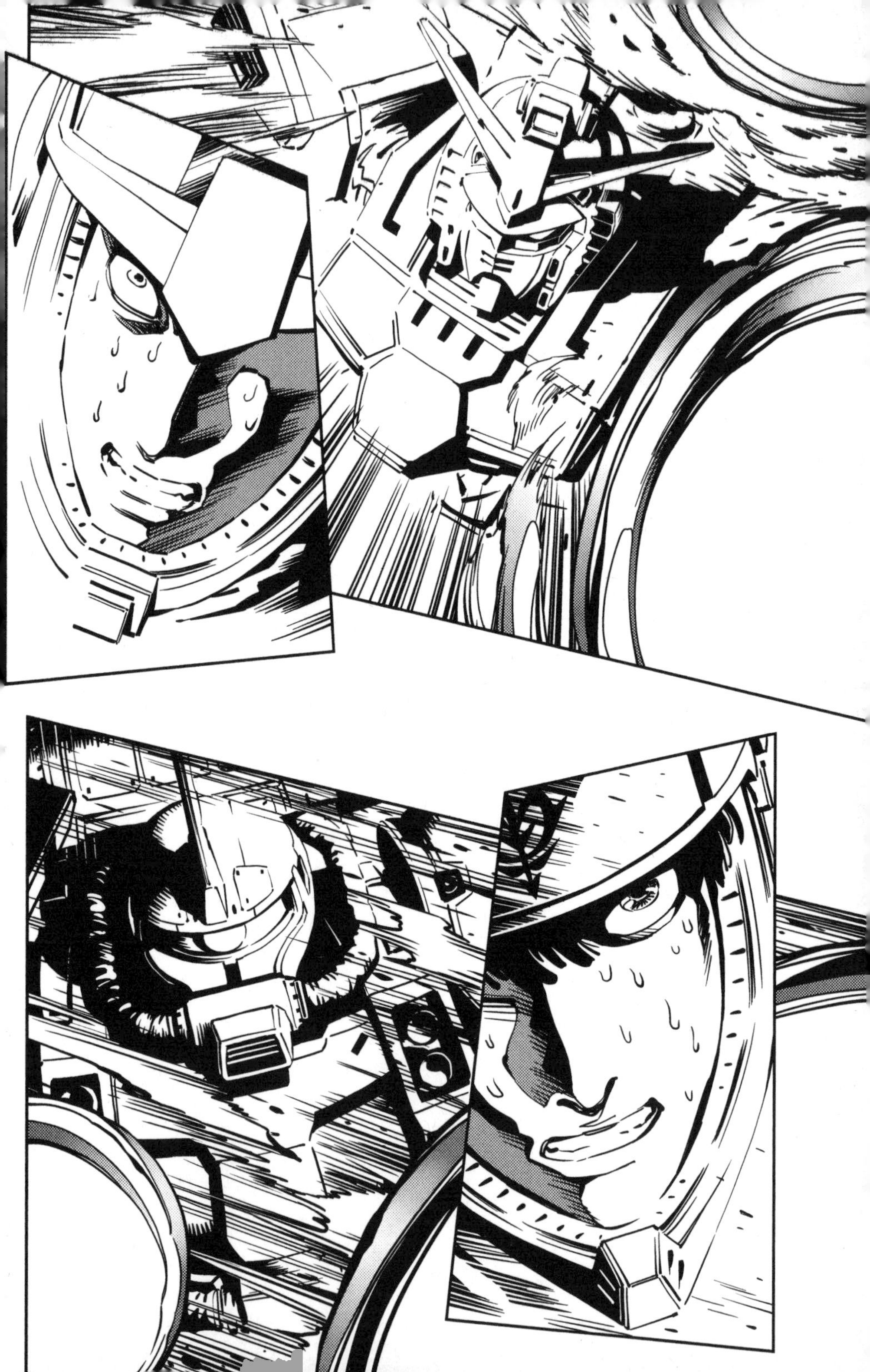

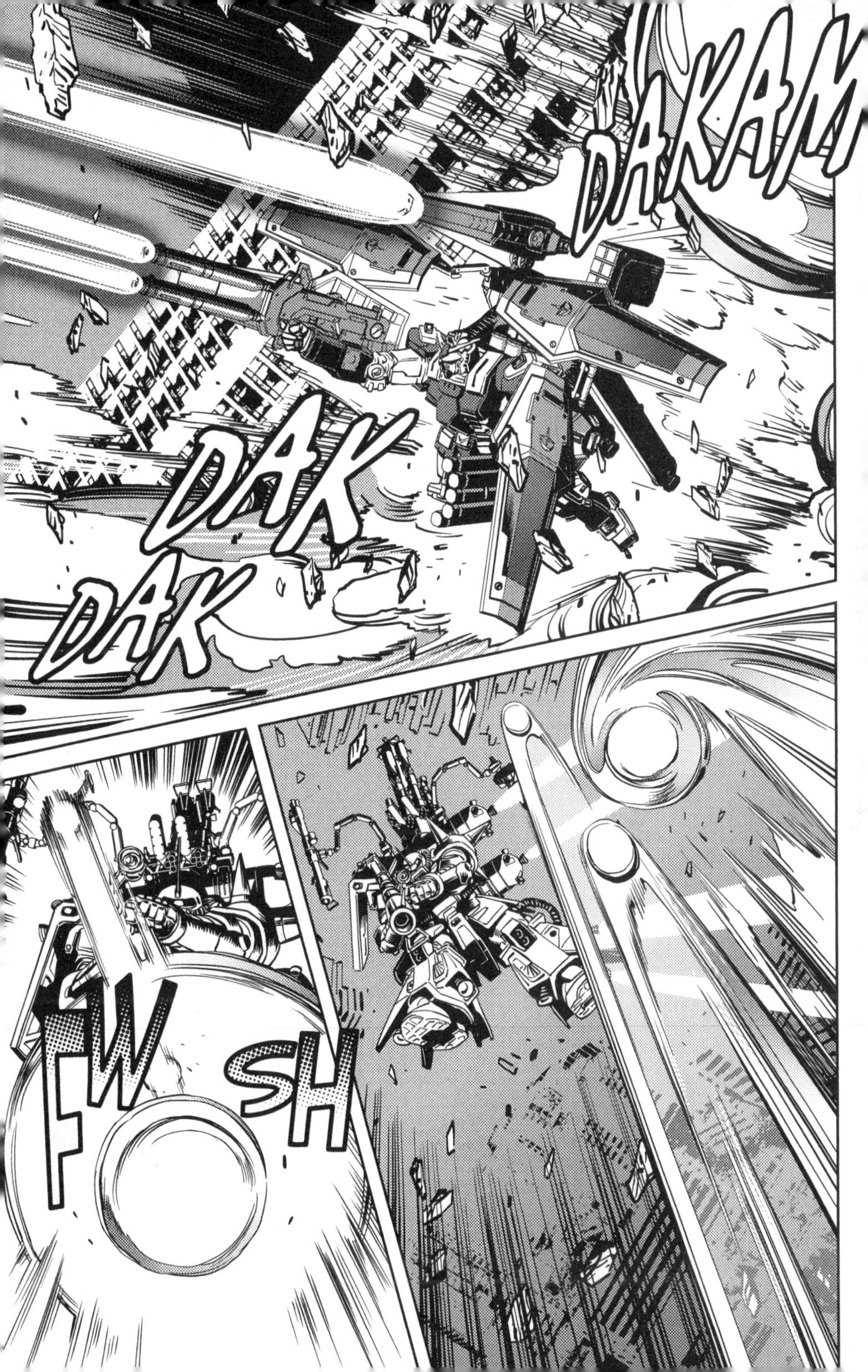
DAKAM
DAK
DAK
FWSH

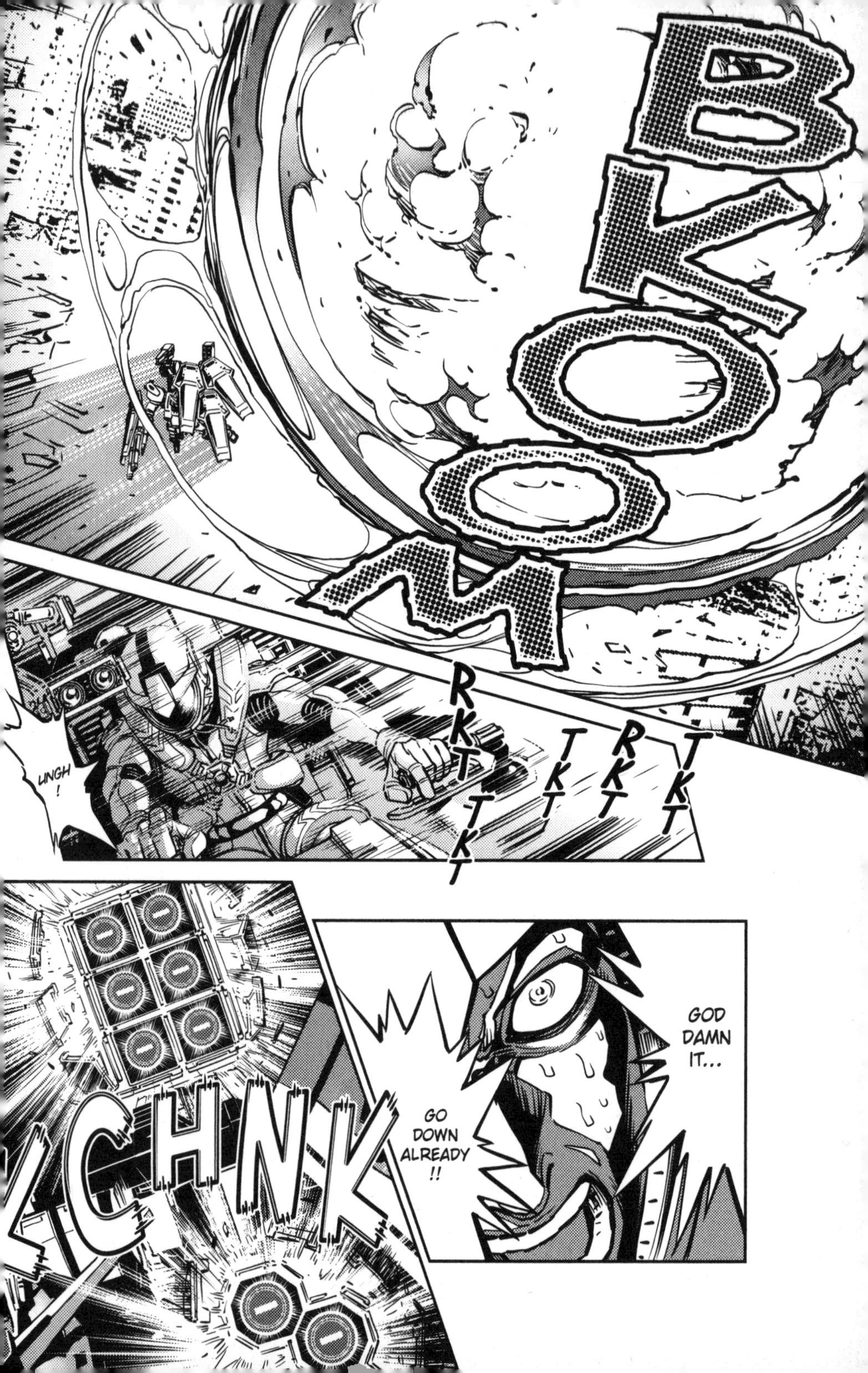
BKOOM
TKT
RKT
TKT
TKT
RKT
TKTKT
UNGH!
GOD DAMN IT...
GO DOWN ALREADY!!
CHNK

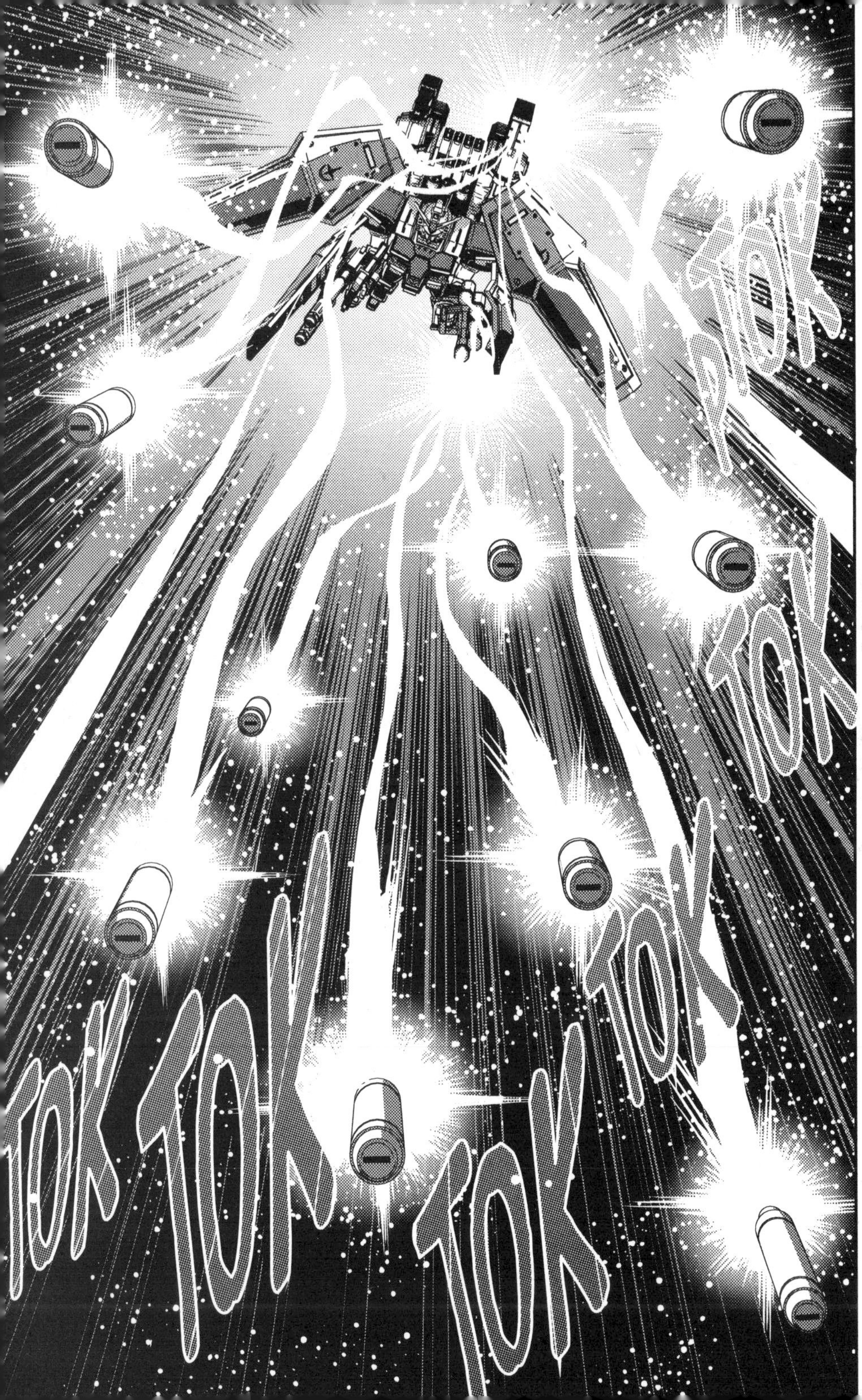
TOK TOK
TOK TOK
TOK TOK TOK
TOK TOK

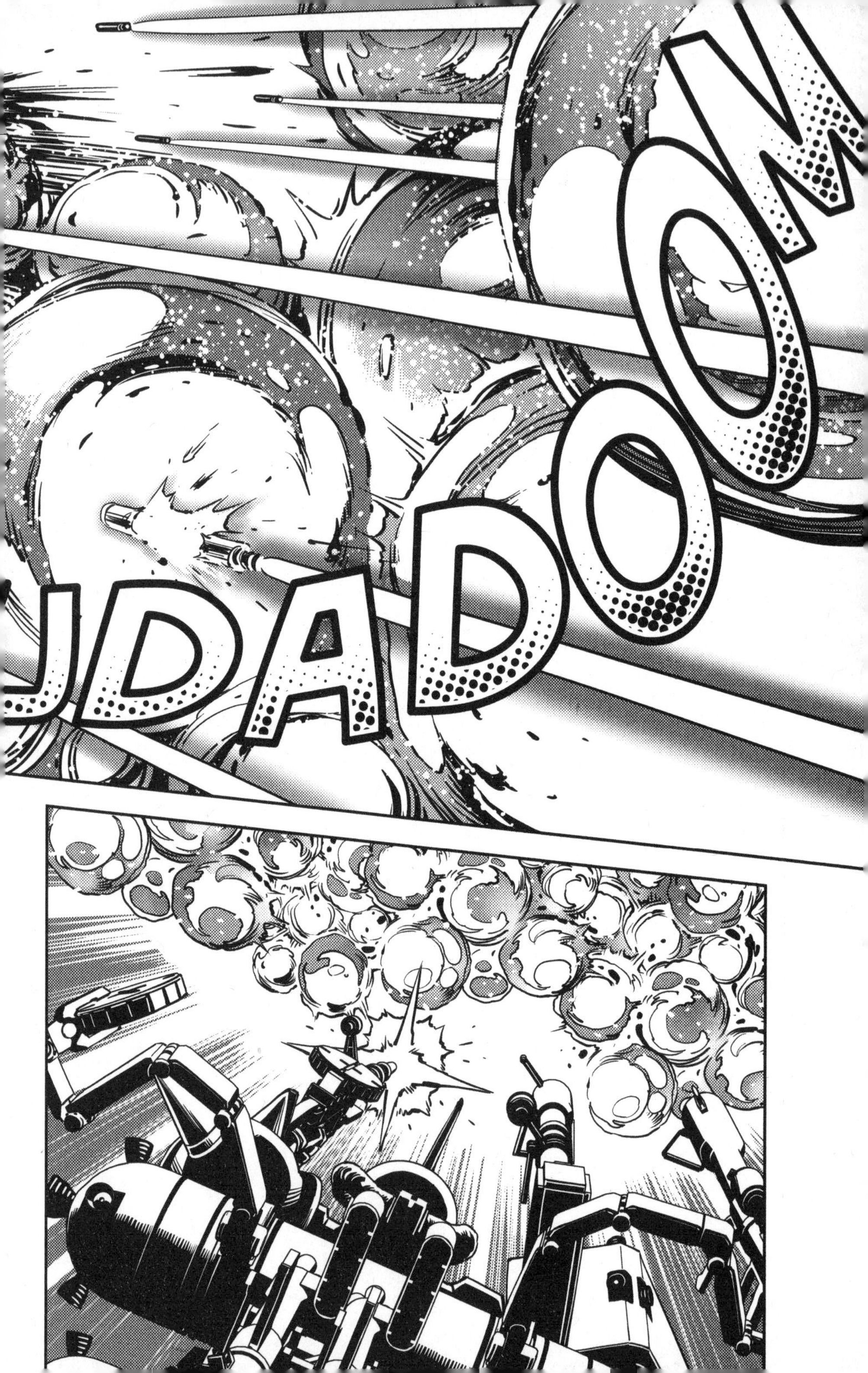
DADOOM

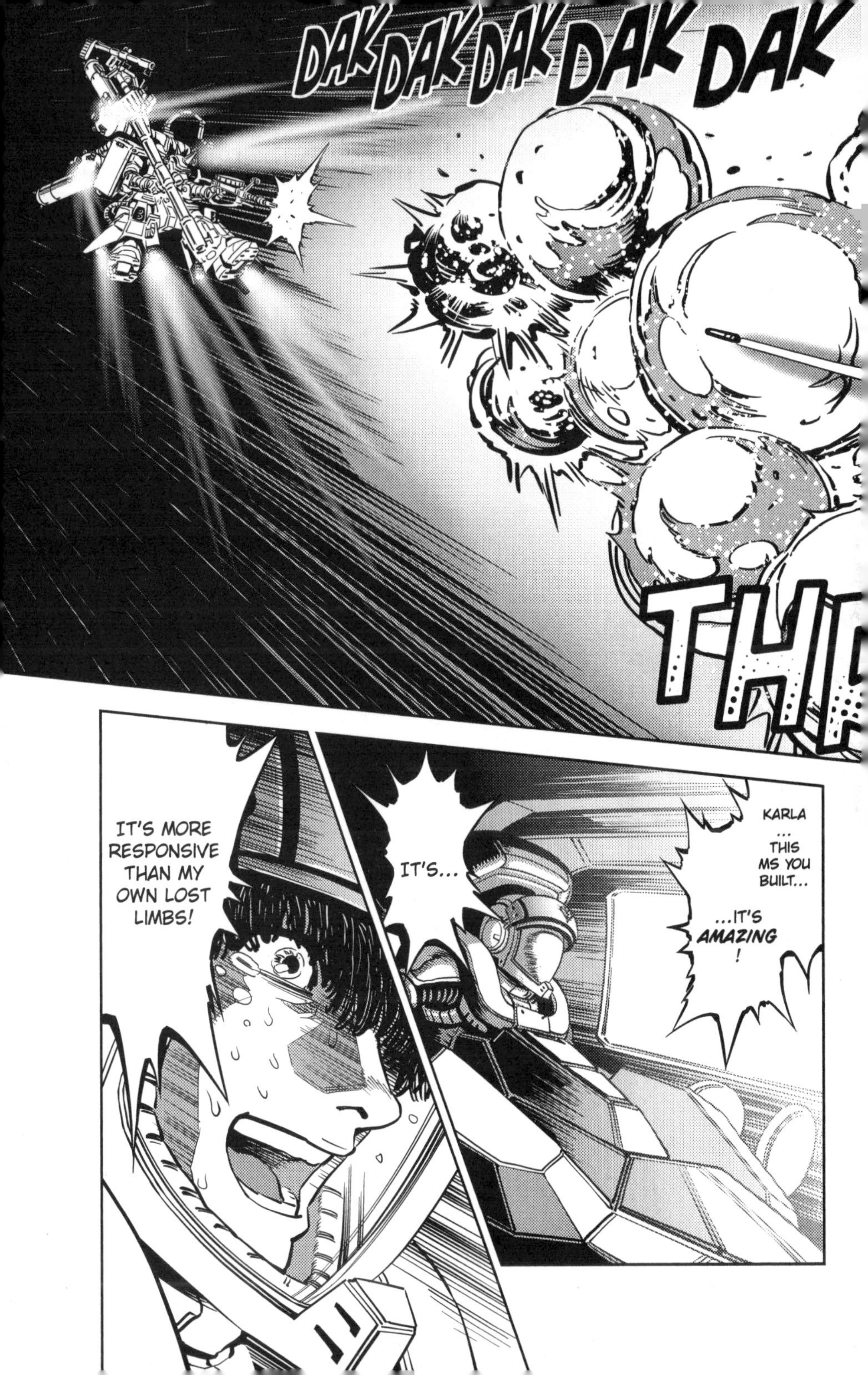
DAK DAK DAK DAK DAK
KARLA ... THIS MS YOU BUILT...
...IT'S *AMAZING* !
IT'S...
IT'S MORE RESPONSIVE THAN MY OWN LOST LIMBS!

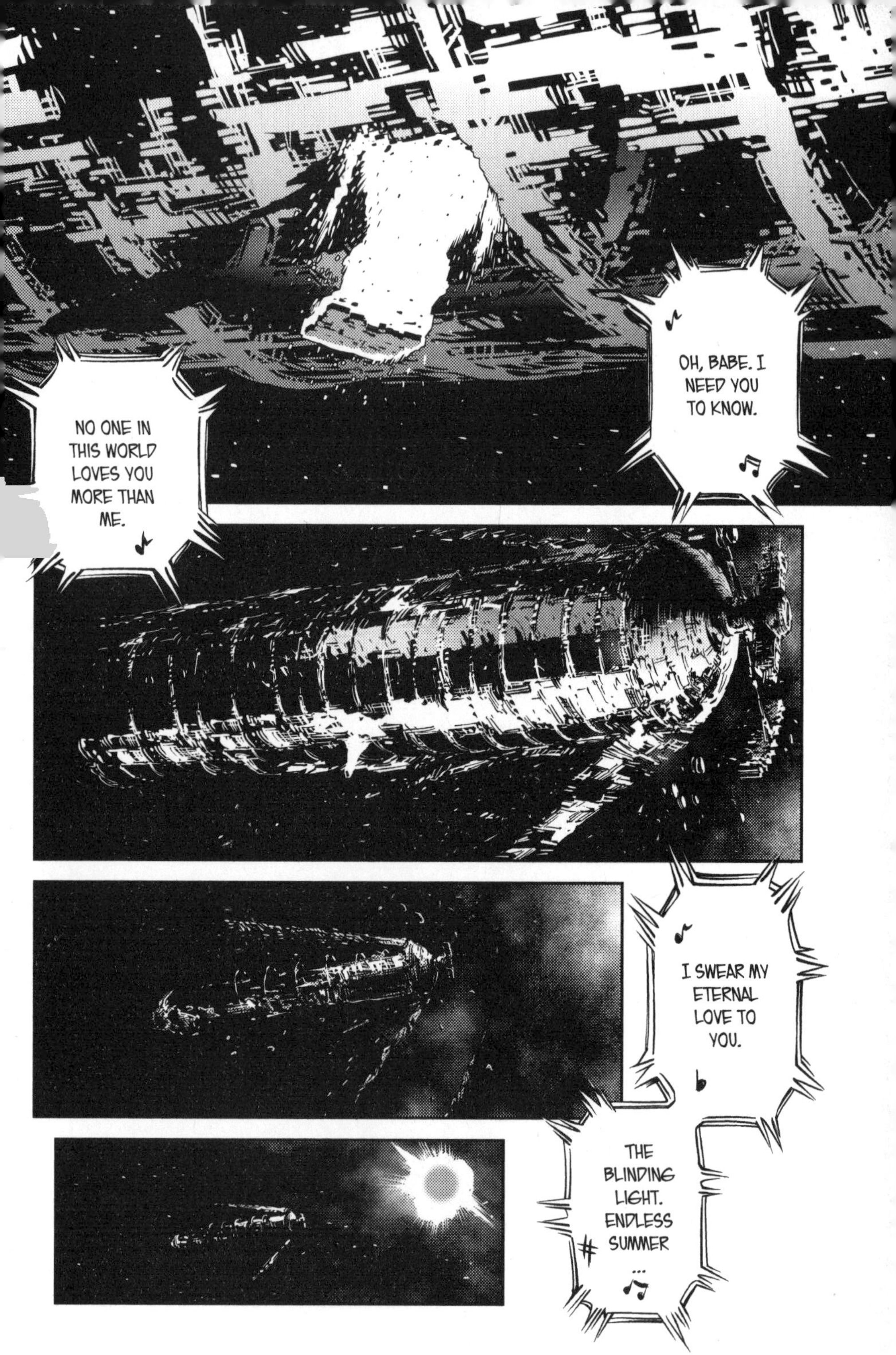
OH, BABE. I NEED YOU TO KNOW.
NO ONE IN THIS WORLD LOVES YOU MORE THAN ME.
I SWEAR MY ETERNAL LOVE TO YOU.
THE BLINDING LIGHT. ENDLESS SUMMER ...

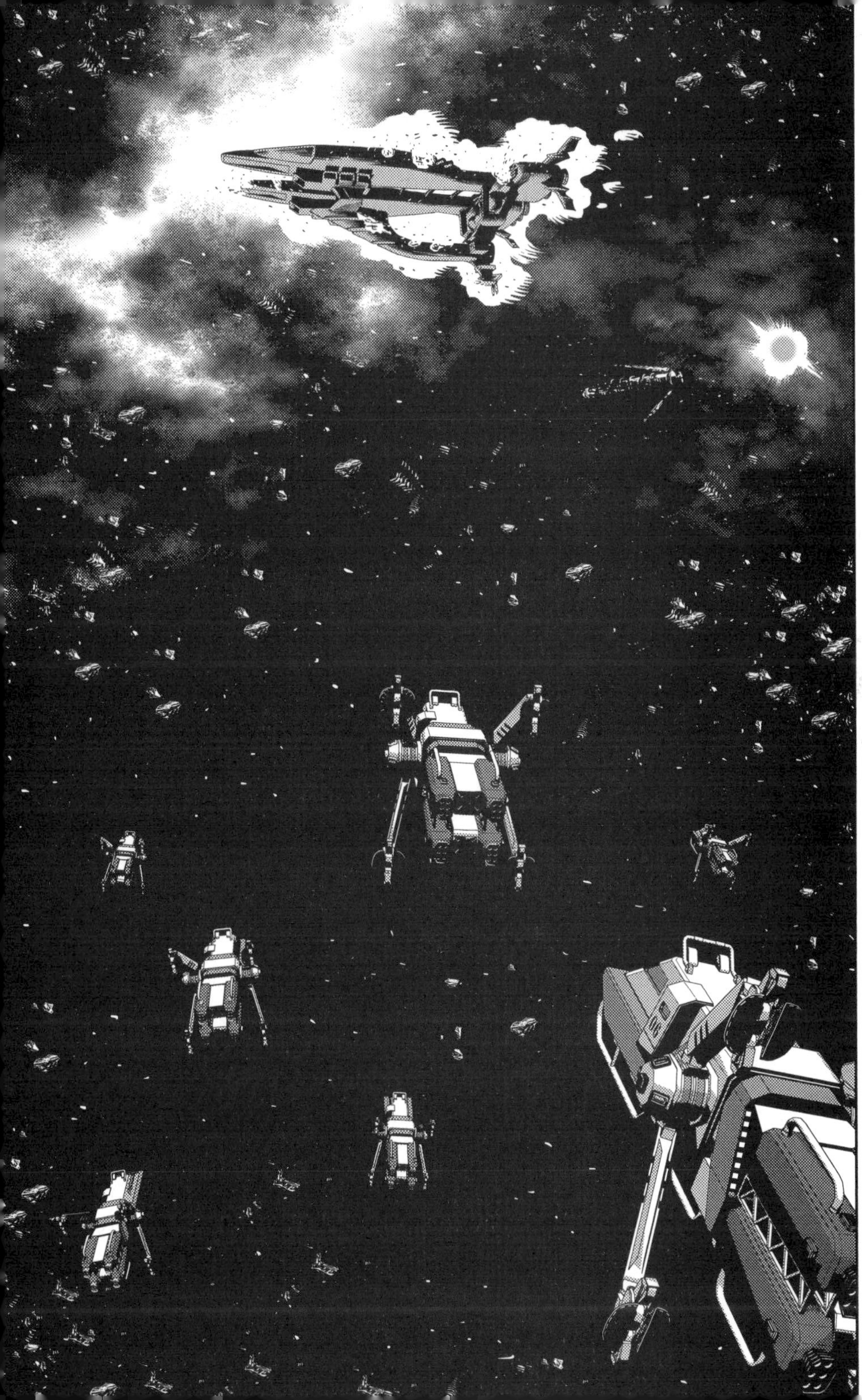

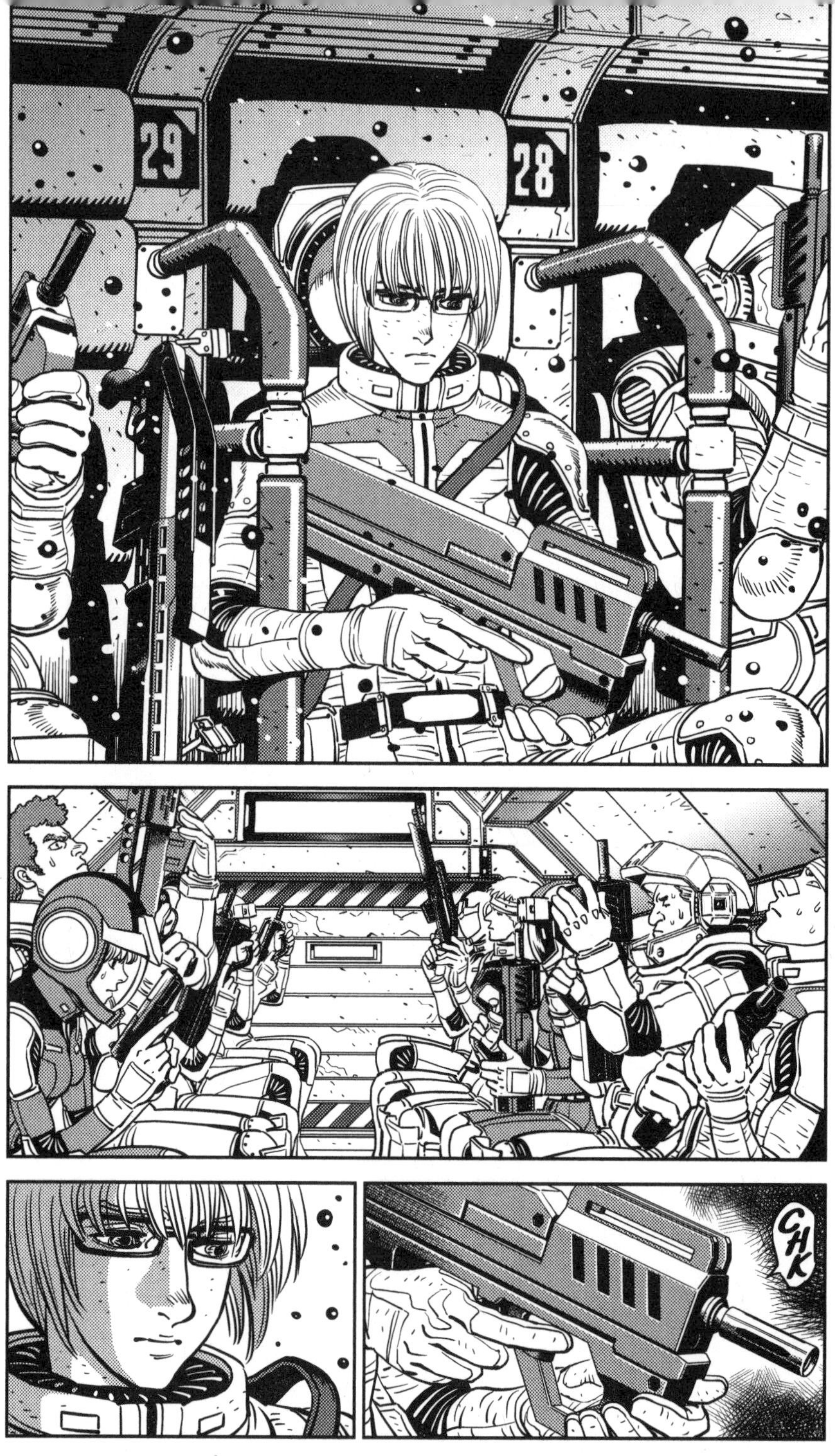
28
29
CHK

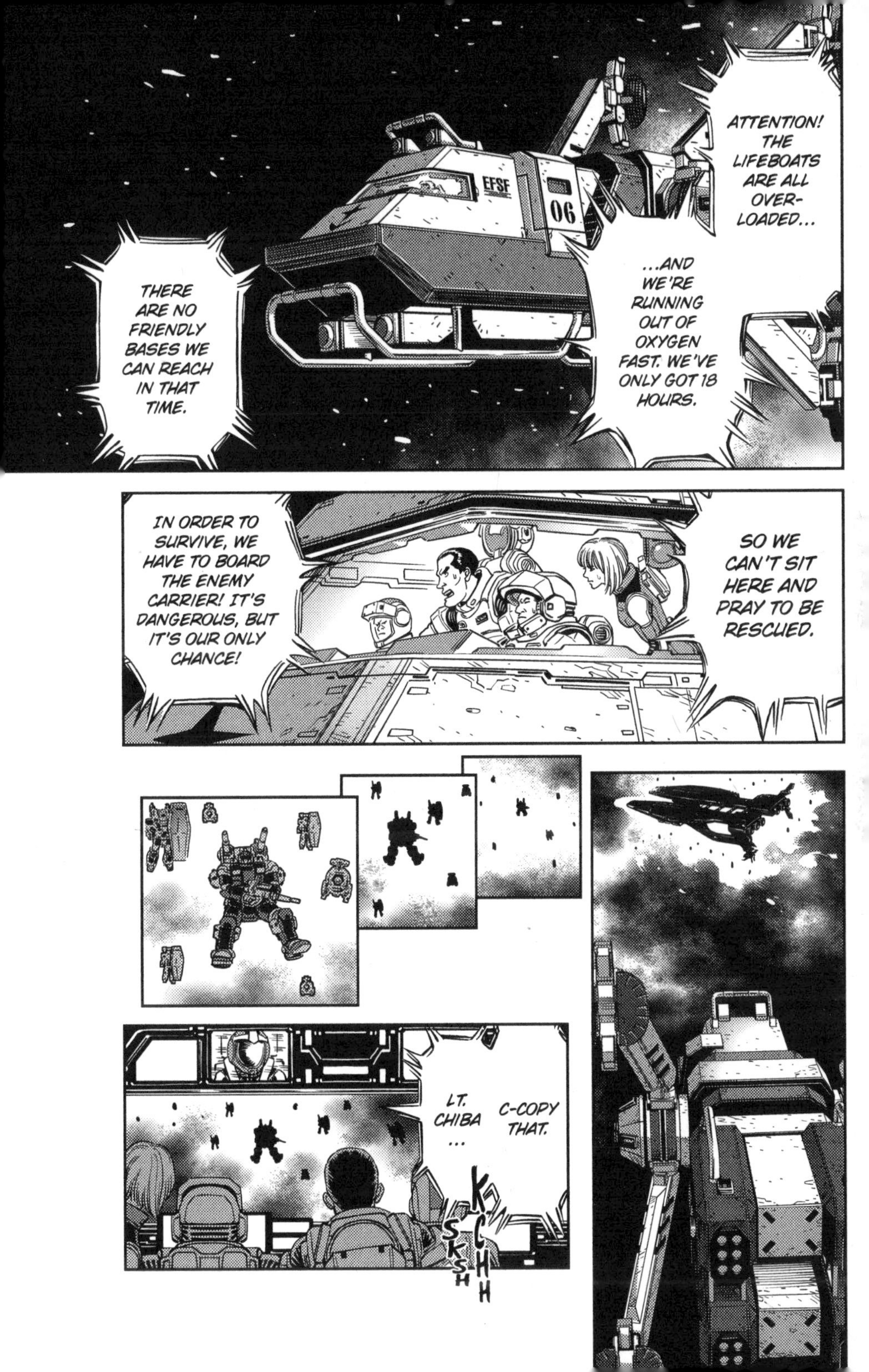
ATTENTION! THE LIFEBOATS ARE ALL OVER-LOADED...
...AND WE'RE RUNNING OUT OF OXYGEN FAST. WE'VE ONLY GOT 18 HOURS.
THERE ARE NO FRIENDLY BASES WE CAN REACH IN THAT TIME.
SO WE CAN'T SIT HERE AND PRAY TO BE RESCUED.
IN ORDER TO SURVIVE, WE HAVE TO BOARD THE ENEMY CARRIER! IT'S DANGEROUS, BUT IT'S OUR ONLY CHANCE!
EFSF
06
C-COPY THAT.
LT. CHIBA ...
KCHH
SKSH

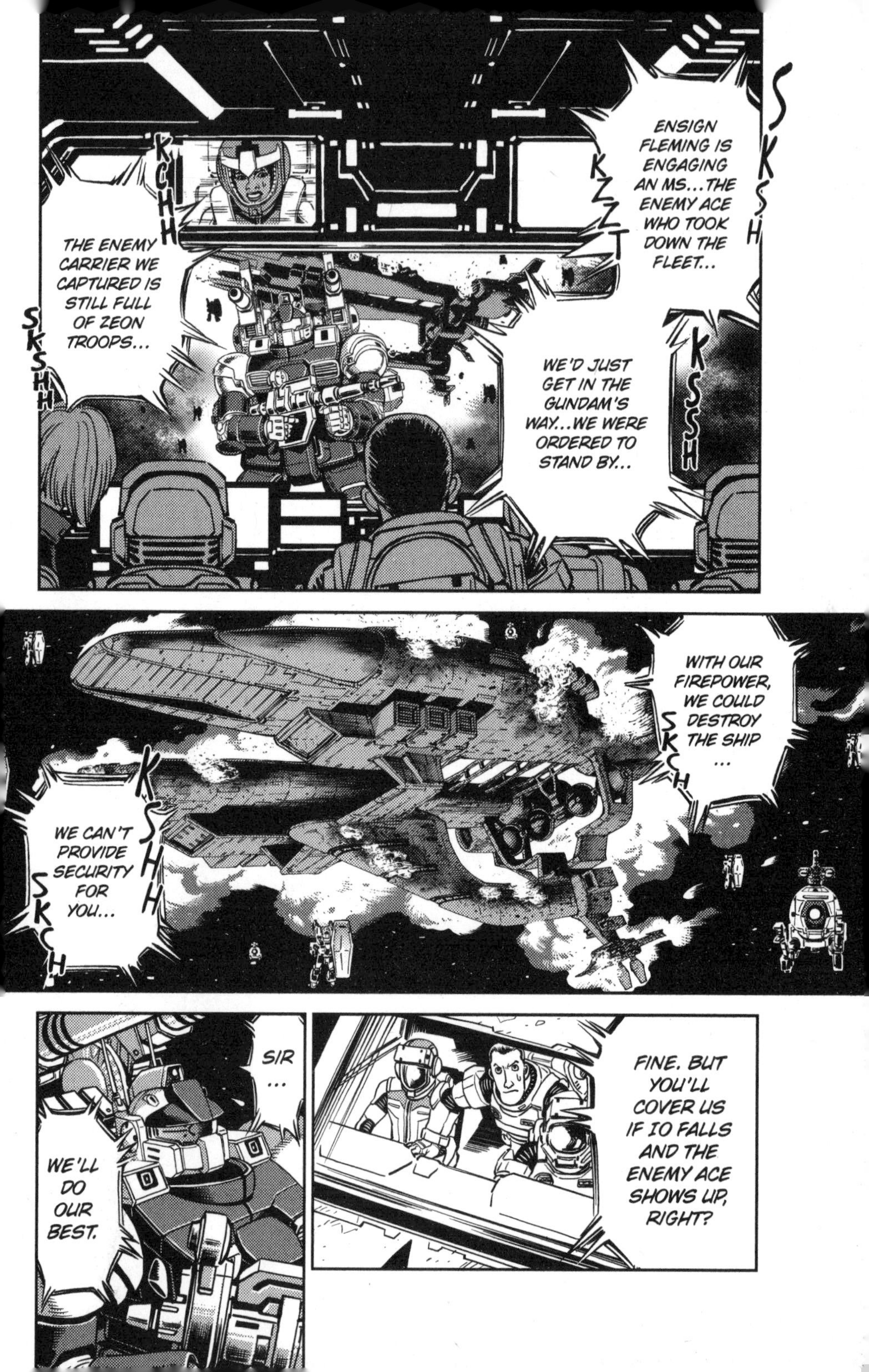
SKSH
KZZT
ENSIGN FLEMING IS ENGAGING AN MS...THE ENEMY ACE WHO TOOK DOWN THE FLEET...
KSSH
WE'D JUST GET IN THE GUNDAM'S WAY...WE WERE ORDERED TO STAND BY...
KCHH
THE ENEMY CARRIER WE CAPTURED IS STILL FULL OF ZEON TROOPS...
SKSHH
SKCH
WITH OUR FIREPOWER, WE COULD DESTROY THE SHIP ...
KSHH
WE CAN'T PROVIDE SECURITY FOR YOU...
SKCH
FINE. BUT YOU'LL COVER US IF IO FALLS AND THE ENEMY ACE SHOWS UP, RIGHT?
SIR ...
WE'LL DO OUR BEST.

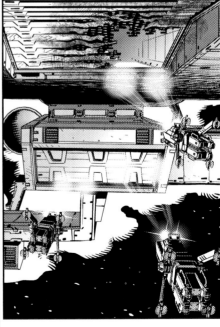

WE'LL GO IN FIRST AND SECURE THE INTERIOR OF THE SHIP!

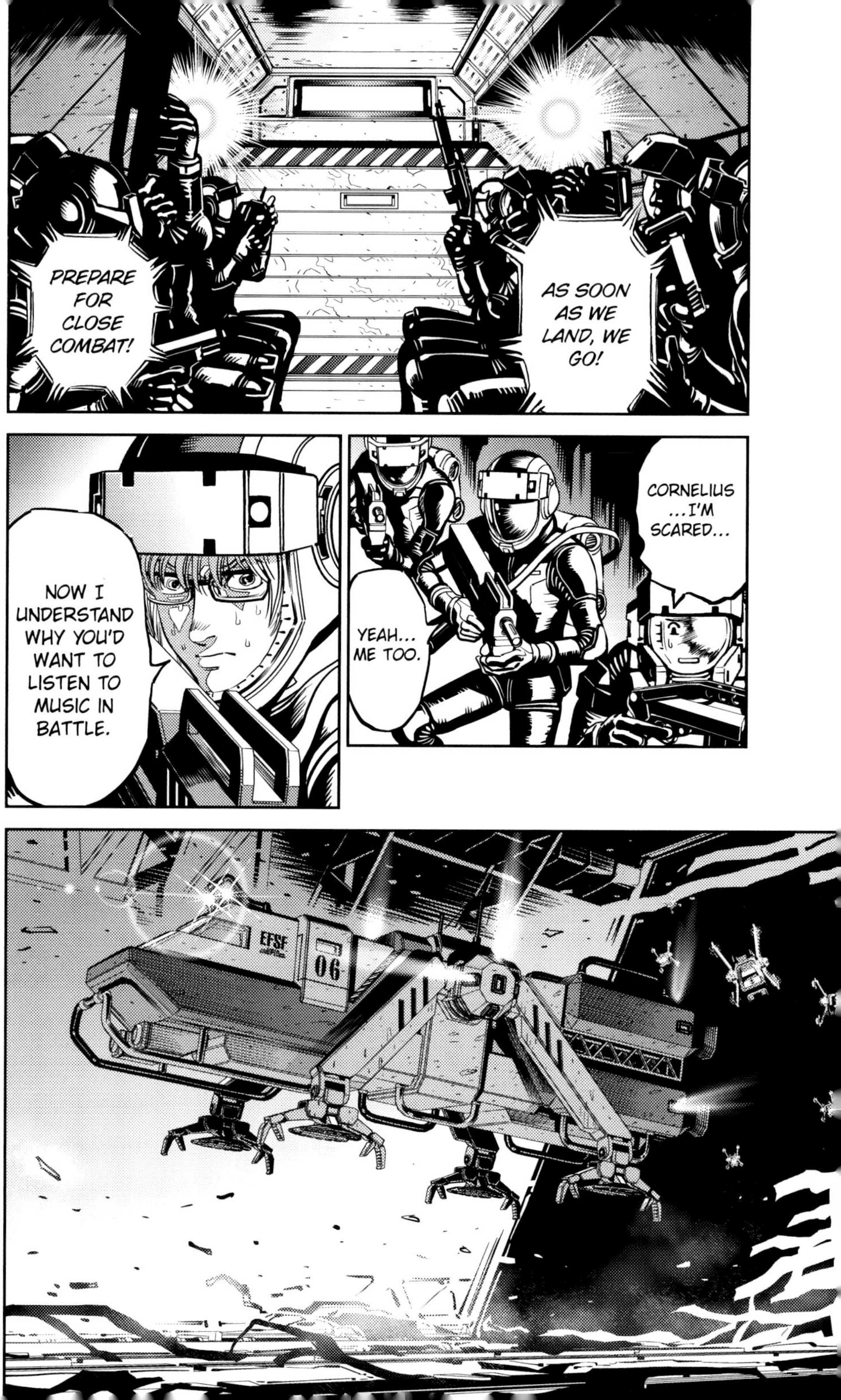
AS SOON AS WE LAND, WE GO!
PREPARE FOR CLOSE COMBAT!
CORNELIUS ...I'M SCARED...
YEAH... ME TOO.
NOW I UNDERSTAND WHY YOU'D WANT TO LISTEN TO MUSIC IN BATTLE.
EFSF
06

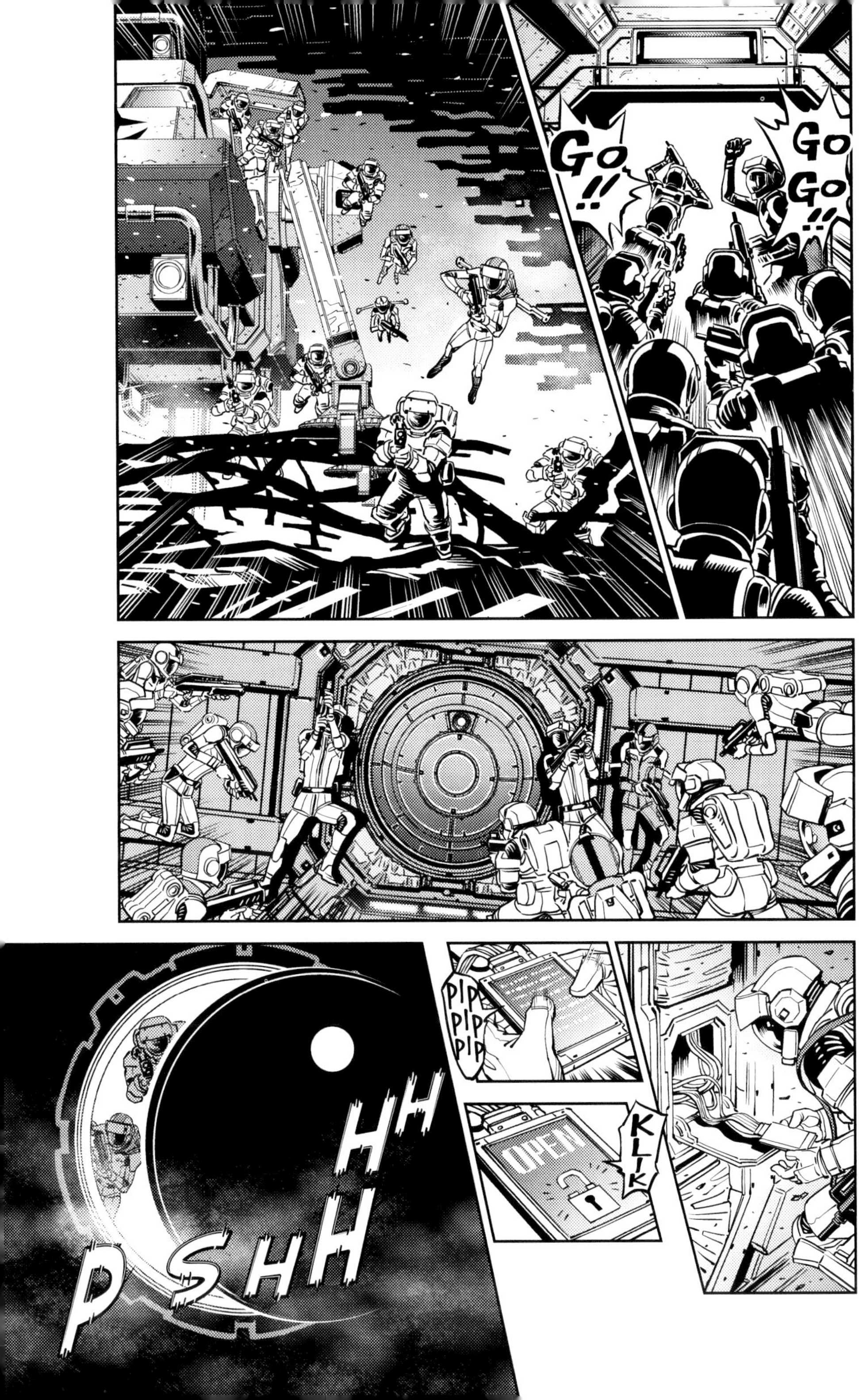
GO GO!!
GO!!
PIP PIP PIP
OPEN
KLIK
PSHHHHH

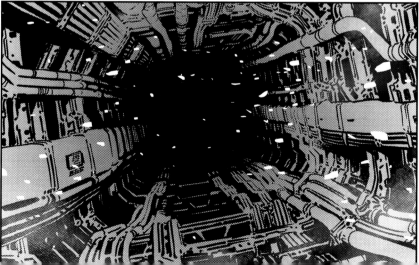

MOBILE SUIT GUNDAM
THUNDERBOLT CHAPTER 22

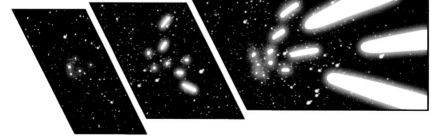

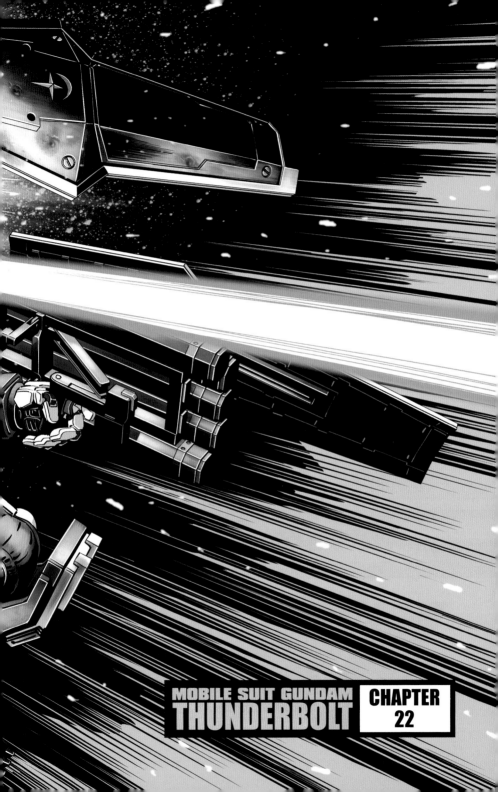

MOBILE SUIT GUNDAM
THUNDERBOLT
CHAPTER 22

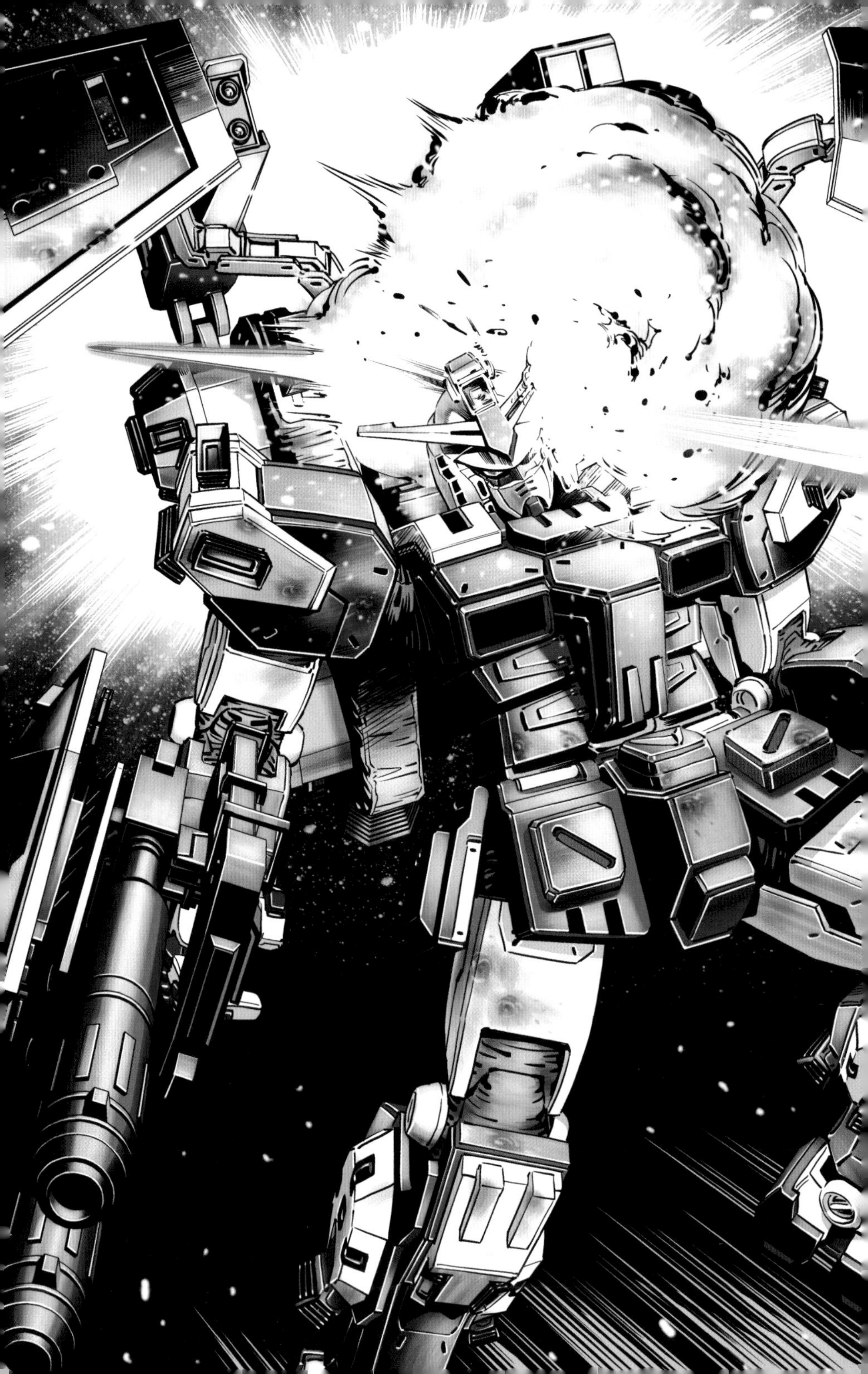

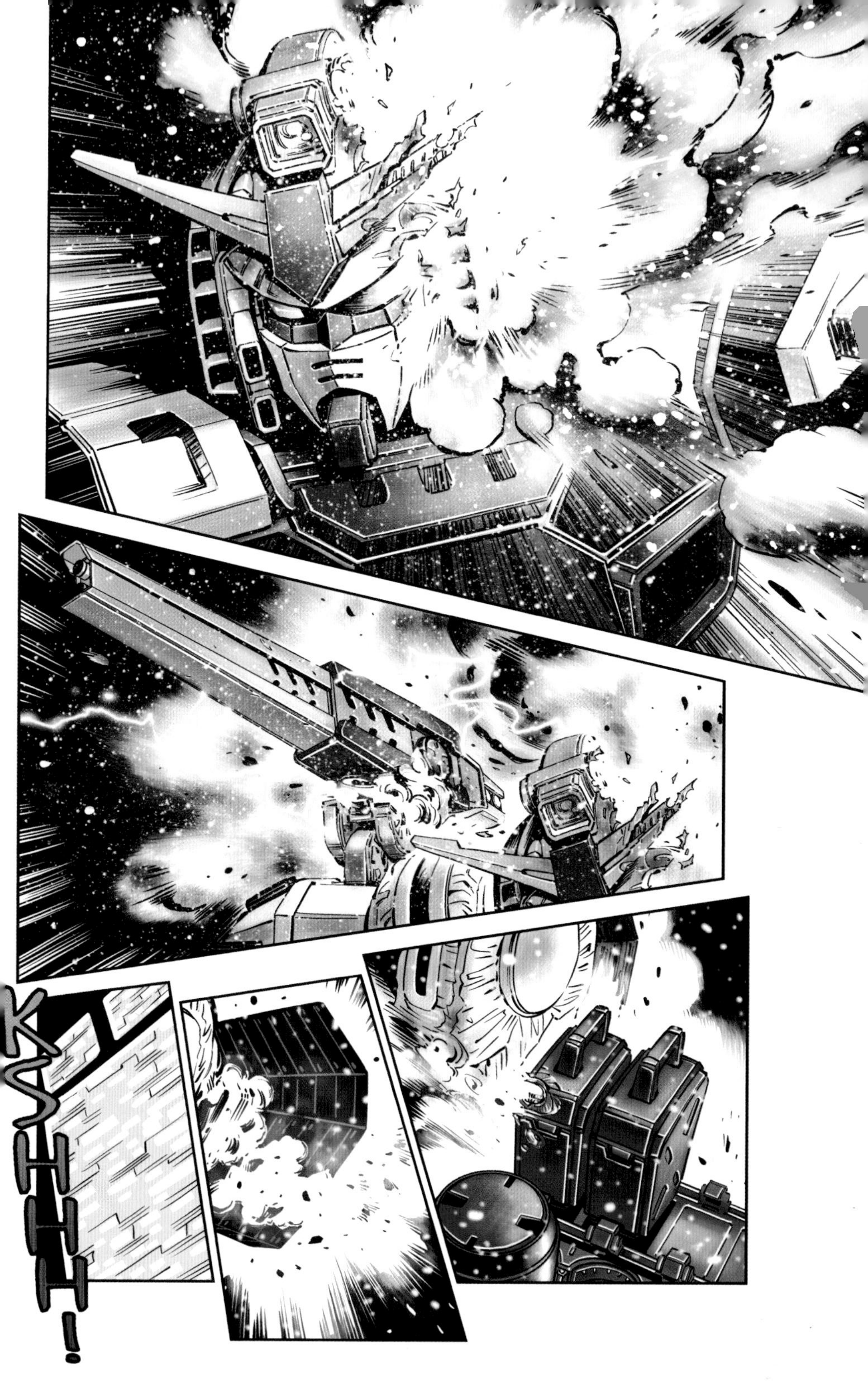
KSHHHH!

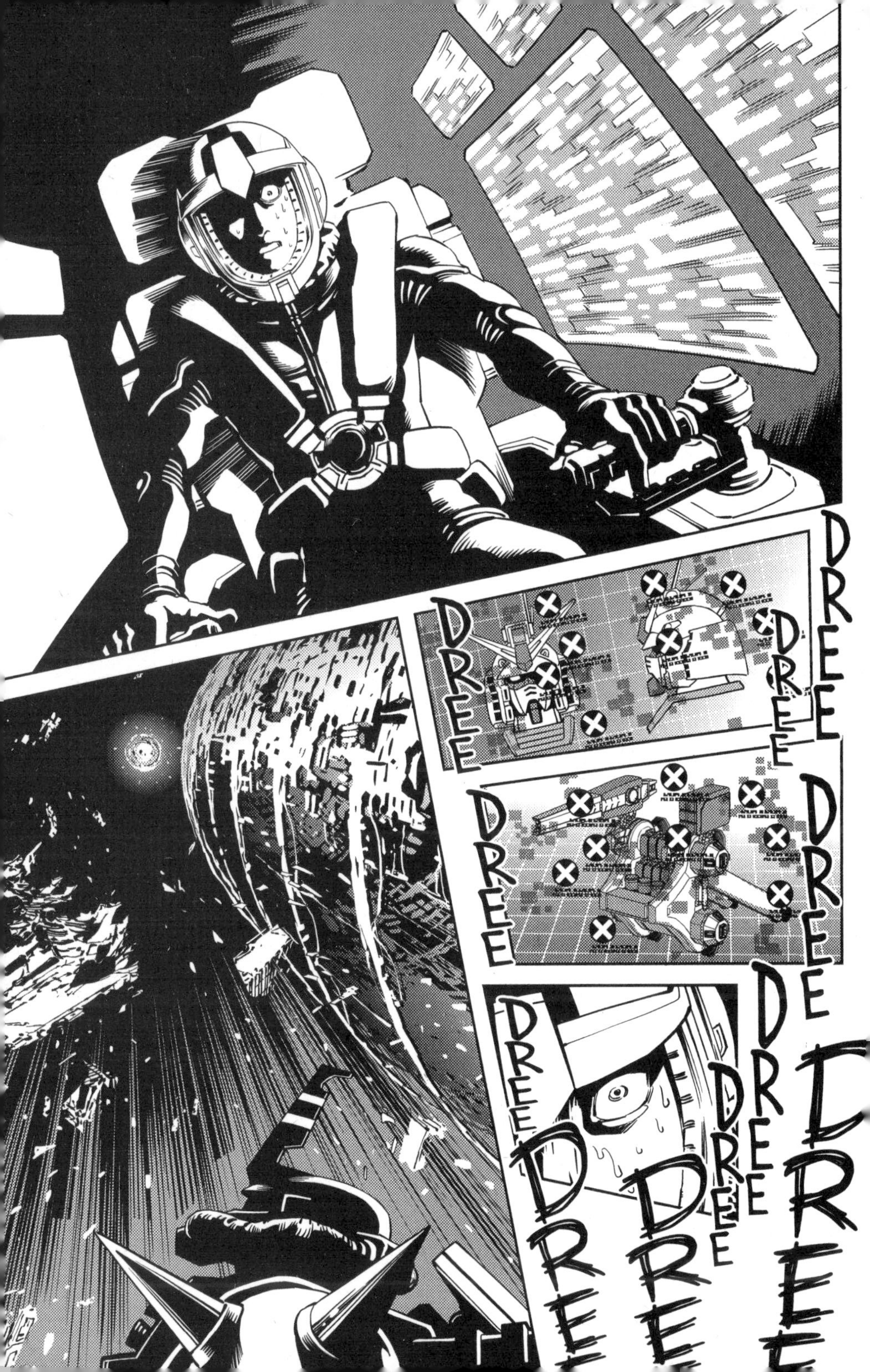
DREE
DREE
DREE
DREE
DREE
DREE
DREE
DREE
DREE
DREE
DREE
DREE

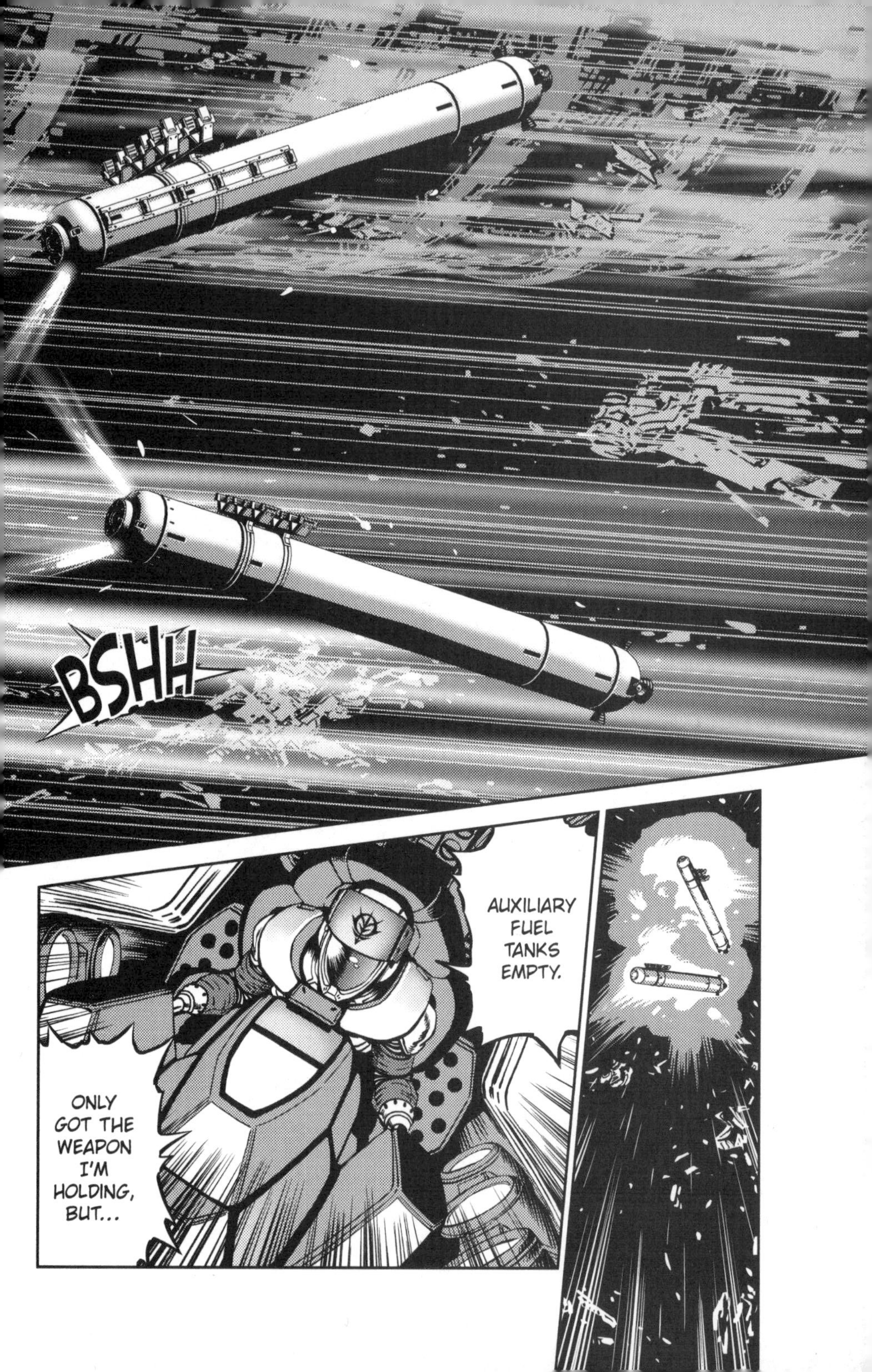
BSHH
AUXILIARY FUEL TANKS EMPTY.
ONLY GOT THE WEAPON I'M HOLDING, BUT...

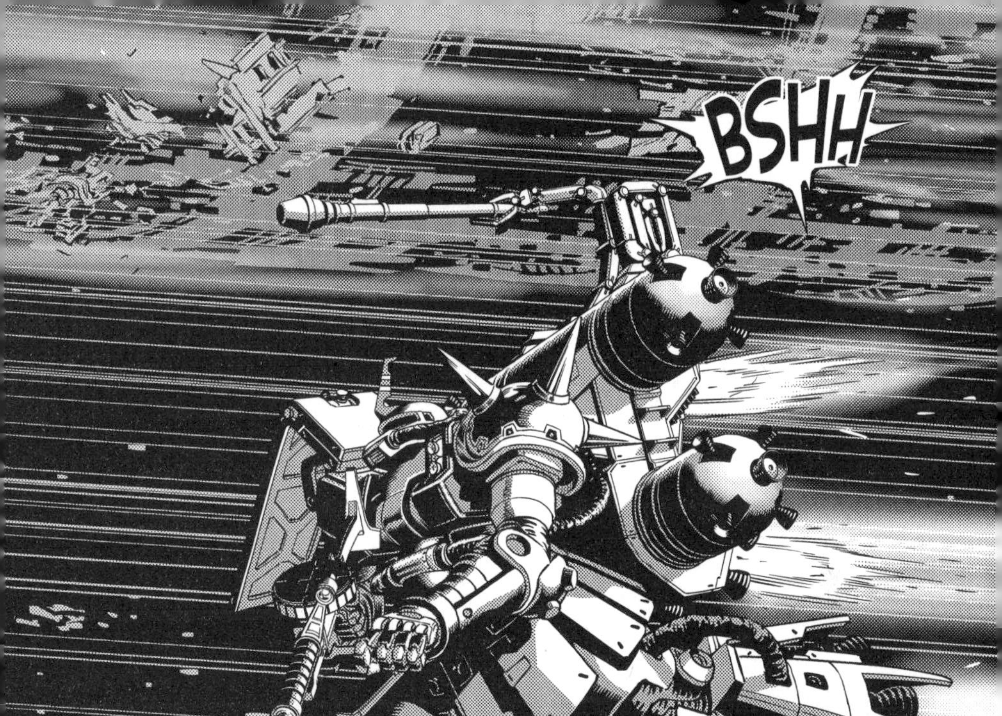
BSHH

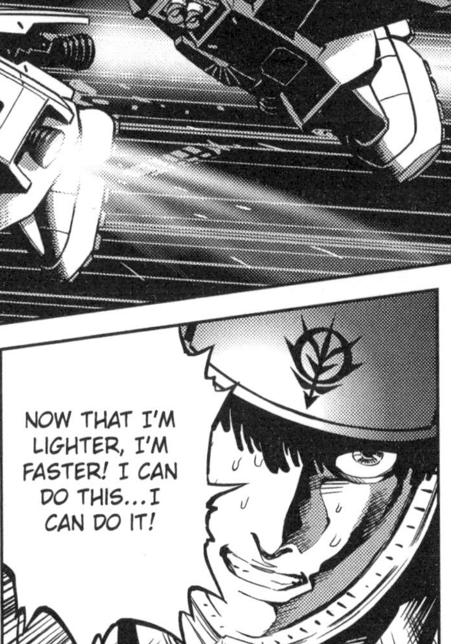
NOW THAT I'M LIGHTER, I'M FASTER! I CAN DO THIS...I CAN DO IT!

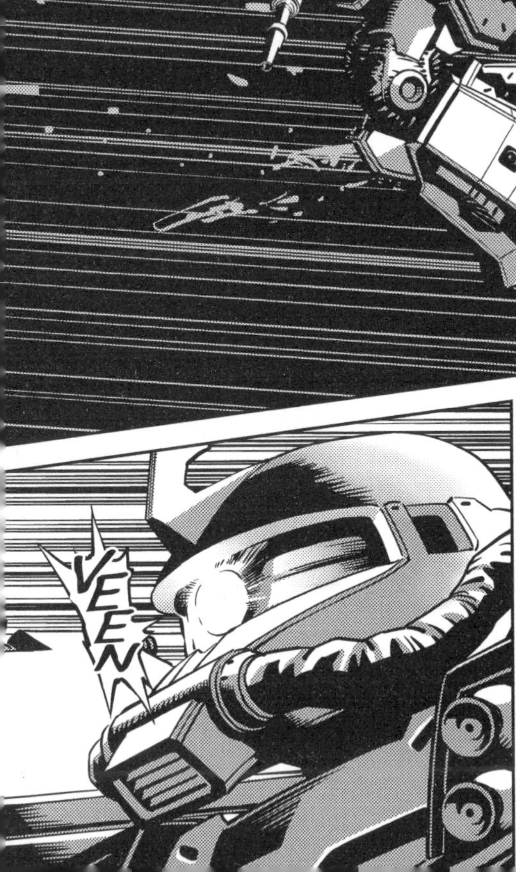
VEEN

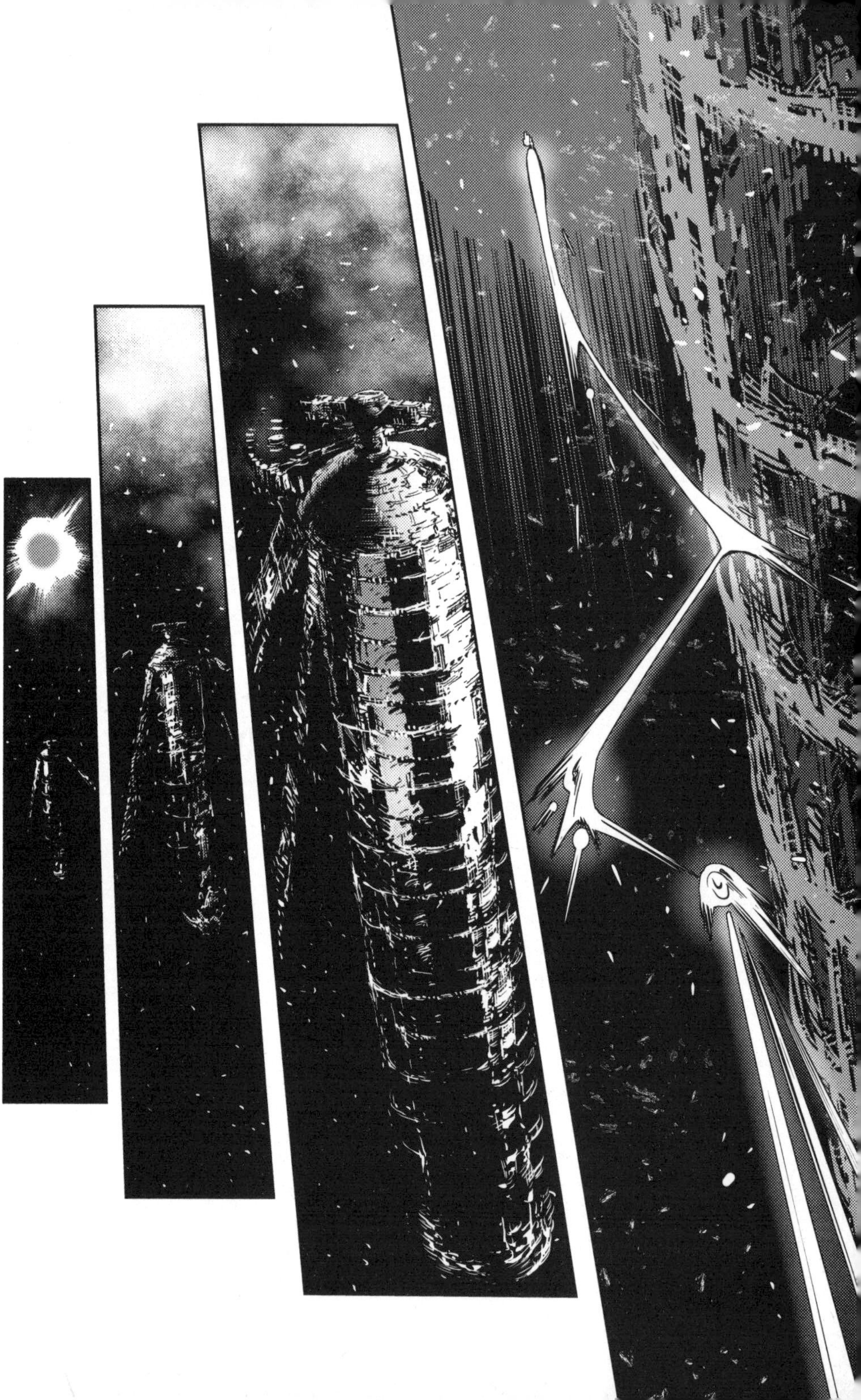

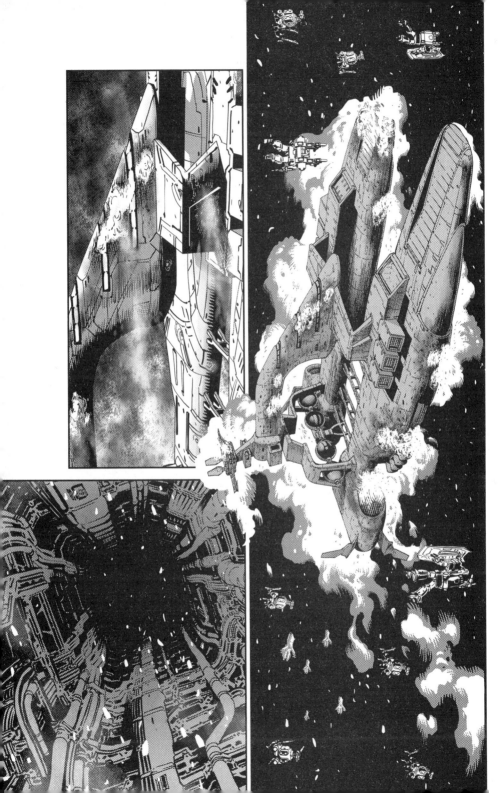

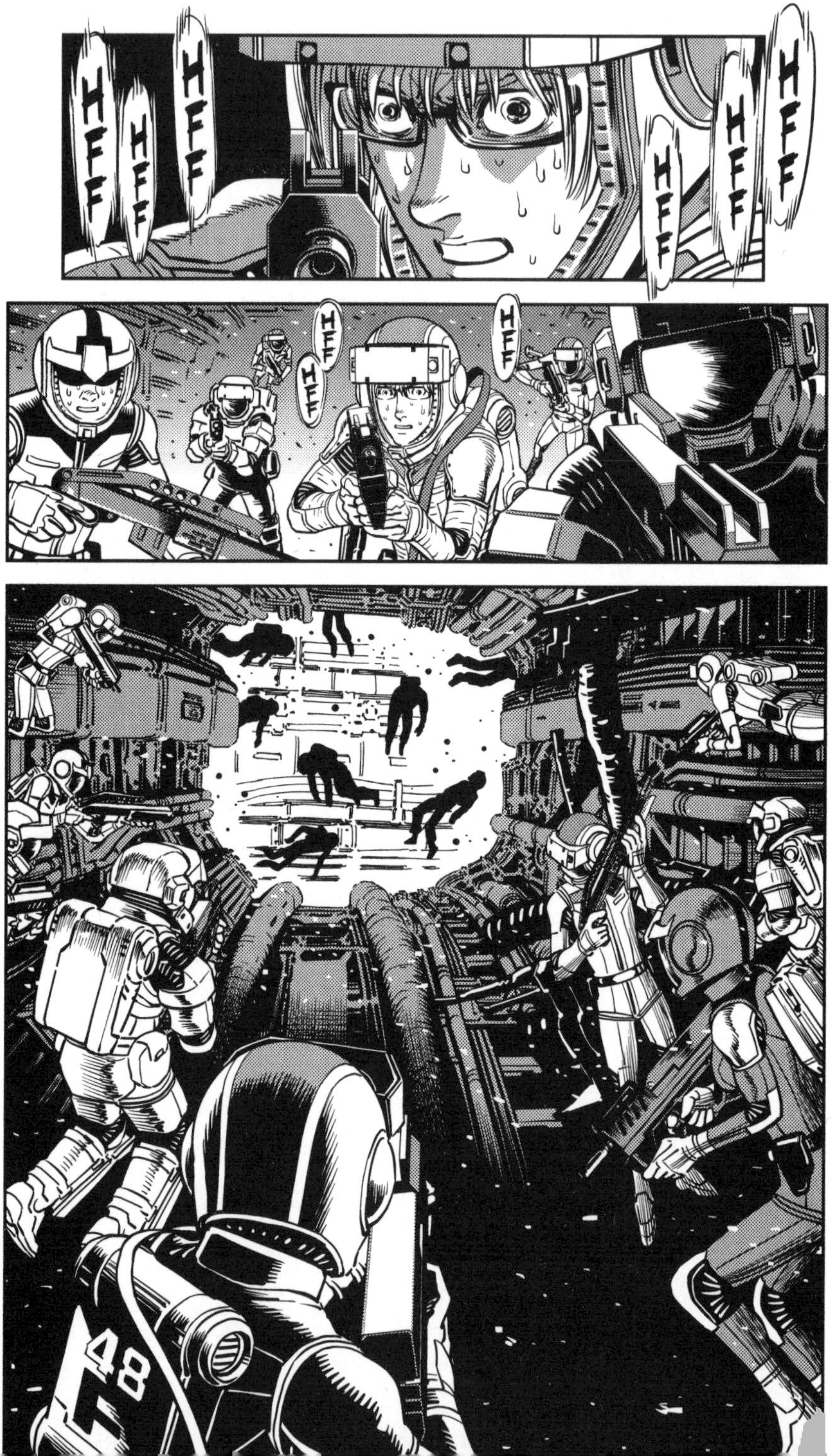
HFF
HFF
HFF
HFF
HFF
HFF
HFF
HFF
HFF
48

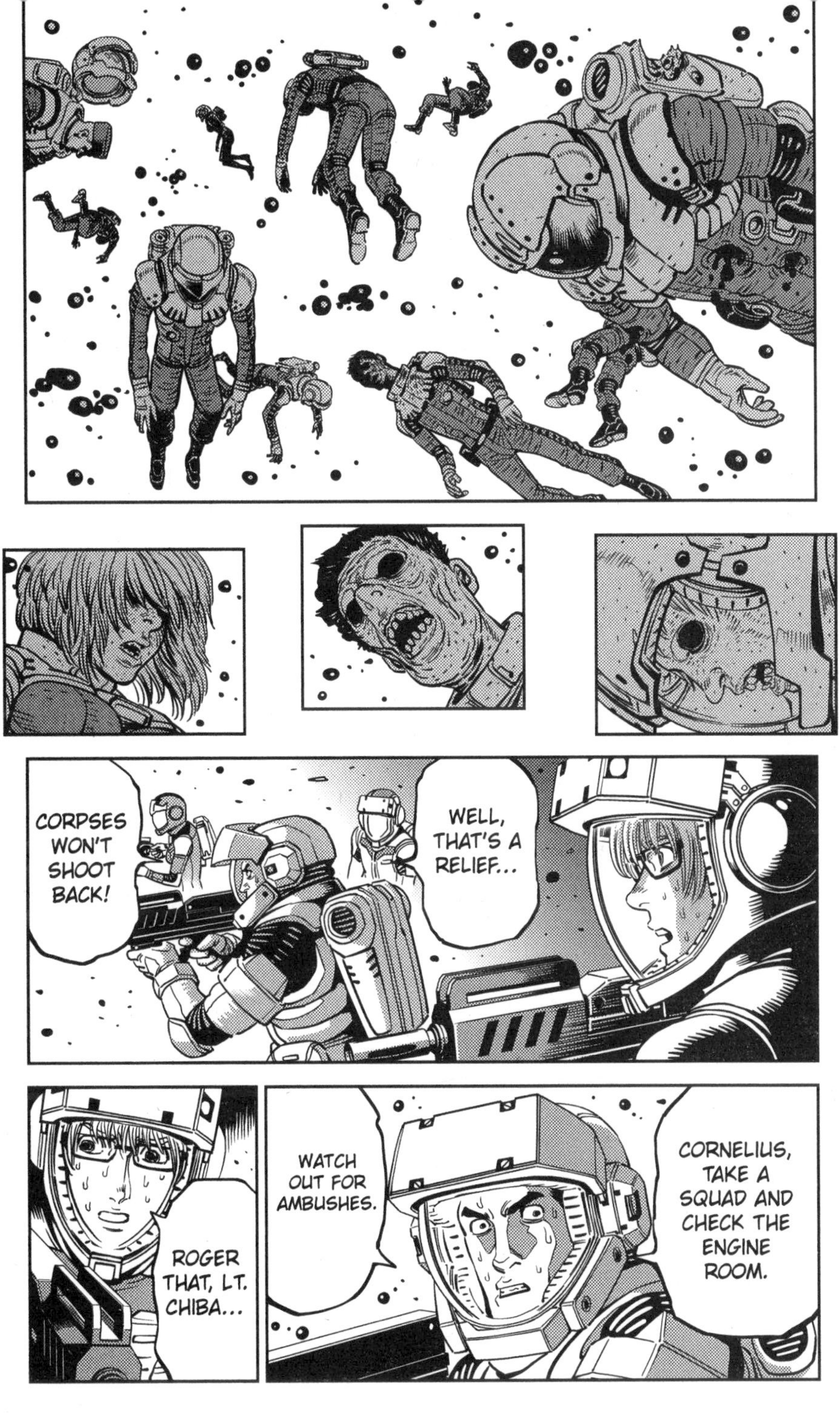
WELL, THAT'S A RELIEF...
CORPSES WON'T SHOOT BACK!
CORNELIUS, TAKE A SQUAD AND CHECK THE ENGINE ROOM.
WATCH OUT FOR AMBUSHES.
ROGER THAT, LT. CHIBA...

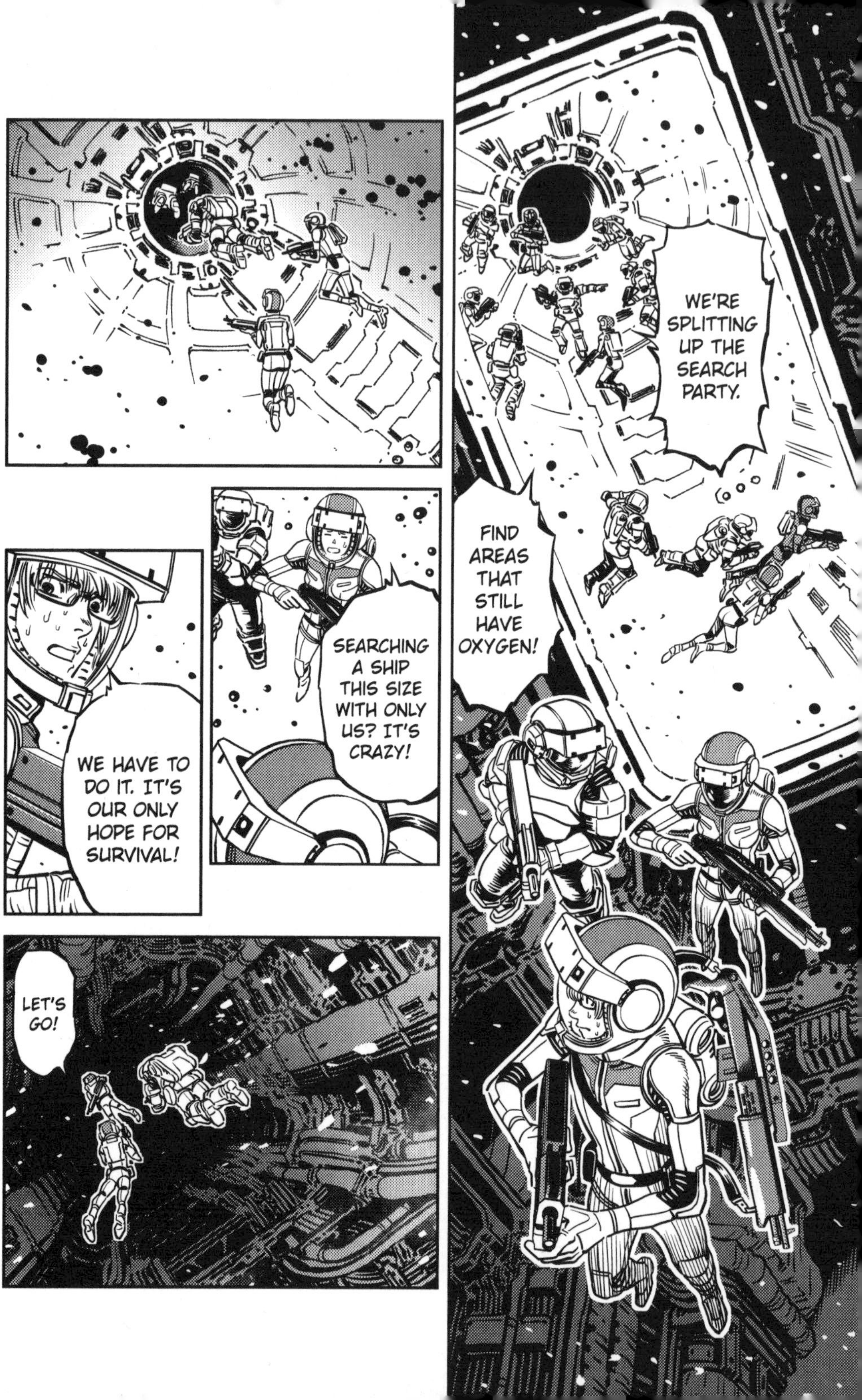
WE'RE SPLITTING UP THE SEARCH PARTY.
FIND AREAS THAT STILL HAVE OXYGEN!
SEARCHING A SHIP THIS SIZE WITH ONLY US? IT'S CRAZY!
WE HAVE TO DO IT. IT'S OUR ONLY HOPE FOR SURVIVAL!
LET'S GO!

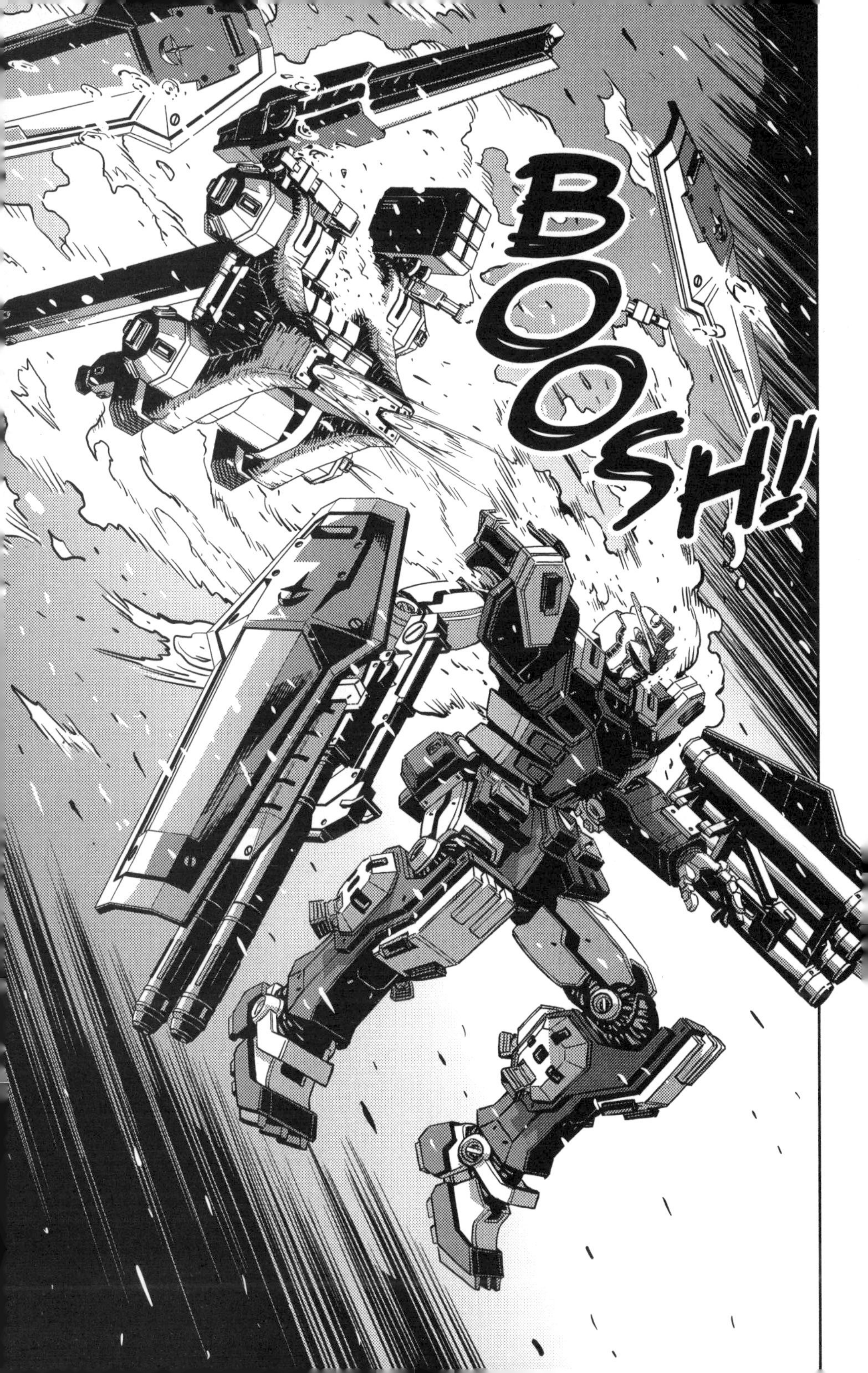
BOOOSH!!

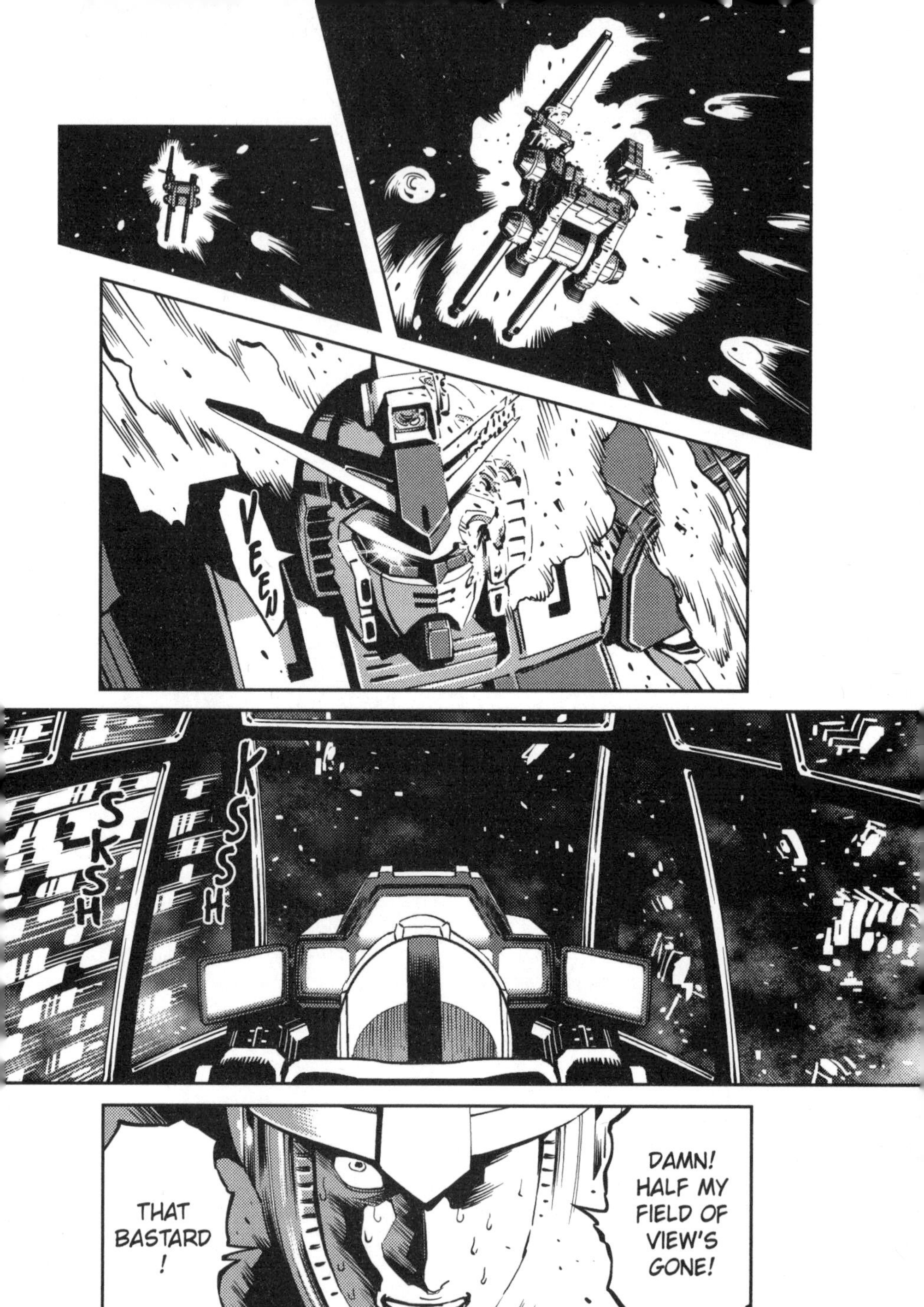
VEEN
KSSH
SKSH
DAMN! HALF MY FIELD OF VIEW'S GONE!
THAT BASTARD!

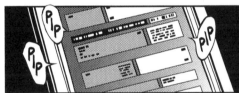

GOOD!

YES! THERE'S OXYGEN IN HERE!

THERE'S EVEN MORE IN THE SECTION UP AHEAD!

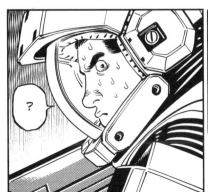

?

?

WHAT? THERE'S MUSIC PLAYING ON THE SHIP'S P.A....

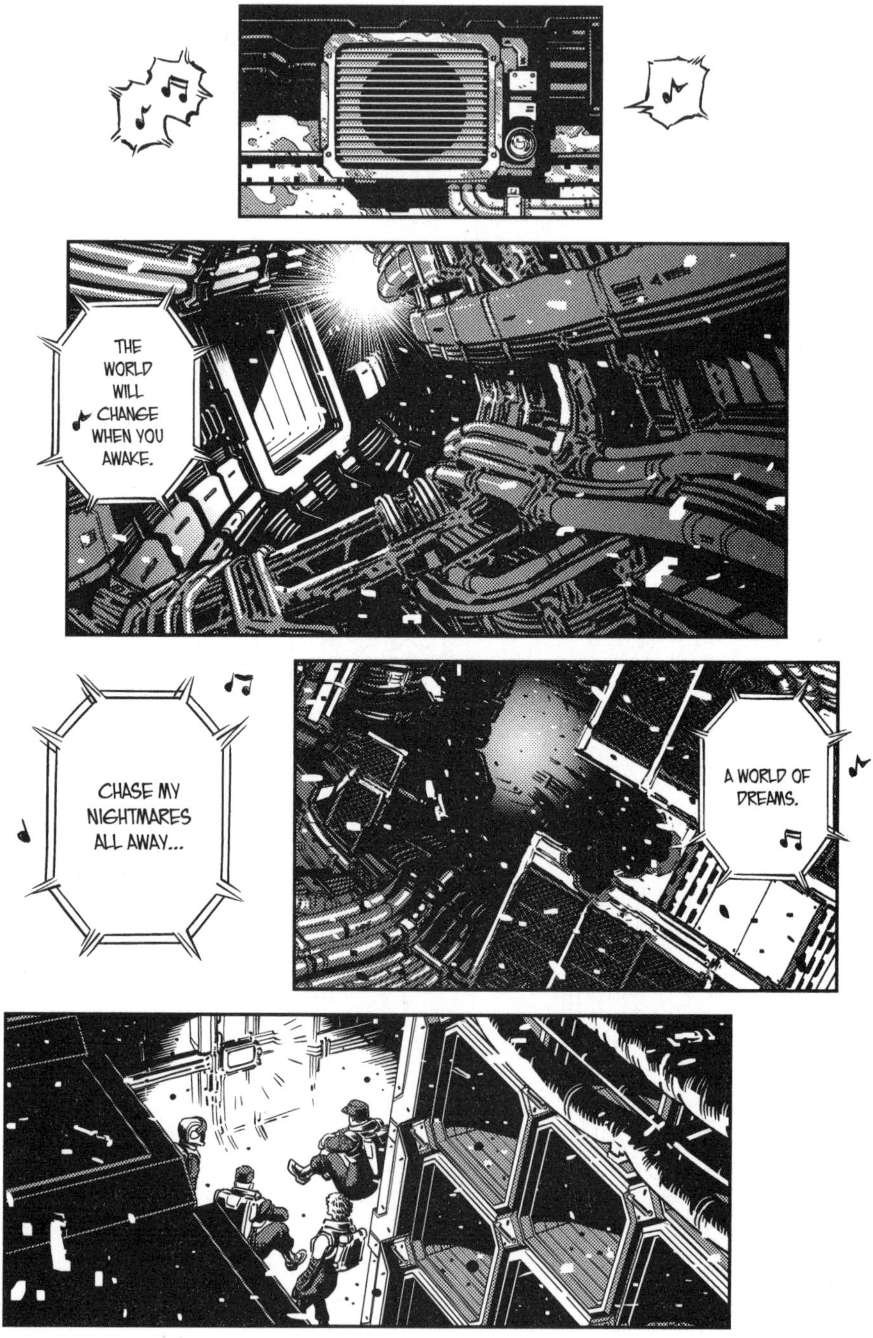
THE WORLD WILL CHANGE WHEN YOU AWAKE.
A WORLD OF DREAMS.
CHASE MY NIGHTMARES ALL AWAY...

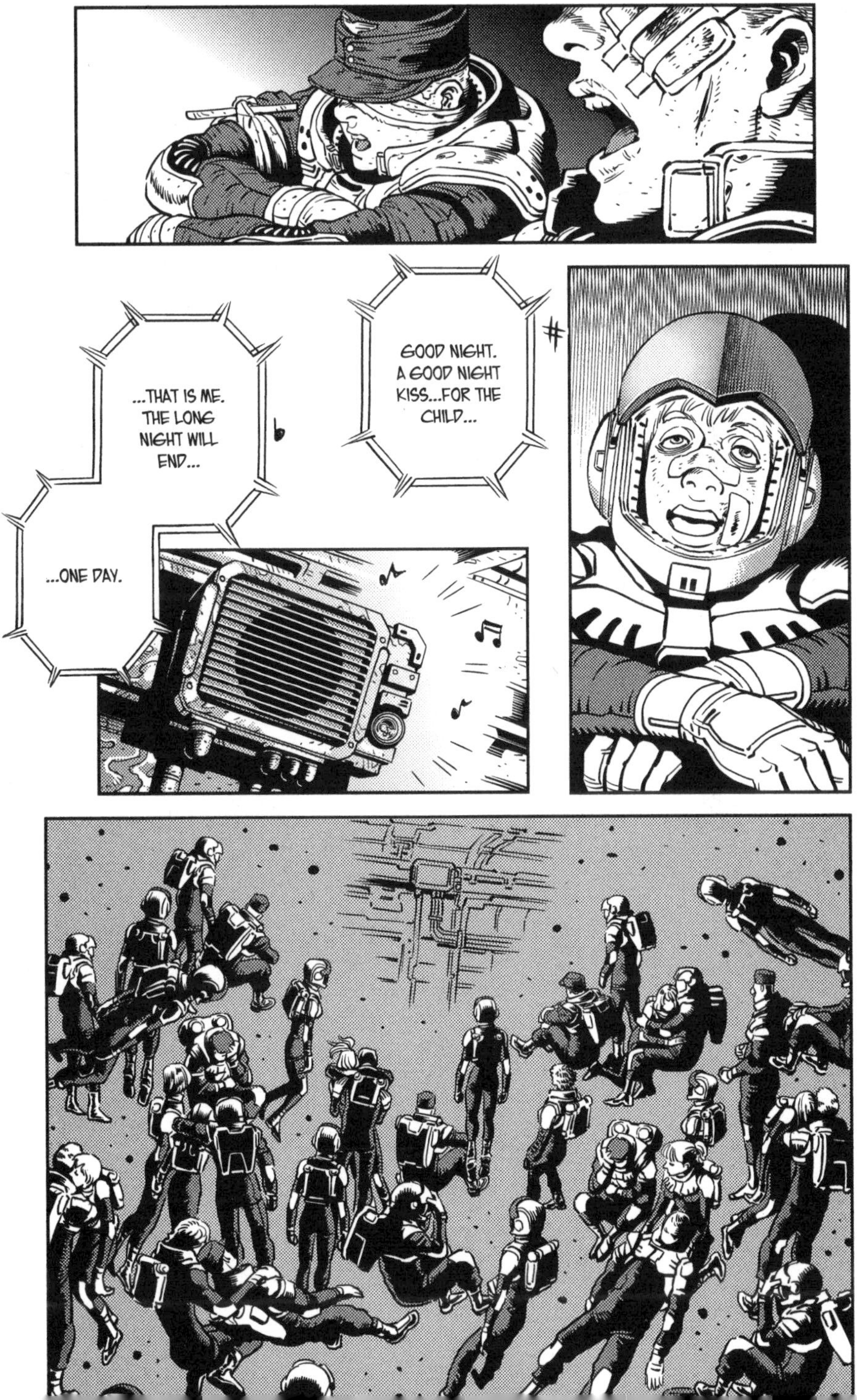
GOOD NIGHT. A GOOD NIGHT KISS...FOR THE CHILD...
...THAT IS ME. THE LONG NIGHT WILL END...
...ONE DAY.

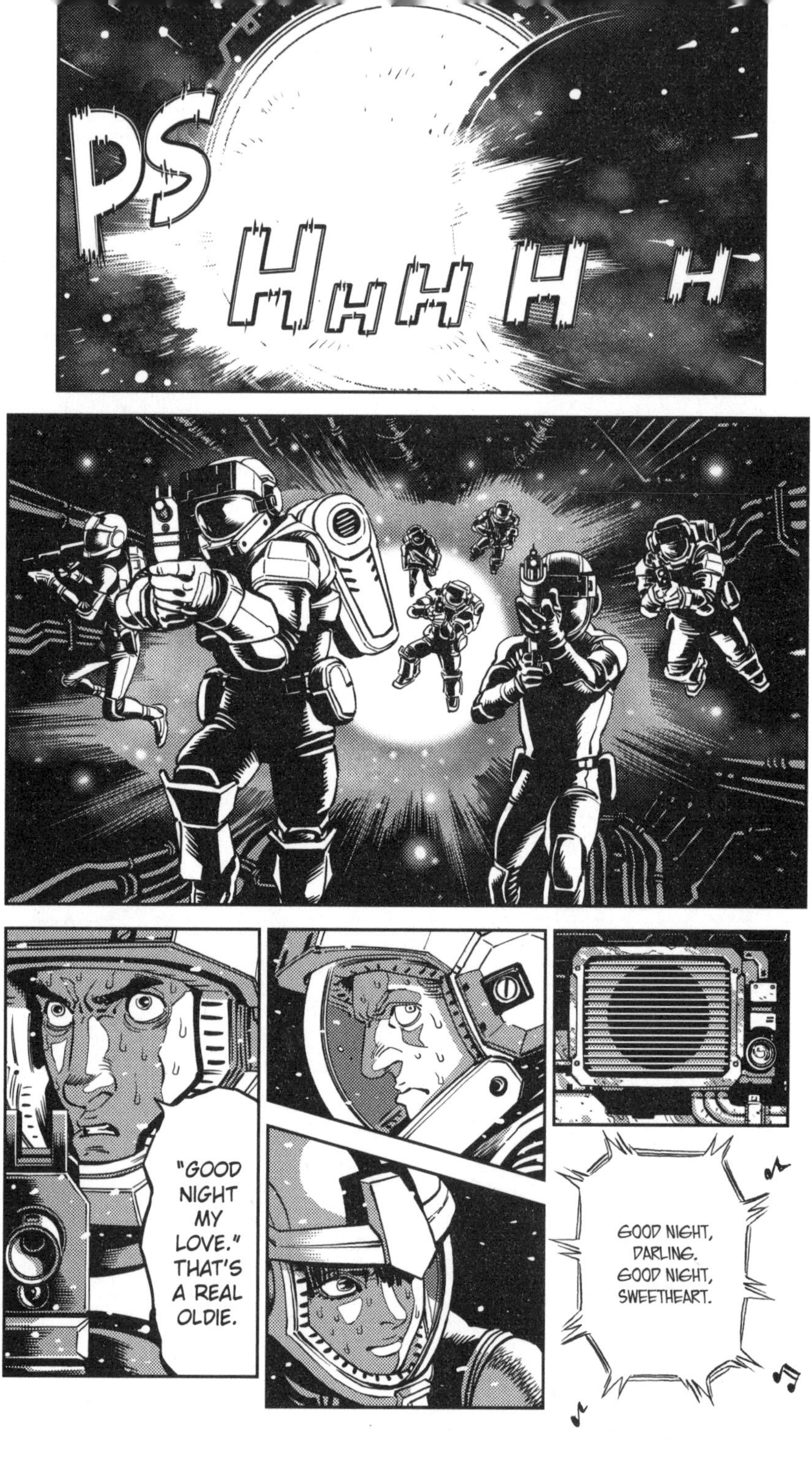
PSHHHHH
GOOD NIGHT, DARLING. GOOD NIGHT, SWEETHEART.
"GOOD NIGHT MY LOVE." THAT'S A REAL OLDIE.

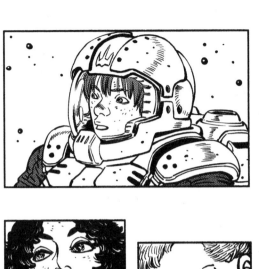

I BELIEVE. THIS NIGHTMARE WILL ONE DAY END.

I BELIEVE. THAT ONE DAY WE WILL ALL LOVE ONE ANOTHER.

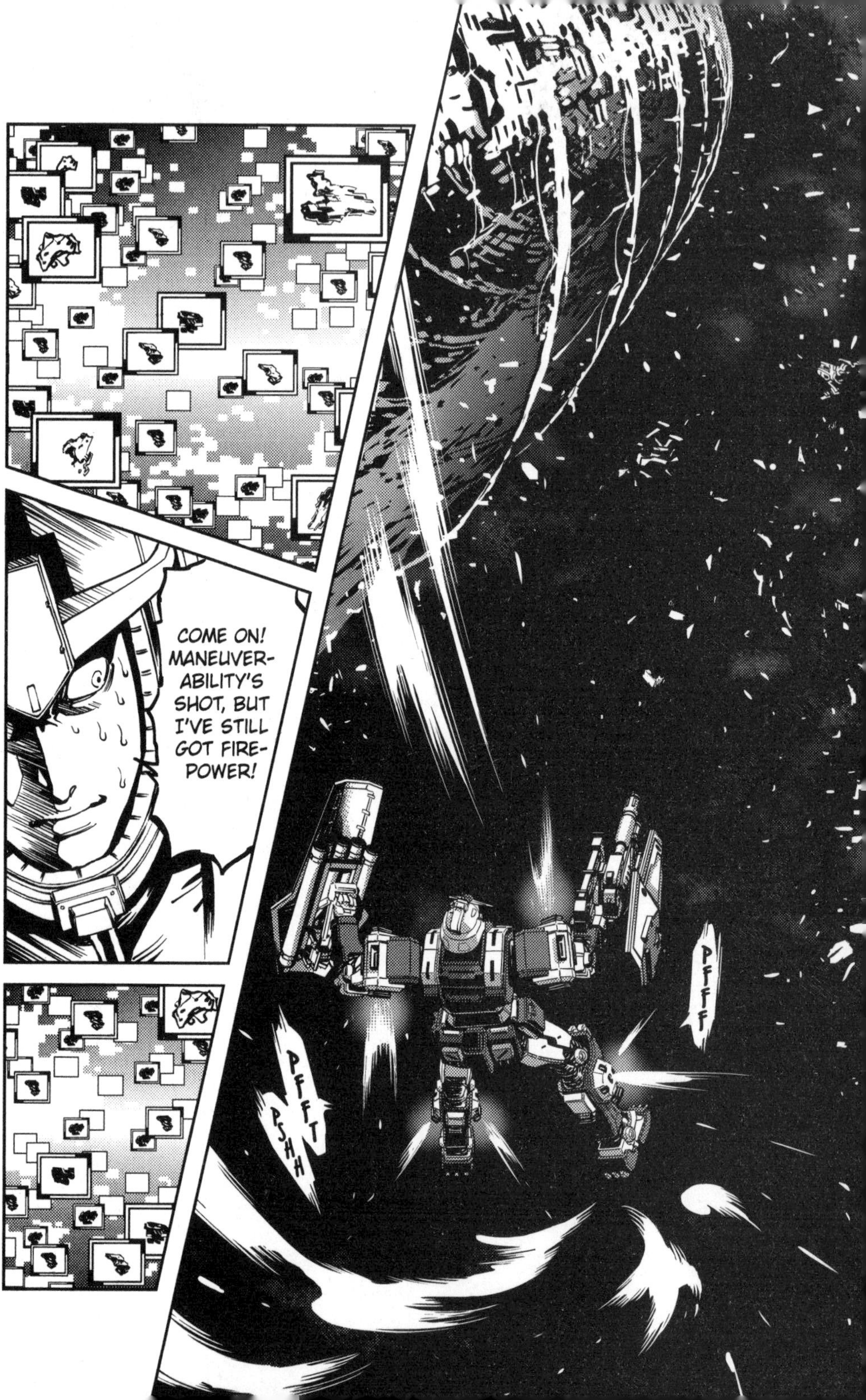
PFFF
PFFT
PSHH
COME ON! MANEUVER-ABILITY'S SHOT, BUT I'VE STILL GOT FIRE-POWER!

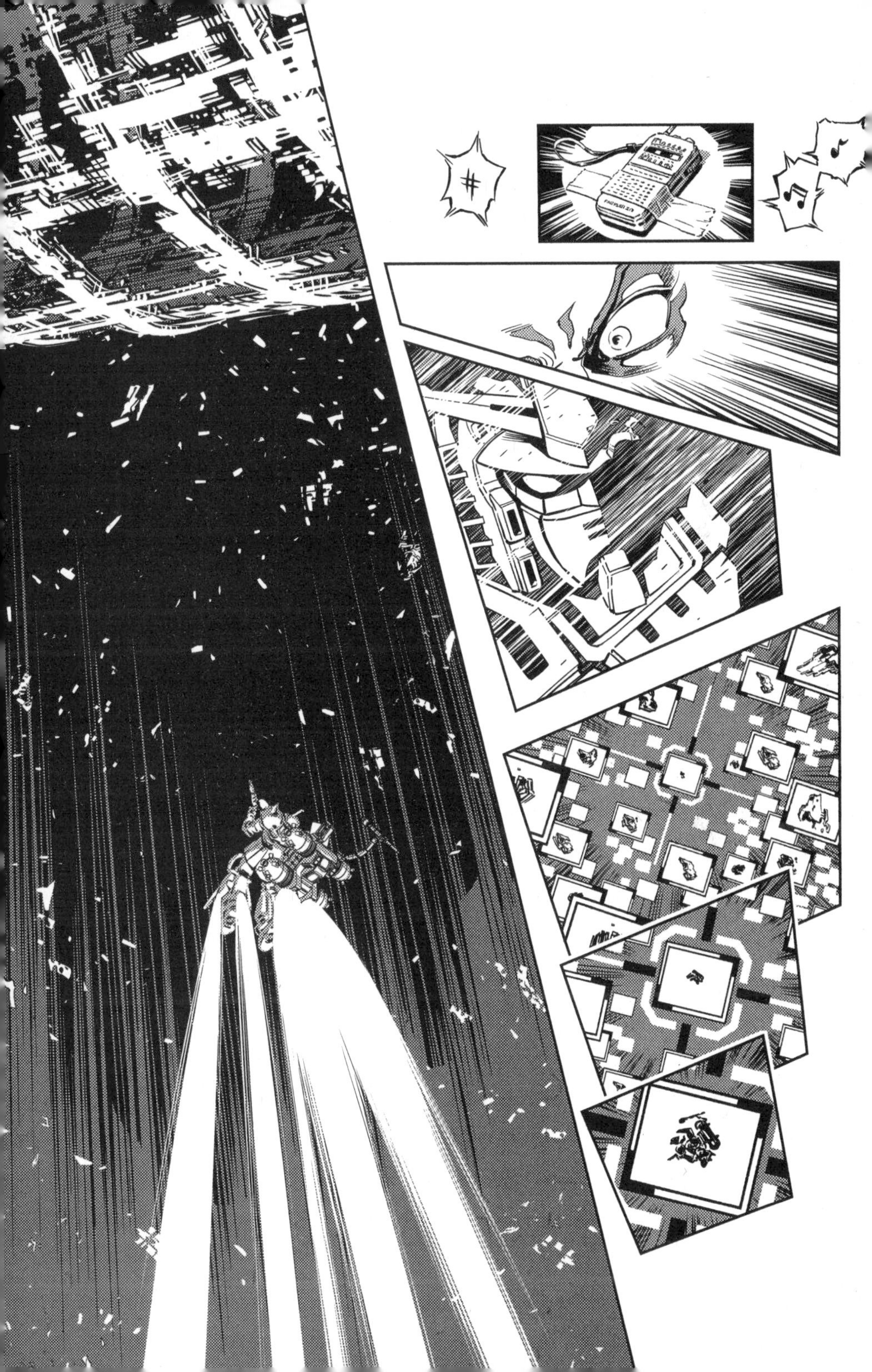

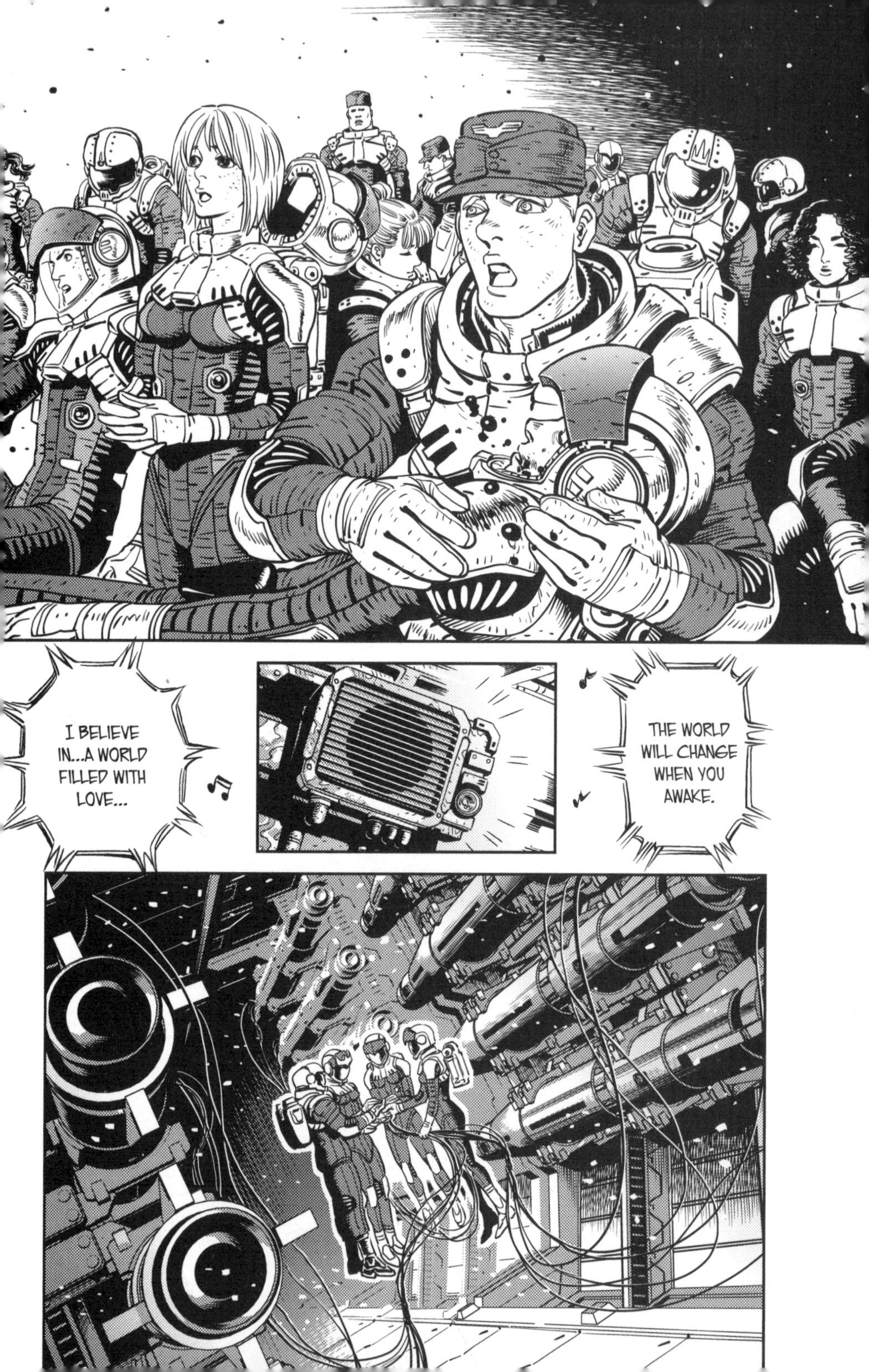
THE WORLD WILL CHANGE WHEN YOU AWAKE.
I BELIEVE IN...A WORLD FILLED WITH LOVE...

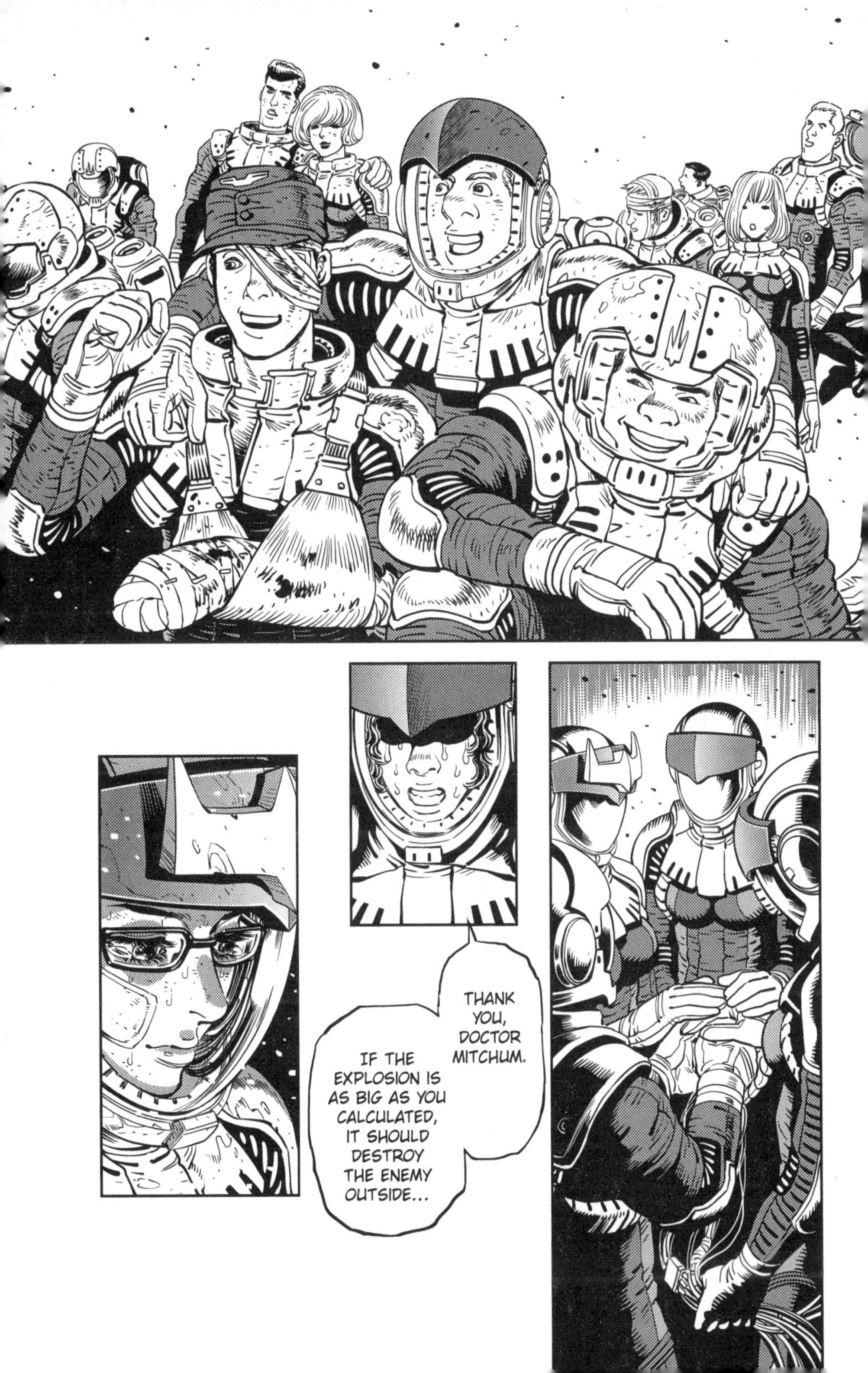
THANK YOU, DOCTOR MITCHUM.
IF THE EXPLOSION IS AS BIG AS YOU CALCULATED, IT SHOULD DESTROY THE ENEMY OUTSIDE...

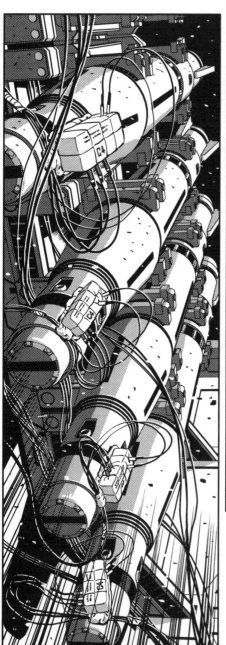

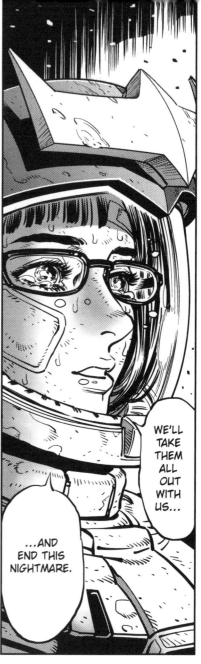

WE'LL TAKE THEM ALL OUT WITH US...

...AND END THIS NIGHTMARE.

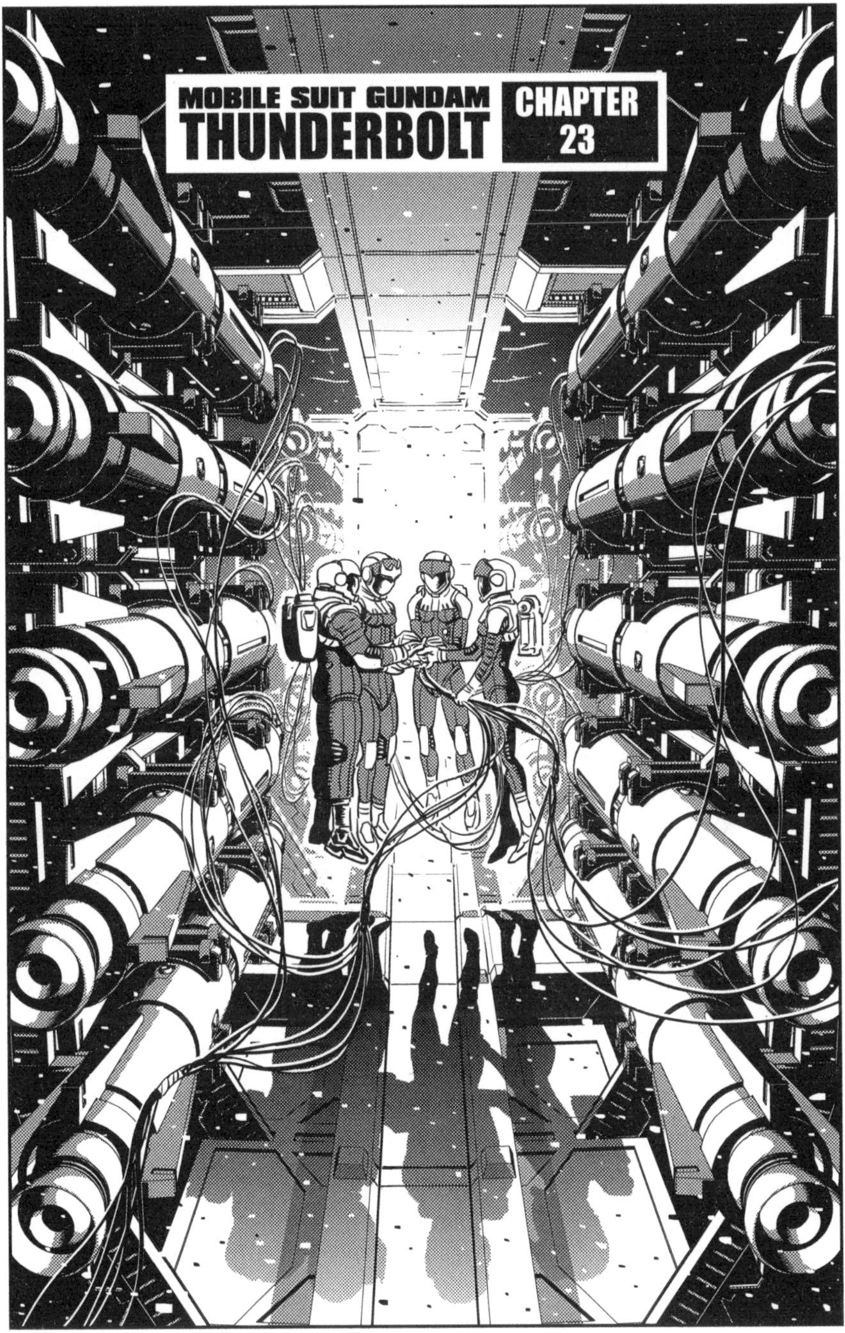
MOBILE SUIT GUNDAM
THUNDERBOLT
CHAPTER
23

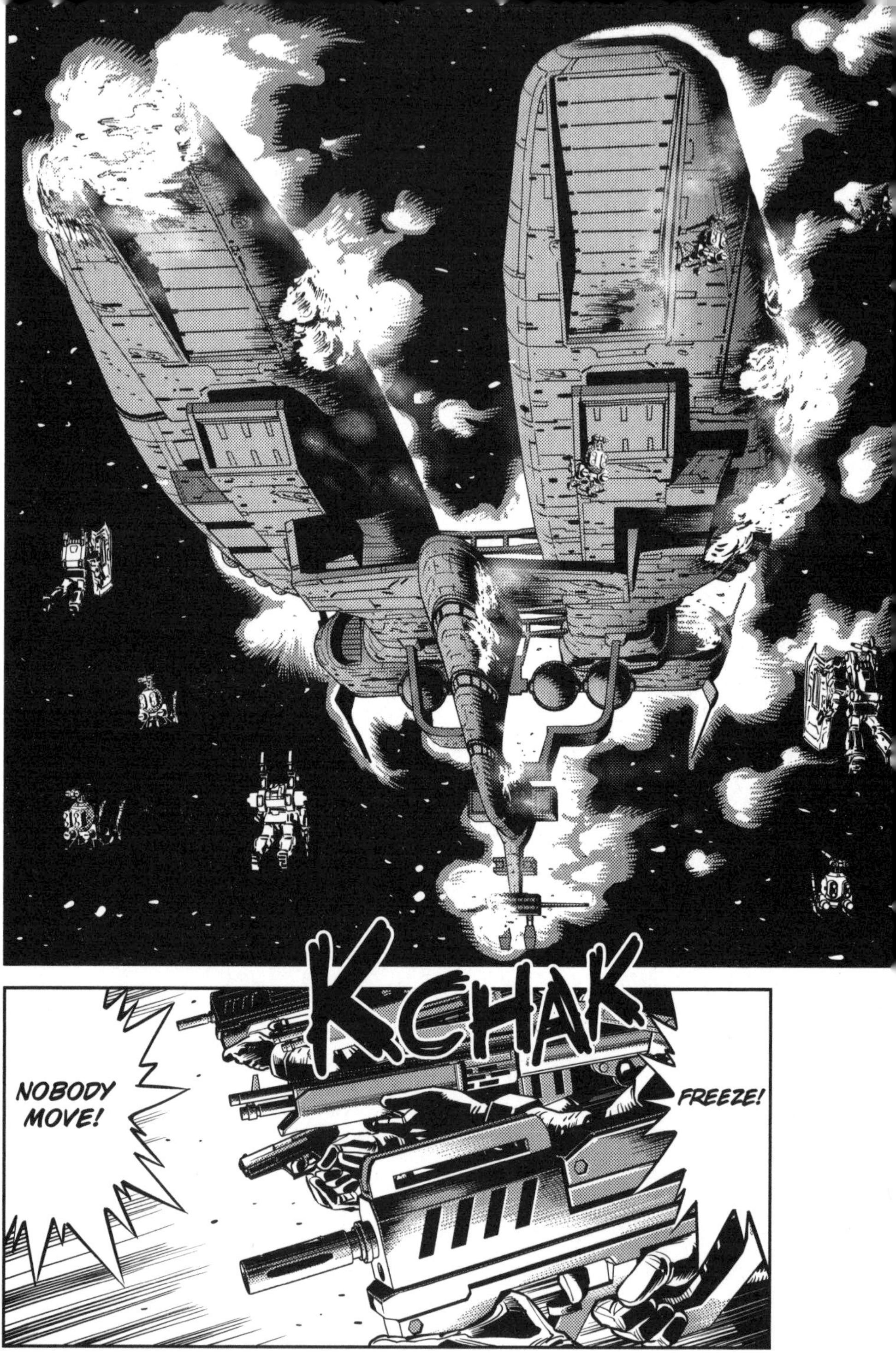
KCHAK
FREEZE!
NOBODY MOVE!

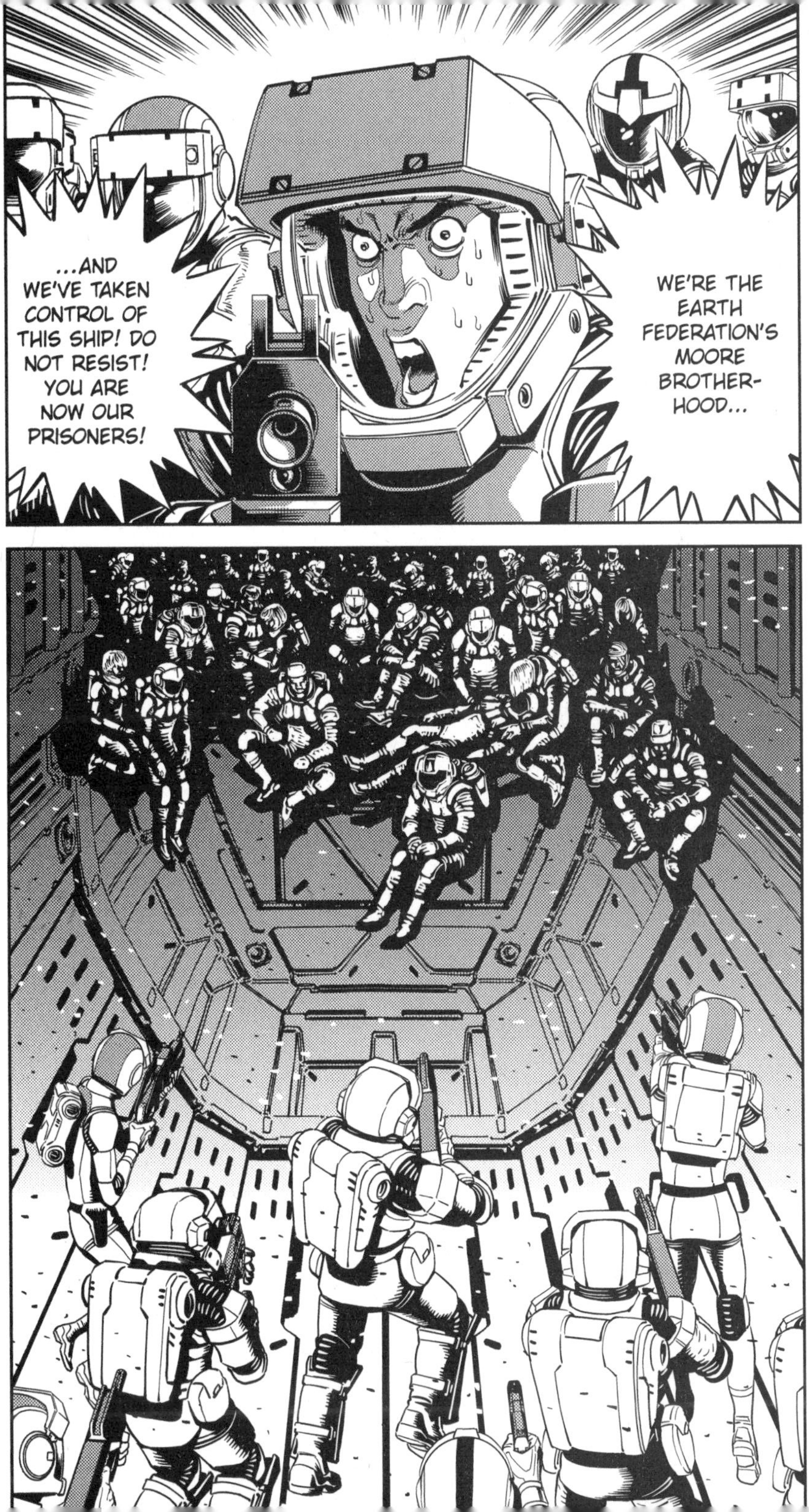
WE'RE THE EARTH FEDERATION'S MOORE BROTHER-HOOD...
...AND WE'VE TAKEN CONTROL OF THIS SHIP! DO NOT RESIST! YOU ARE NOW OUR PRISONERS!

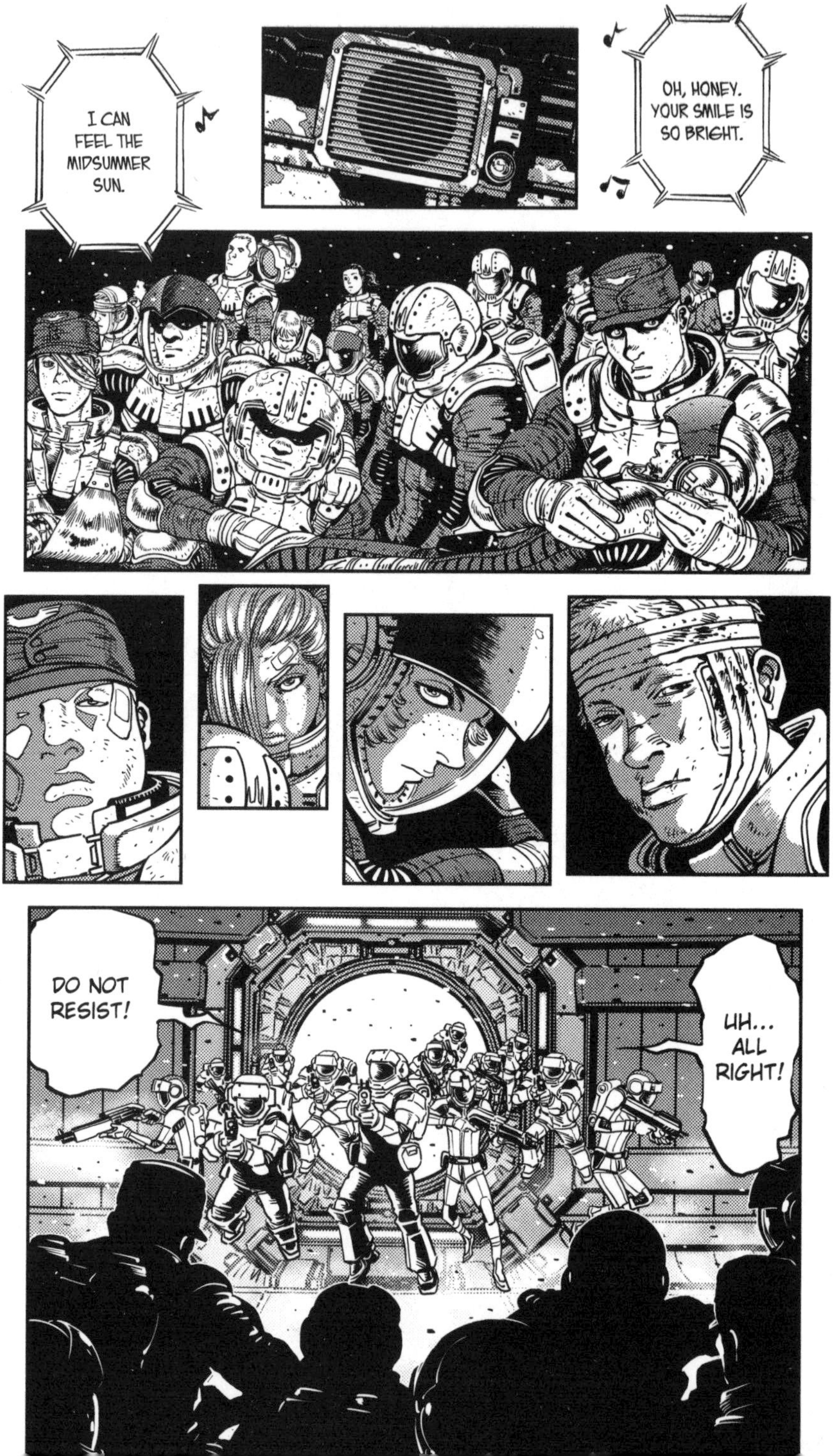
OH, HONEY. YOUR SMILE IS SO BRIGHT.
I CAN FEEL THE MIDSUMMER SUN.
UH... ALL RIGHT!
DO NOT RESIST!

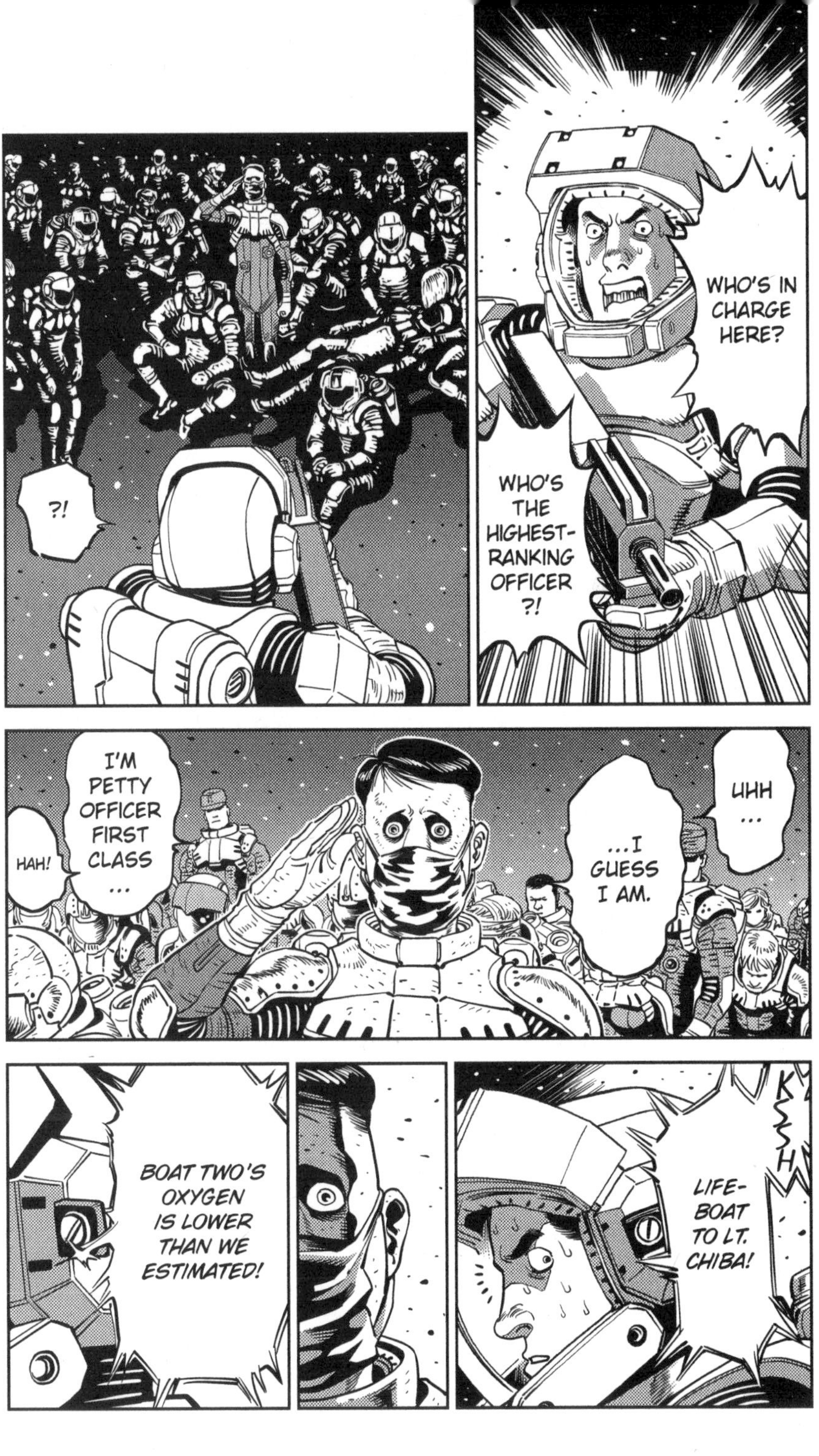
WHO'S IN CHARGE HERE?
WHO'S THE HIGHEST-RANKING OFFICER ?!
?!
UHH ...
...I GUESS I AM.
I'M PETTY OFFICER FIRST CLASS ...
HAH!
KSSH
LIFE-BOAT TO LT. CHIBA!
BOAT TWO'S OXYGEN IS LOWER THAN WE ESTIMATED!

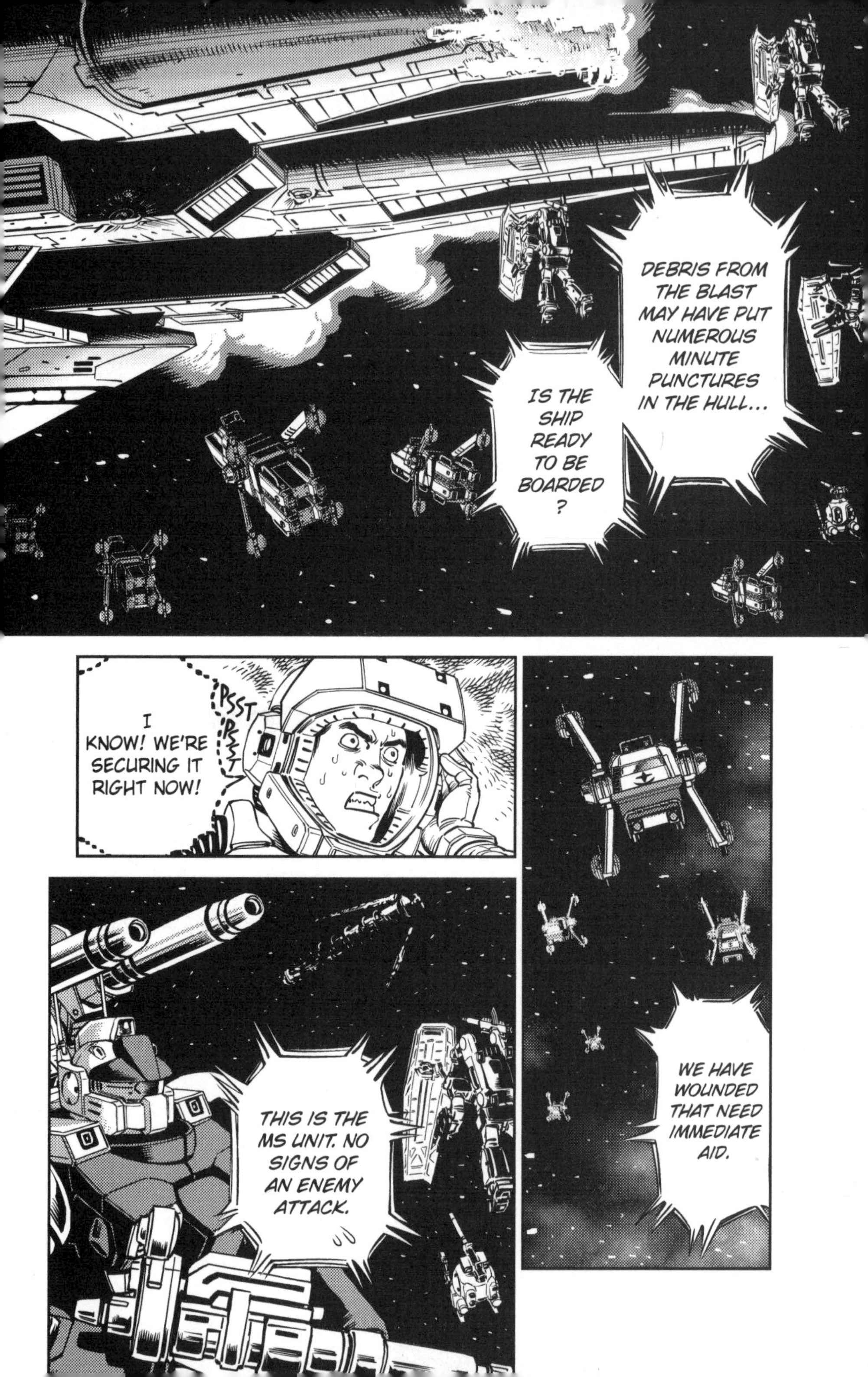
DEBRIS FROM THE BLAST MAY HAVE PUT NUMEROUS MINUTE PUNCTURES IN THE HULL...
IS THE SHIP READY TO BE BOARDED?
WE HAVE WOUNDED THAT NEED IMMEDIATE AID.
PSST
PSST
I KNOW! WE'RE SECURING IT RIGHT NOW!
THIS IS THE MS UNIT. NO SIGNS OF AN ENEMY ATTACK.

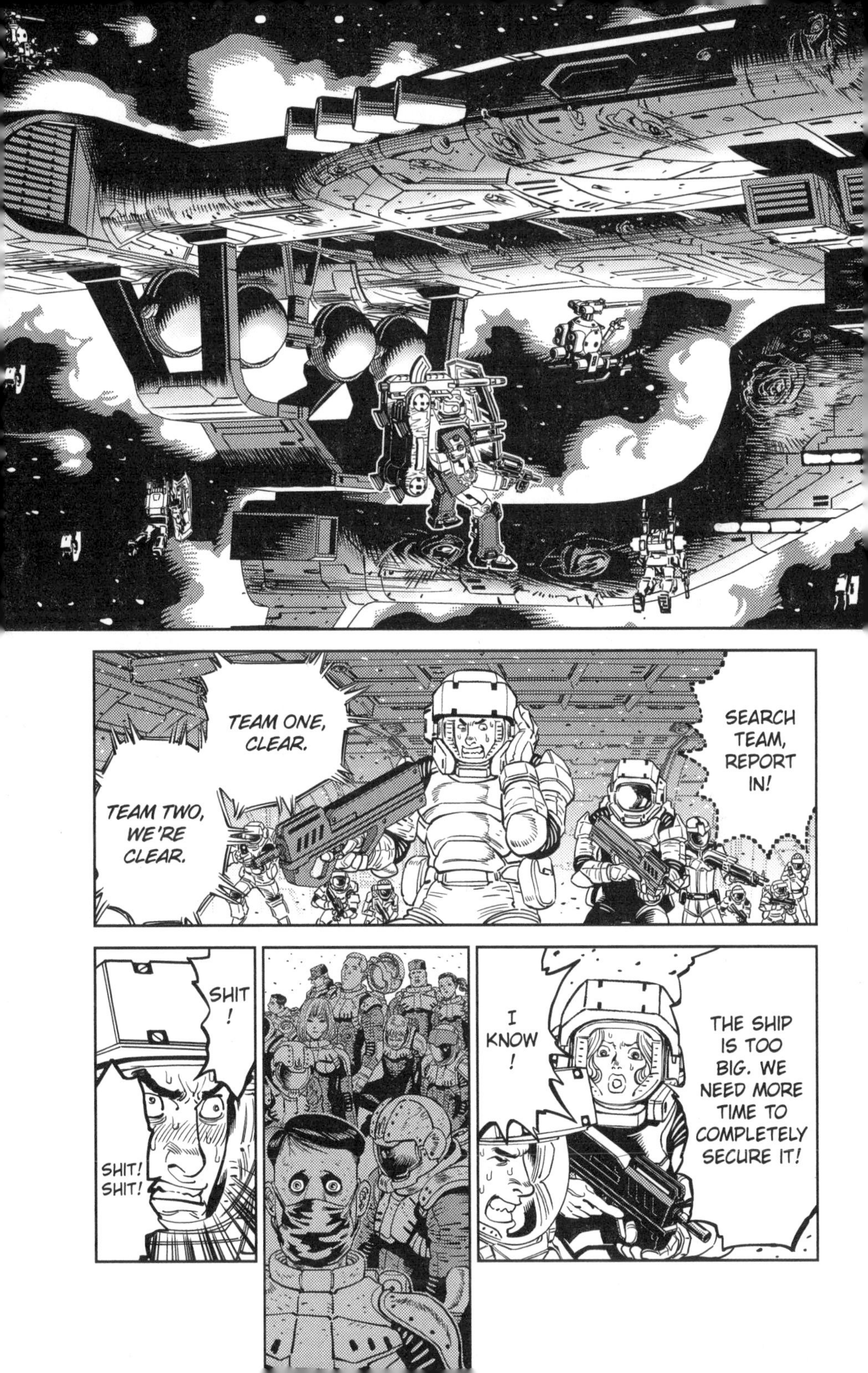
SEARCH TEAM, REPORT IN!
TEAM ONE, CLEAR.
TEAM TWO, WE'RE CLEAR.
THE SHIP IS TOO BIG. WE NEED MORE TIME TO COMPLETELY SECURE IT!
I KNOW!
SHIT!
SHIT! SHIT!

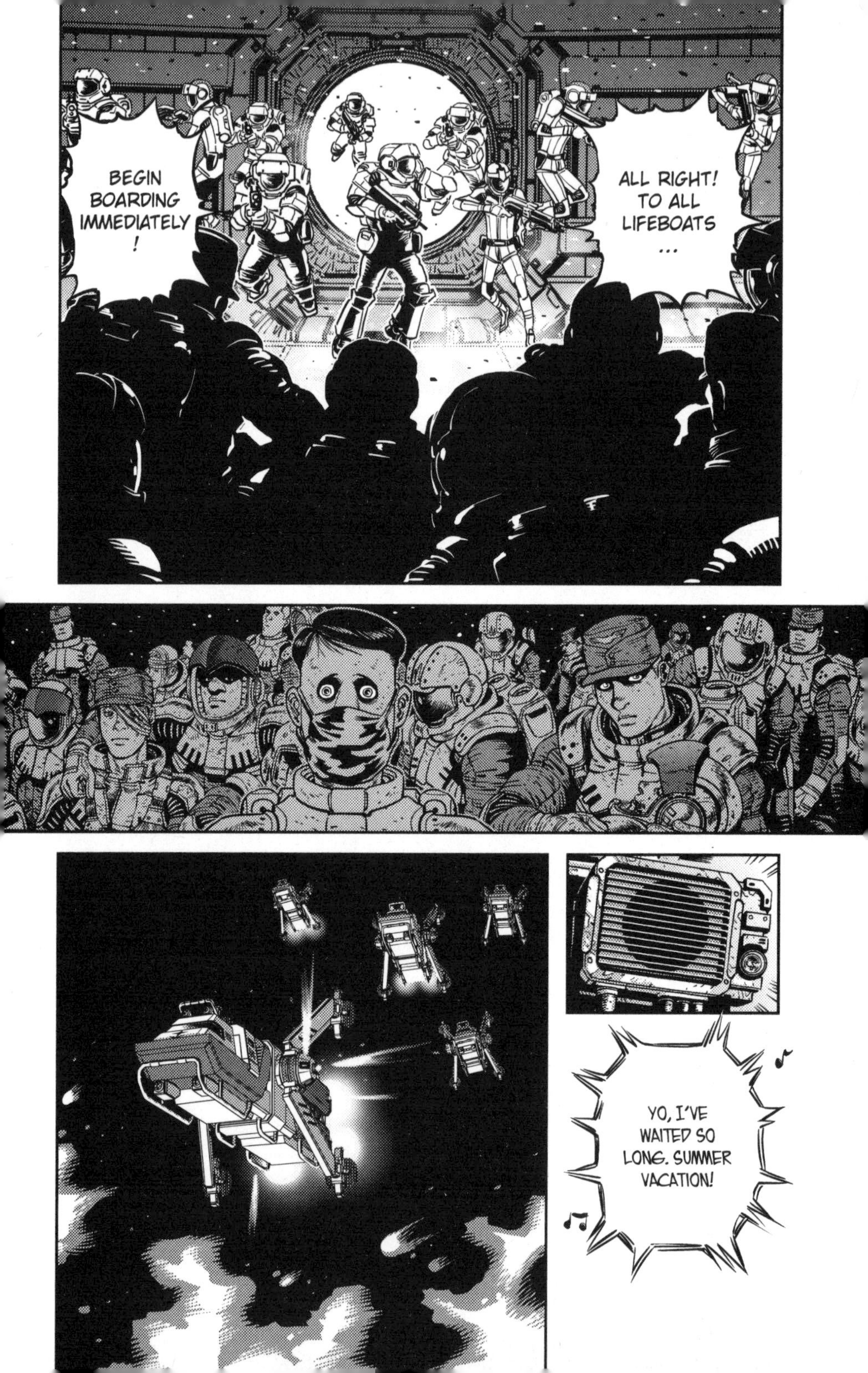
ALL RIGHT! TO ALL LIFEBOATS...
BEGIN BOARDING IMMEDIATELY!
YO, I'VE WAITED SO LONG. SUMMER VACATION!

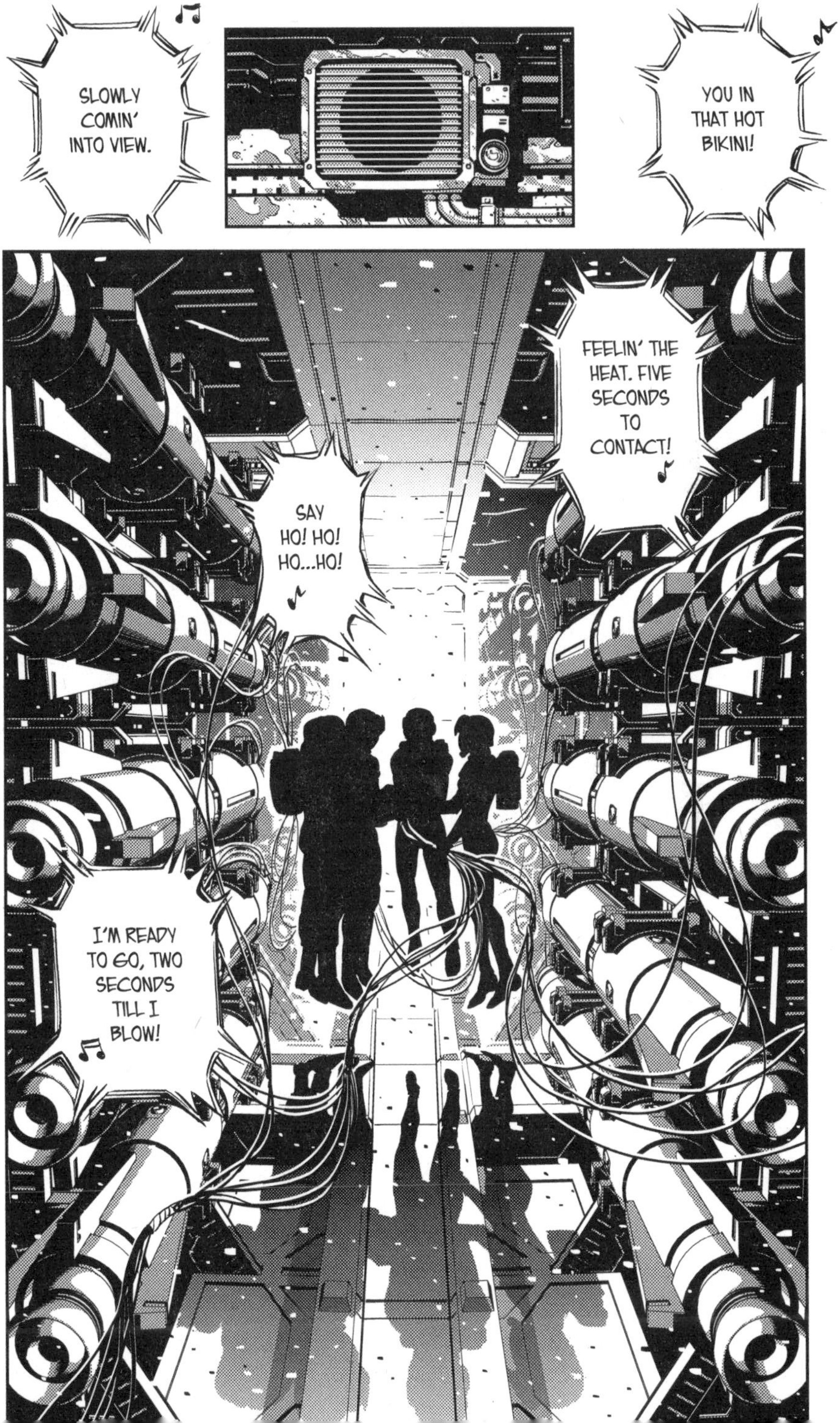
YOU IN THAT HOT BIKINI!
SLOWLY COMIN' INTO VIEW.
FEELIN' THE HEAT. FIVE SECONDS TO CONTACT!
SAY HO! HO! HO...HO!
I'M READY TO GO, TWO SECONDS TILL I BLOW!

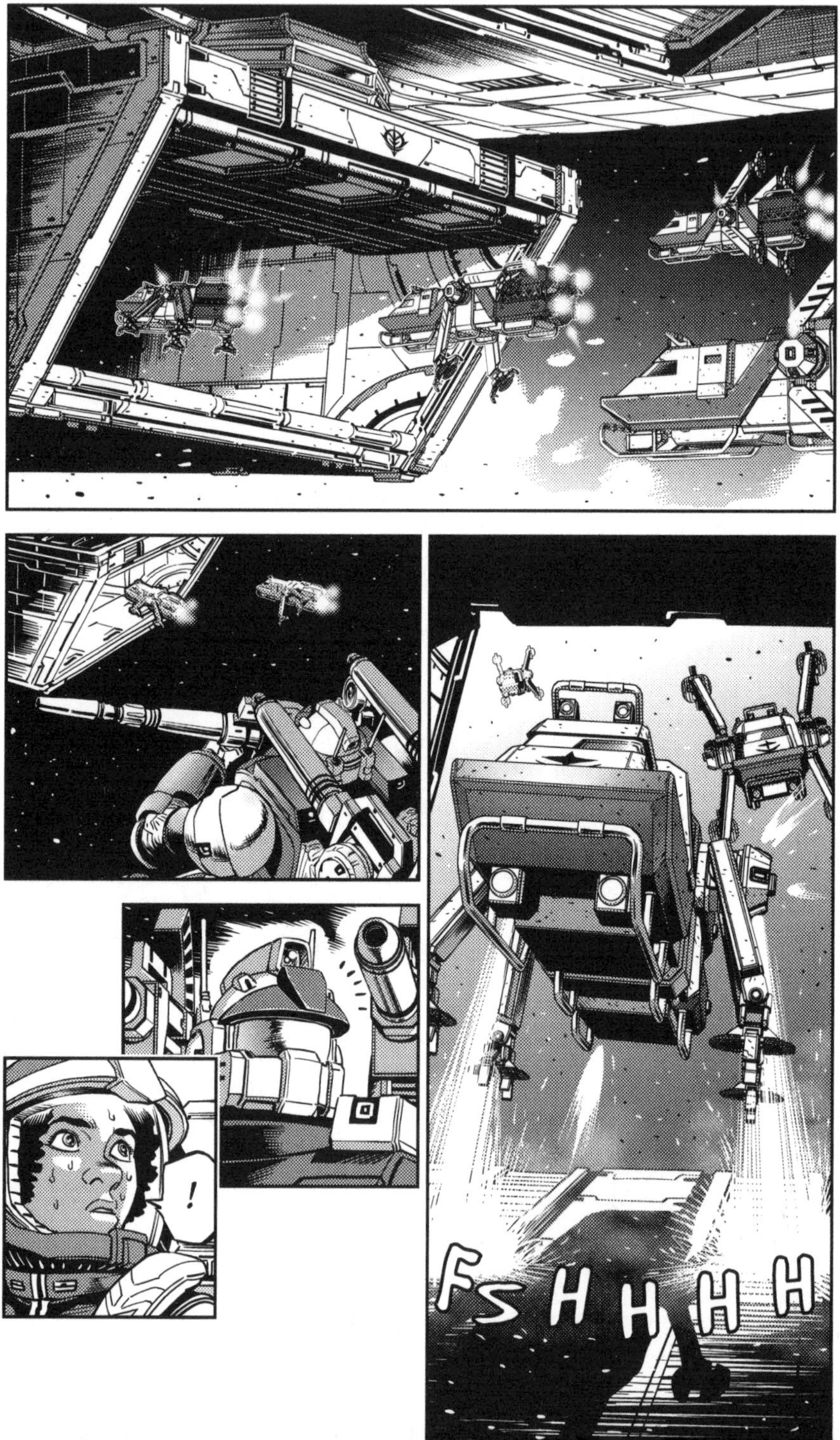
FSHHHH
!

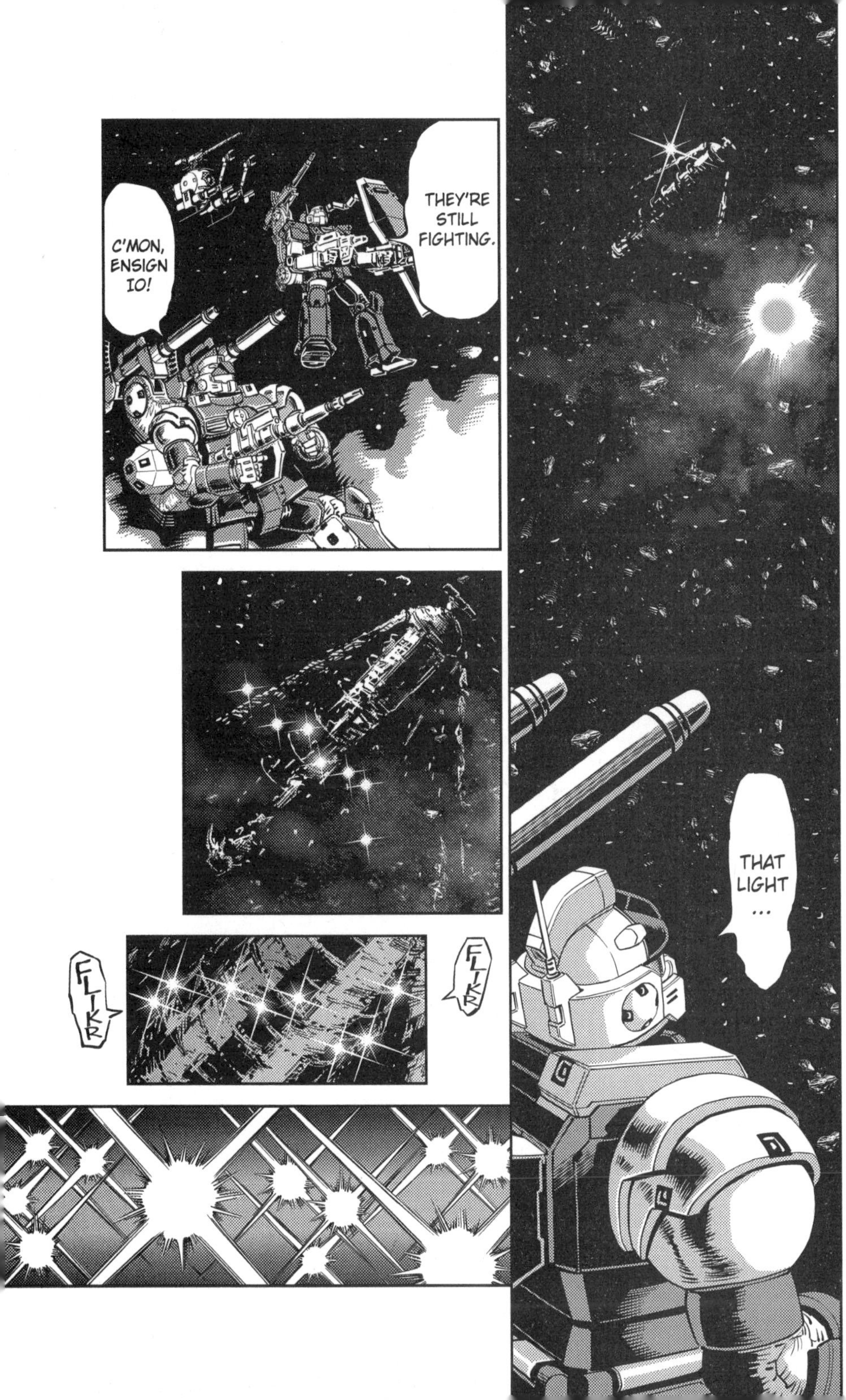
THAT LIGHT ...
THEY'RE STILL FIGHTING.
C'MON, ENSIGN IO!
FLIKR
FLIKR

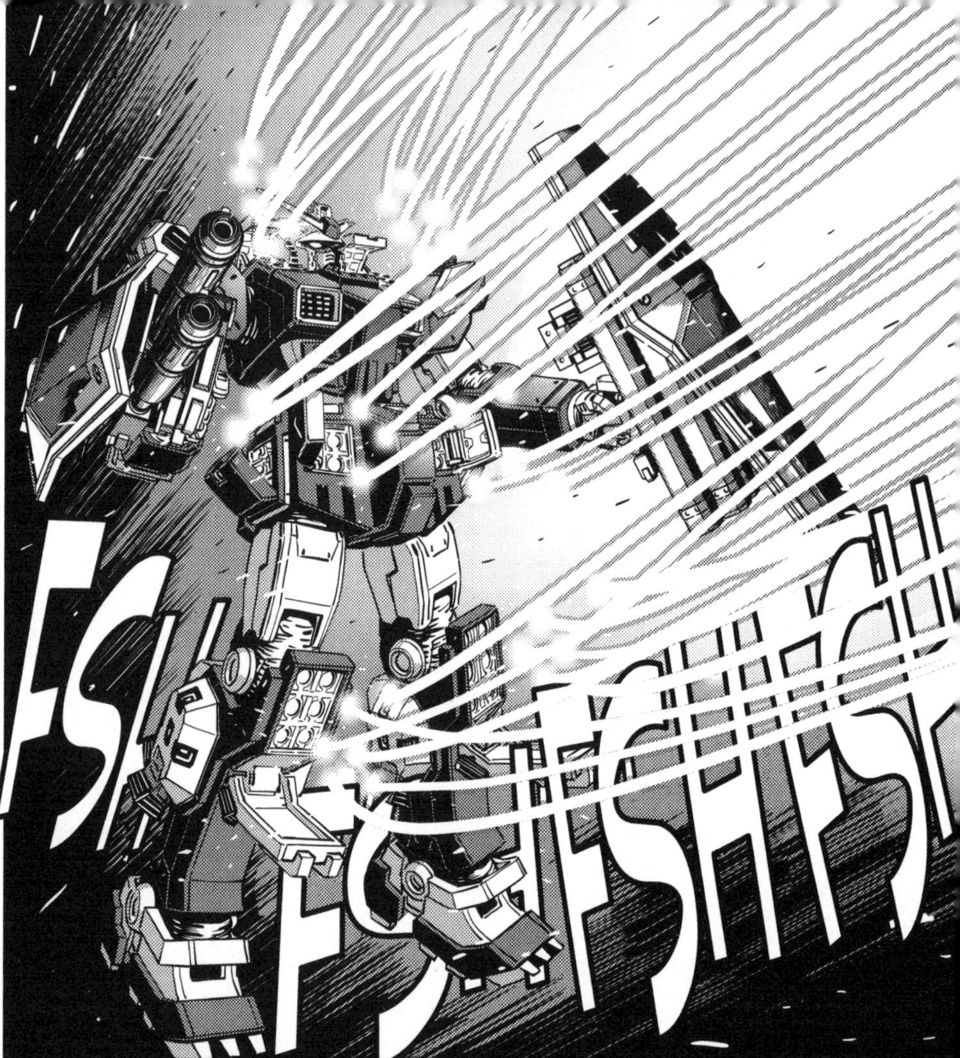
FSH FSH FSH FSH FSH
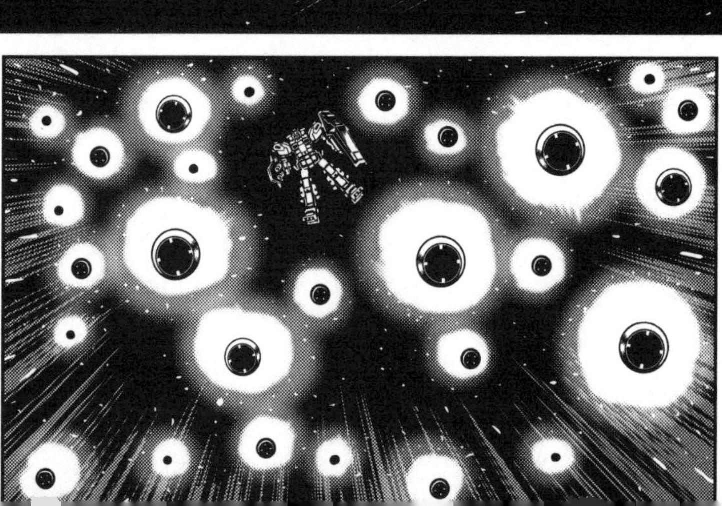

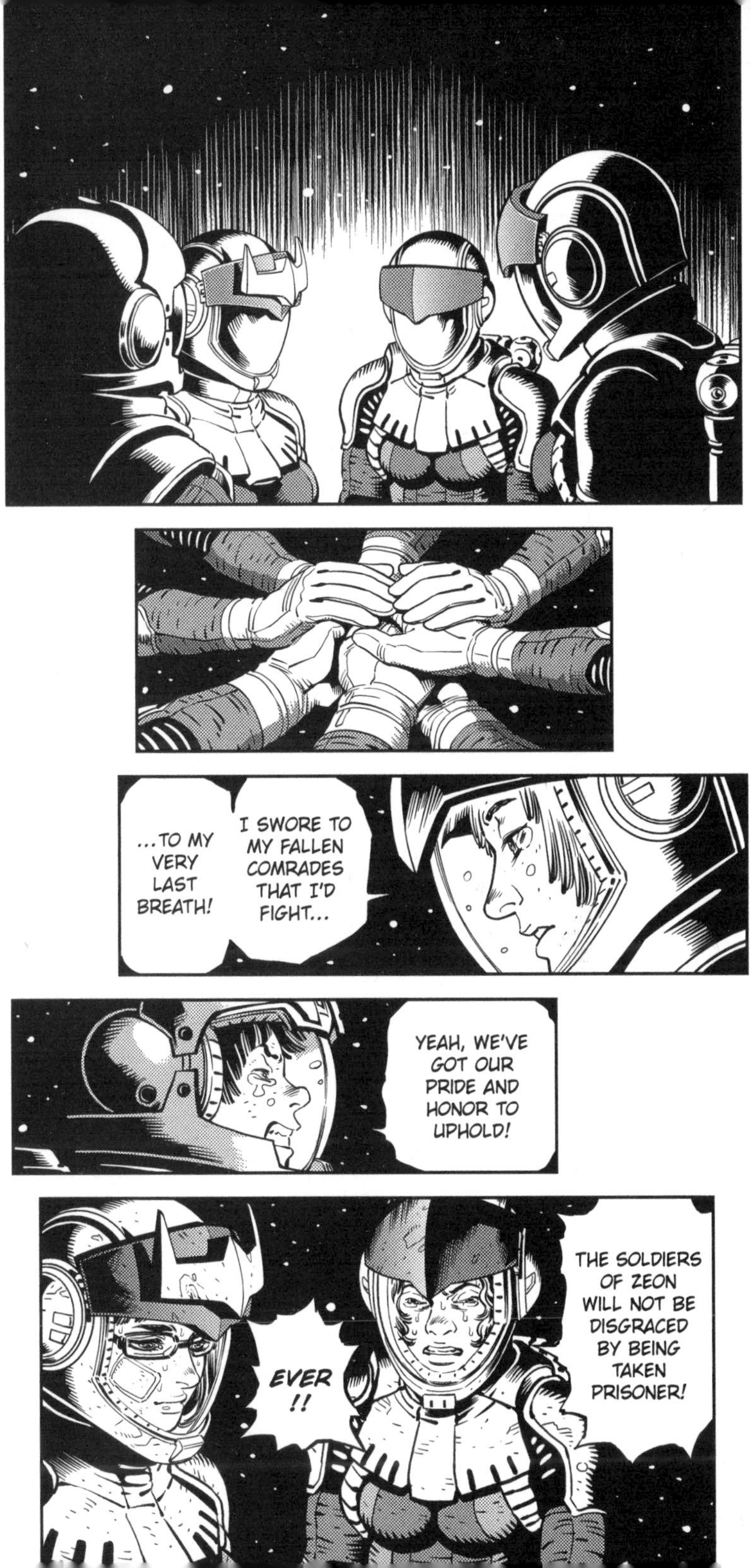
I SWORE TO MY FALLEN COMRADES THAT I'D FIGHT...
...TO MY VERY LAST BREATH!
YEAH, WE'VE GOT OUR PRIDE AND HONOR TO UPHOLD!
THE SOLDIERS OF ZEON WILL NOT BE DISGRACED BY BEING TAKEN PRISONER!
EVER !!

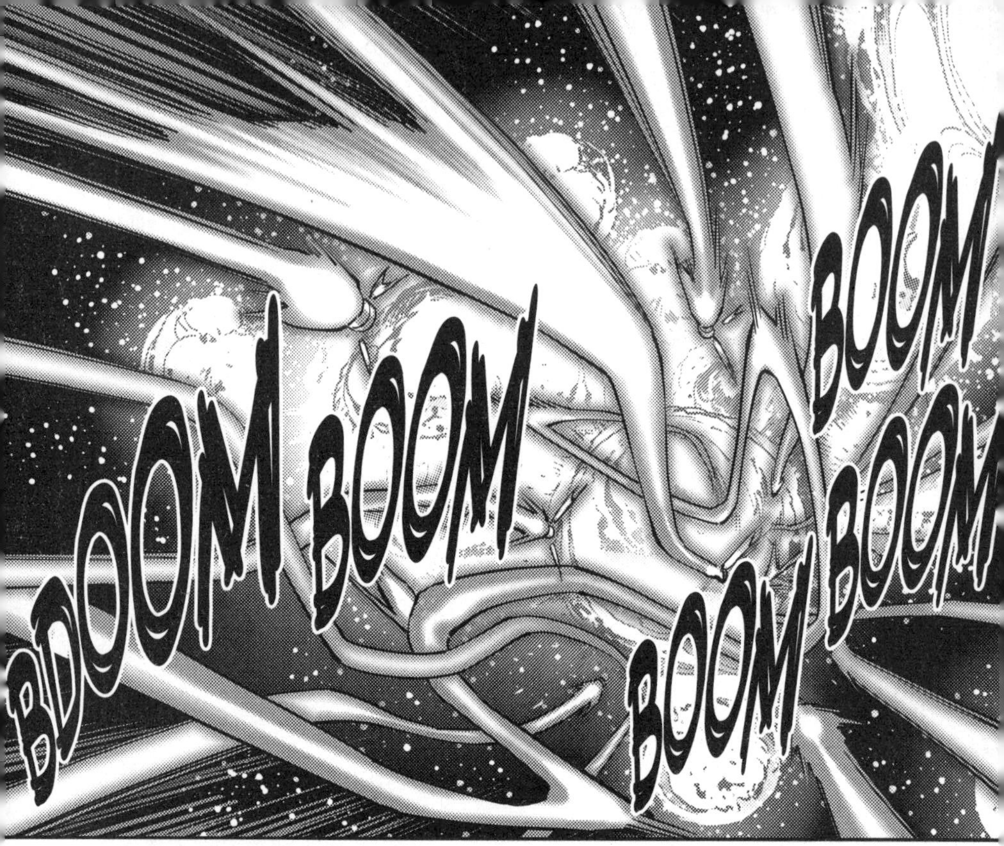
BOOM
BOOM BOOM
BDOOM BOOM
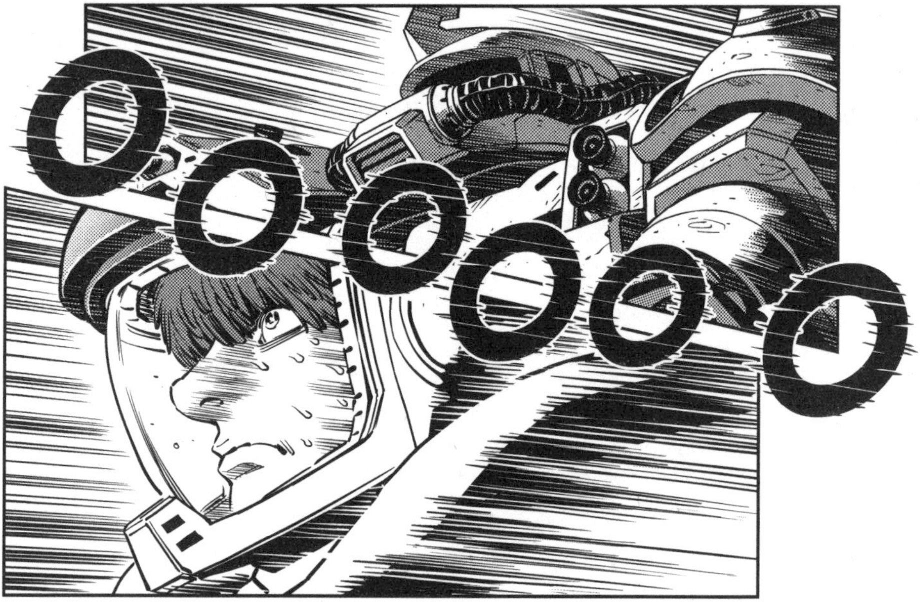
OOOOOO

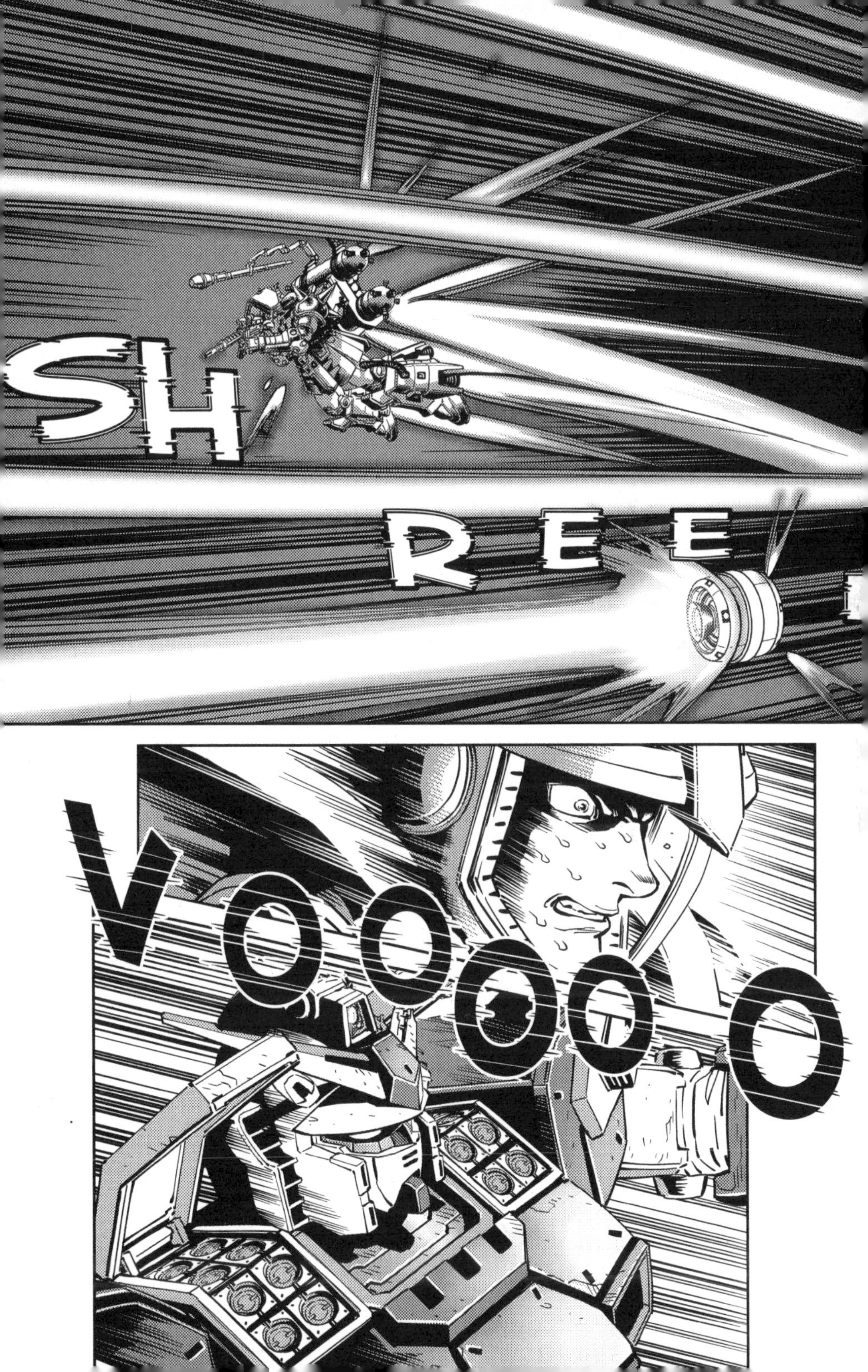
SH
REEE
VOOOOO

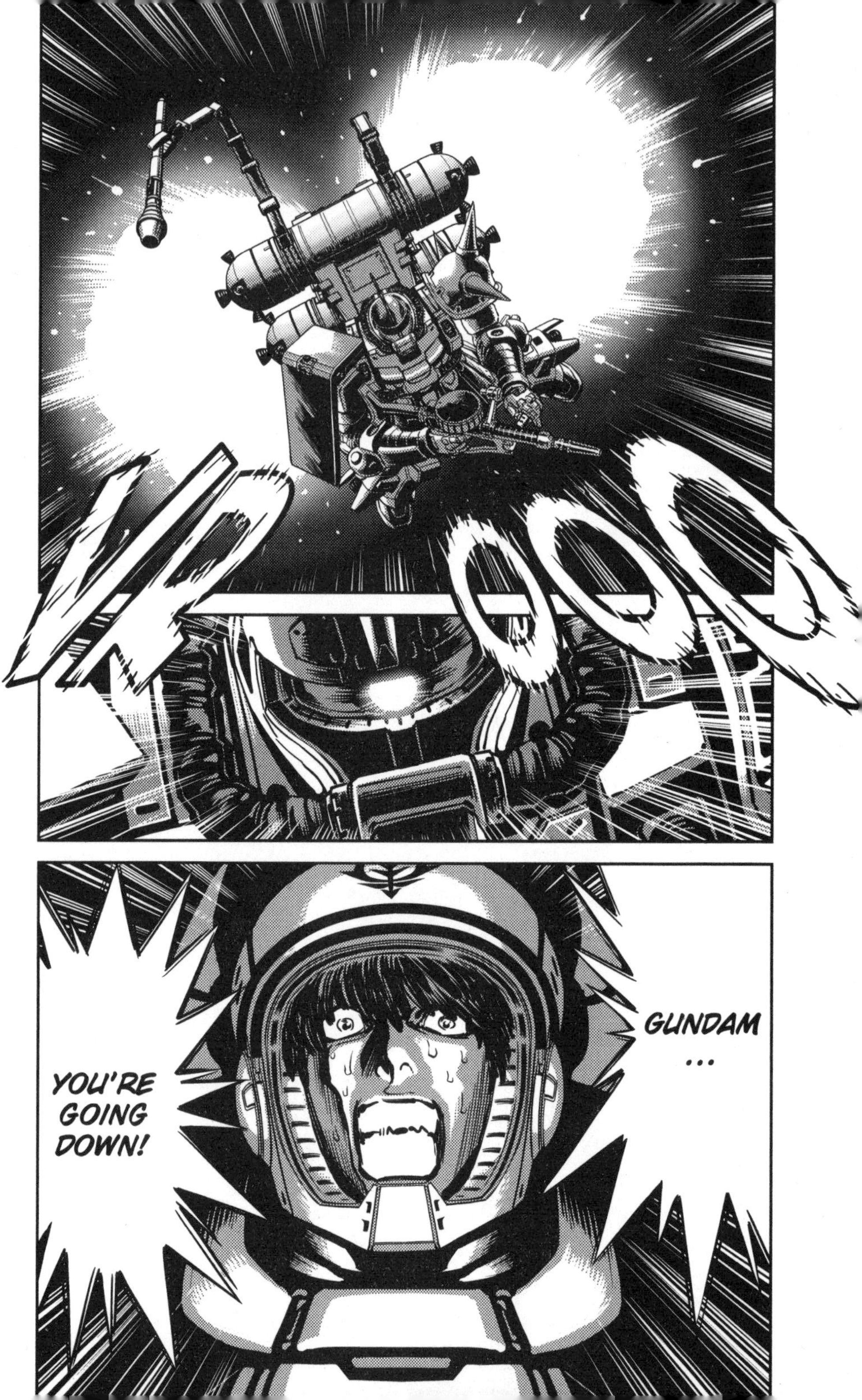
WHOOO
GUNDAM ...
YOU'RE GOING DOWN!

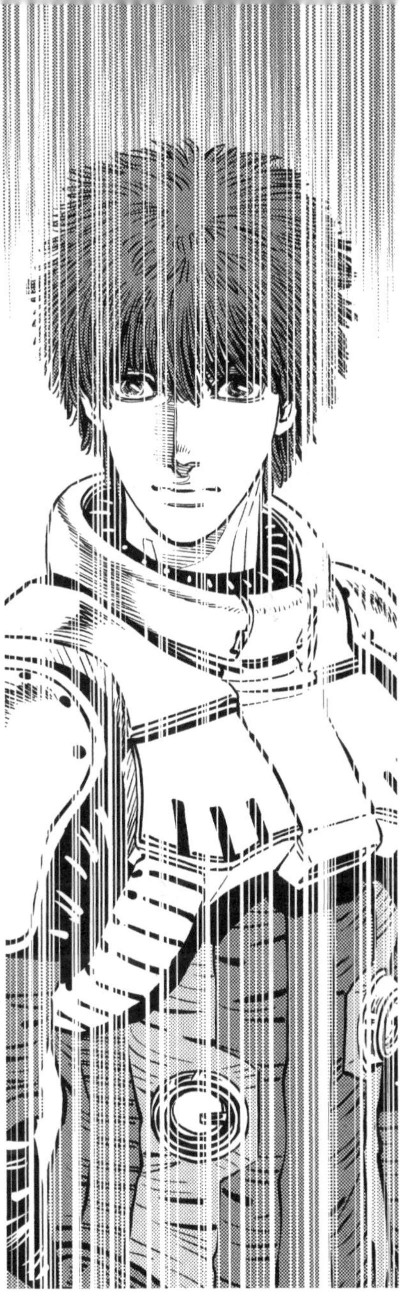
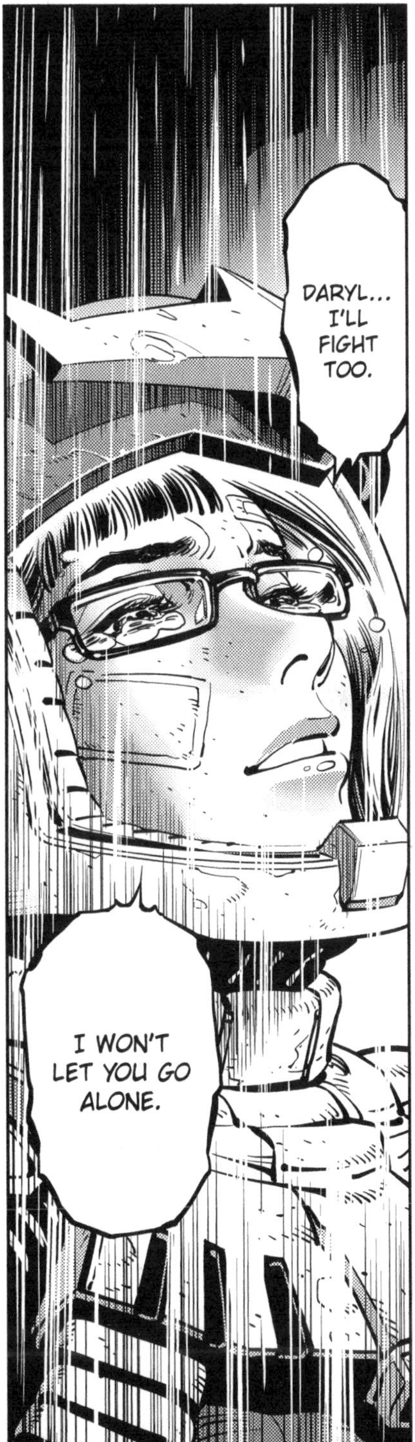
DARYL... I'LL FIGHT TOO.
I WON'T LET YOU GO ALONE.

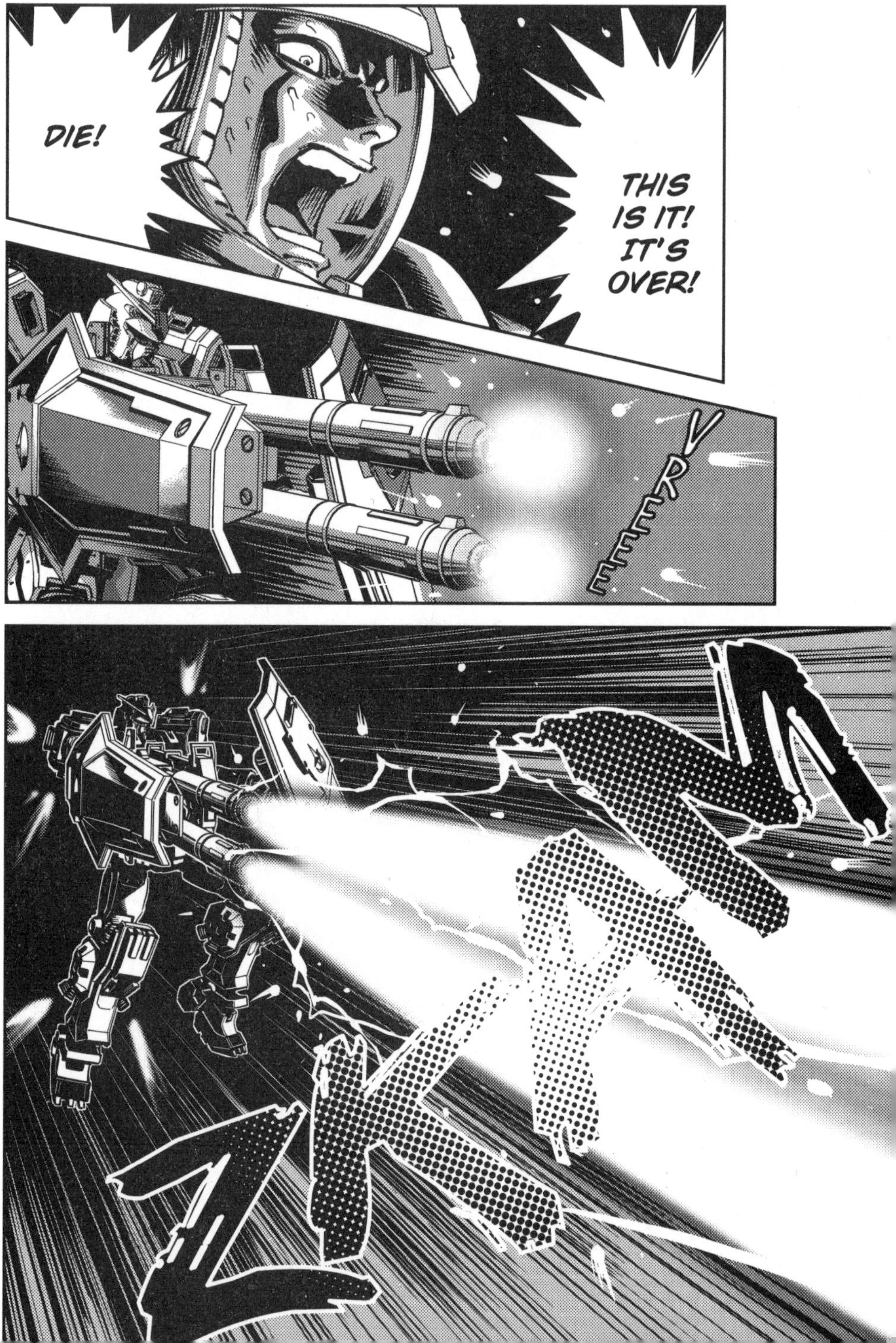
THIS IS IT! IT'S OVER!
DIE!
VREEEE

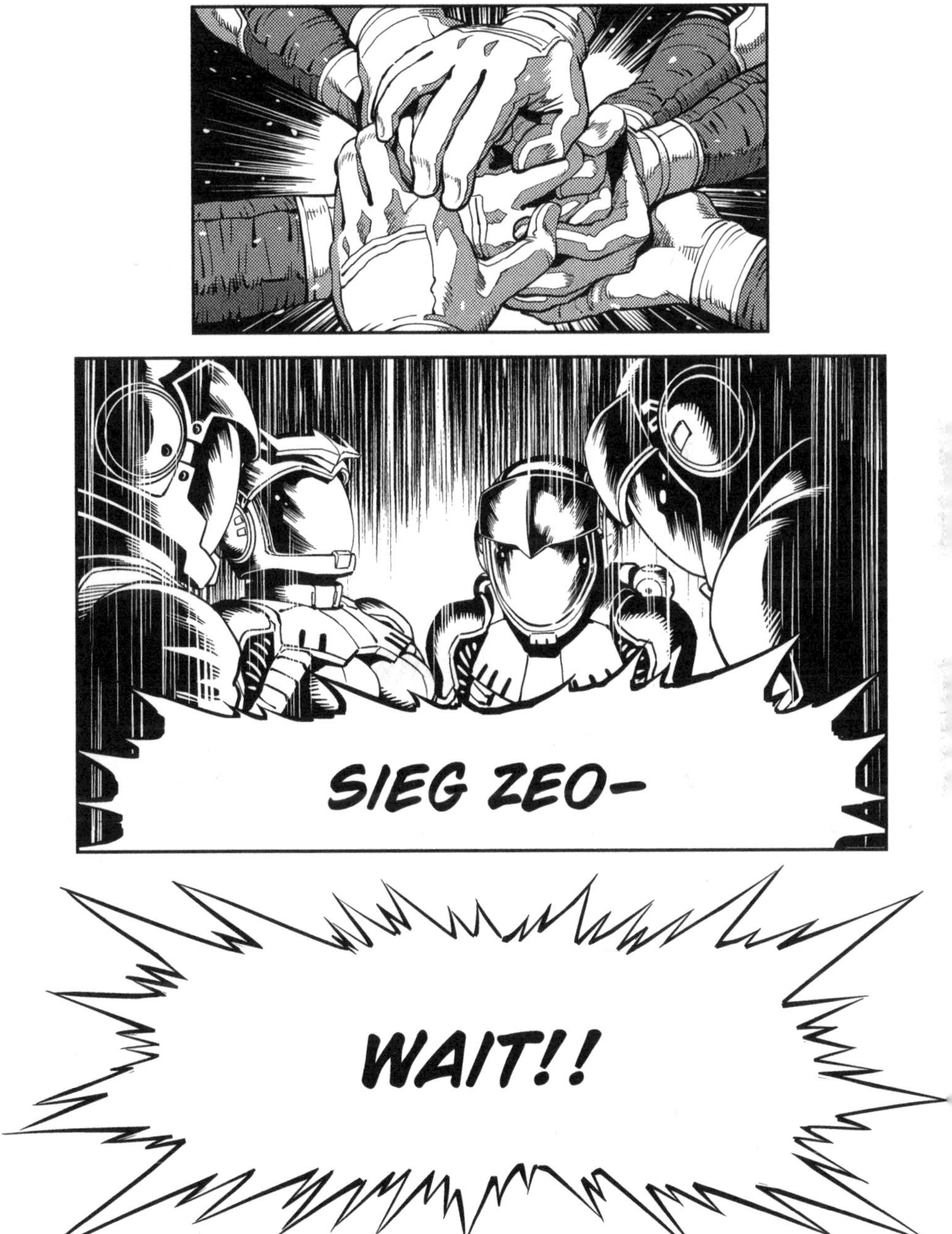
SIEG ZEO-
WAIT!!

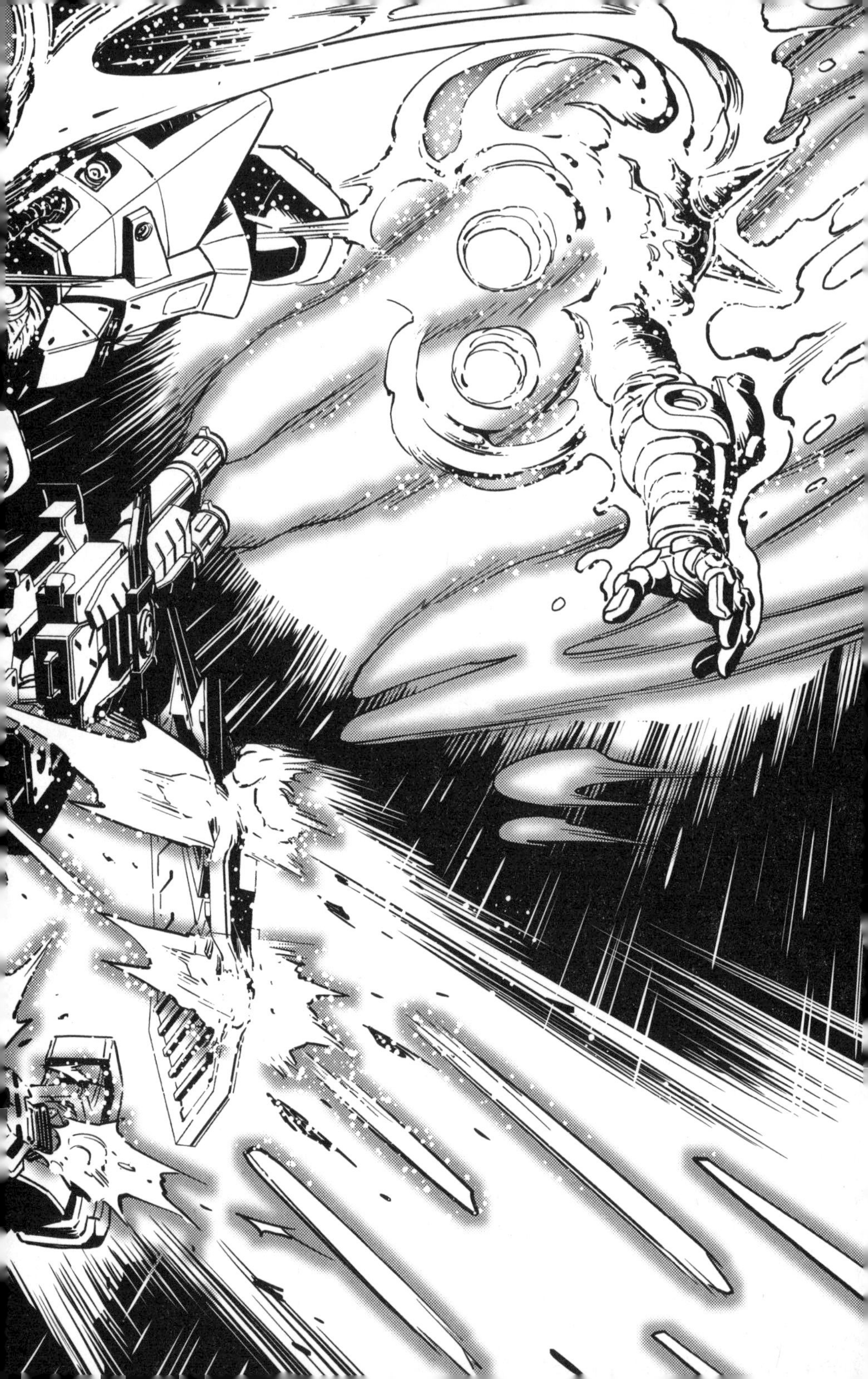

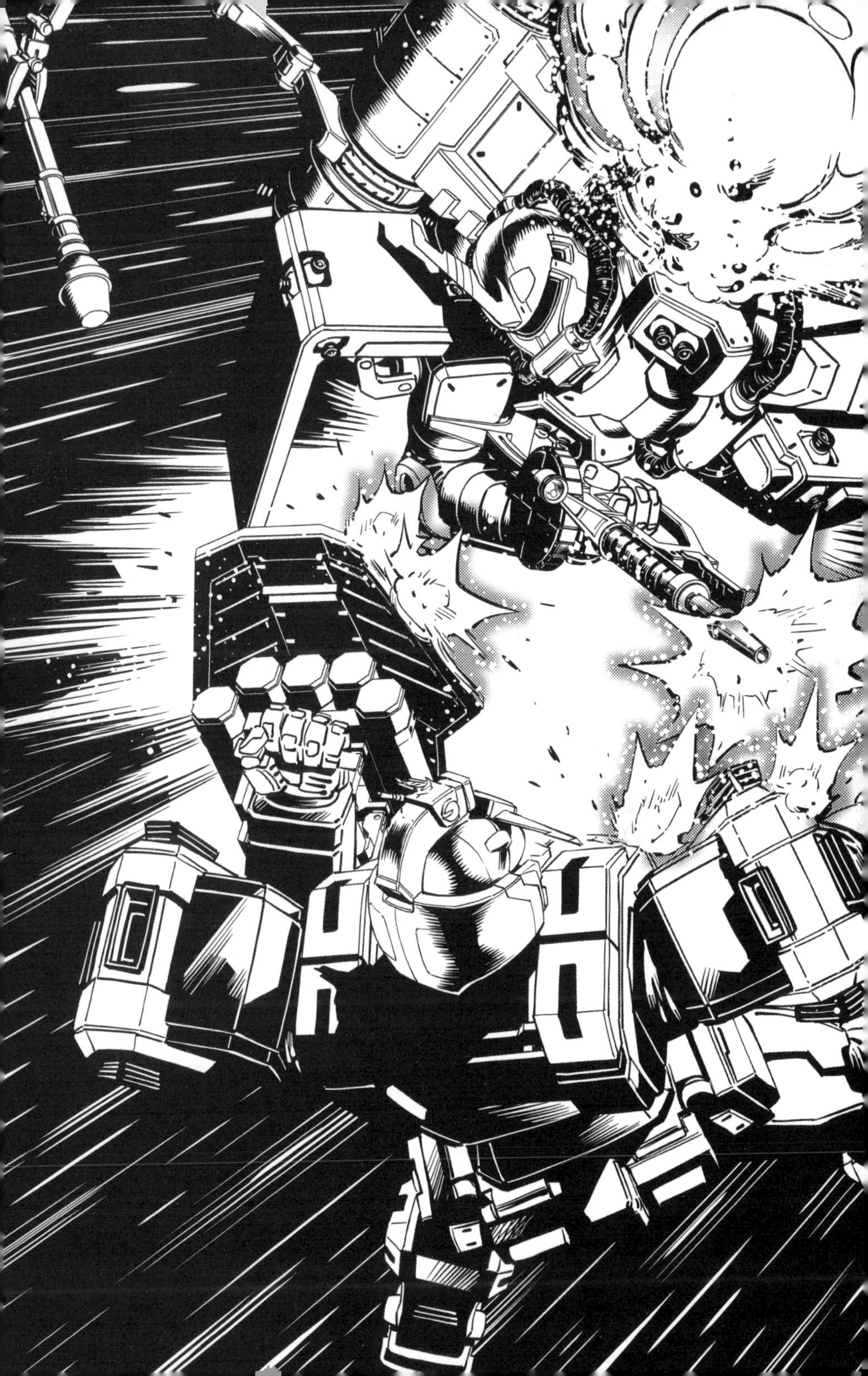

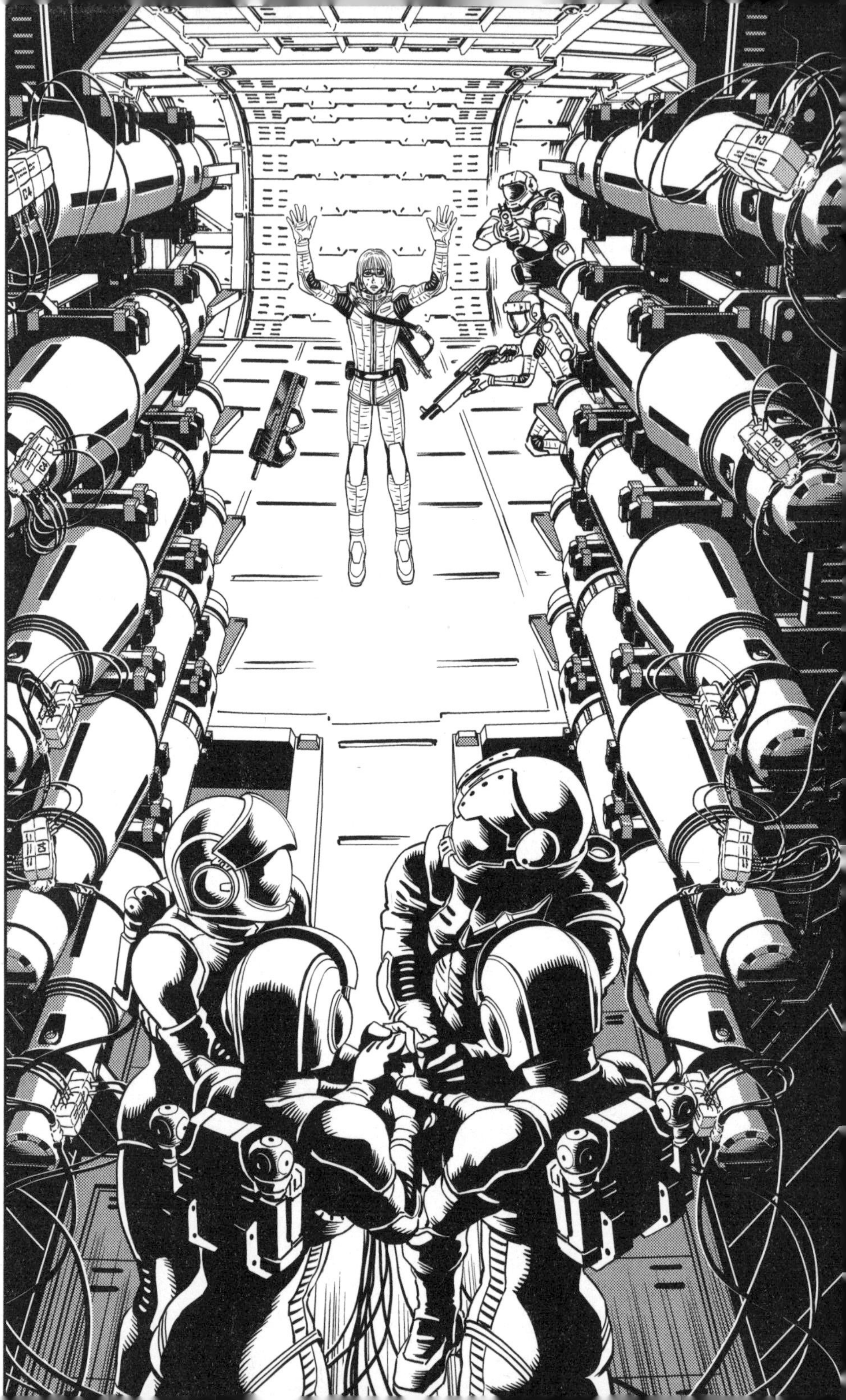
C4

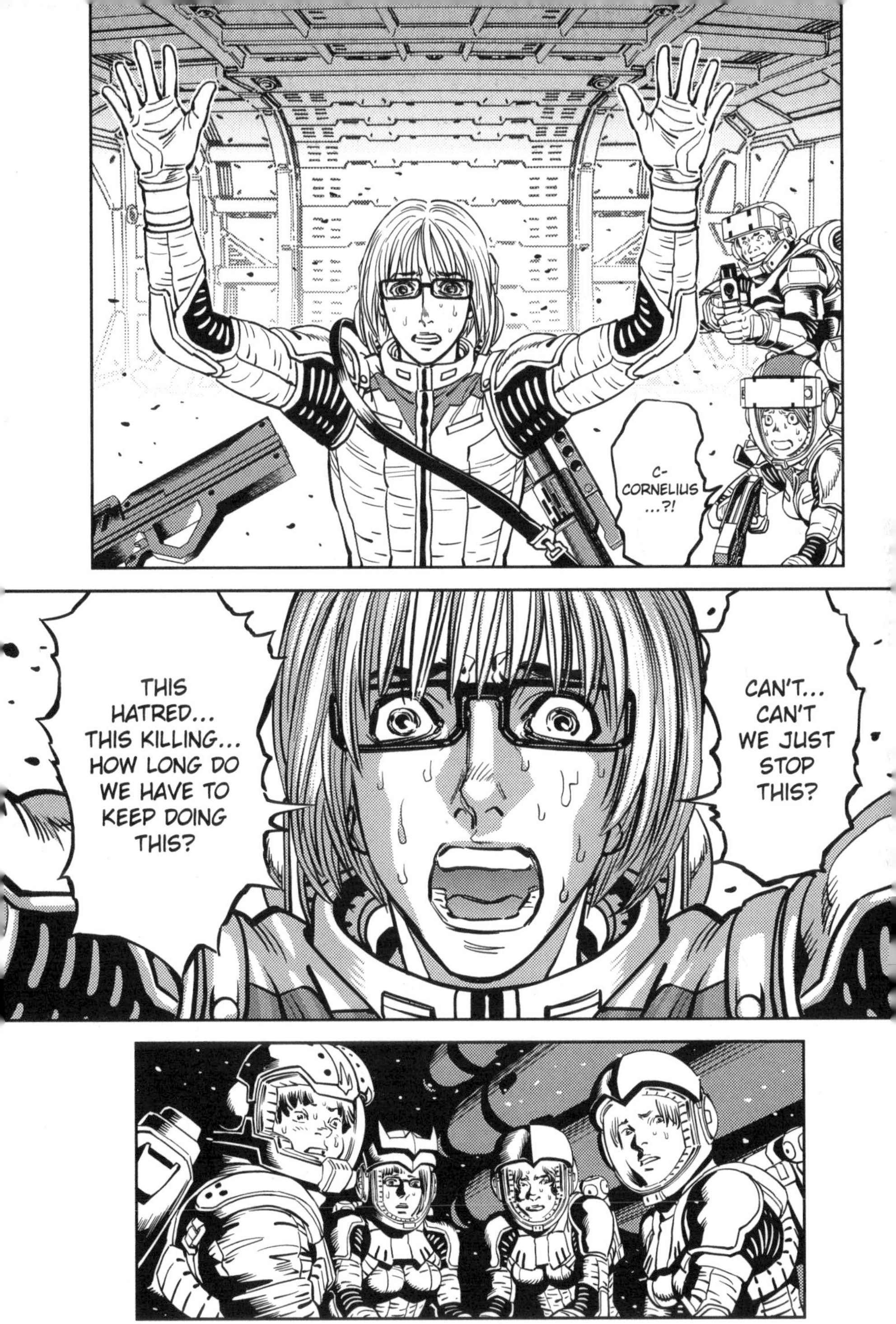
C-CORNELIUS...?!
CAN'T... CAN'T WE JUST STOP THIS?
THIS HATRED... THIS KILLING... HOW LONG DO WE HAVE TO KEEP DOING THIS?

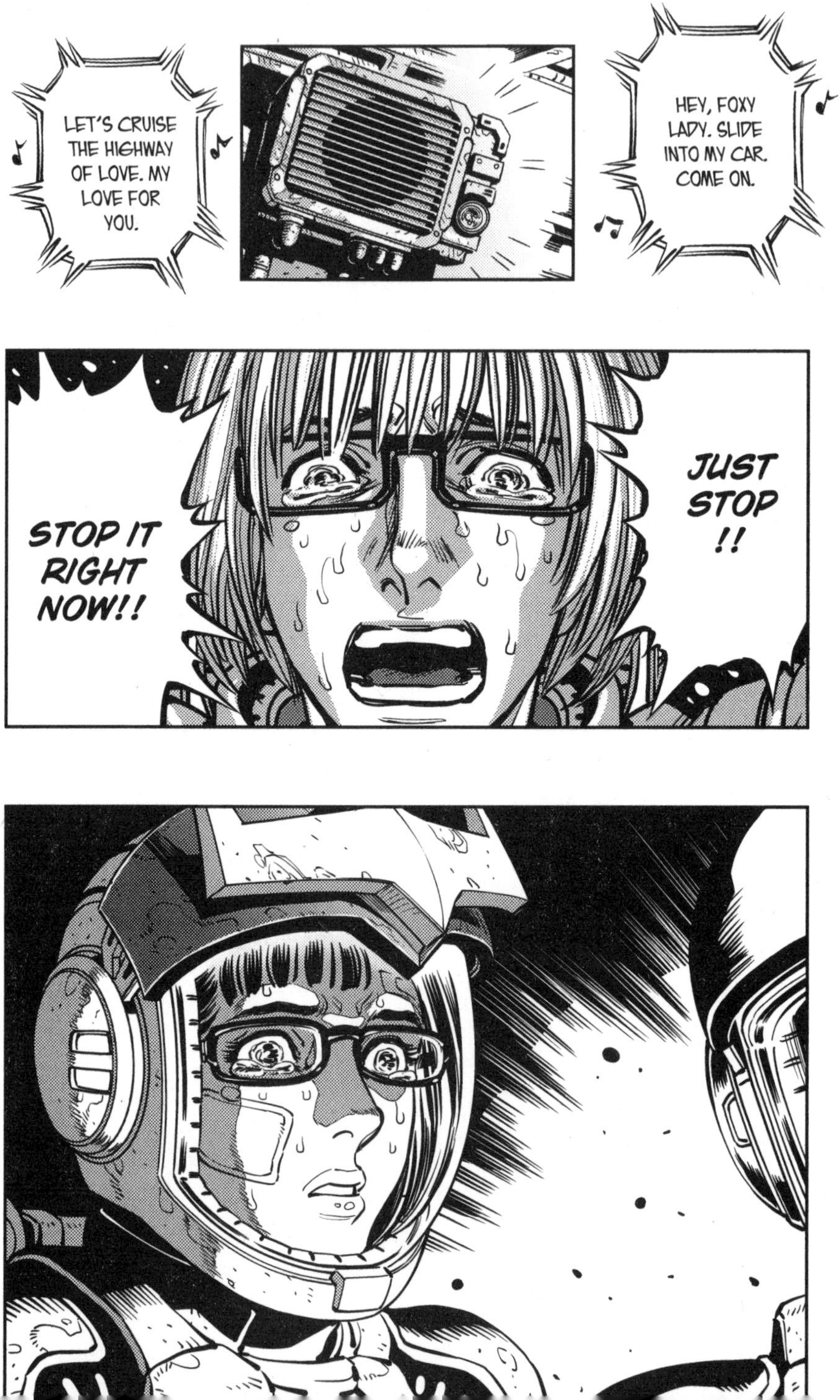
HEY, FOXY LADY. SLIDE INTO MY CAR. COME ON.
LET'S CRUISE THE HIGHWAY OF LOVE. MY LOVE FOR YOU.
JUST STOP !!
STOP IT RIGHT NOW!!

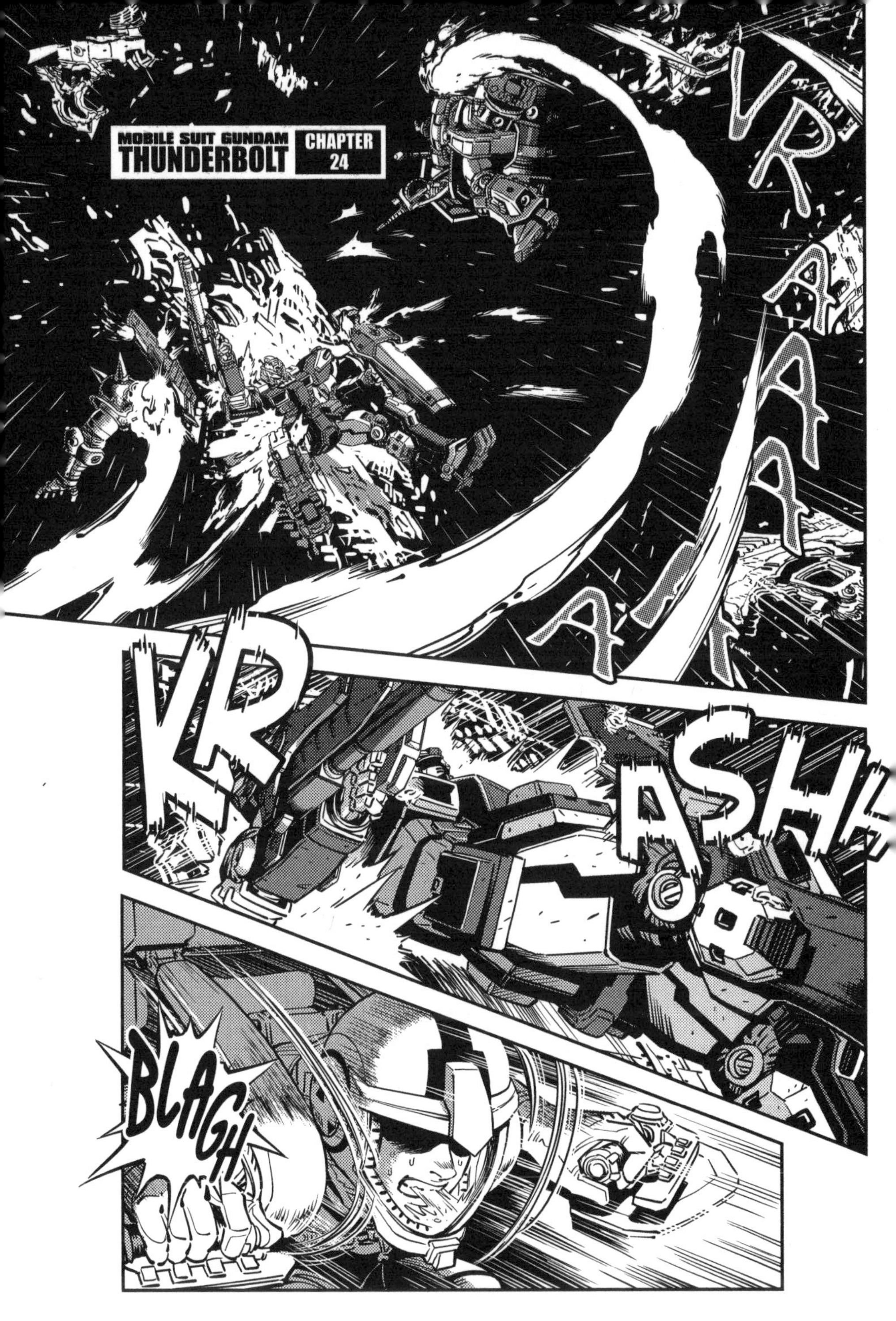
VRAAAAA
MOBILE SUIT GUNDAM THUNDERBOLT
CHAPTER 24
VRASH
BLAGH

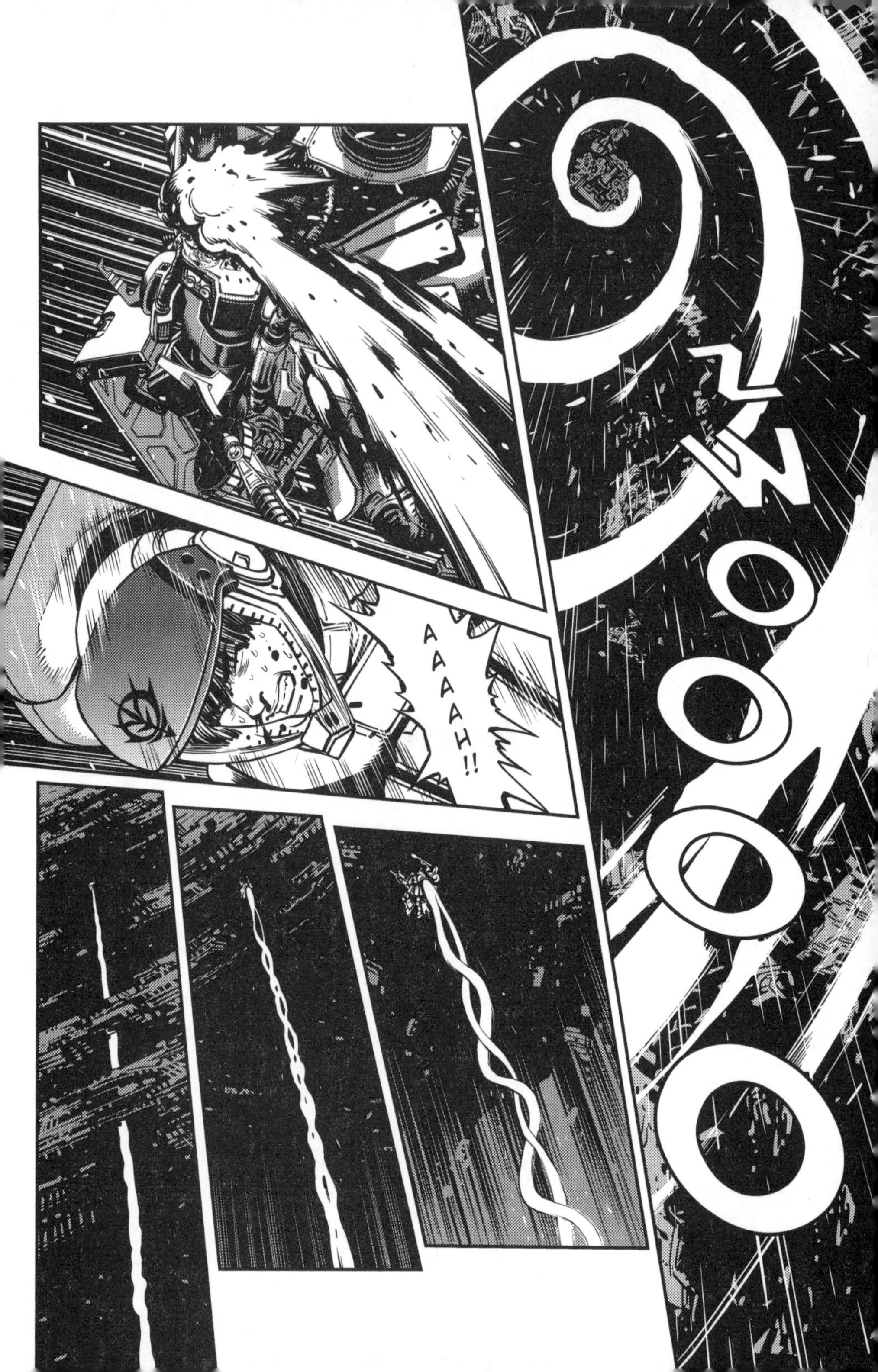
ZWOOOOO
AAAAAH!!

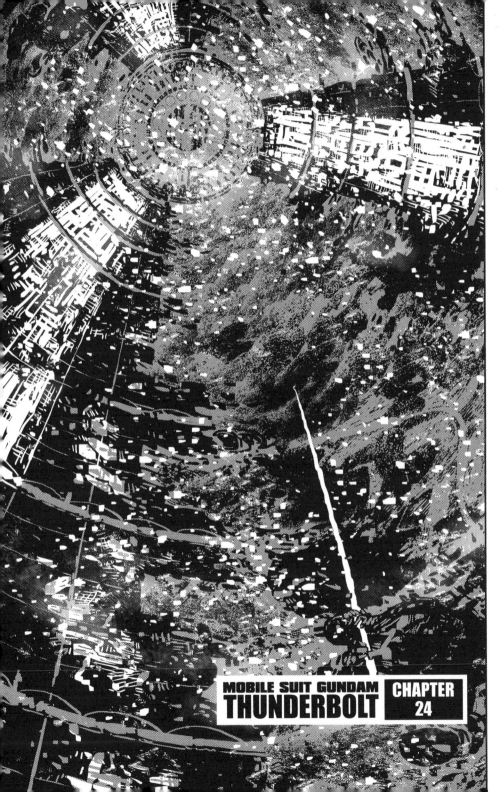

MOBILE SUIT GUNDAM
THUNDERBOLT | CHAPTER 24

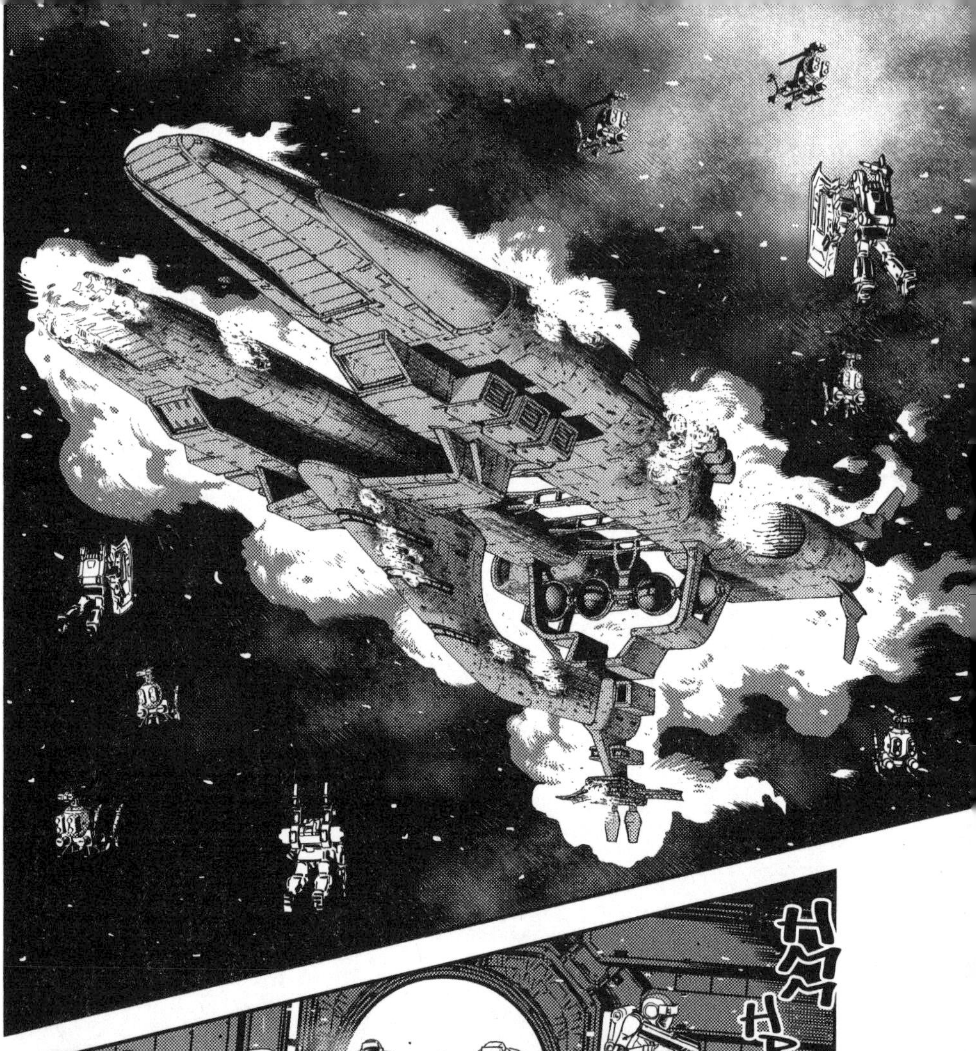

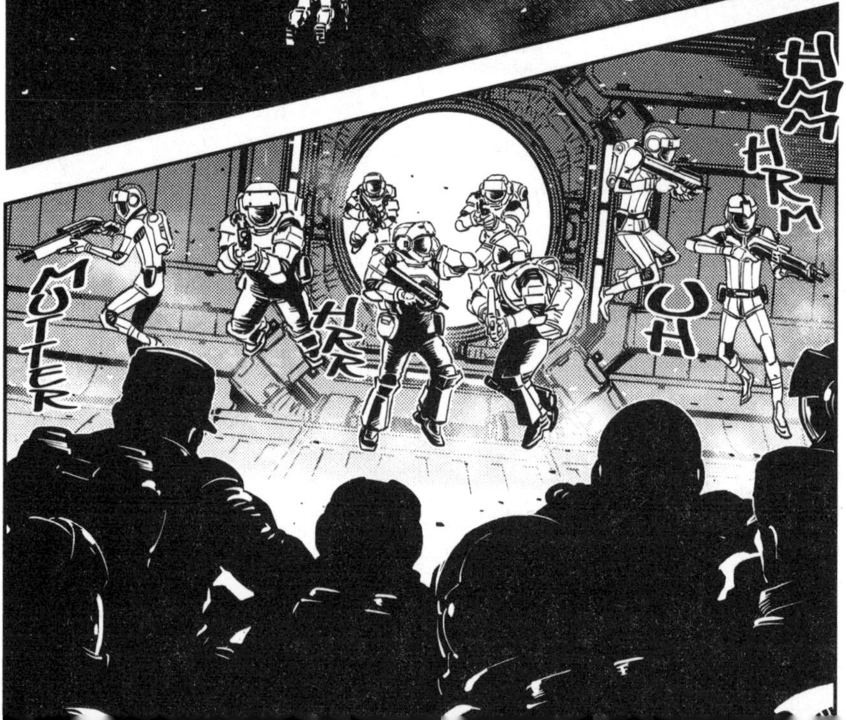
HMM
HRM
UH
HRR
MUTTER

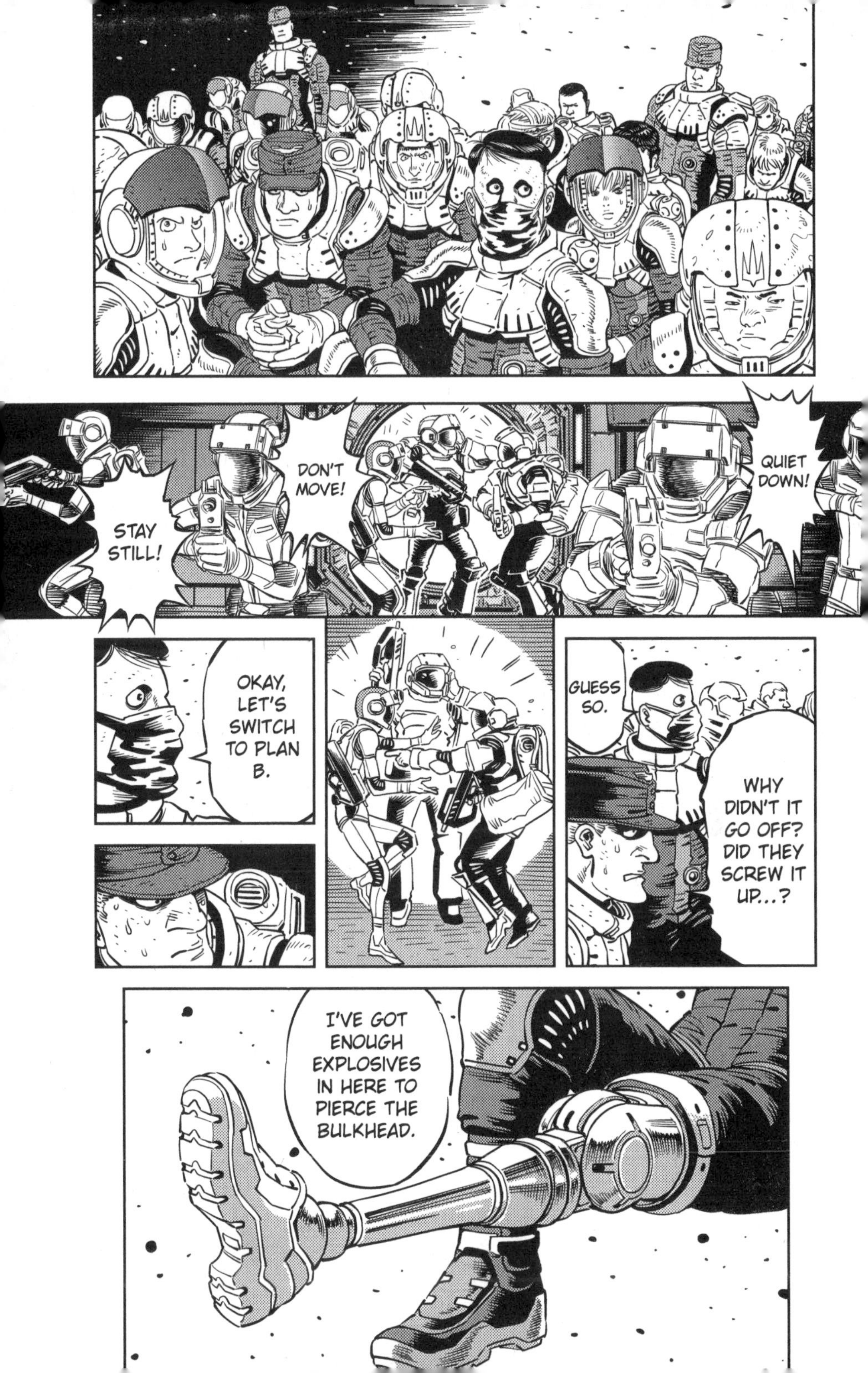
QUIET DOWN!
DON'T MOVE!
STAY STILL!
GUESS SO.
WHY DIDN'T IT GO OFF? DID THEY SCREW IT UP...?
OKAY, LET'S SWITCH TO PLAN B.
I'VE GOT ENOUGH EXPLOSIVES IN HERE TO PIERCE THE BULKHEAD.

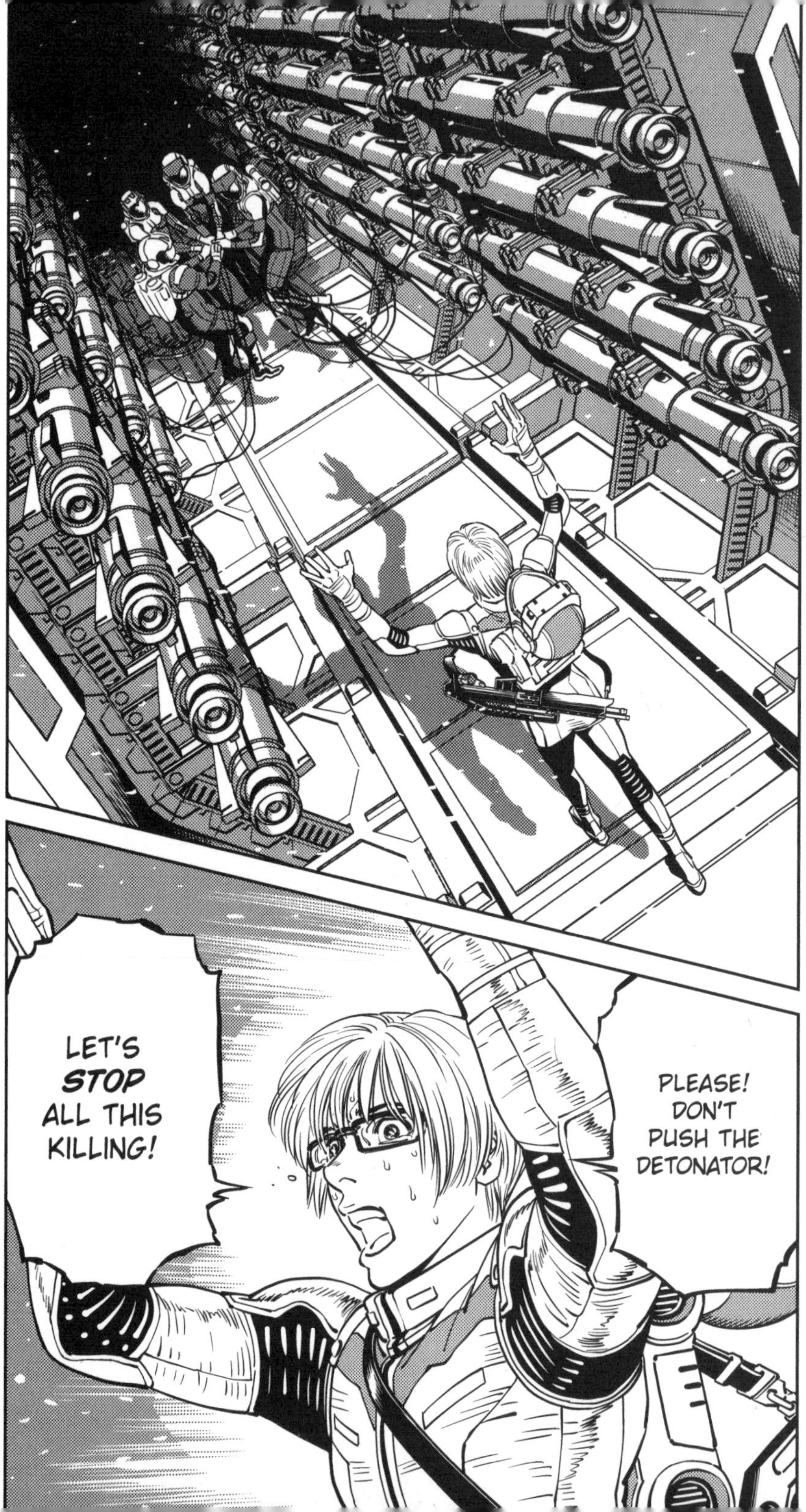
PLEASE! DON'T PUSH THE DETONATOR!
LET'S STOP ALL THIS KILLING!

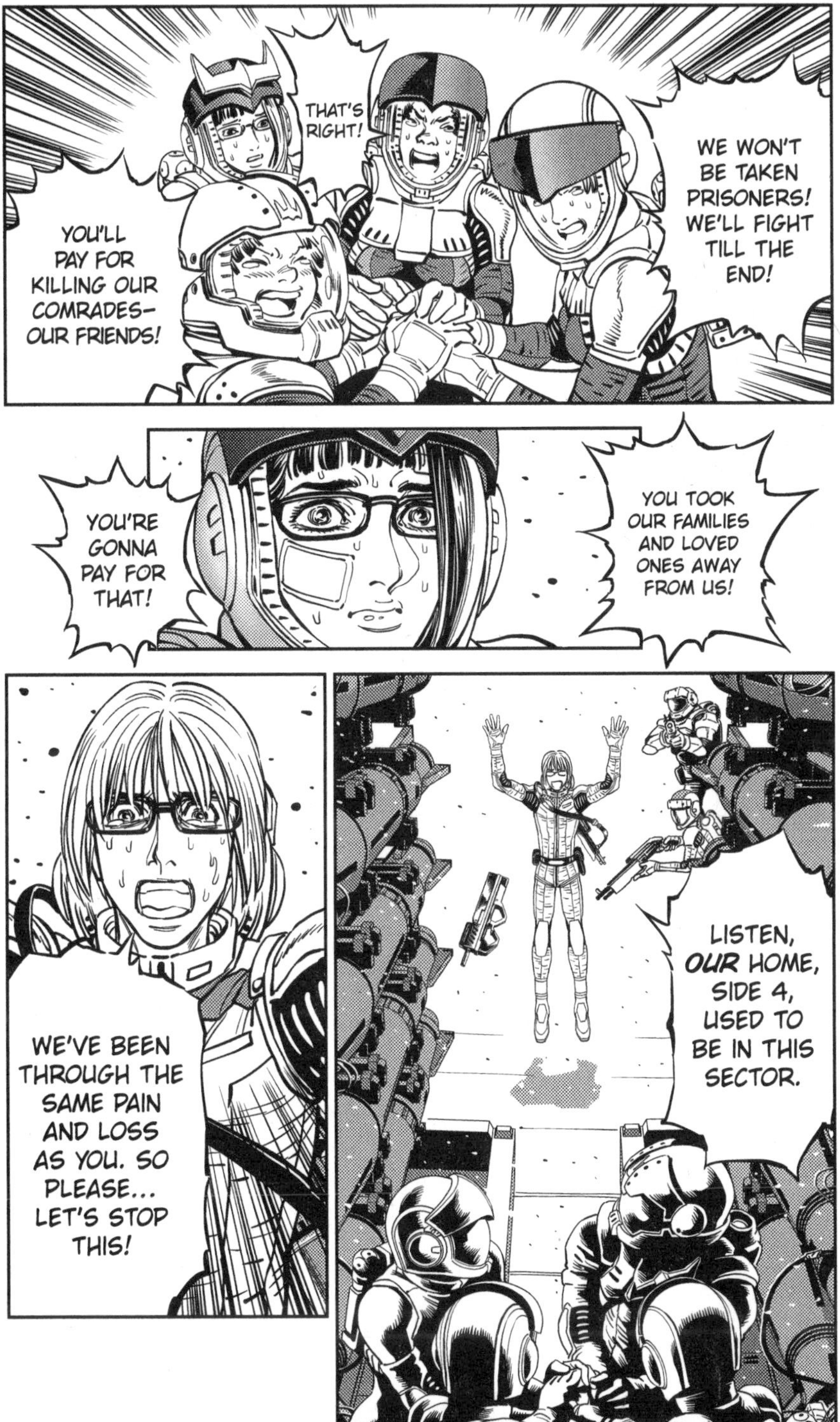
WE WON'T BE TAKEN PRISONERS! WE'LL FIGHT TILL THE END!
THAT'S RIGHT!
YOU'LL PAY FOR KILLING OUR COMRADES— OUR FRIENDS!
YOU TOOK OUR FAMILIES AND LOVED ONES AWAY FROM US!
YOU'RE GONNA PAY FOR THAT!
LISTEN, ***OUR*** HOME, SIDE 4, USED TO BE IN THIS SECTOR.
WE'VE BEEN THROUGH THE SAME PAIN AND LOSS AS YOU. SO PLEASE... LET'S STOP THIS!

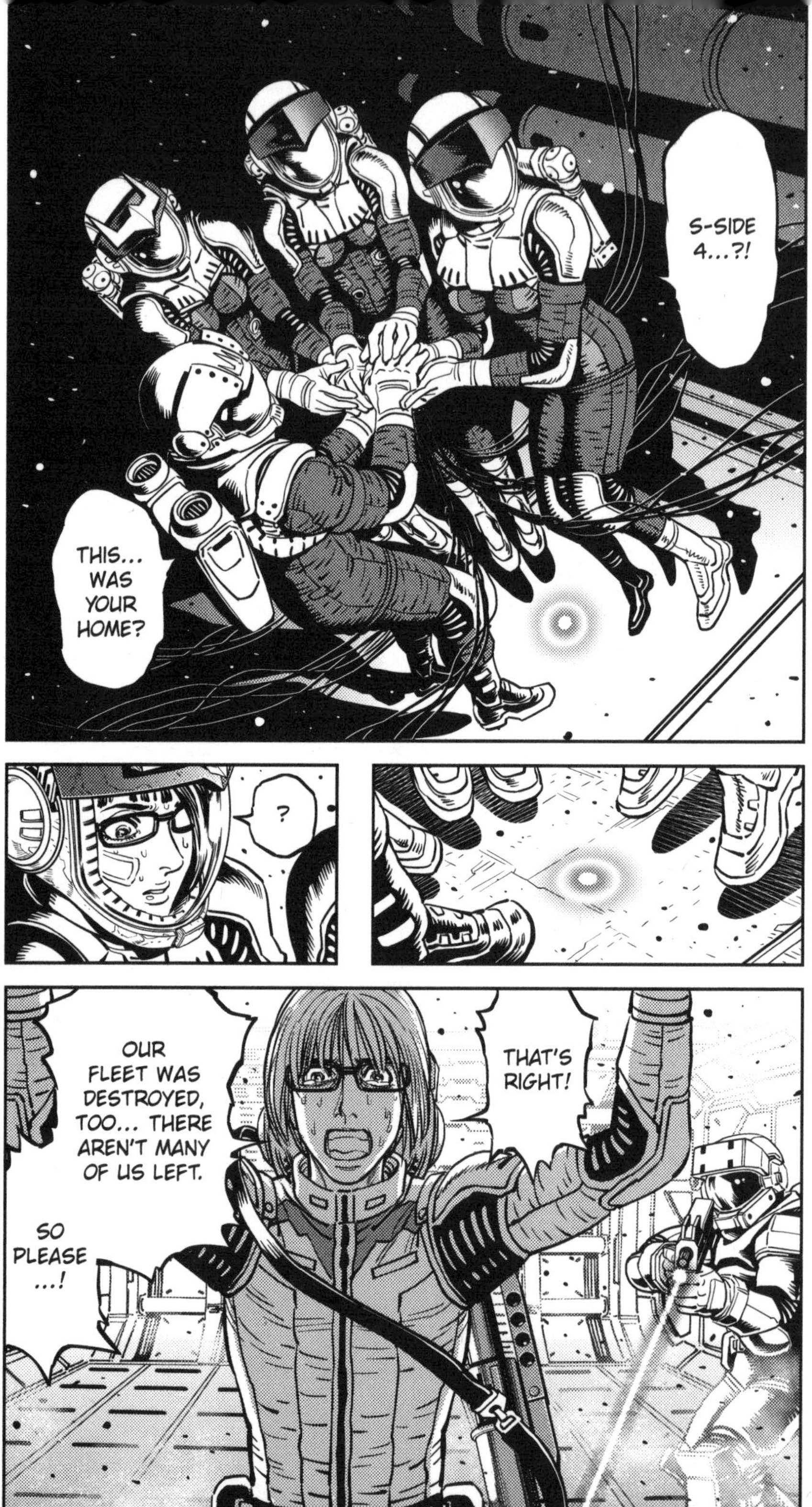
S-SIDE 4...?!
THIS... WAS YOUR HOME?
?
THAT'S RIGHT!
OUR FLEET WAS DESTROYED, TOO... THERE AREN'T MANY OF US LEFT.
SO PLEASE ...!

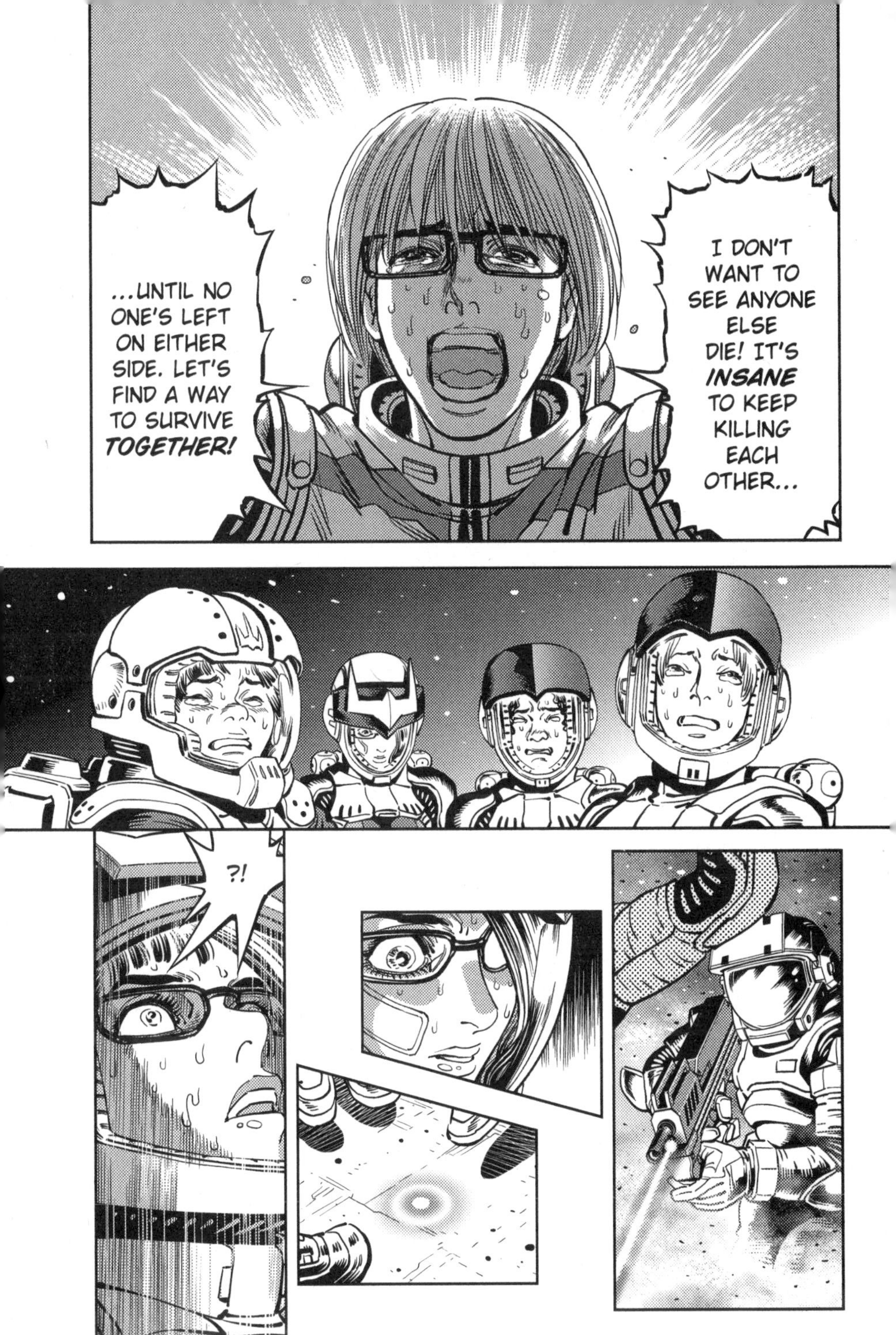
I DON'T WANT TO SEE ANYONE ELSE DIE! IT'S ***INSANE*** TO KEEP KILLING EACH OTHER...
...UNTIL NO ONE'S LEFT ON EITHER SIDE. LET'S FIND A WAY TO SURVIVE ***TOGETHER!***
?!

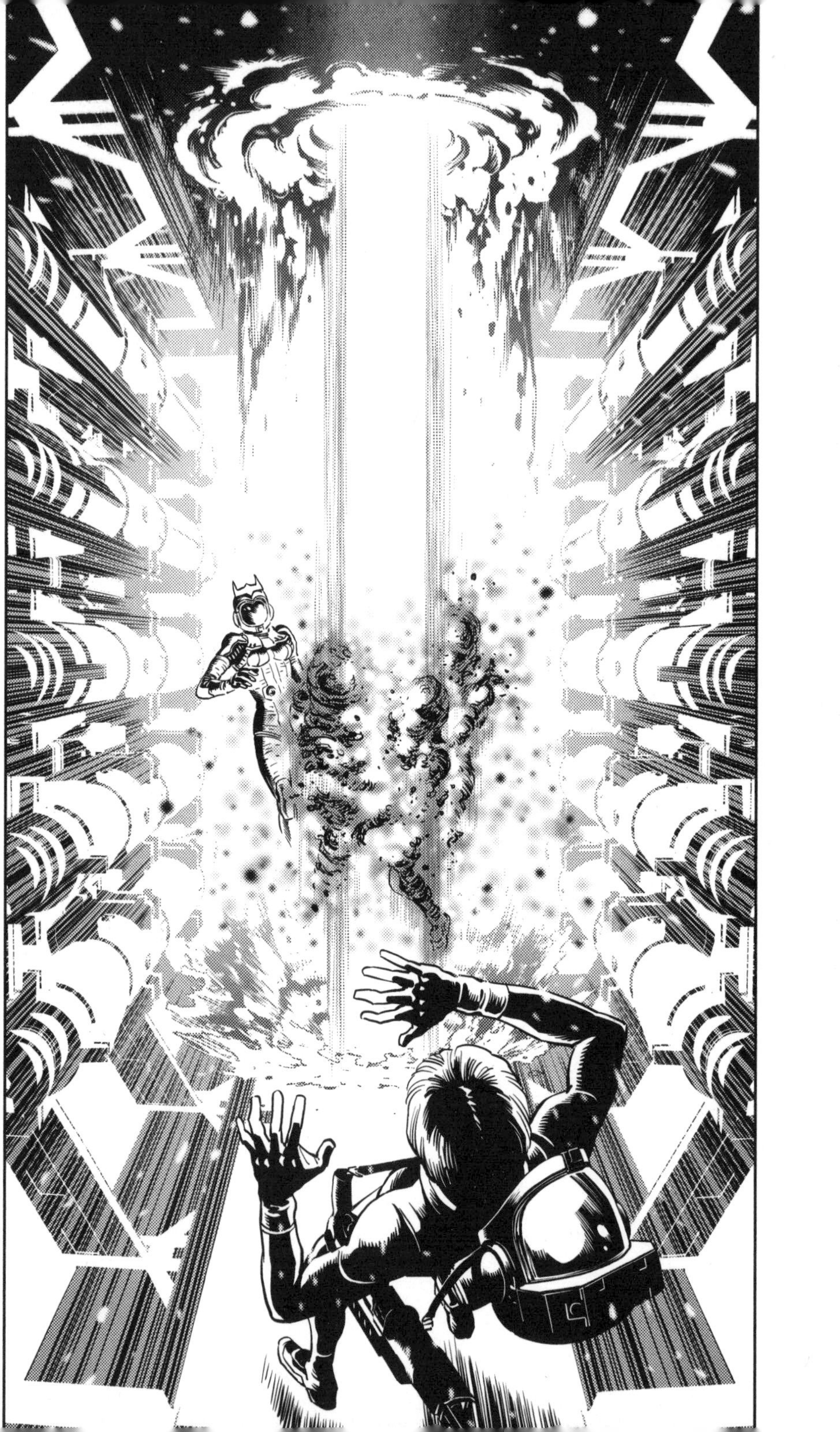

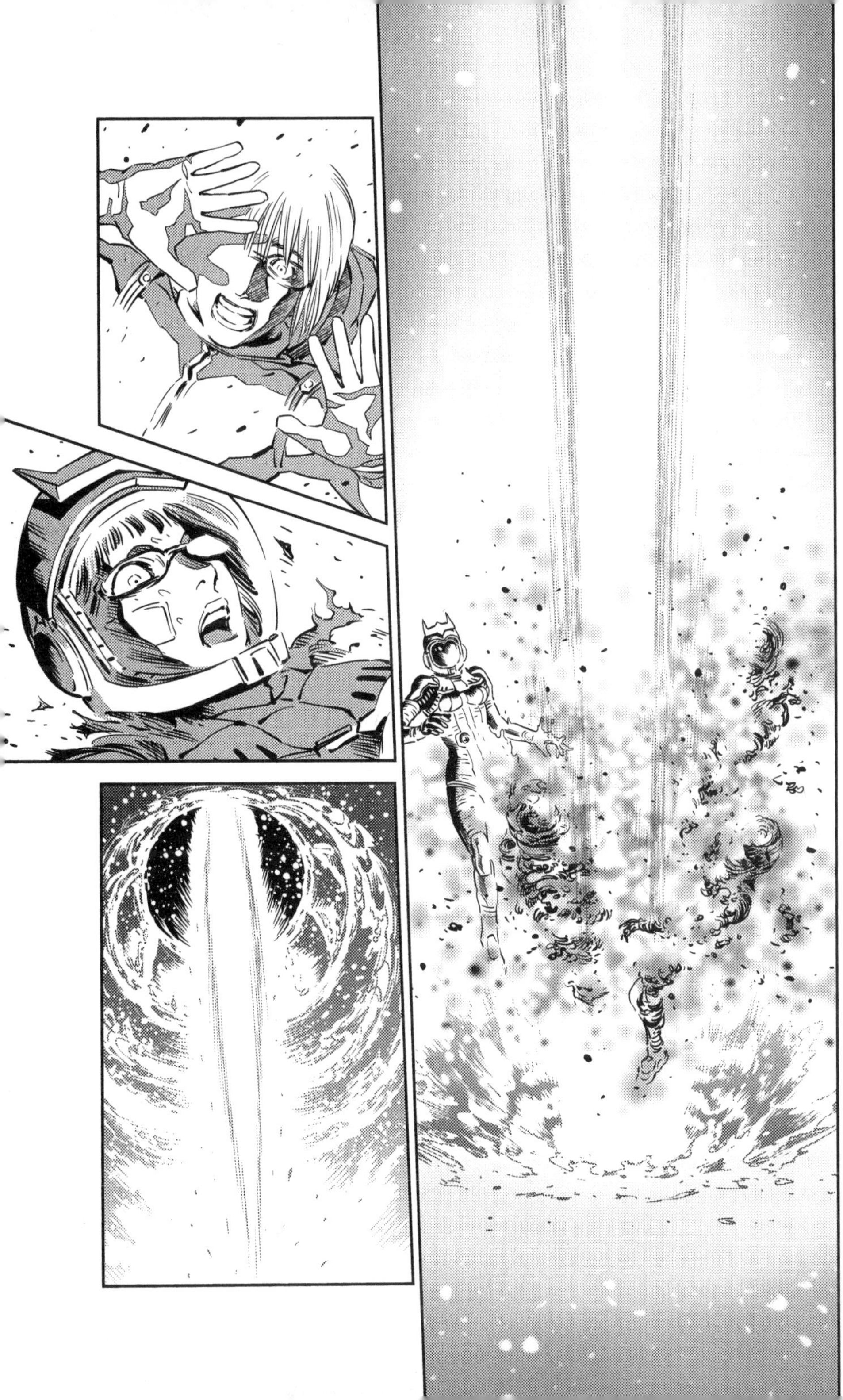

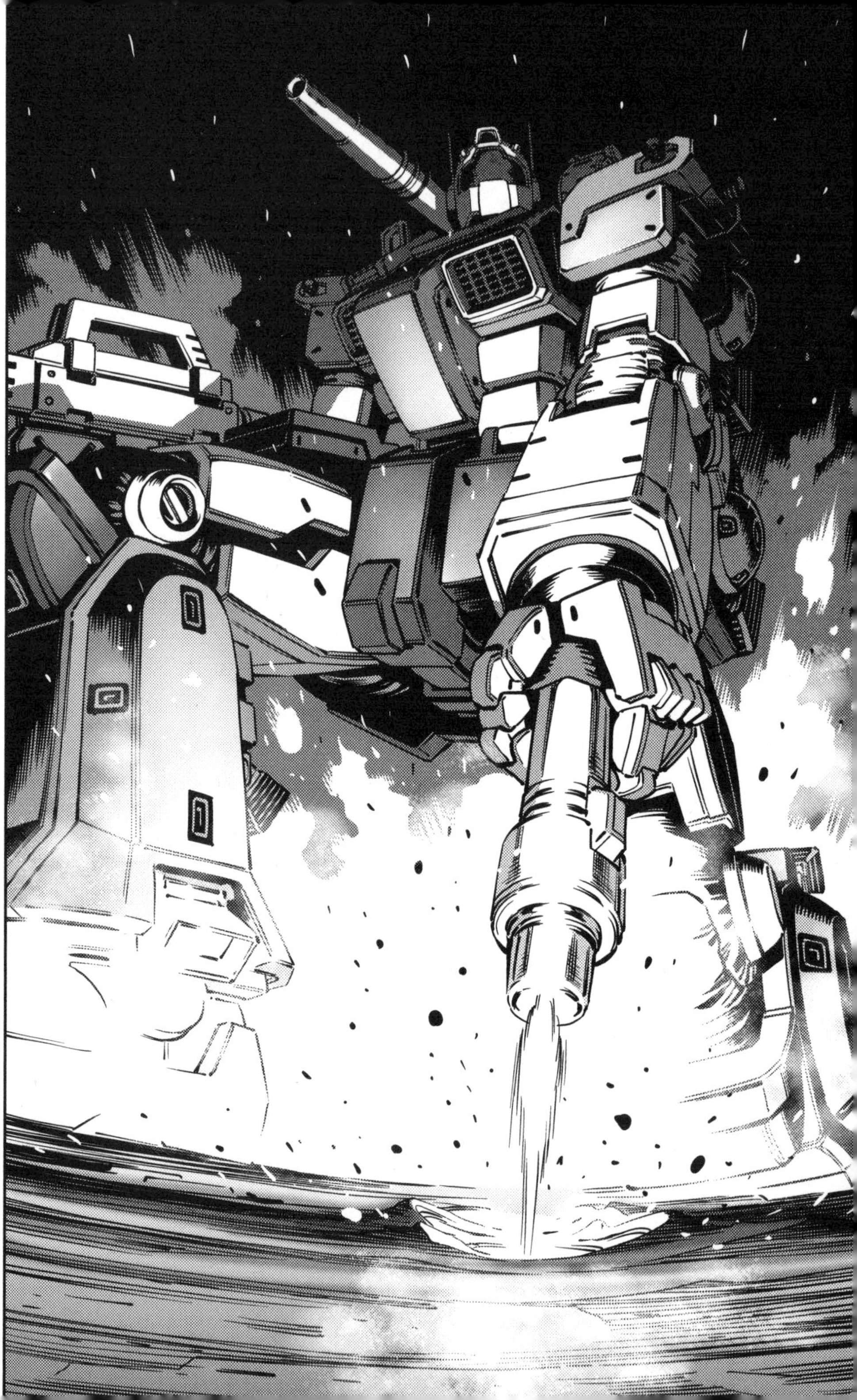

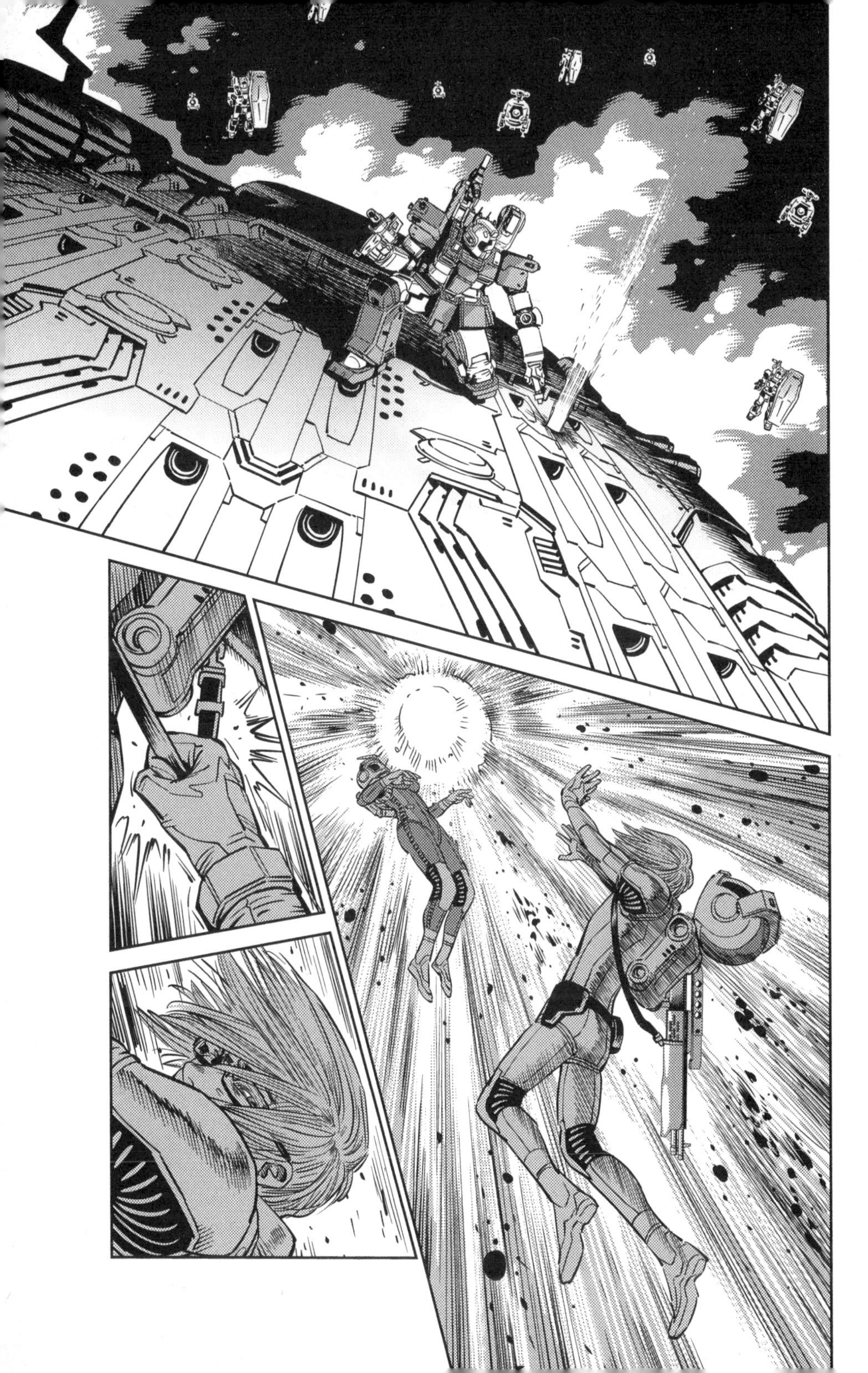

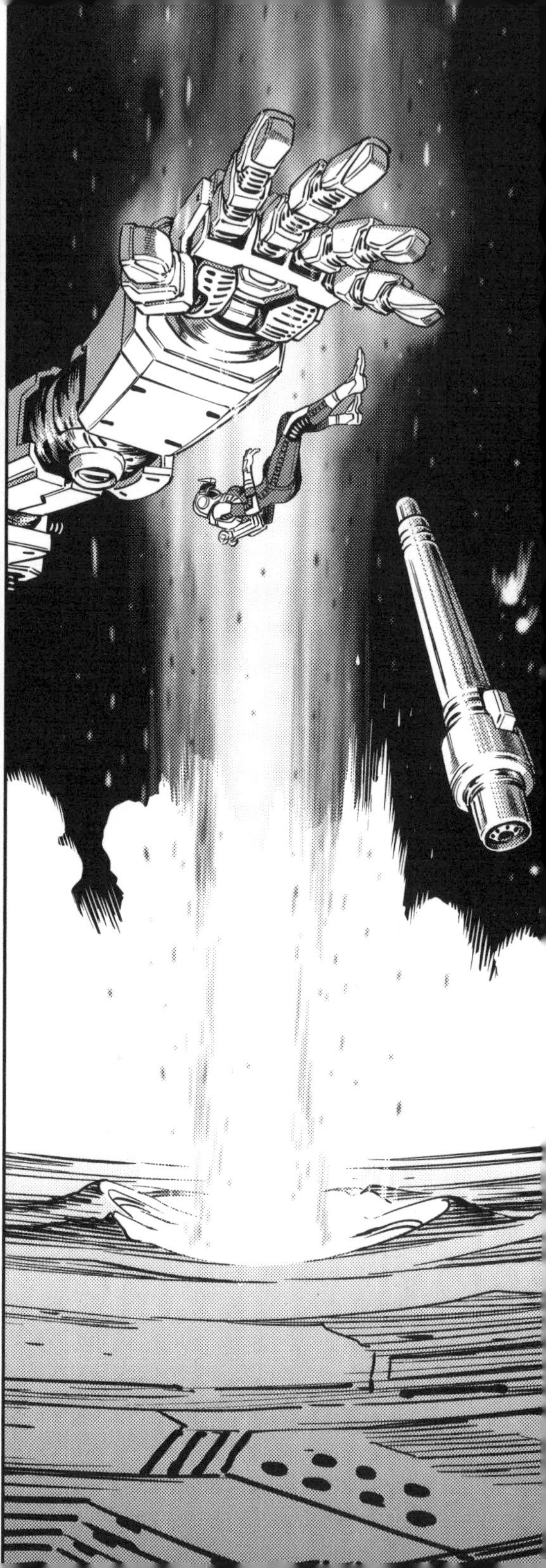
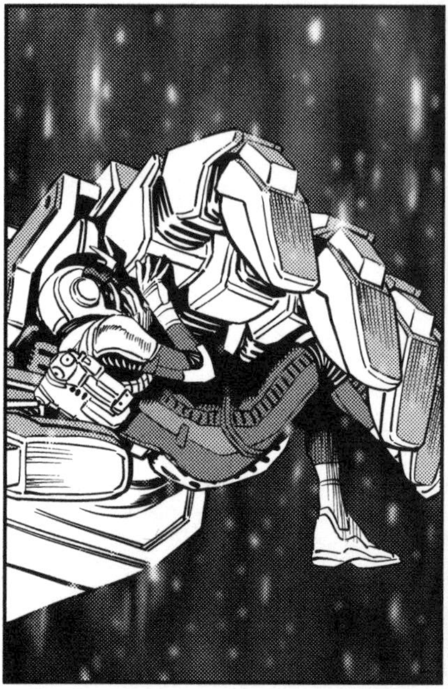
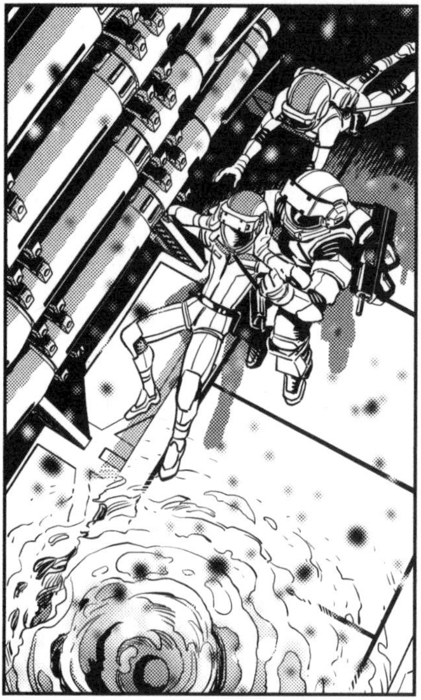

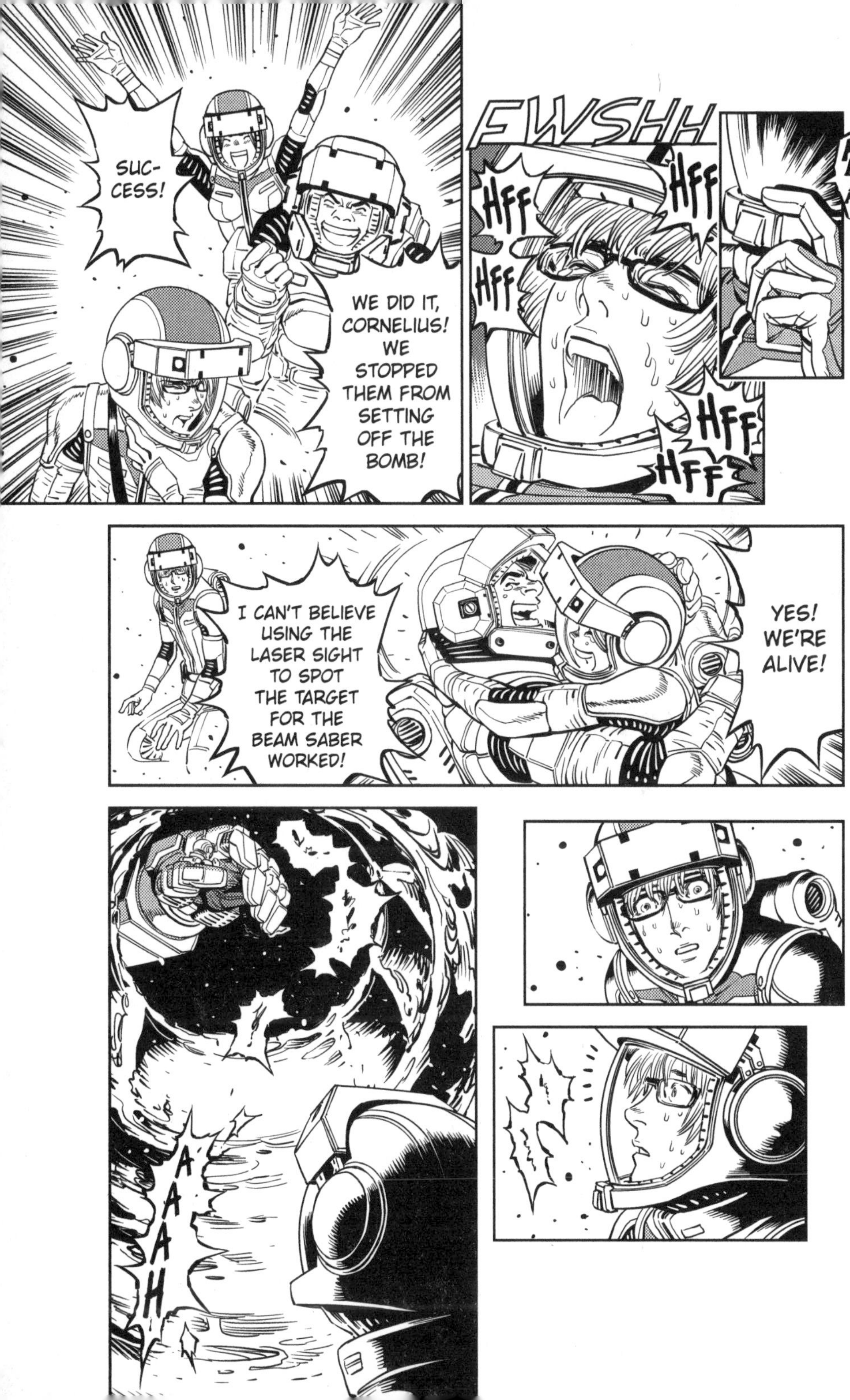
KLIK
FWSHH
HFF
HFF
HFF
HFF
HFF
SUC-CESS!
WE DID IT, CORNELIUS! WE STOPPED THEM FROM SETTING OFF THE BOMB!
YES! WE'RE ALIVE!
I CAN'T BELIEVE USING THE LASER SIGHT TO SPOT THE TARGET FOR THE BEAM SABER WORKED!
AAAAH

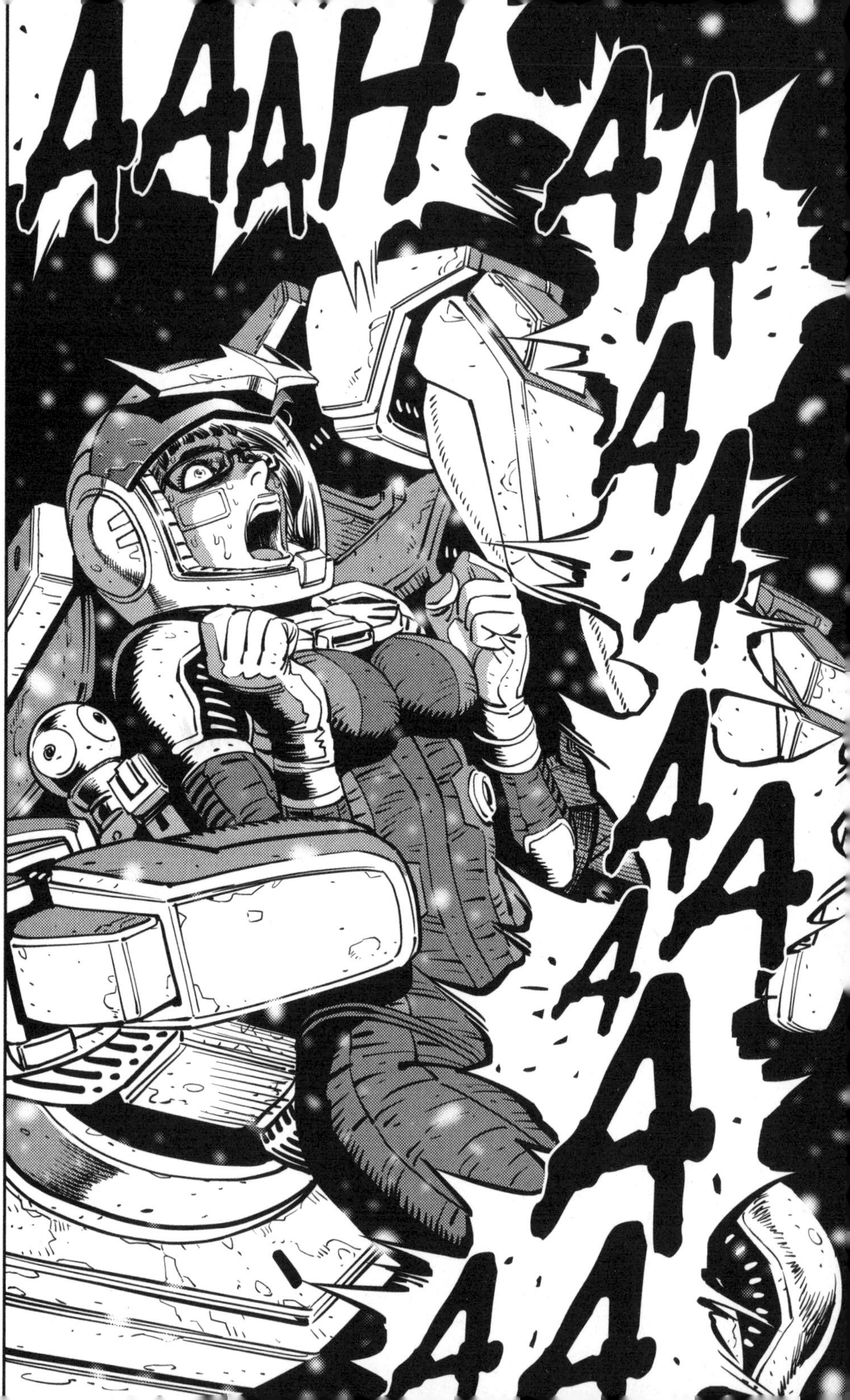
AAAH AAAAAAAAAAAAAA

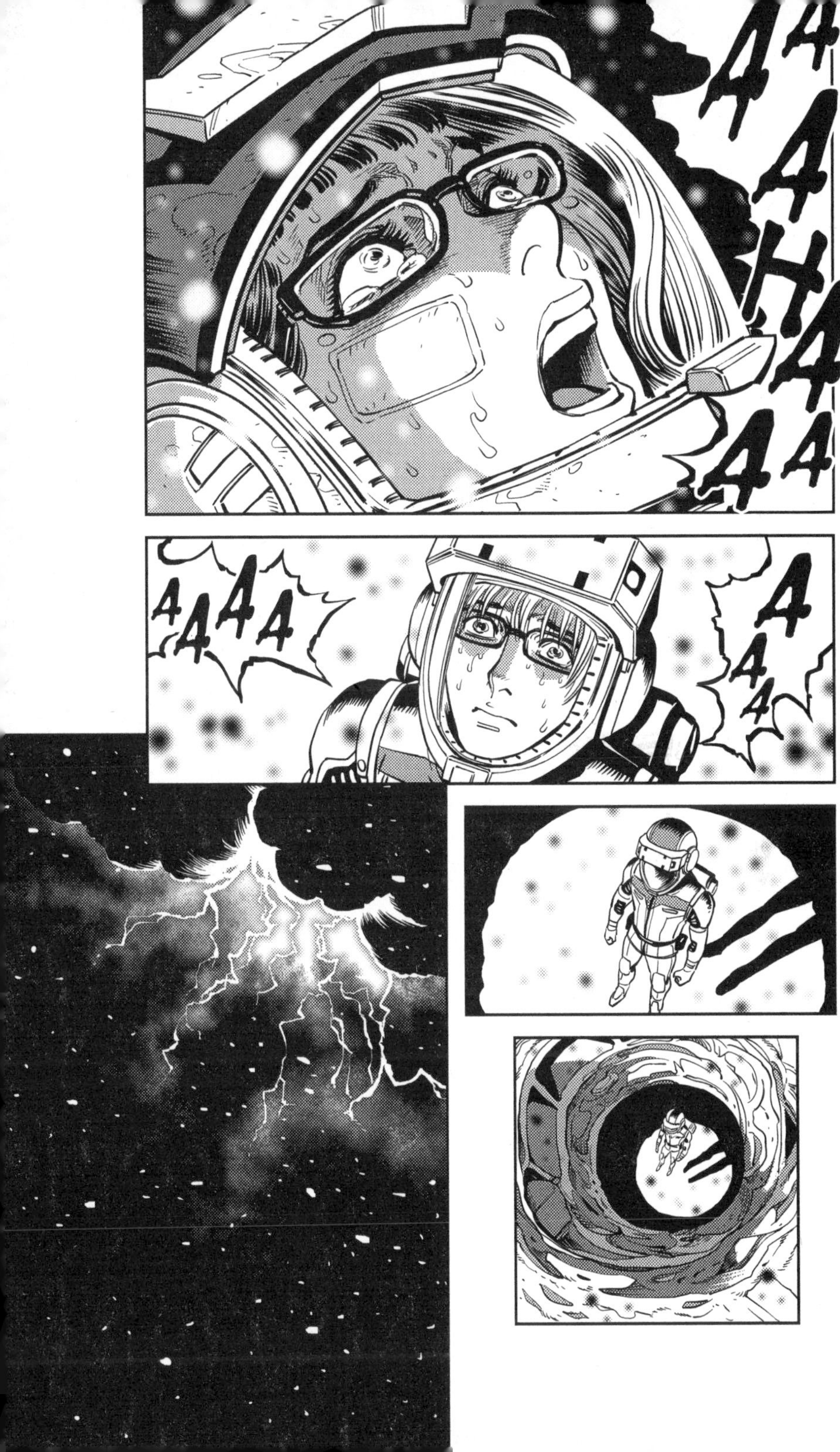
AAAAHAAAA
AAAA
AAAA

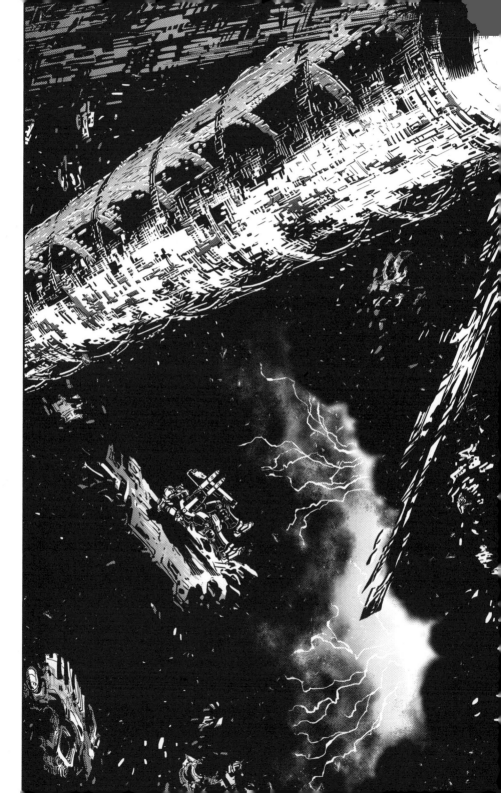

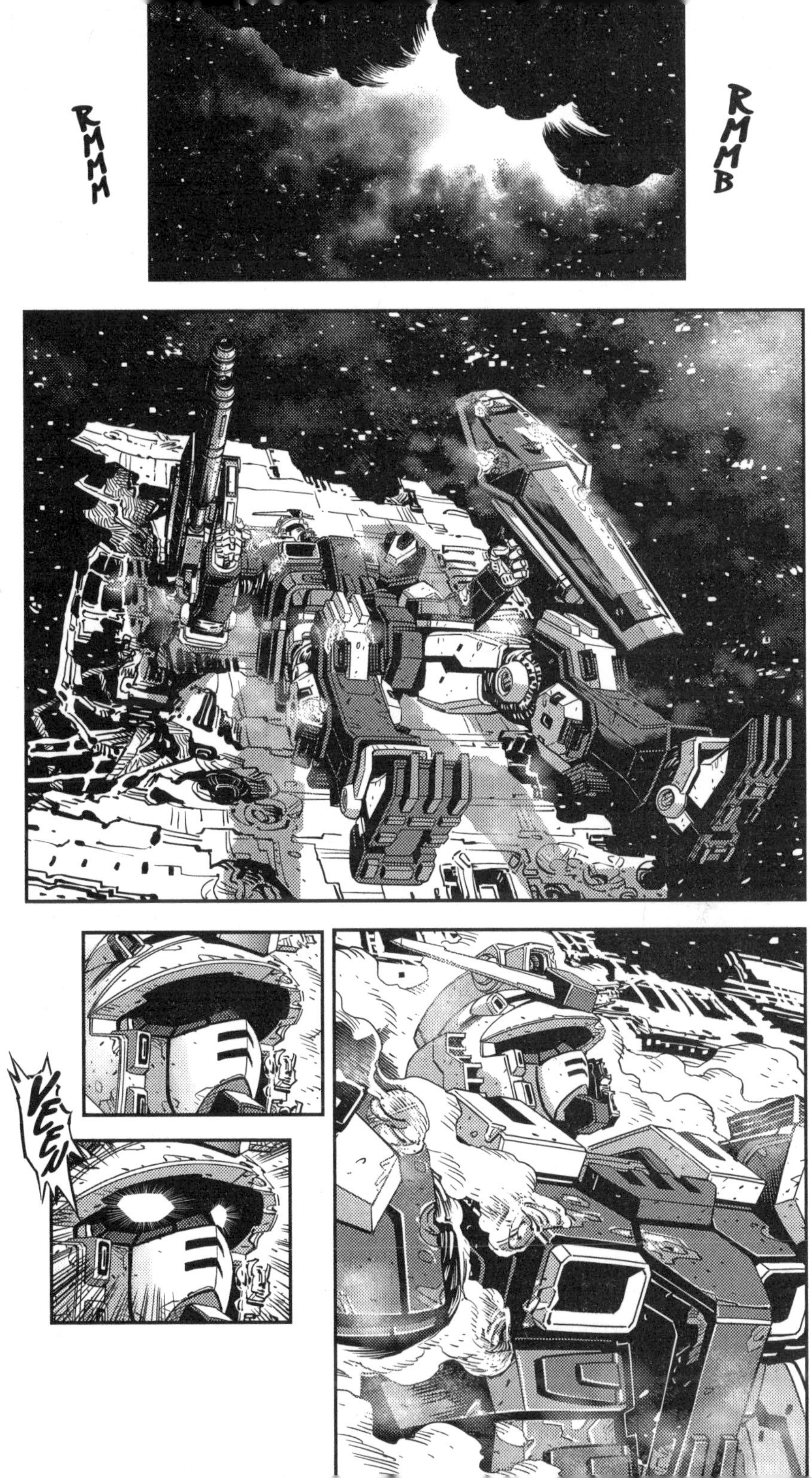
RMMM
RMMB
VEEN

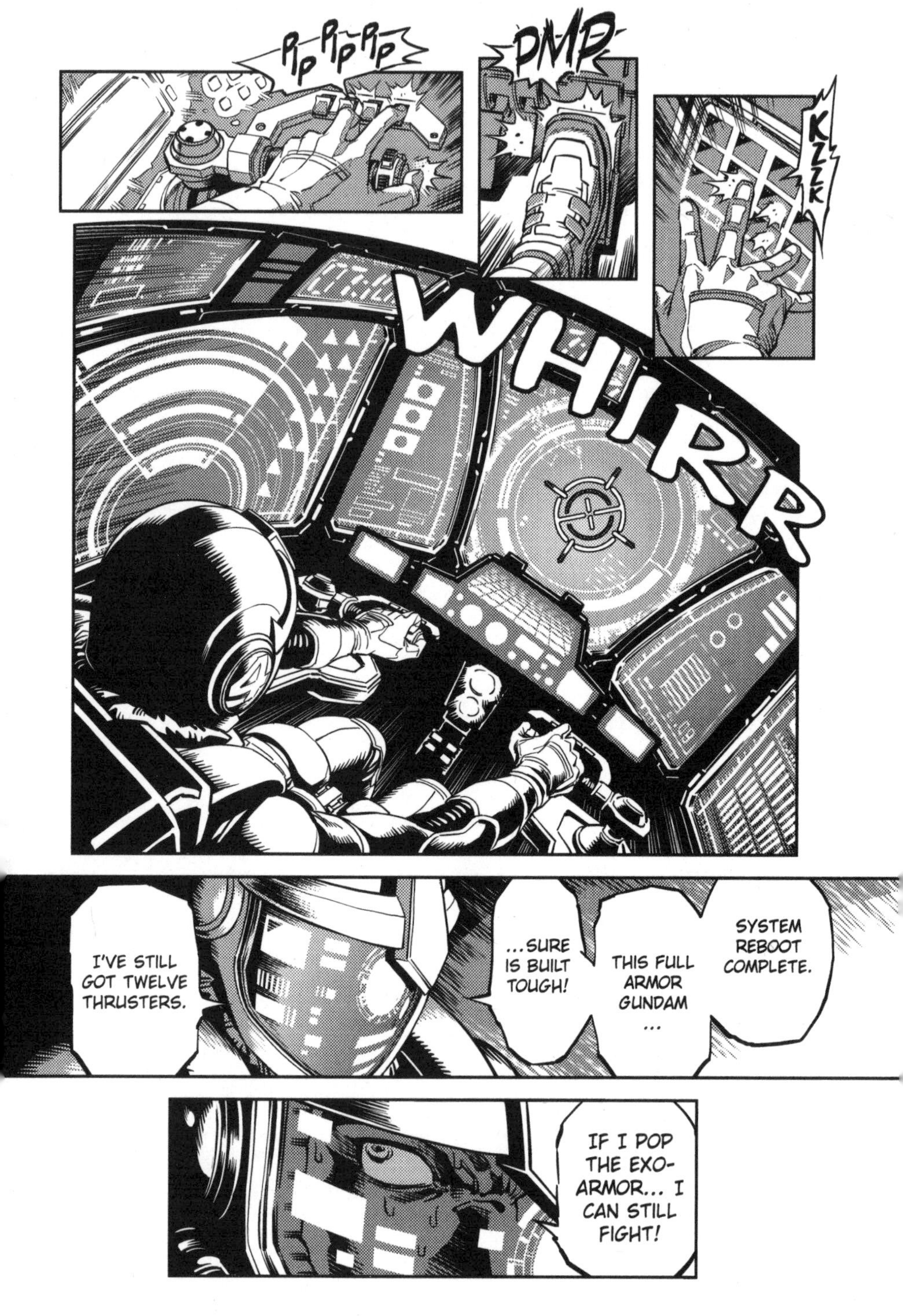
KZZK
DMP
RIP RIP RIP
WHIRR
SYSTEM REBOOT COMPLETE.
THIS FULL ARMOR GUNDAM ...
...SURE IS BUILT TOUGH!
I'VE STILL GOT TWELVE THRUSTERS.
IF I POP THE EXO-ARMOR... I CAN STILL FIGHT!

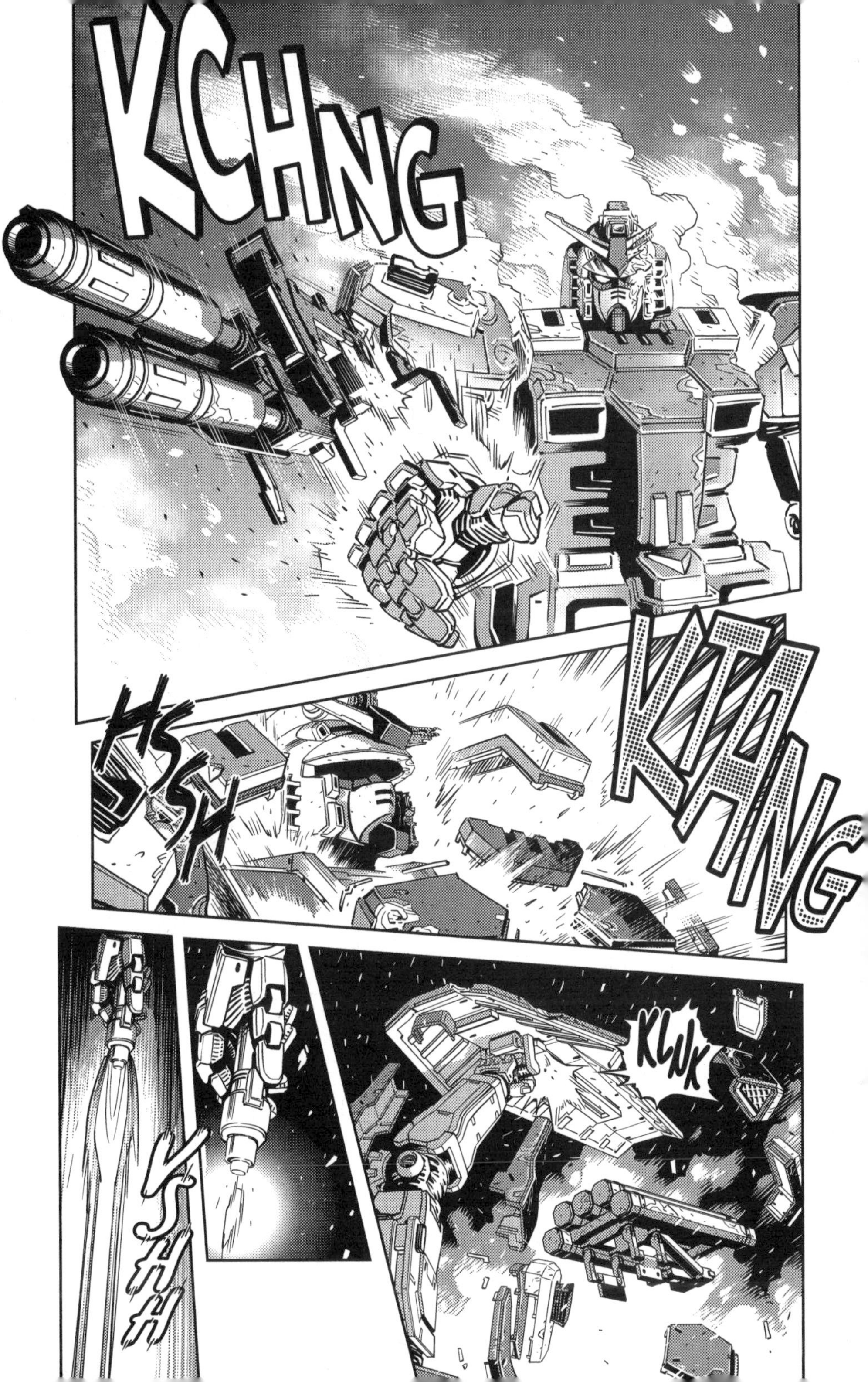
KCHNG
KTANG
HSSH
KLNK
VSHH

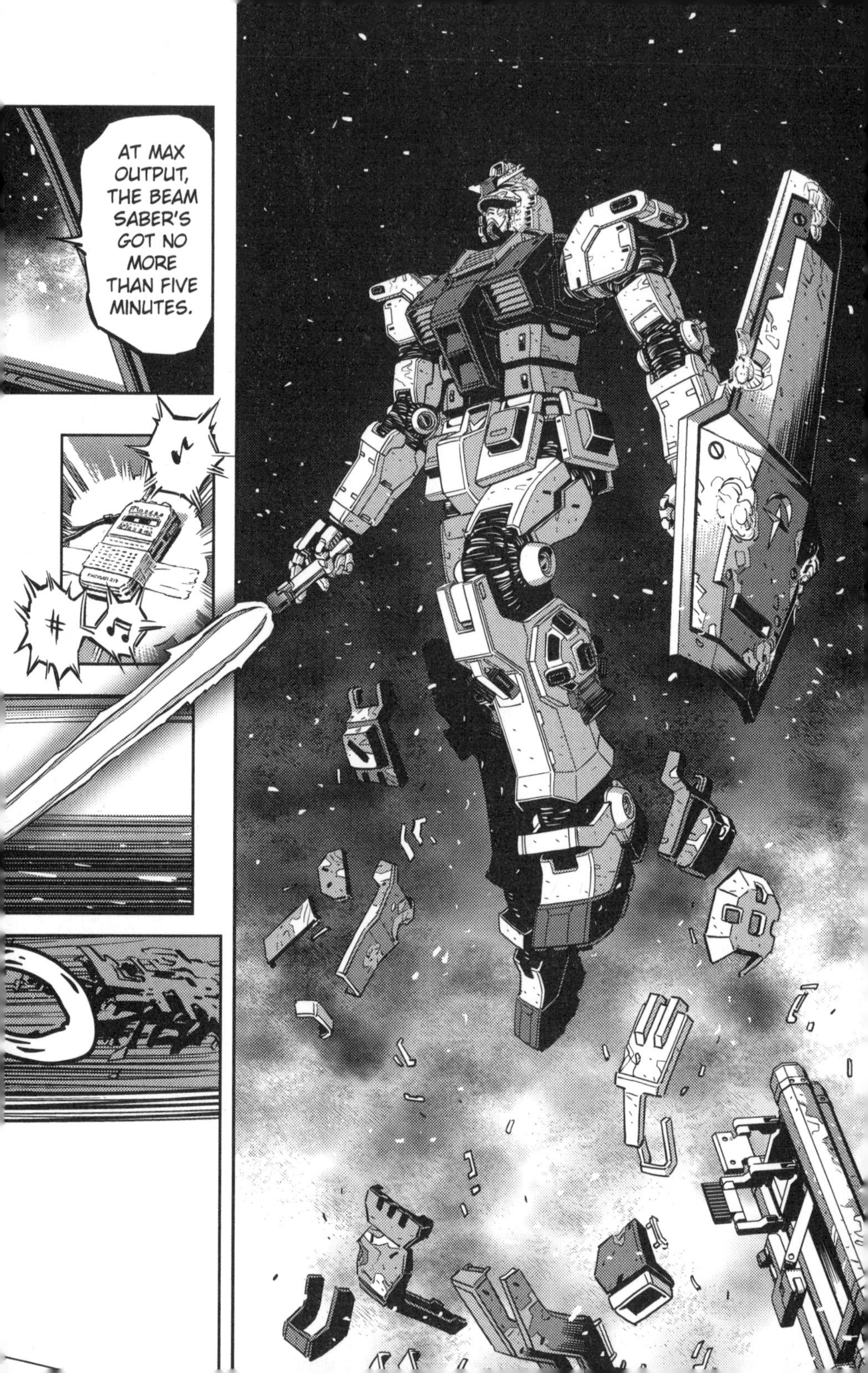
AT MAX OUTPUT, THE BEAM SABER'S GOT NO MORE THAN FIVE MINUTES.

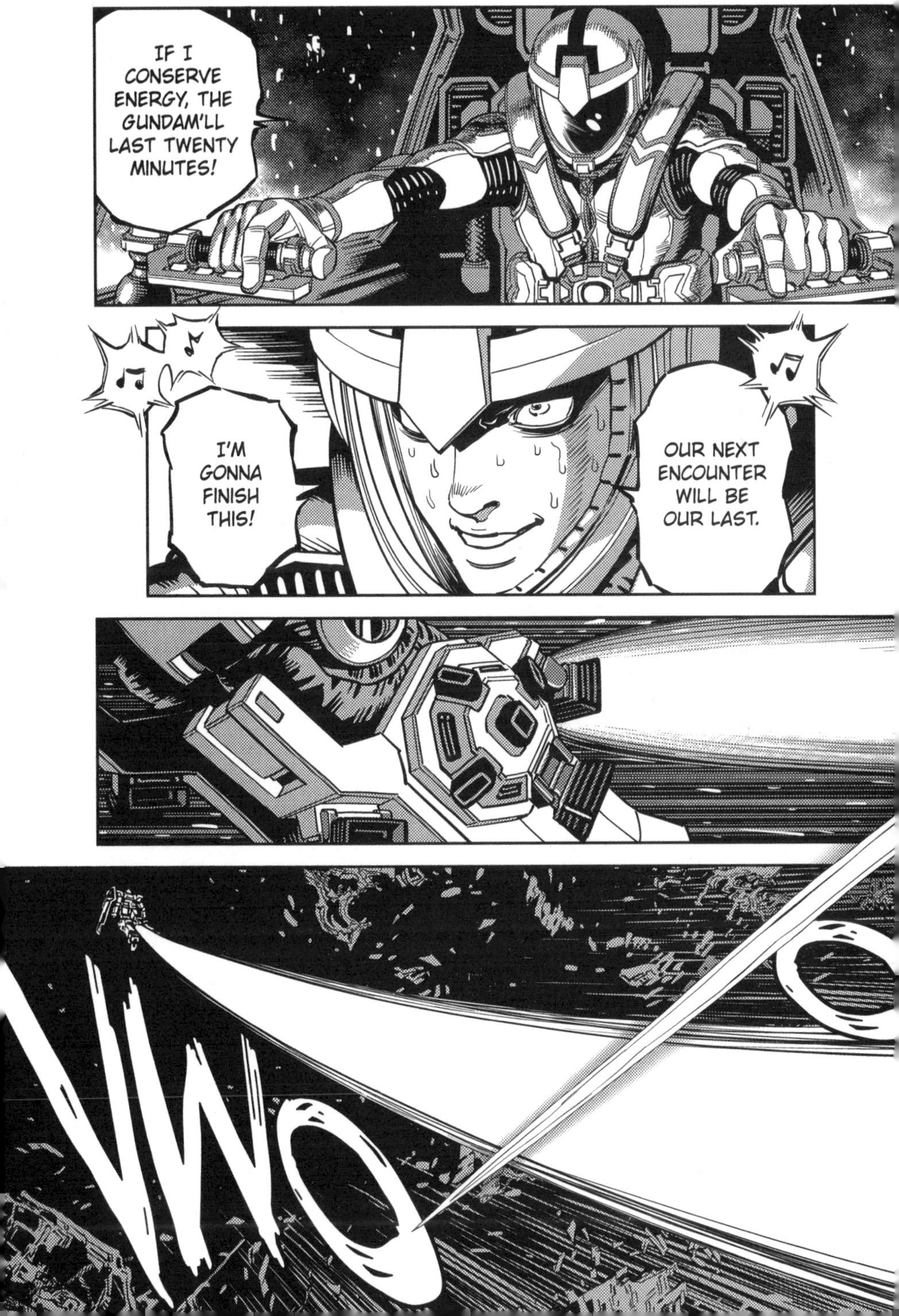
IF I CONSERVE ENERGY, THE GUNDAM'LL LAST TWENTY MINUTES!
OUR NEXT ENCOUNTER WILL BE OUR LAST.
I'M GONNA FINISH THIS!
VWOO

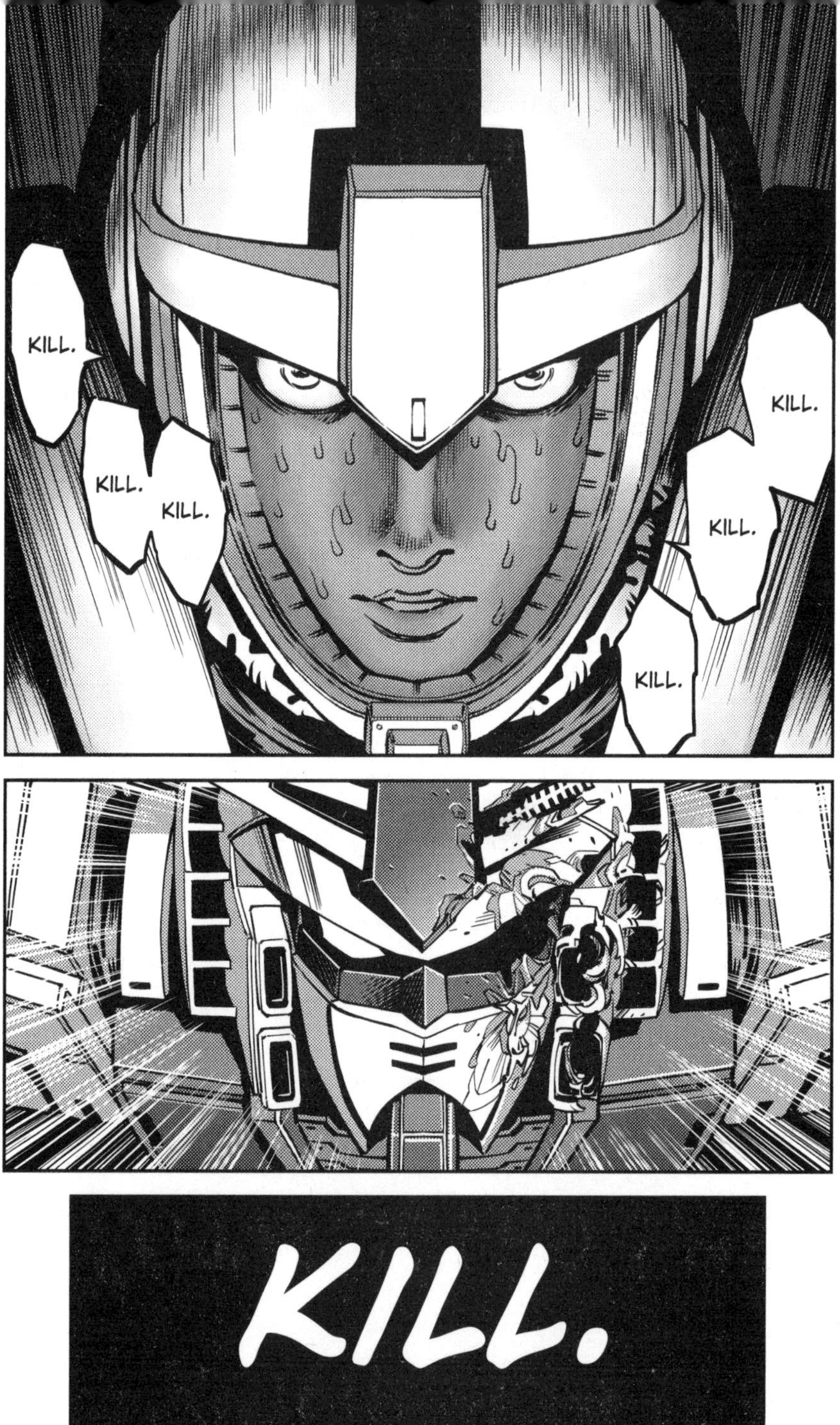
KILL.
KILL.
KILL.
KILL.
KILL.
KILL.
KILL.

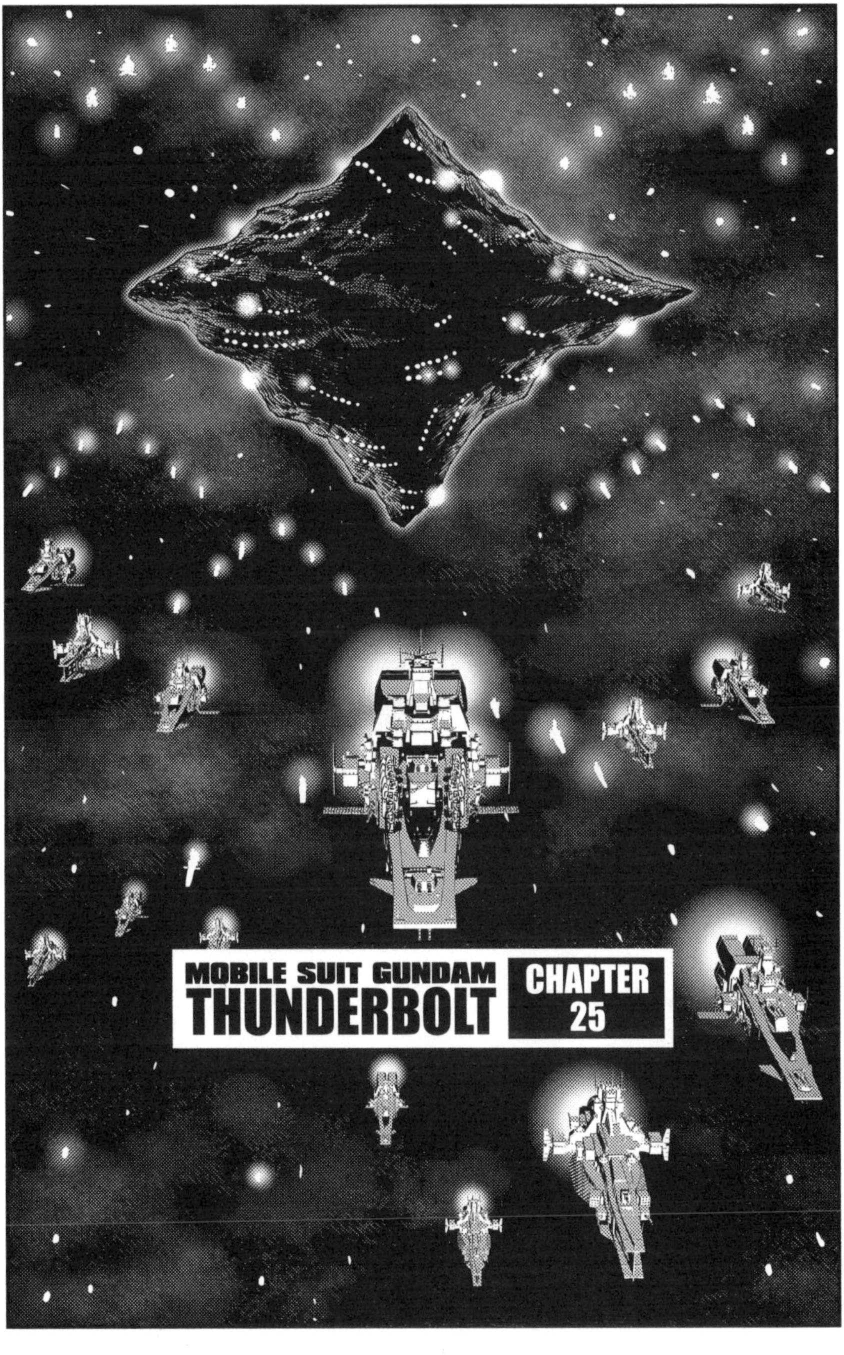
MOBILE SUIT GUNDAM
THUNDERBOLT
CHAPTER
25

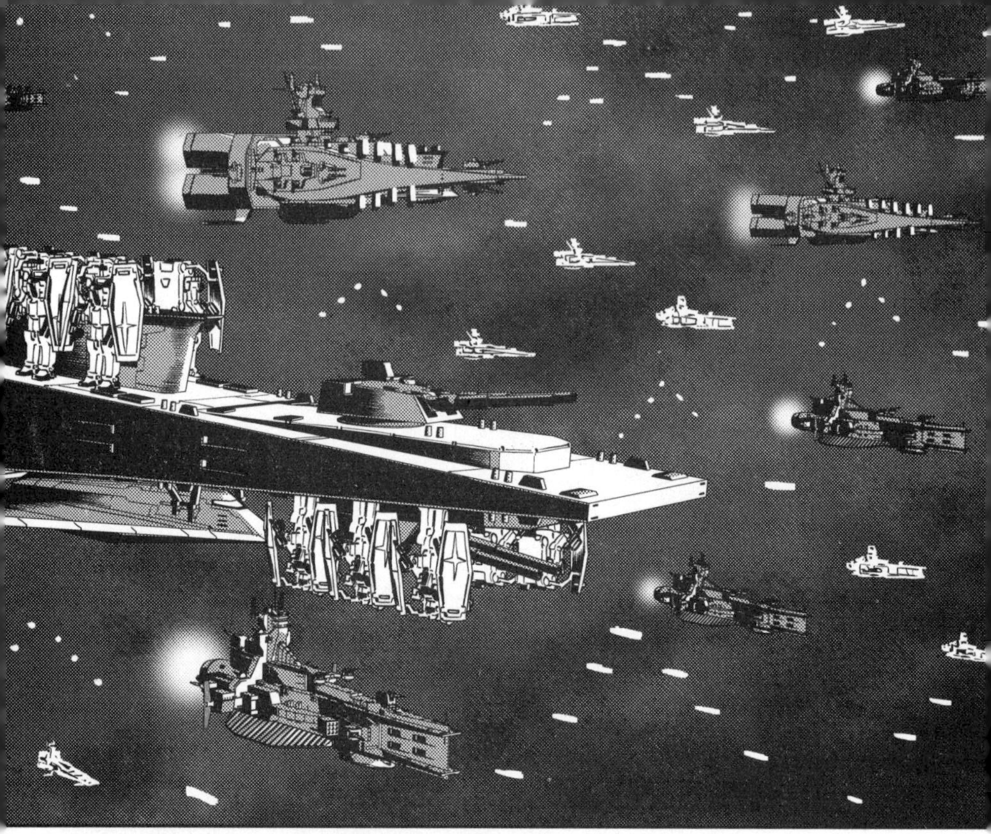

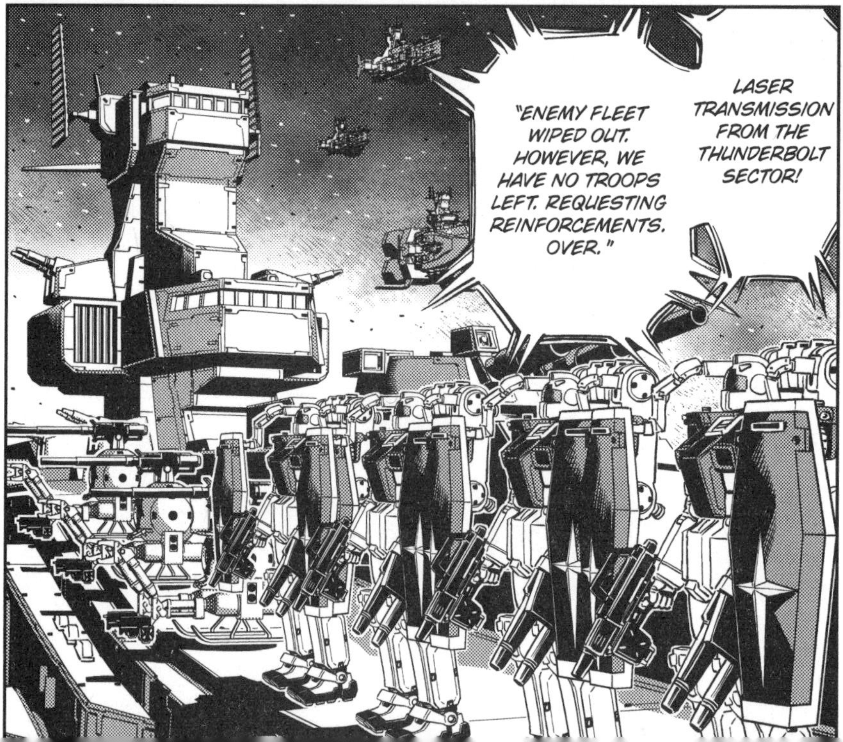
LASER TRANSMISSION FROM THE THUNDERBOLT SECTOR!
"ENEMY FLEET WIPED OUT. HOWEVER, WE HAVE NO TROOPS LEFT. REQUESTING REINFORCEMENTS. OVER."

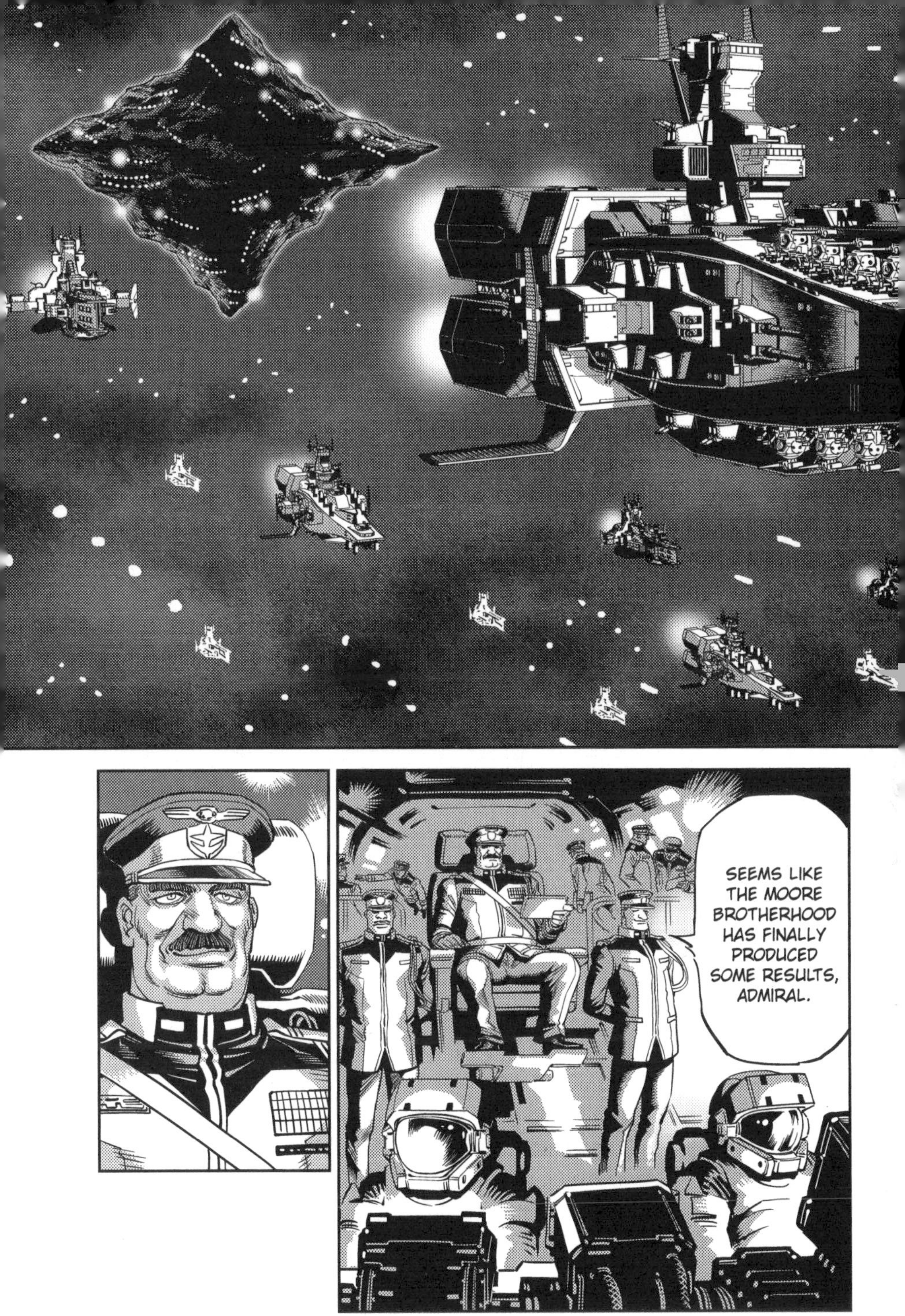
SEEMS LIKE THE MOORE BROTHERHOOD HAS FINALLY PRODUCED SOME RESULTS, ADMIRAL.

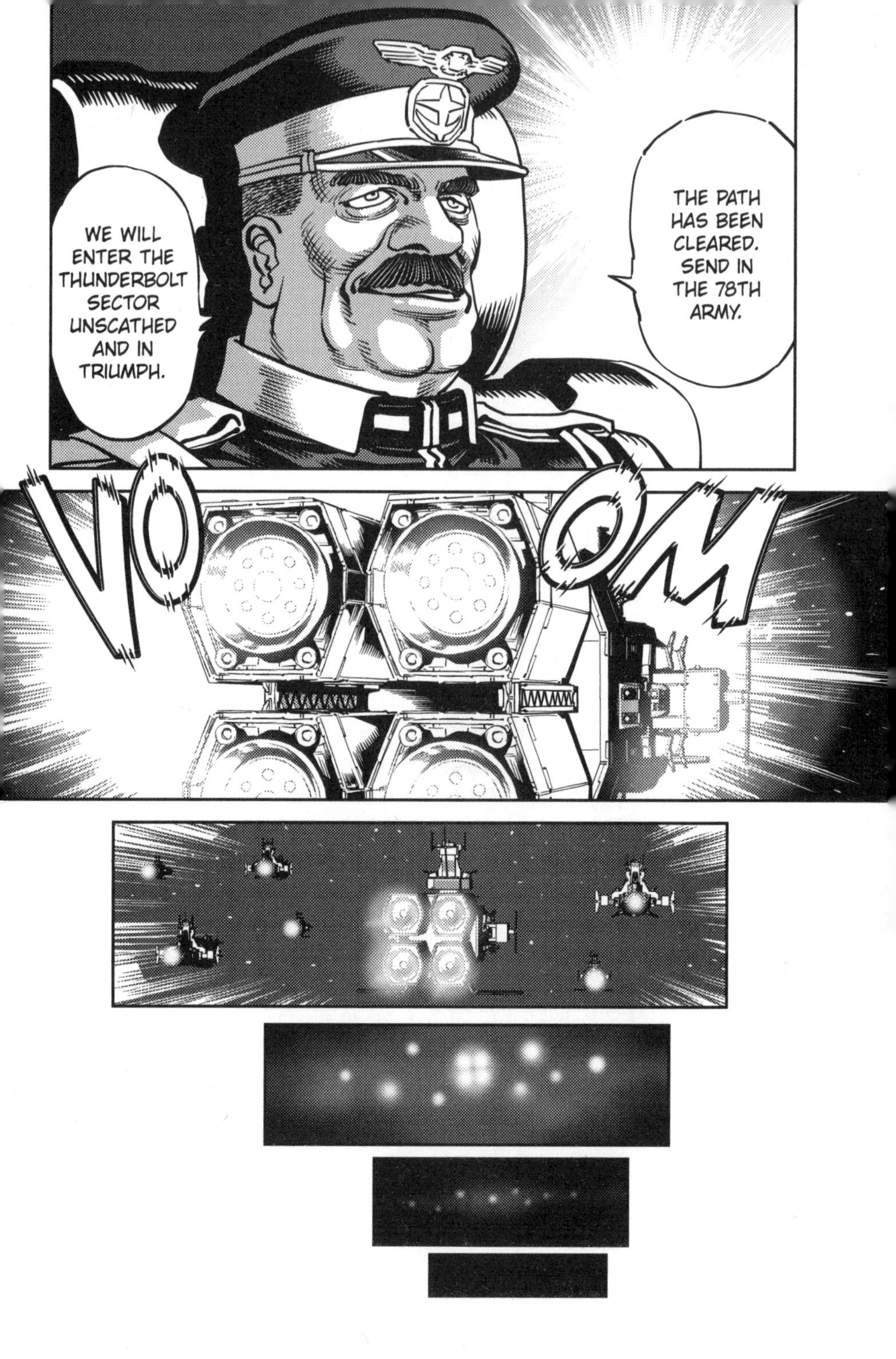
THE PATH HAS BEEN CLEARED. SEND IN THE 78TH ARMY.
WE WILL ENTER THE THUNDERBOLT SECTOR UNSCATHED AND IN TRIUMPH.
VOOOM

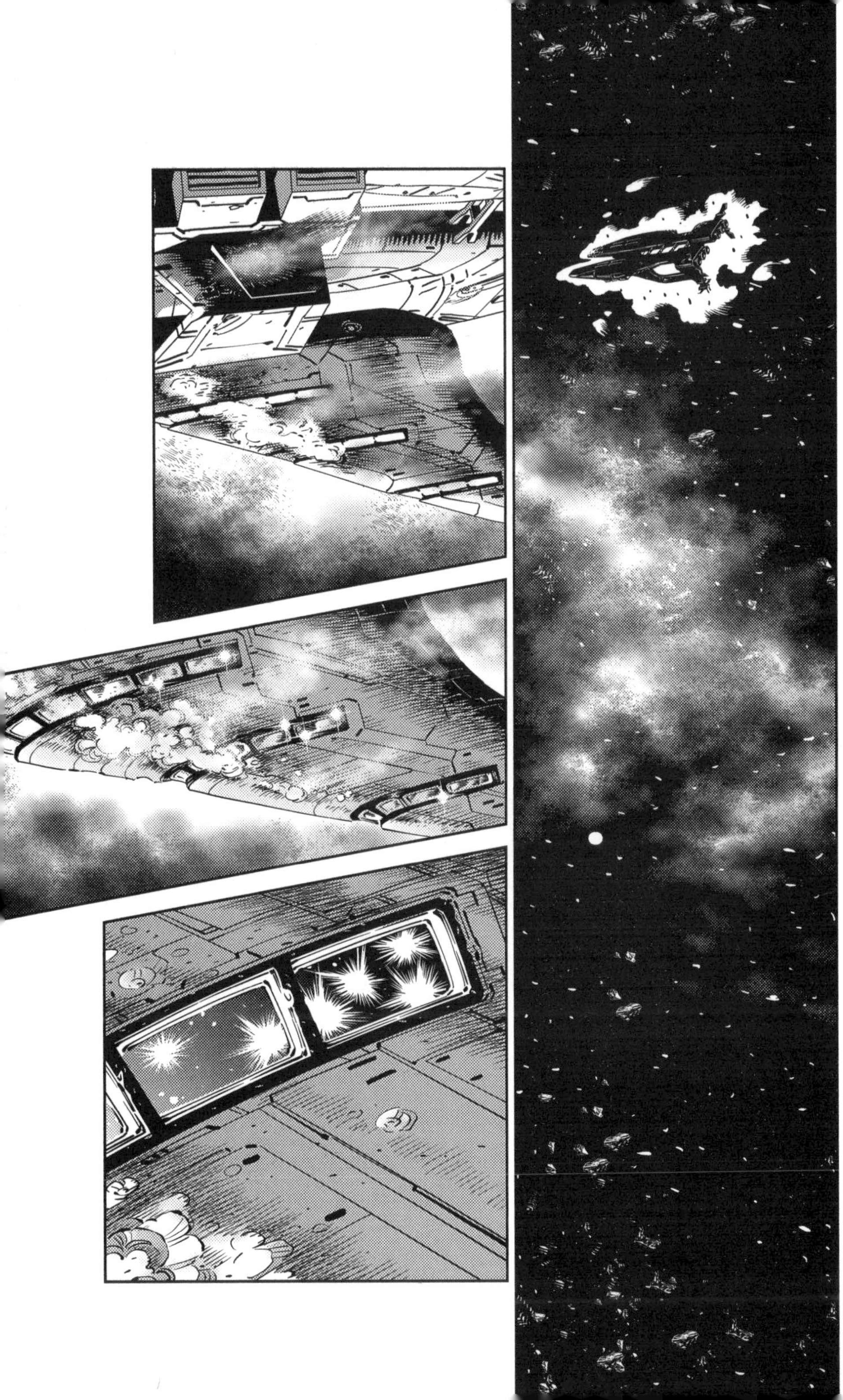

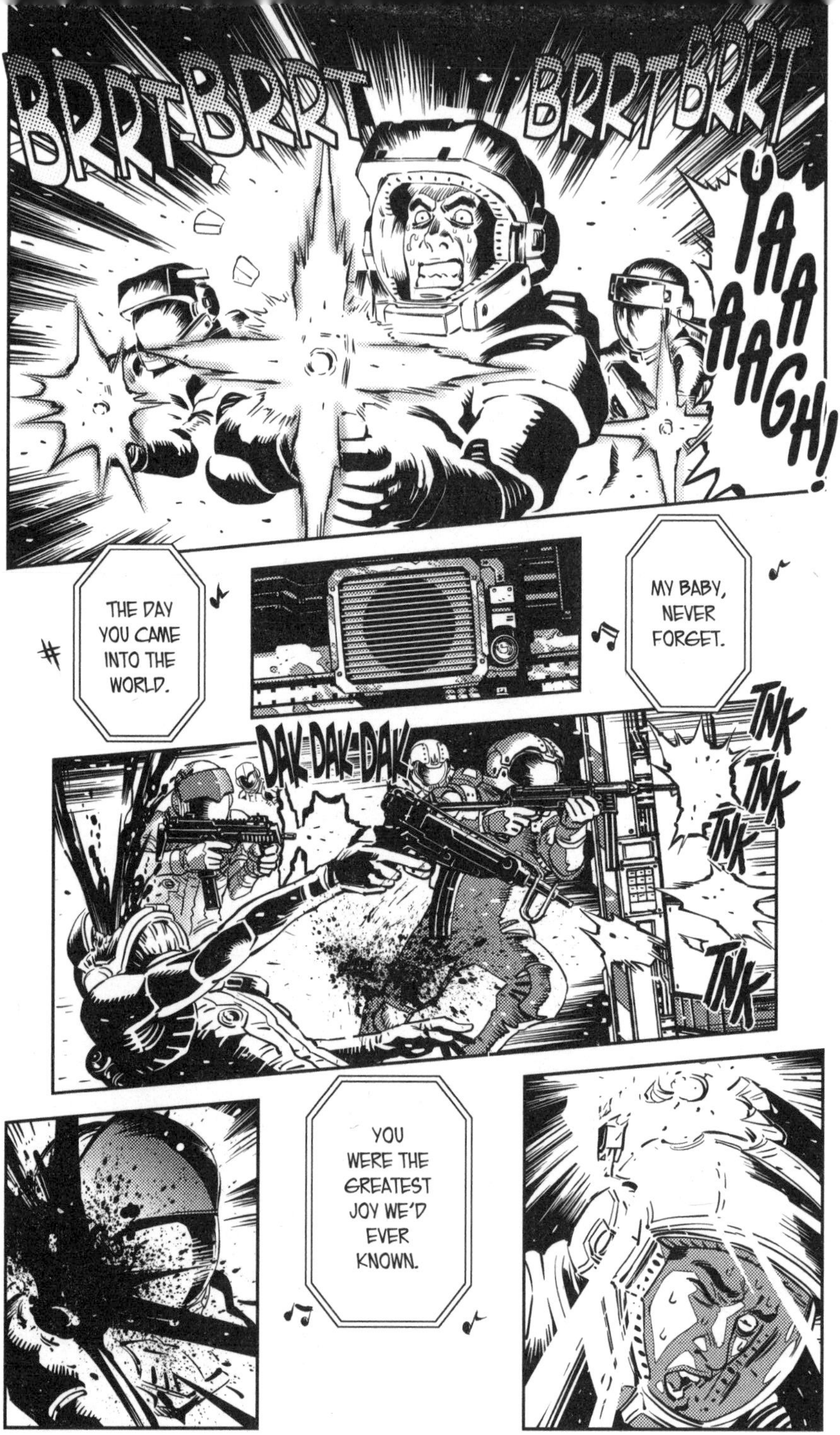
BRRT BRRT
YAAAAGH!
BRRT-BRRT
MY BABY, NEVER FORGET.
THE DAY YOU CAME INTO THE WORLD.
TNK TNK TNK
TNK
DAK DAK DAK
YOU WERE THE GREATEST JOY WE'D EVER KNOWN.

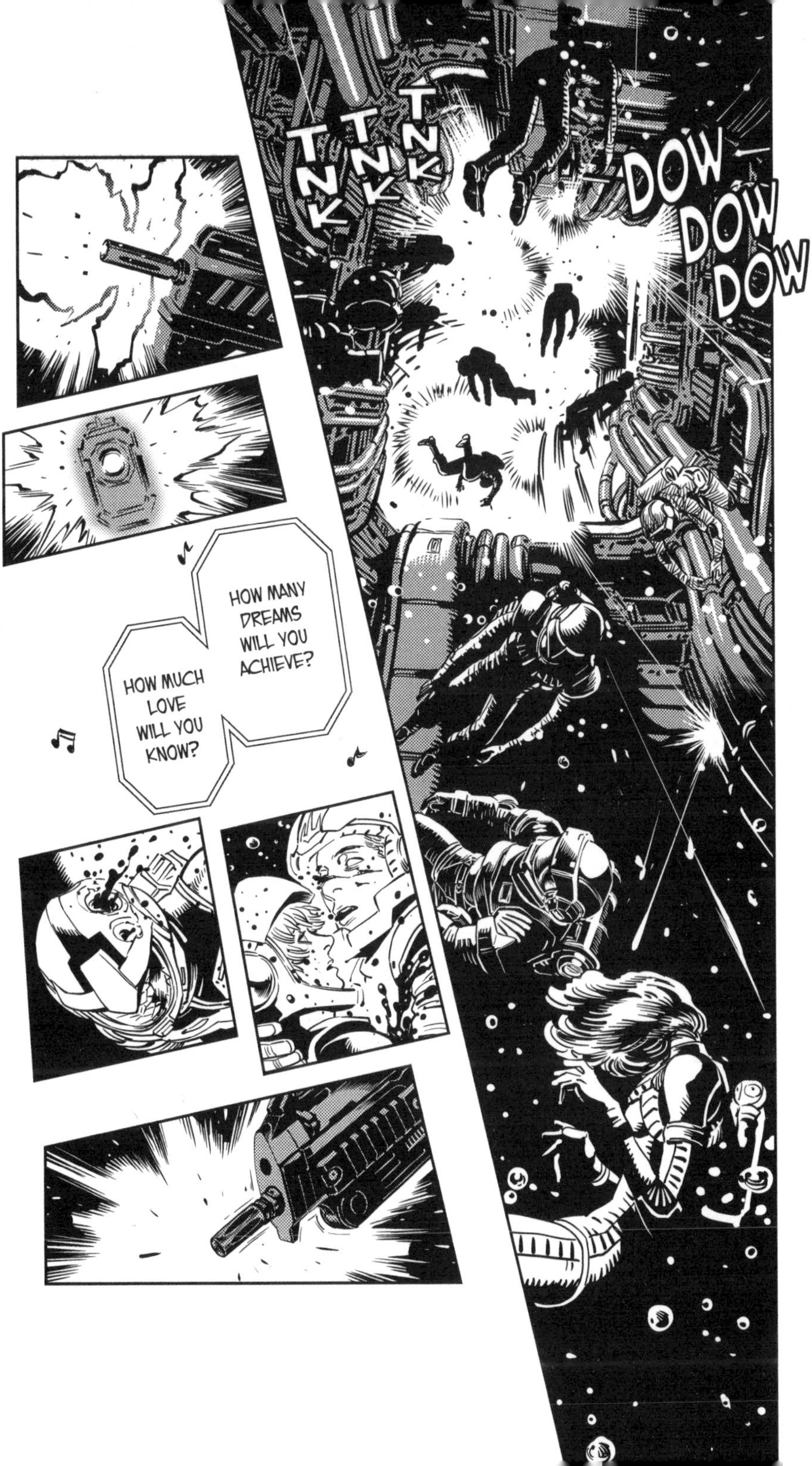
TNK
TNK
TNK
DOW
DOW
DOW
HOW MANY DREAMS WILL YOU ACHIEVE?
HOW MUCH LOVE WILL YOU KNOW?

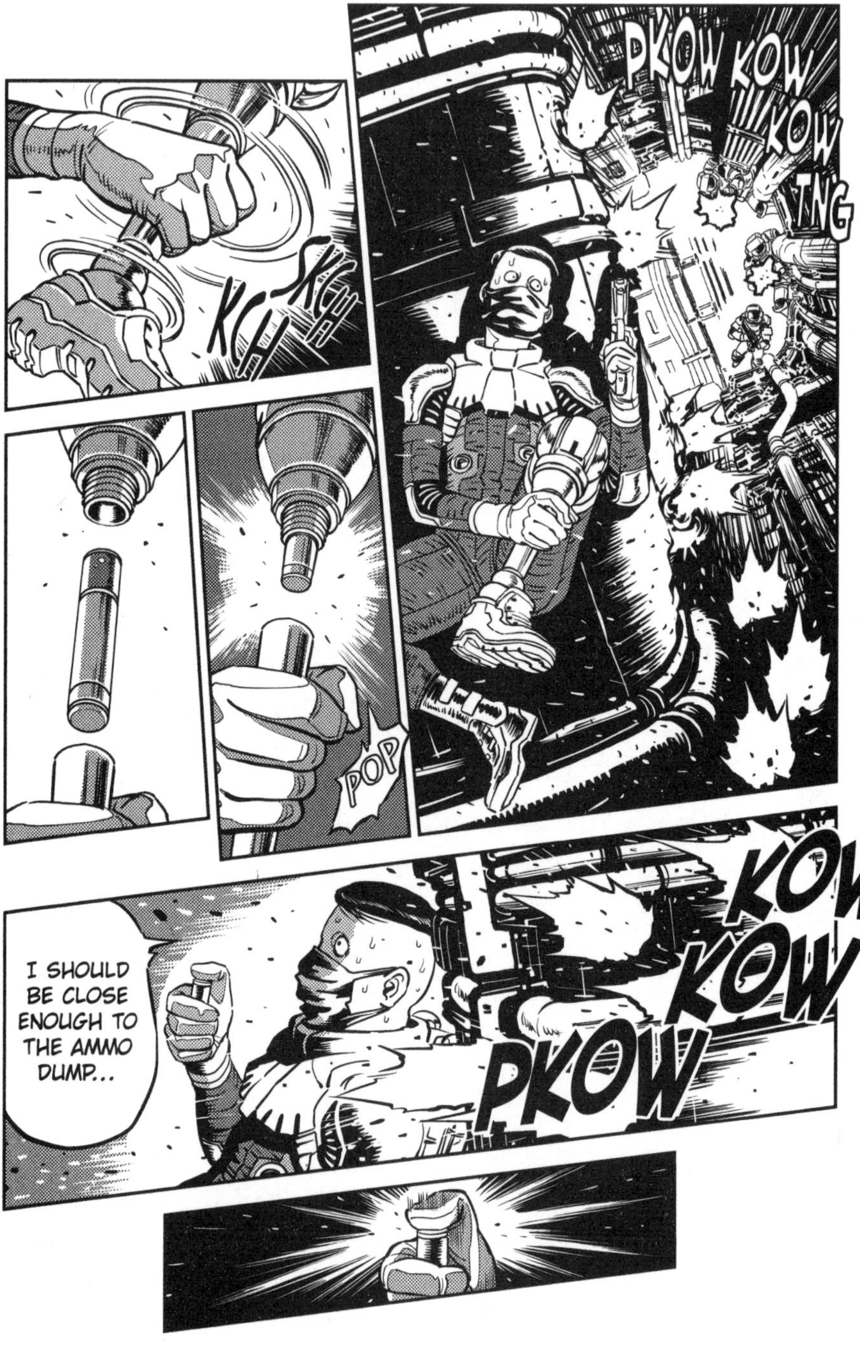
PKOW KOW KOW
TNG
KCH KCH
POP
KOW KOW PKOW
I SHOULD BE CLOSE ENOUGH TO THE AMMO DUMP...

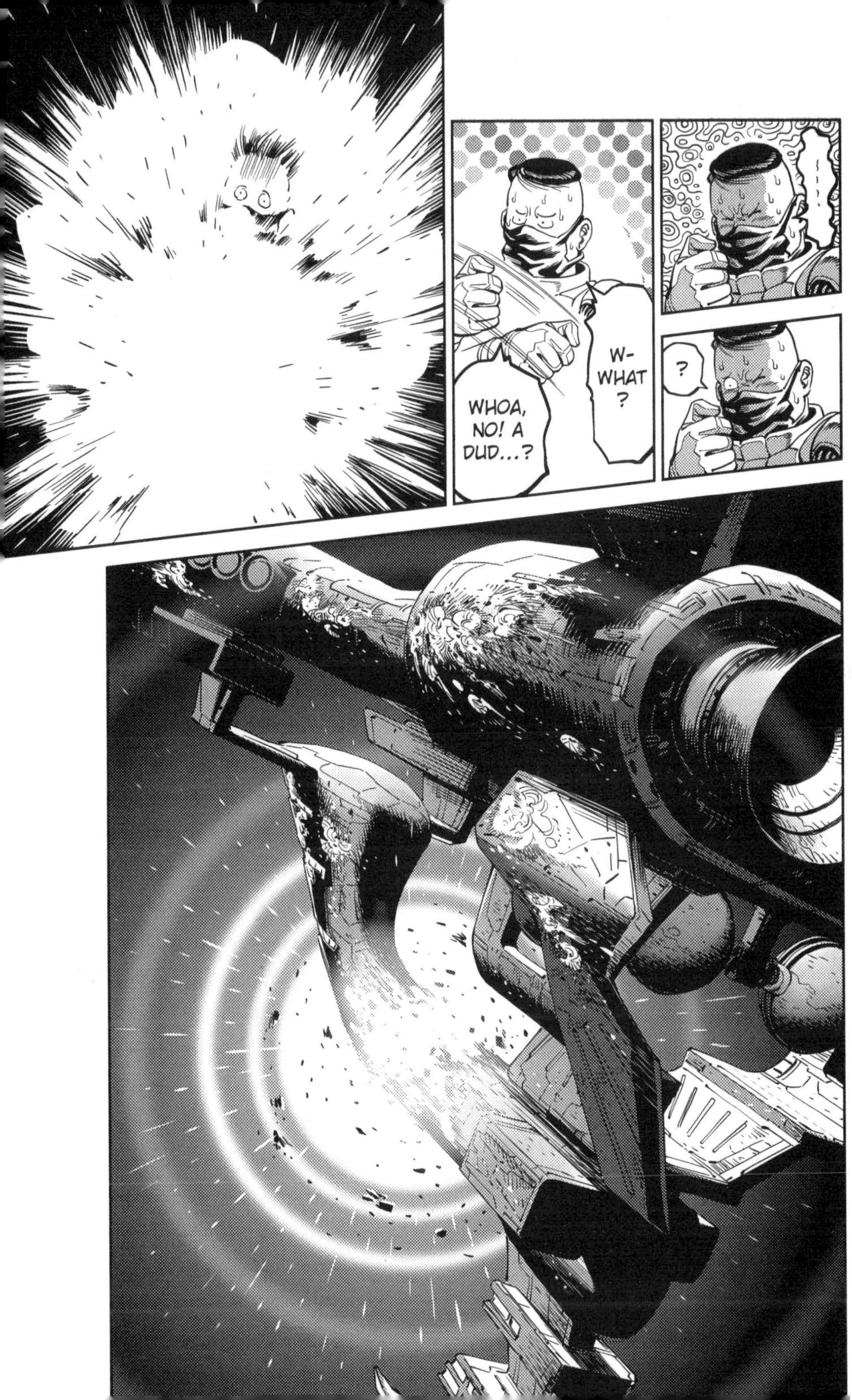
?
W-
WHAT
?
WHOA,
NO! A
DUD...?

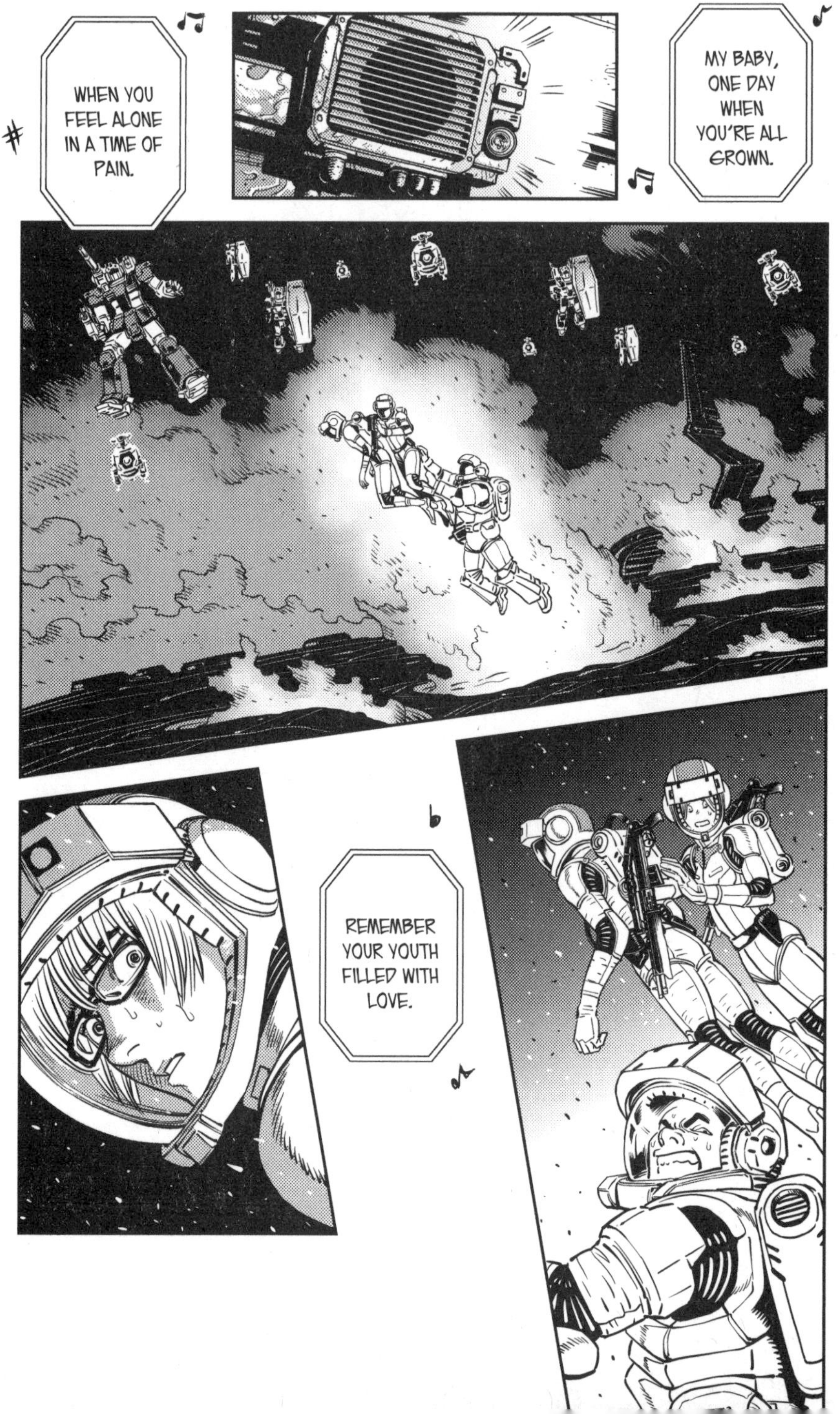
MY BABY, ONE DAY WHEN YOU'RE ALL GROWN.
WHEN YOU FEEL ALONE IN A TIME OF PAIN.
REMEMBER YOUR YOUTH FILLED WITH LOVE.

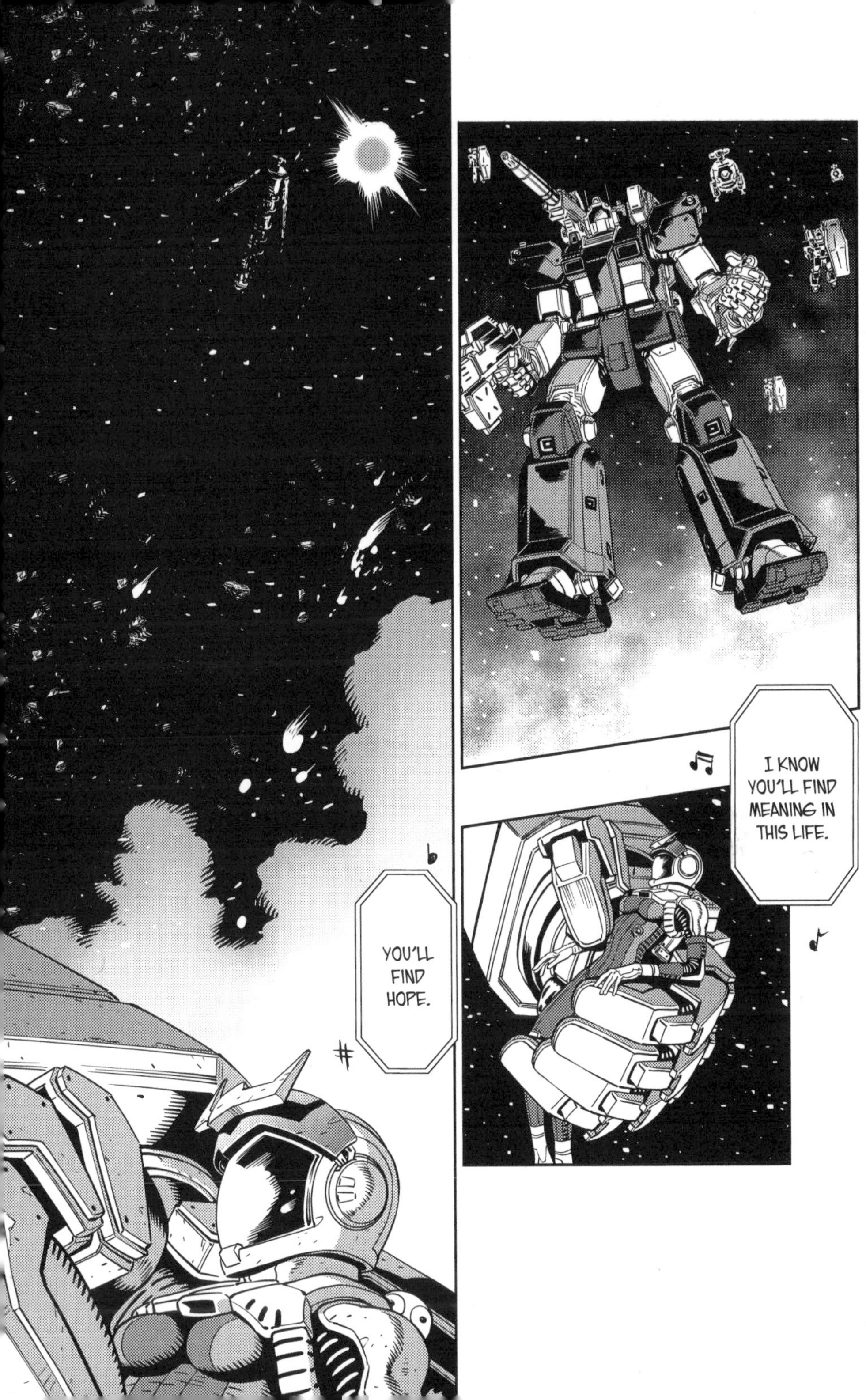
I KNOW YOU'LL FIND MEANING IN THIS LIFE.
YOU'LL FIND HOPE.

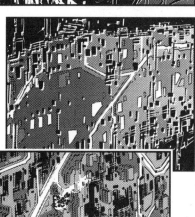

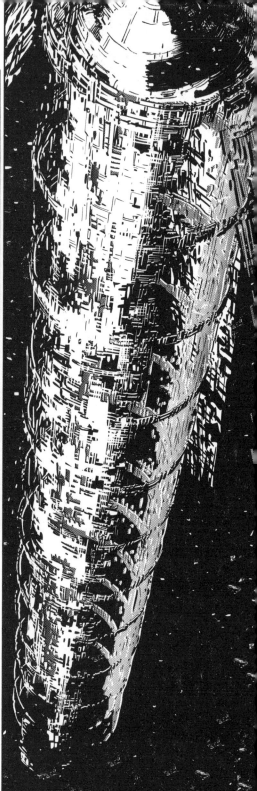

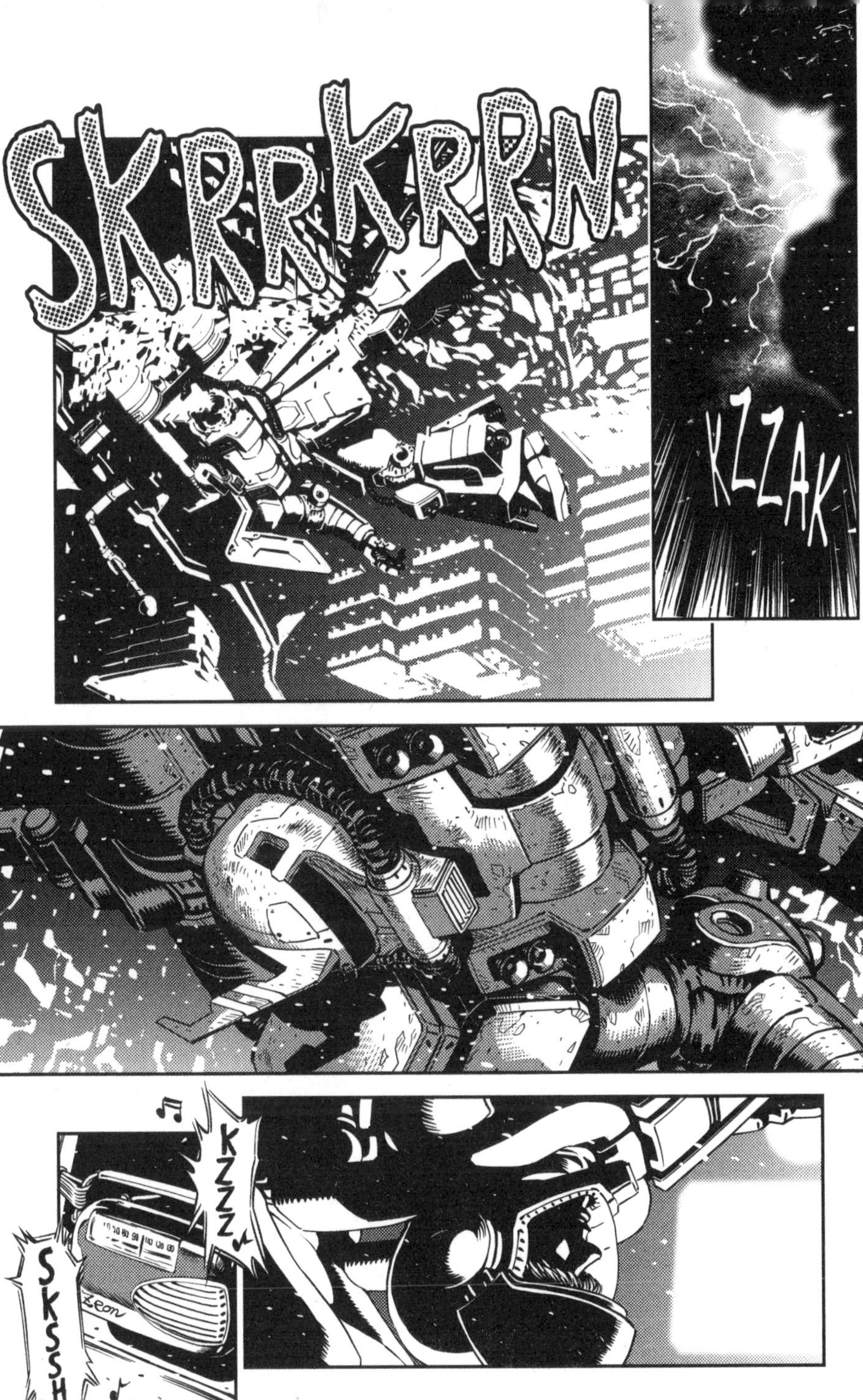
KZZAK
SKRRKRRRN
KZZZ
SKSSH
Zeon

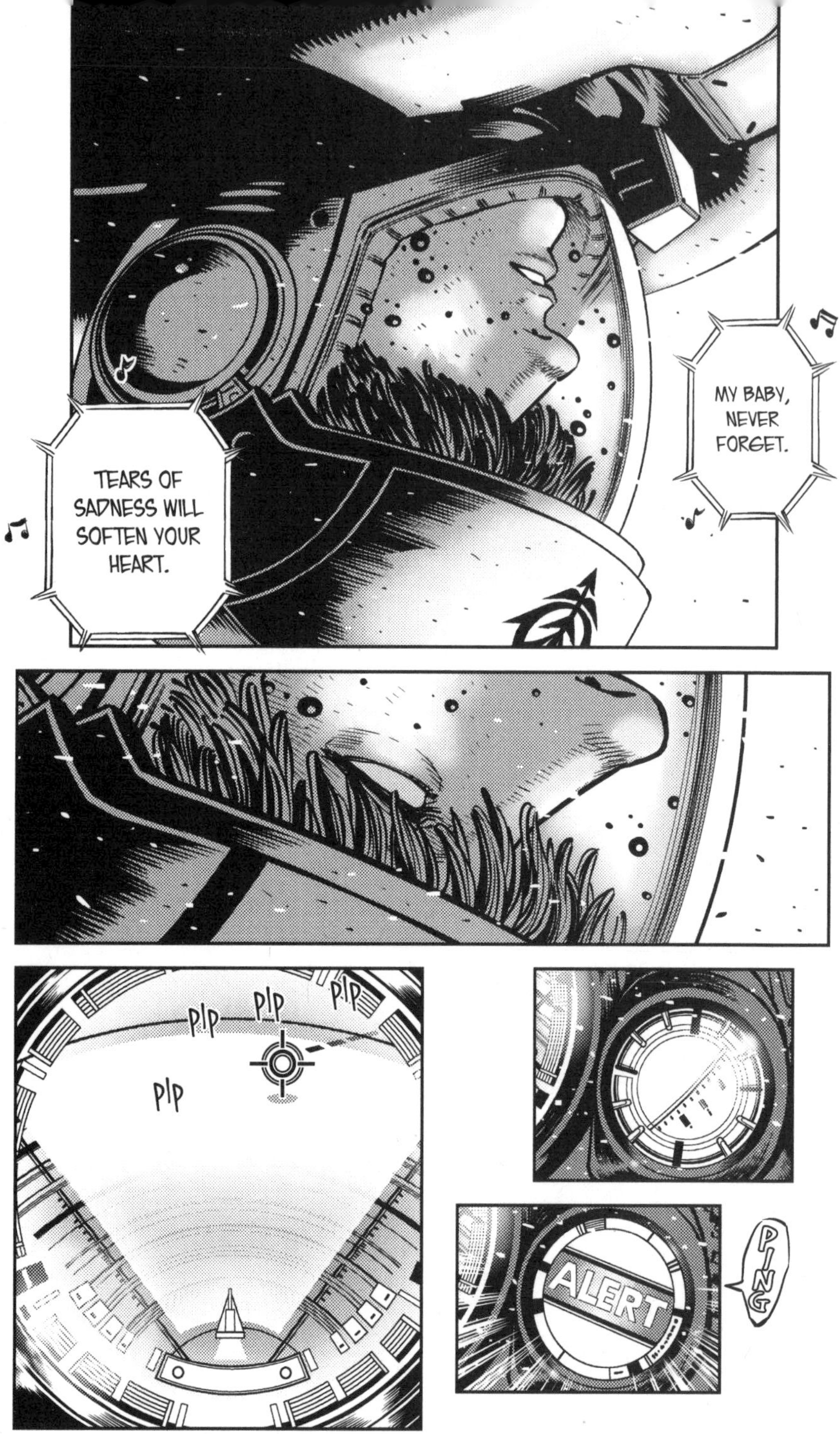
MY BABY, NEVER FORGET.
TEARS OF SADNESS WILL SOFTEN YOUR HEART.
ALERT
PING
PIP
PIP
PIP
PIP

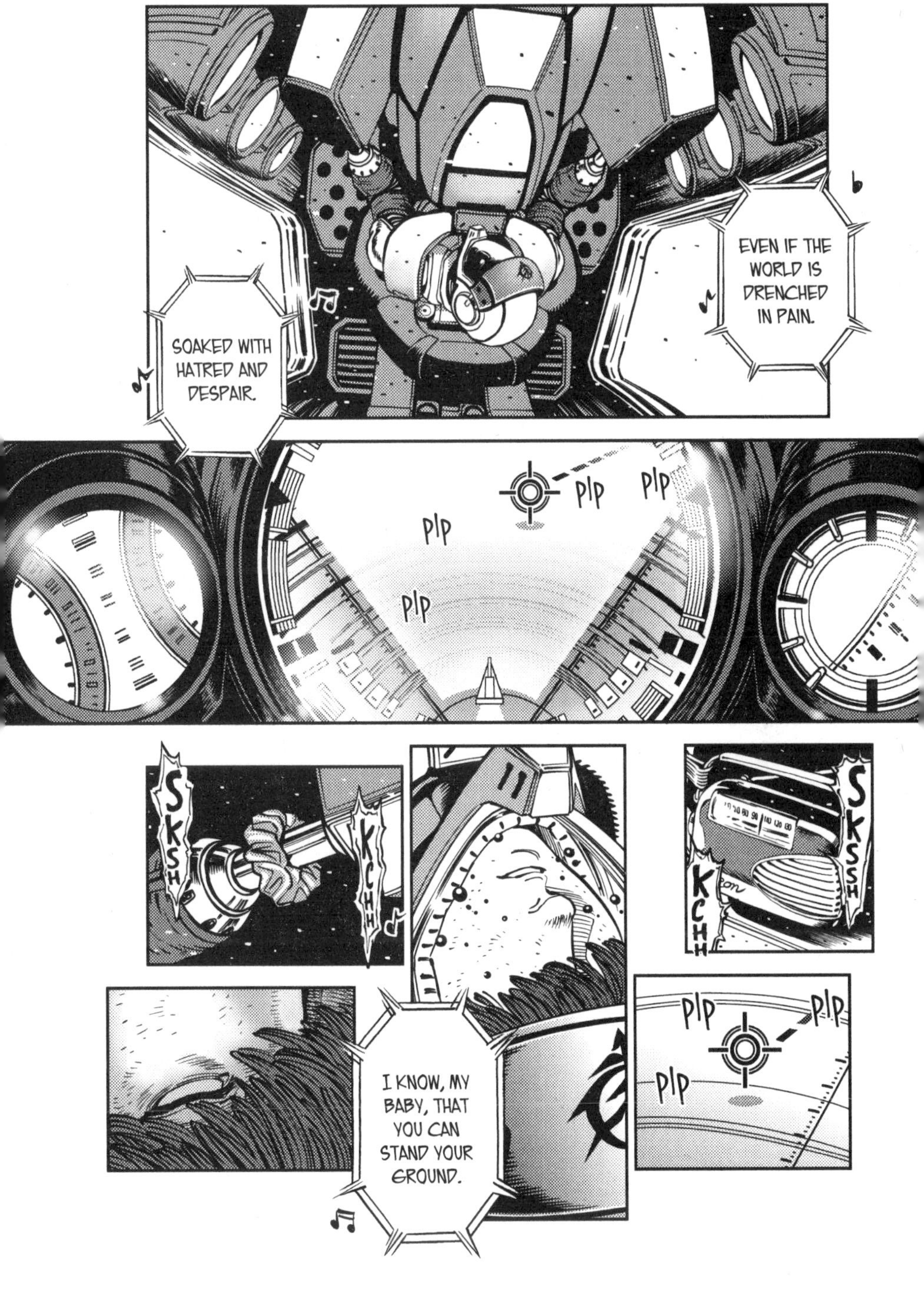
EVEN IF THE WORLD IS DRENCHED IN PAIN.
SOAKED WITH HATRED AND DESPAIR.
PIP
PIP
PIP
PIP
SKSSH
KCHH
SKSH
KCHH
PIP
PIP
PIP
I KNOW, MY BABY, THAT YOU CAN STAND YOUR GROUND.

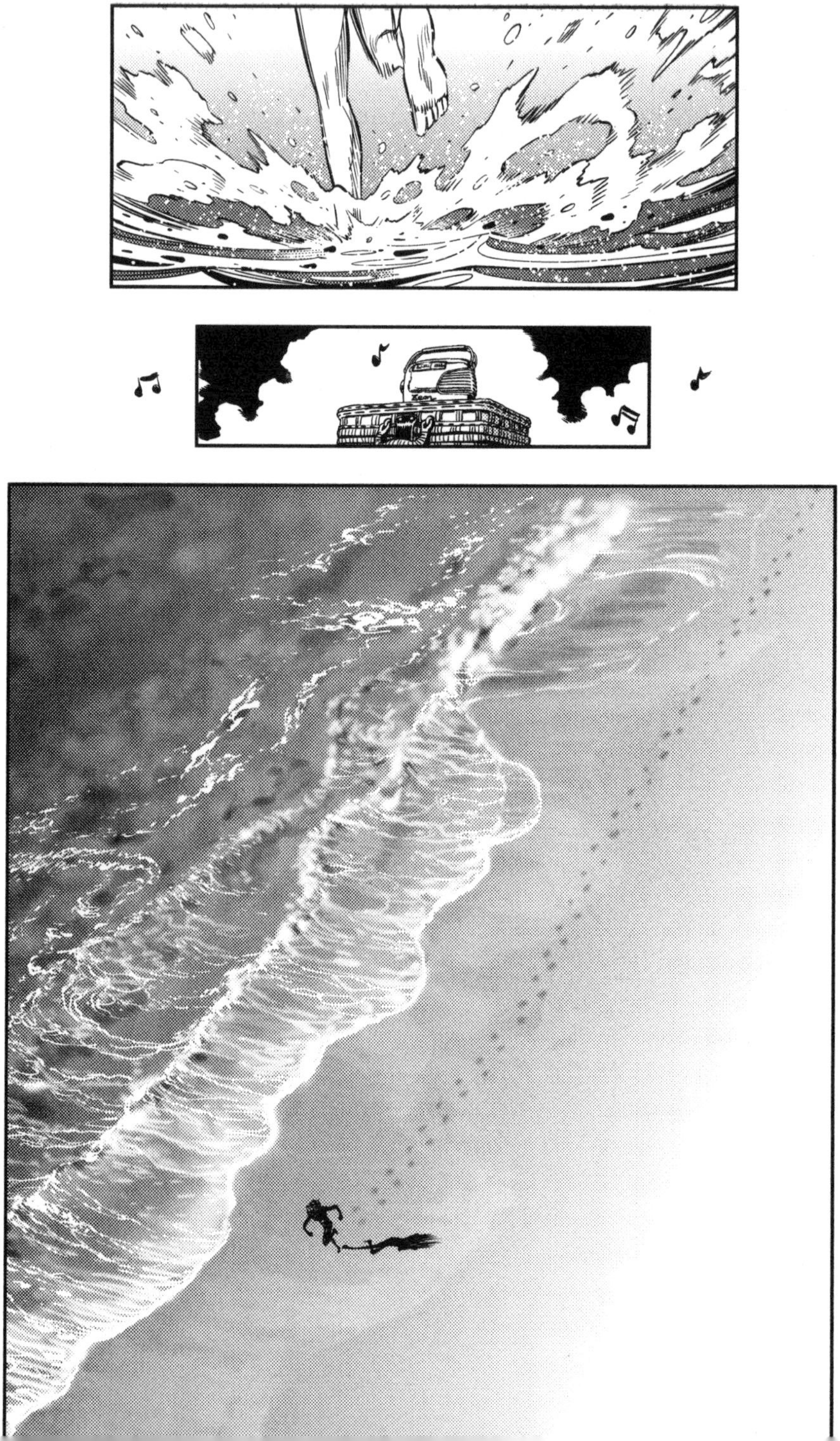

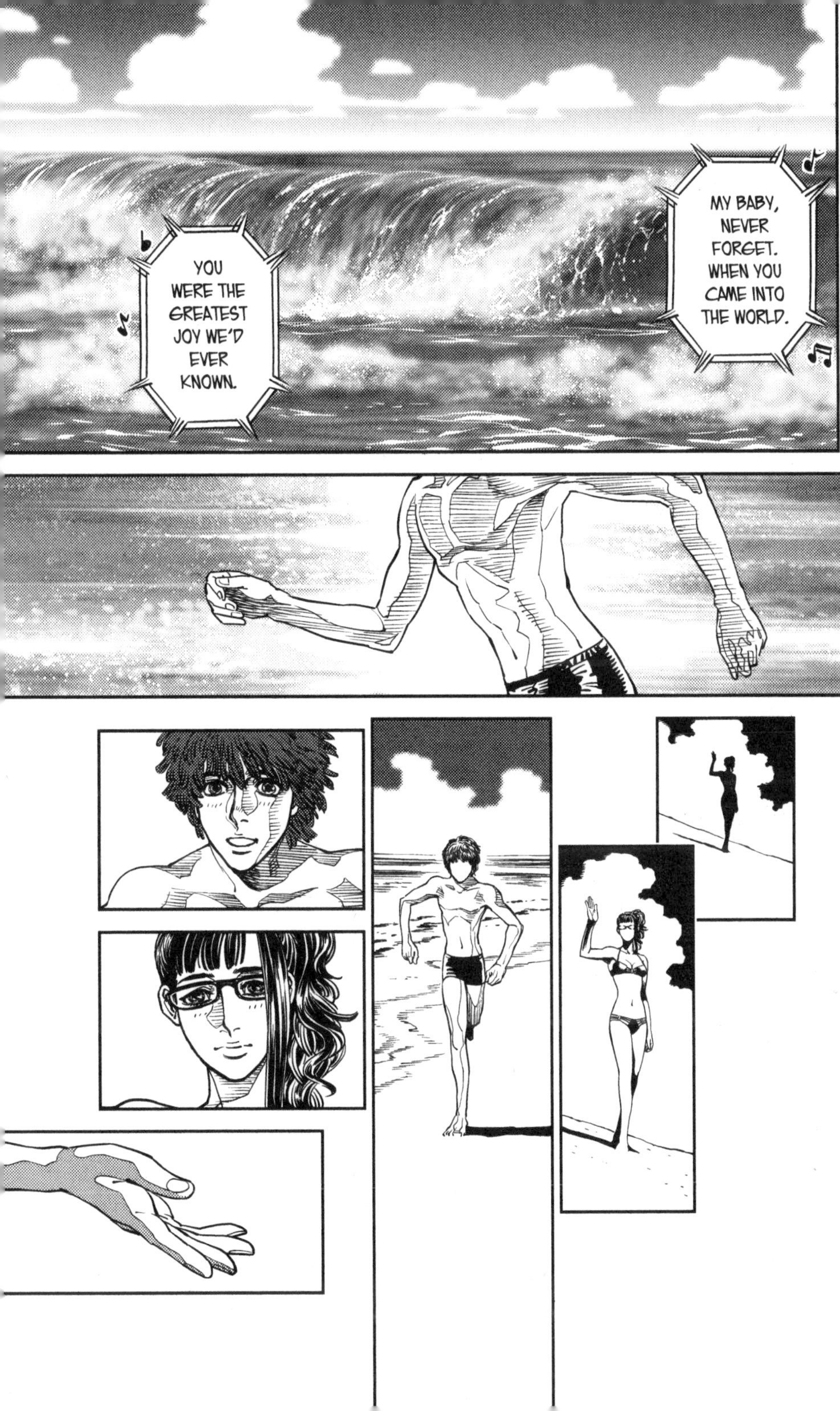
MY BABY, NEVER FORGET. WHEN YOU CAME INTO THE WORLD.
YOU WERE THE GREATEST JOY WE'D EVER KNOWN.

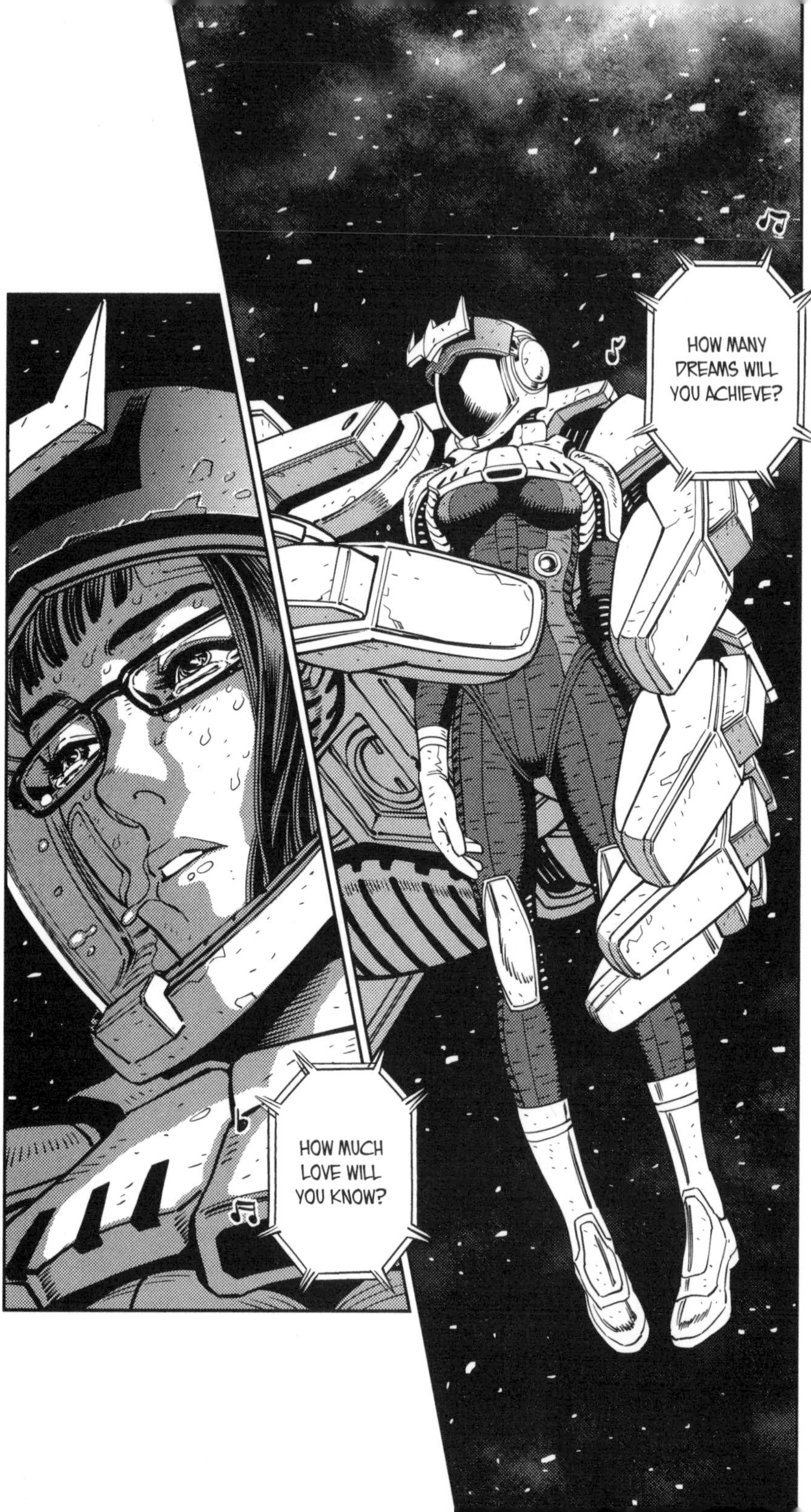
HOW MANY DREAMS WILL YOU ACHIEVE?
HOW MUCH LOVE WILL YOU KNOW?

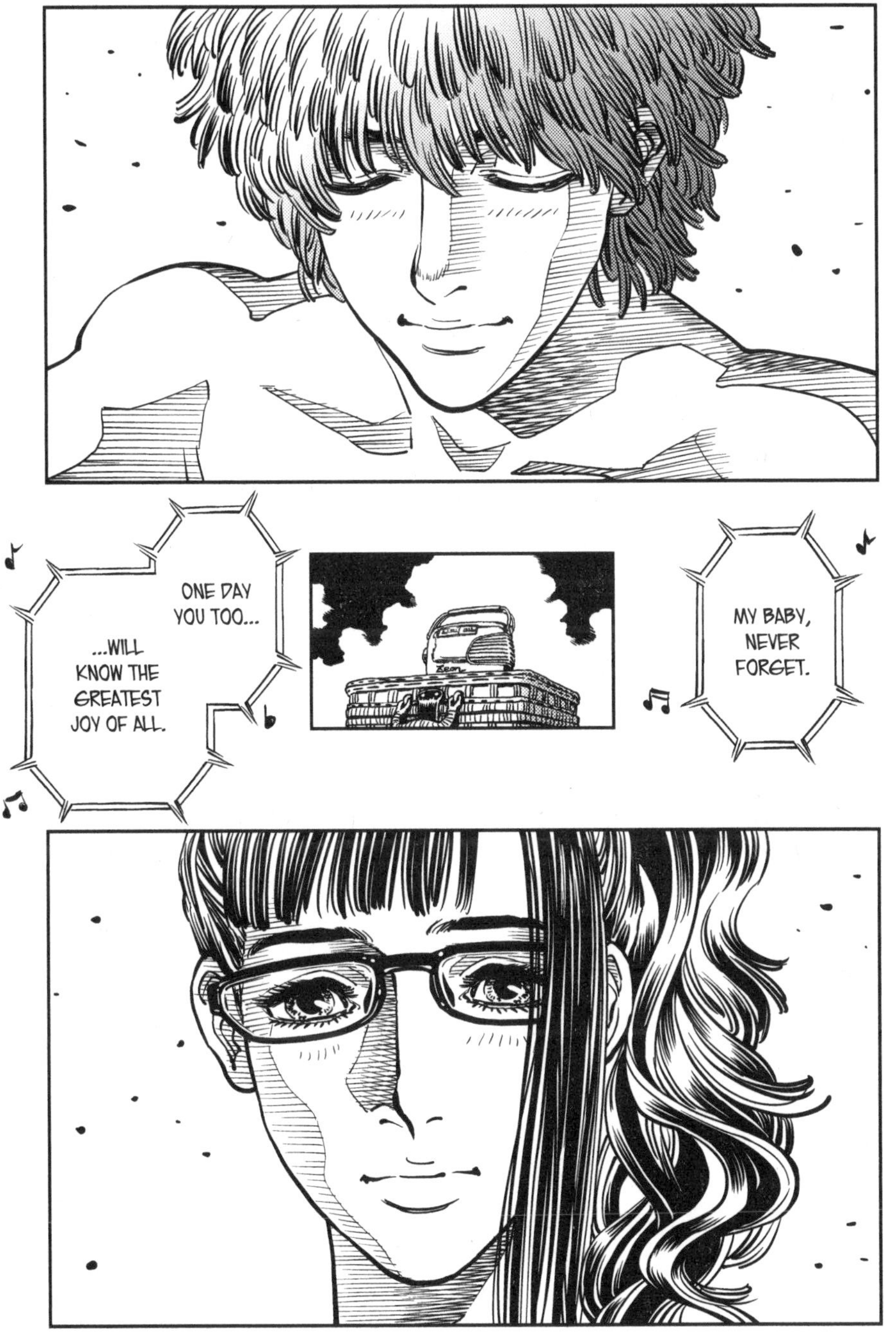
MY BABY, NEVER FORGET.
ONE DAY YOU TOO...
...WILL KNOW THE GREATEST JOY OF ALL.

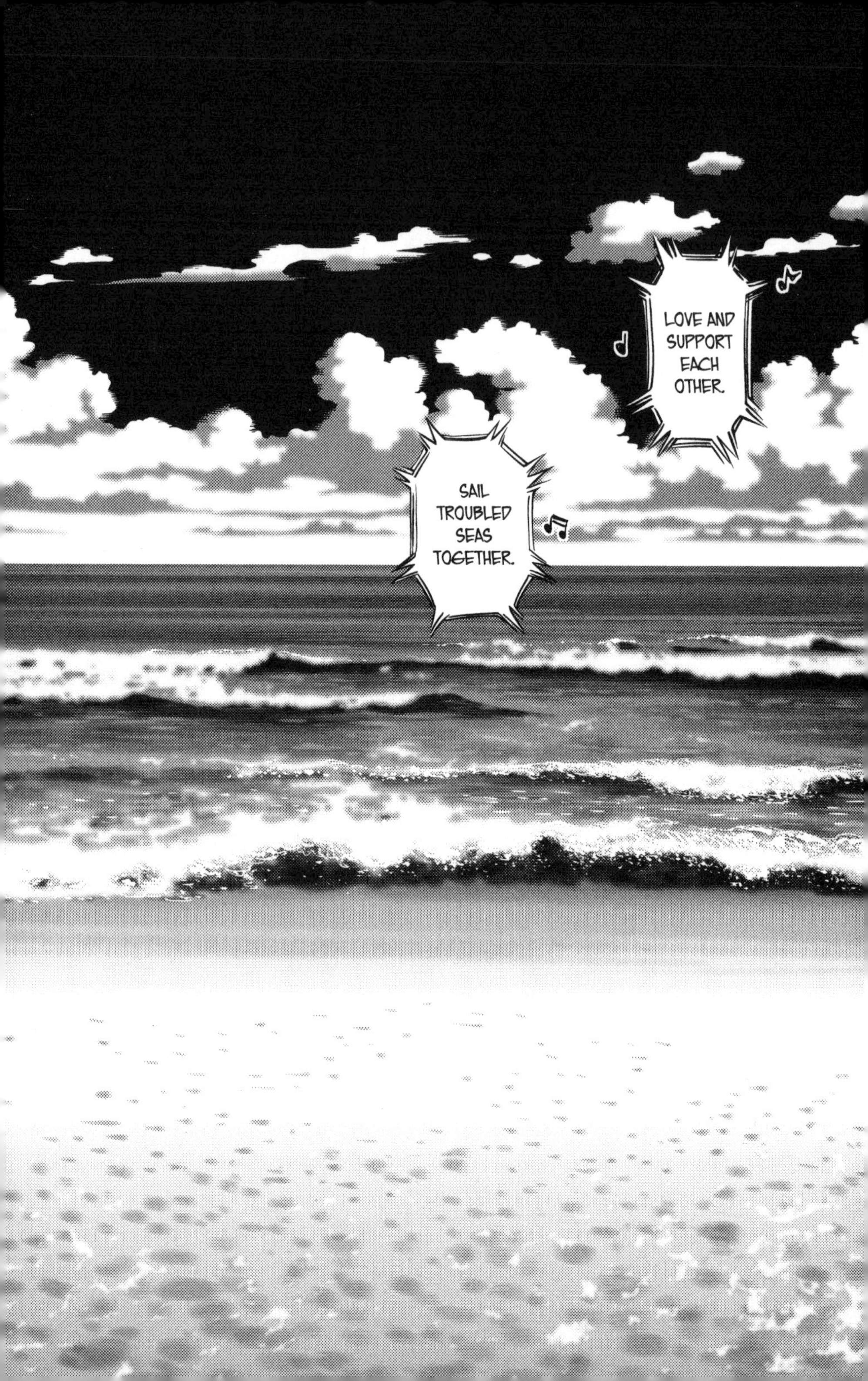
LOVE AND SUPPORT EACH OTHER.
SAIL TROUBLED SEAS TOGETHER.

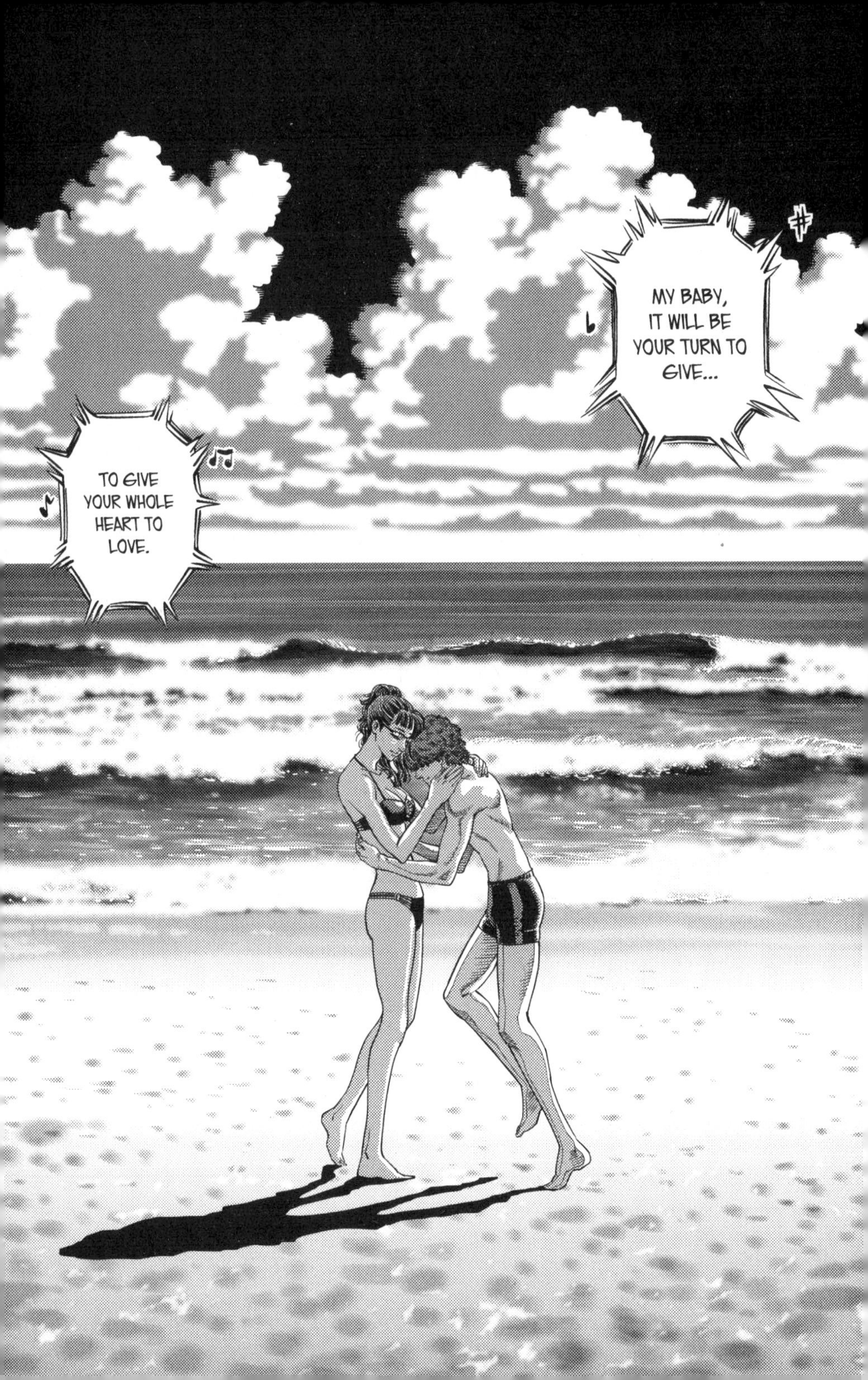
MY BABY, IT WILL BE YOUR TURN TO GIVE...
TO GIVE YOUR WHOLE HEART TO LOVE.

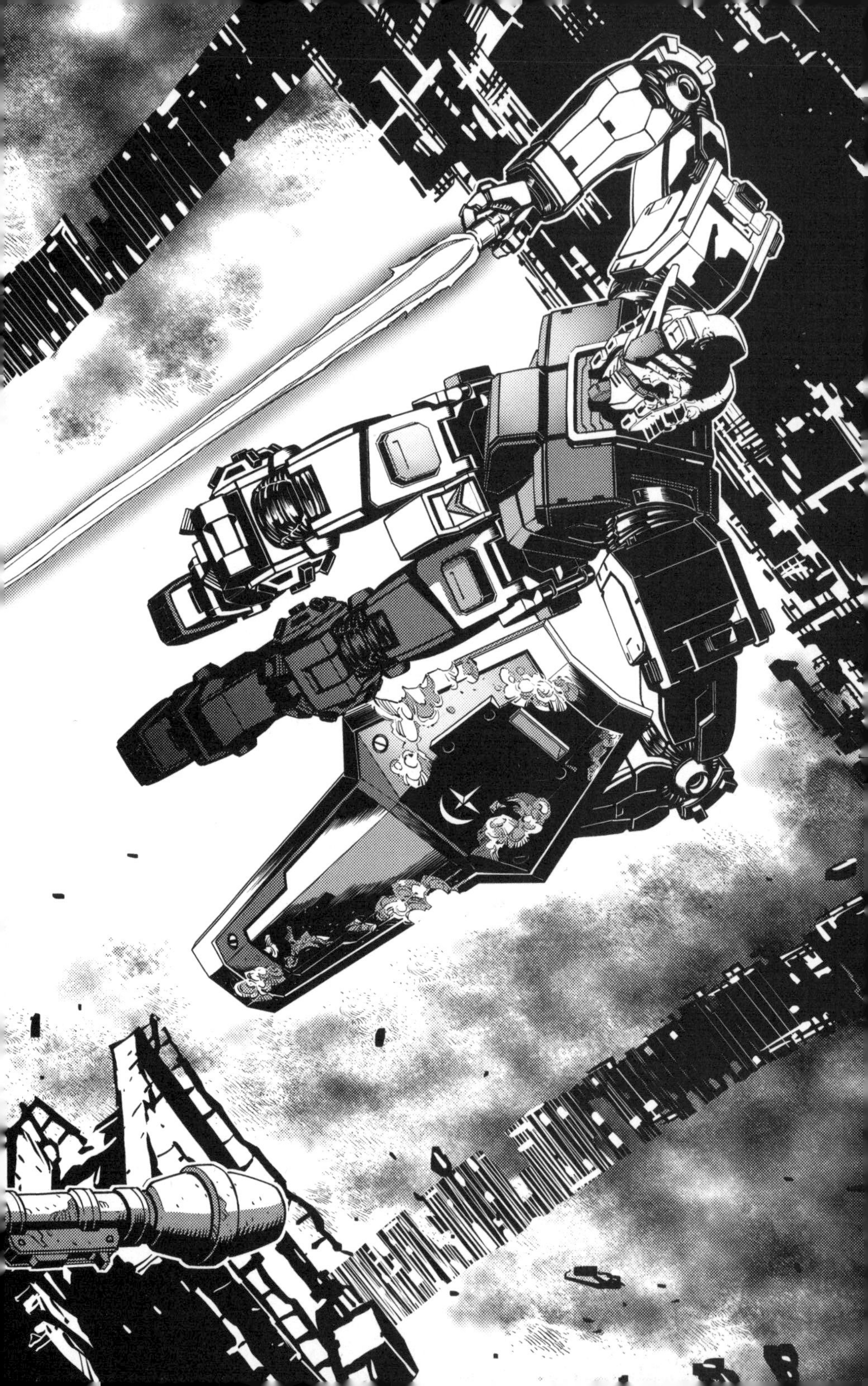

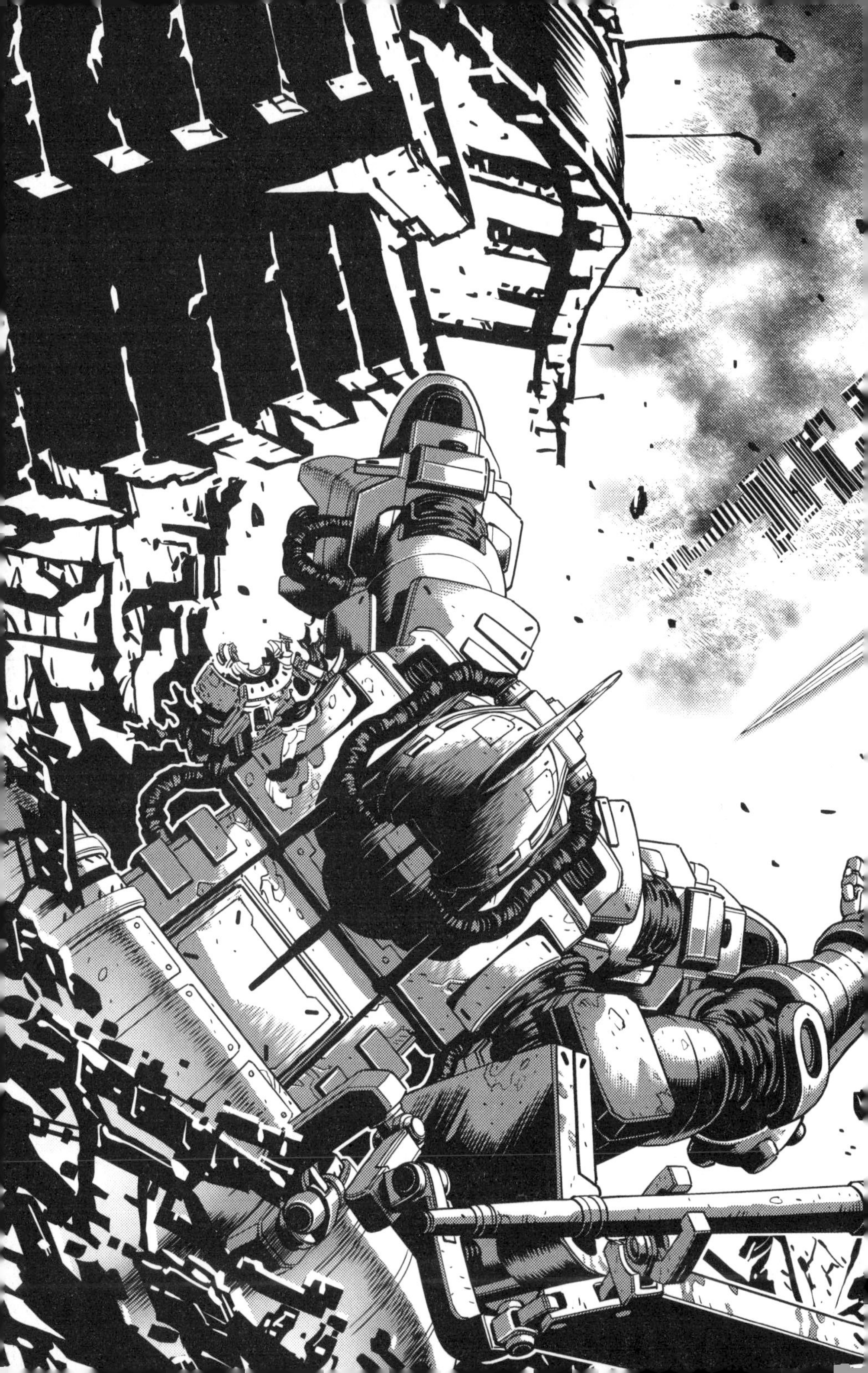

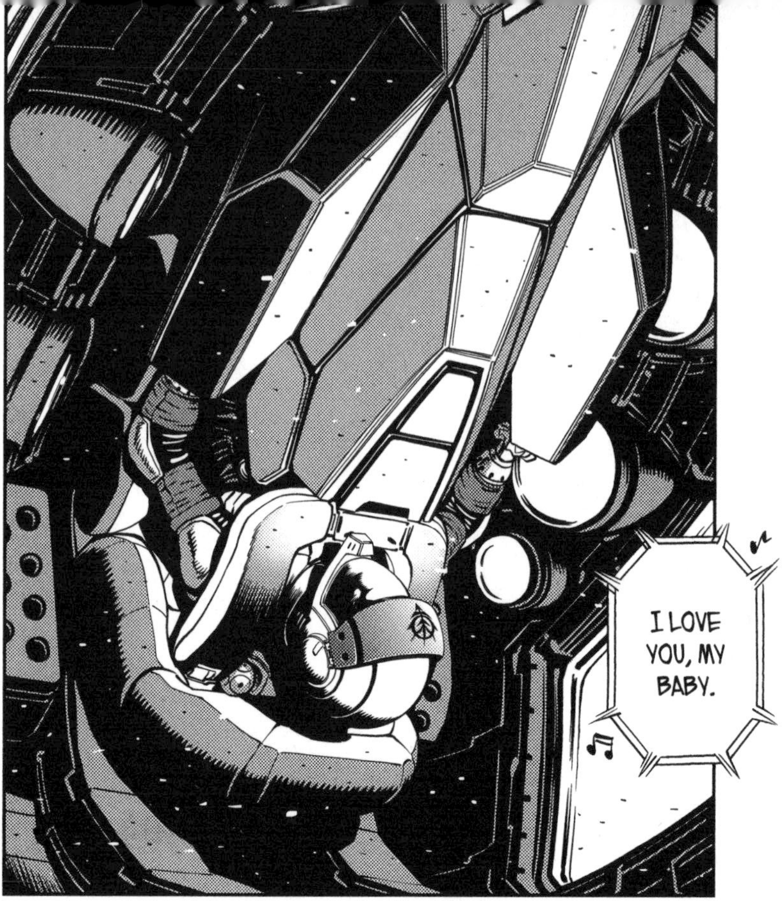
I LOVE YOU, MY BABY.
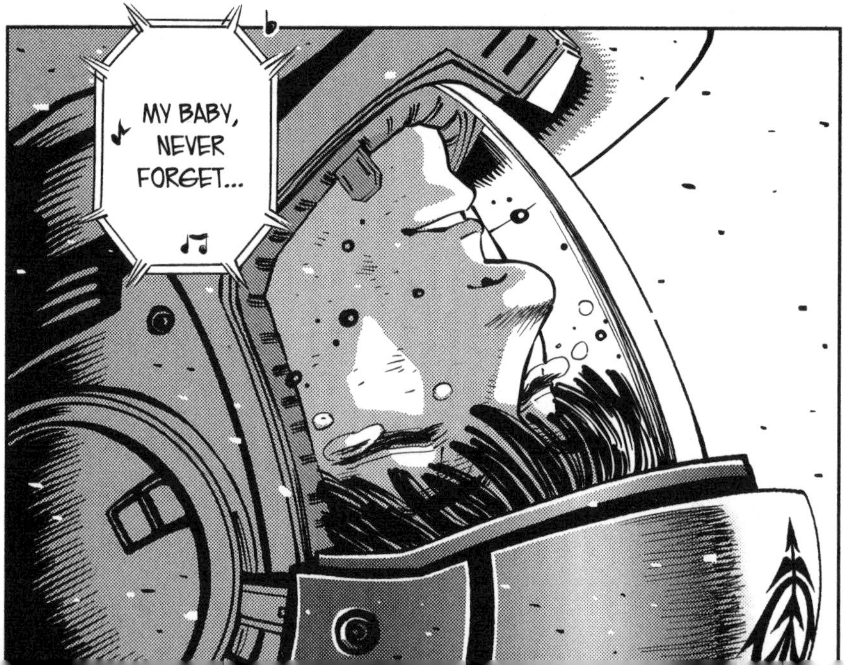
MY BABY, NEVER FORGET...

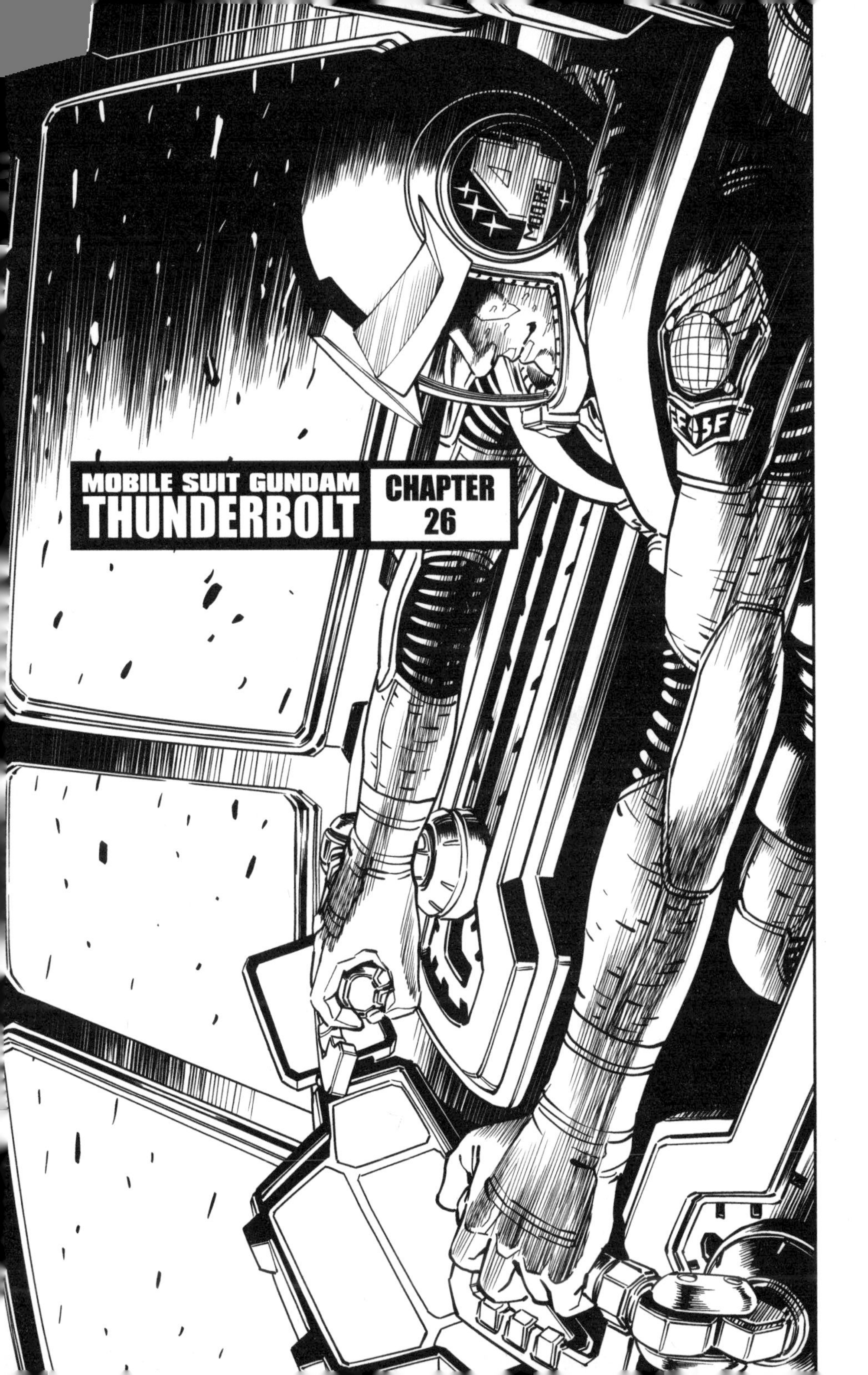
MOBILE SUIT GUNDAM
THUNDERBOLT
CHAPTER
26

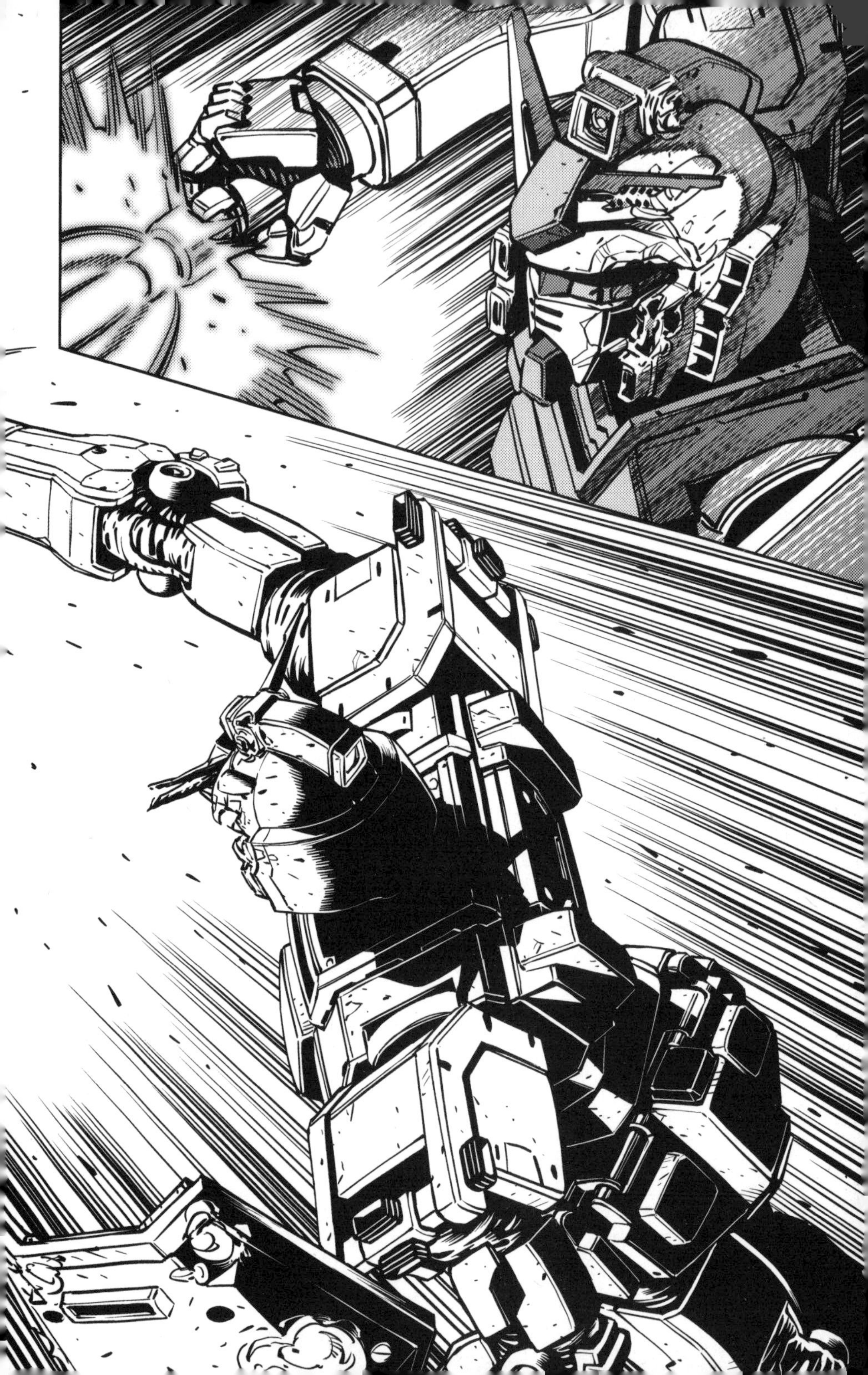

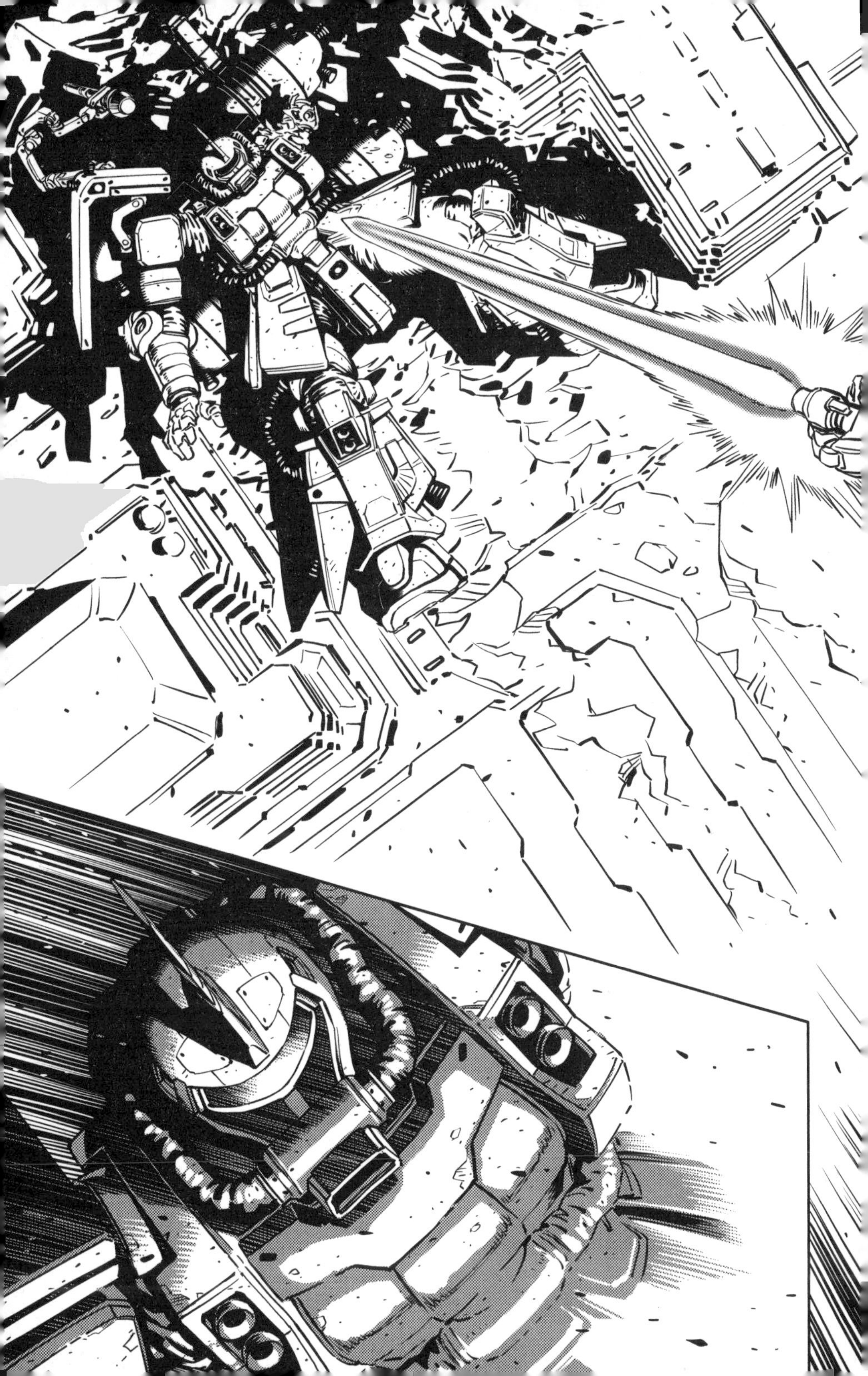

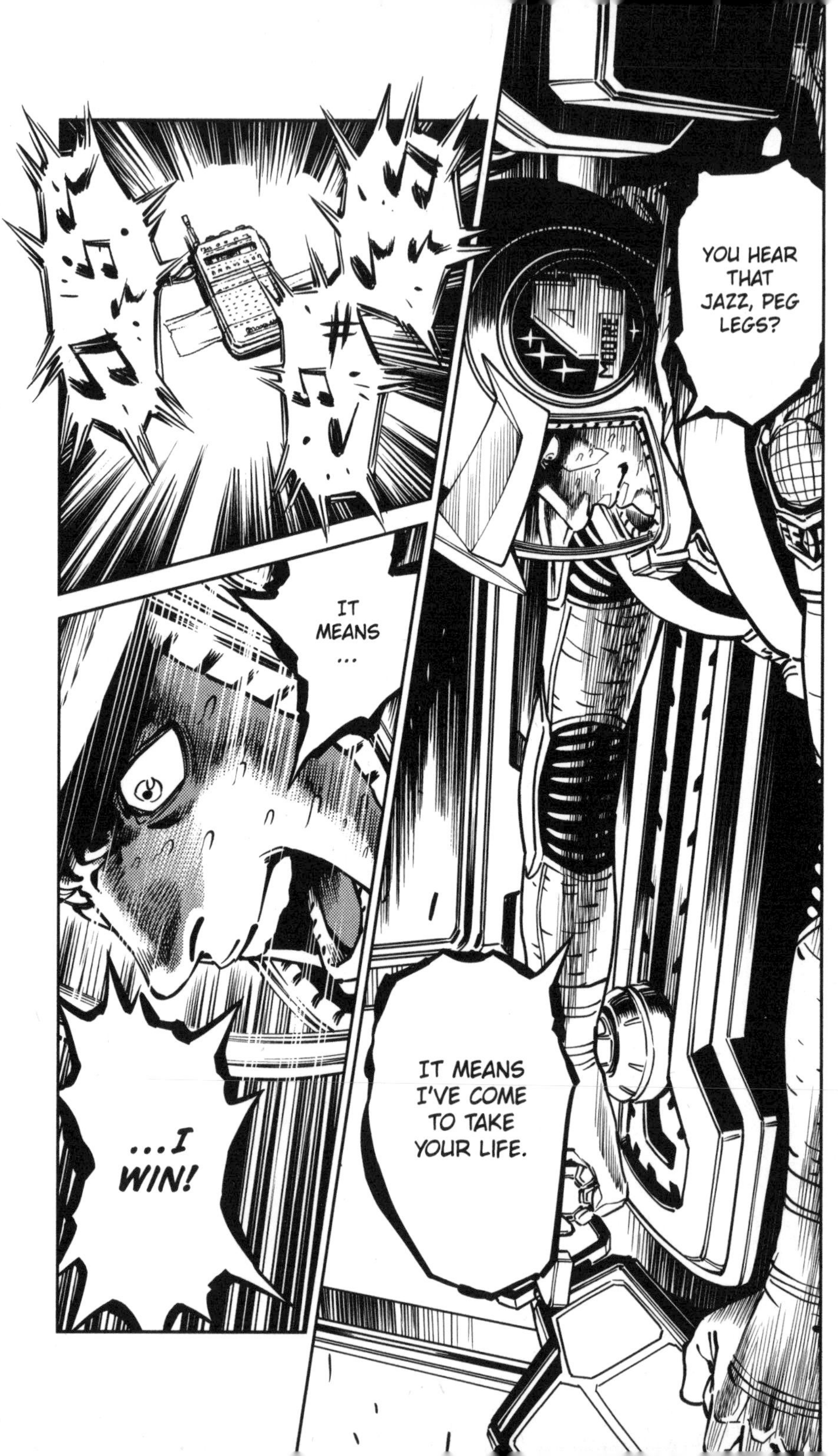
YOU HEAR THAT JAZZ, PEG LEGS?
IT MEANS ...
...I WIN!
IT MEANS I'VE COME TO TAKE YOUR LIFE.

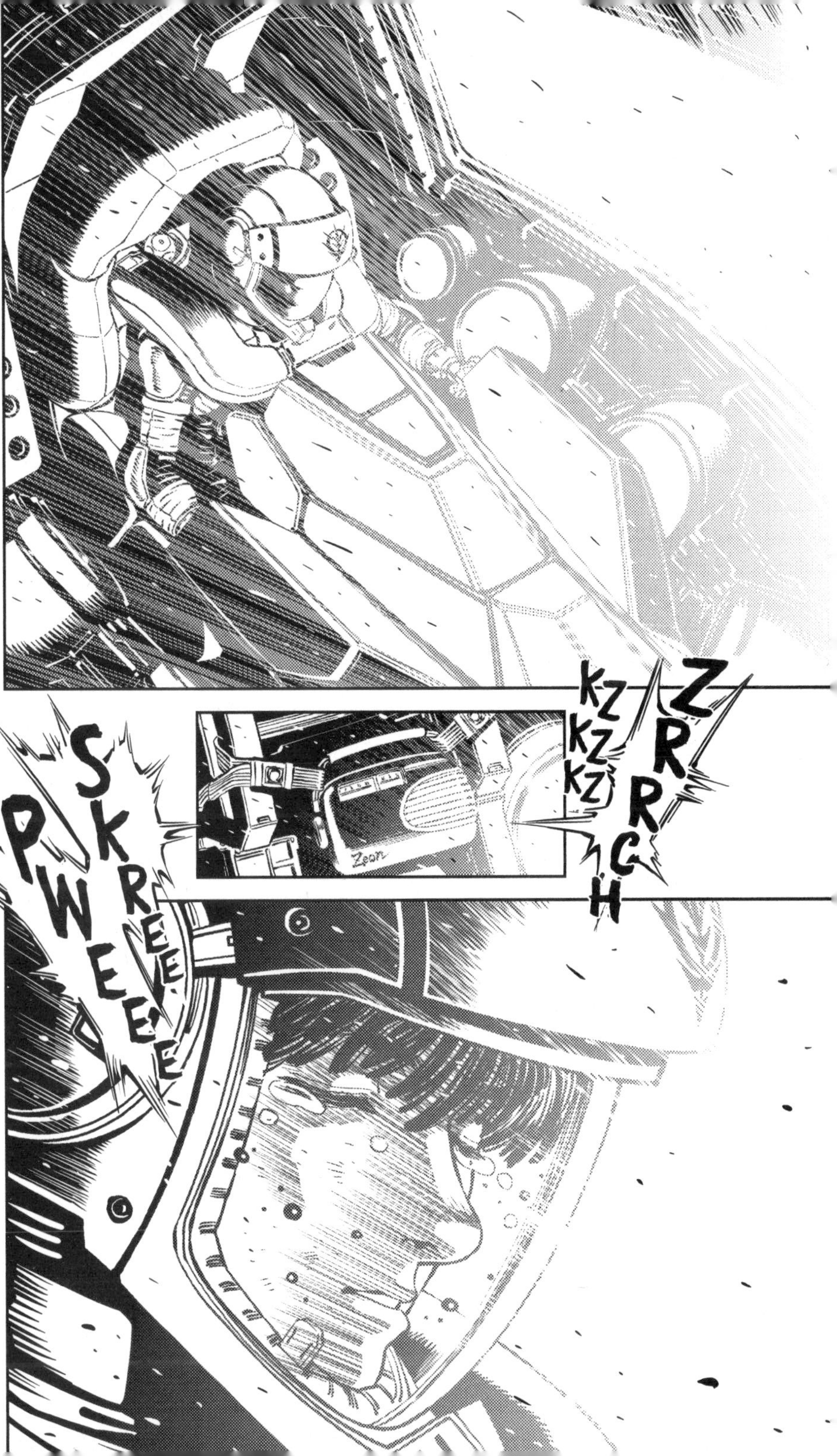
ZRRRCH
KZ KZ KZ
Zeon
SKREE
PWEEE

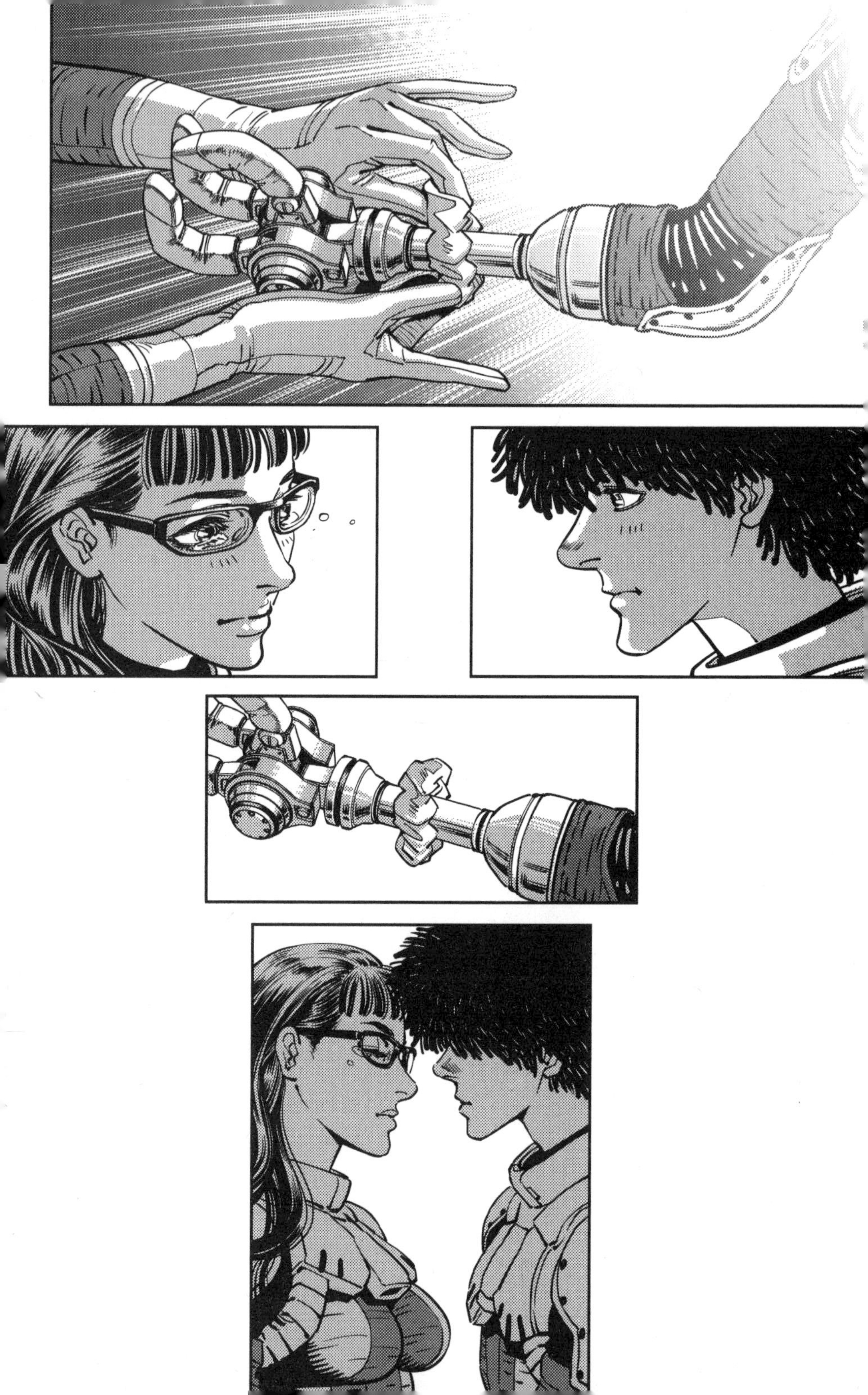

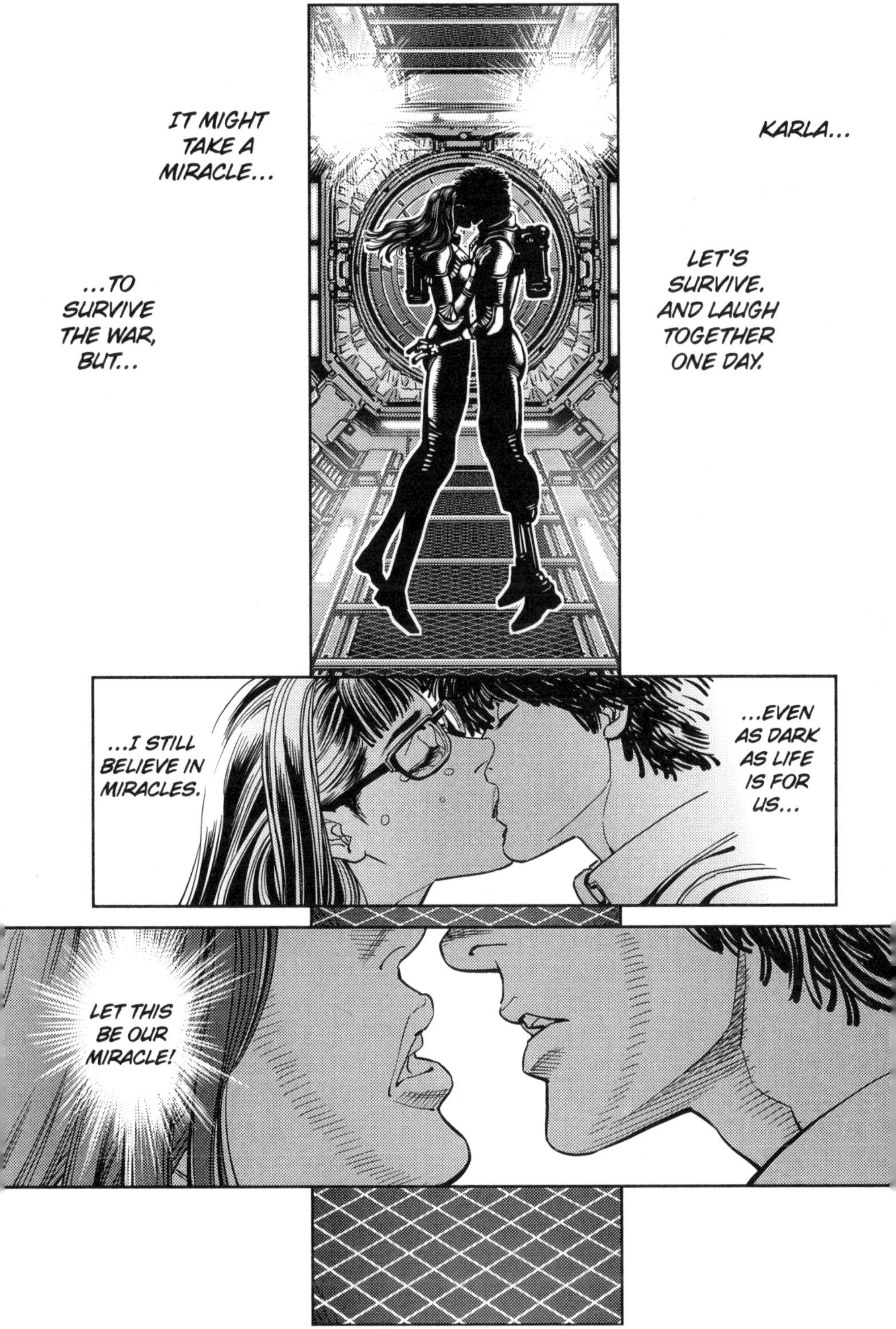
KARLA...
LET'S SURVIVE. AND LAUGH TOGETHER ONE DAY.
IT MIGHT TAKE A MIRACLE...
...TO SURVIVE THE WAR, BUT...
...EVEN AS DARK AS LIFE IS FOR US...
...I STILL BELIEVE IN MIRACLES.
LET THIS BE OUR MIRACLE!

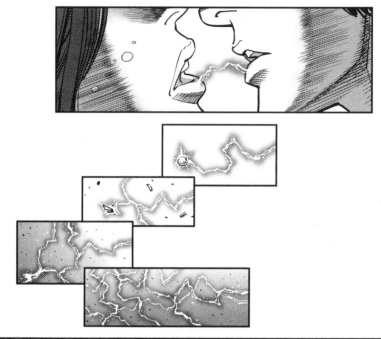

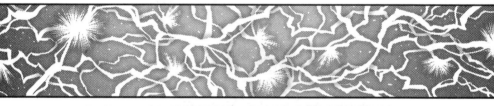

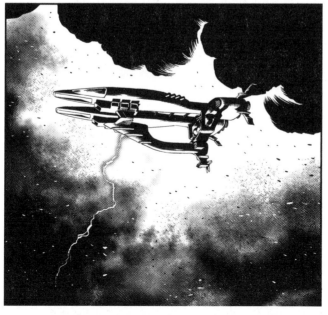

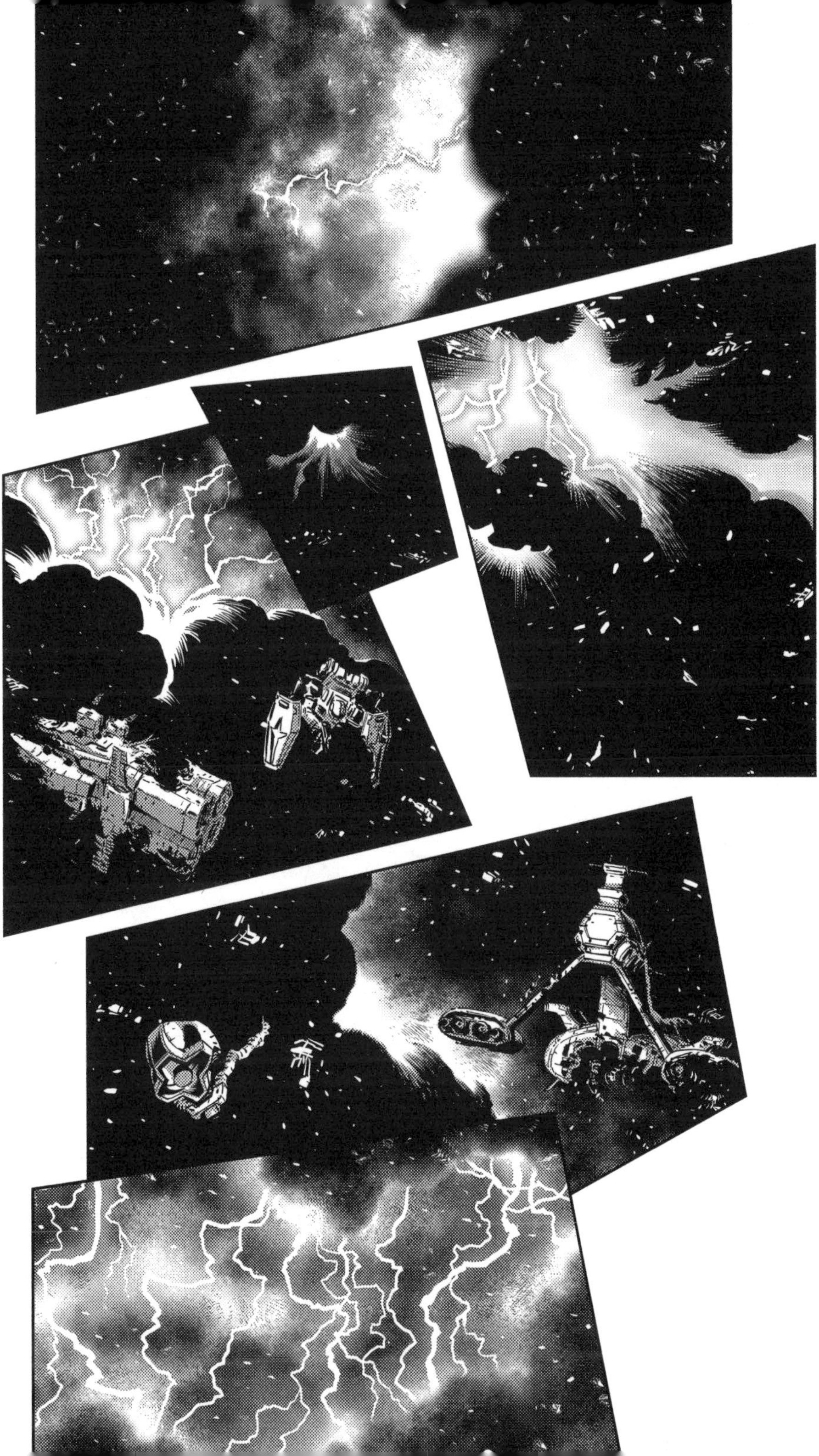

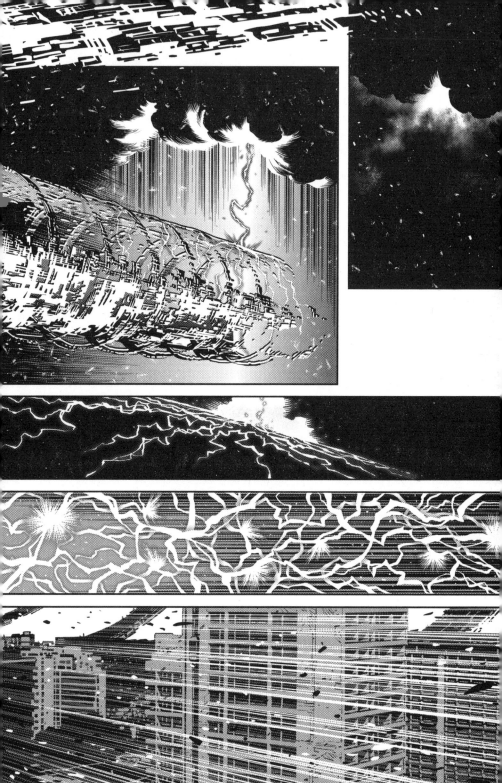

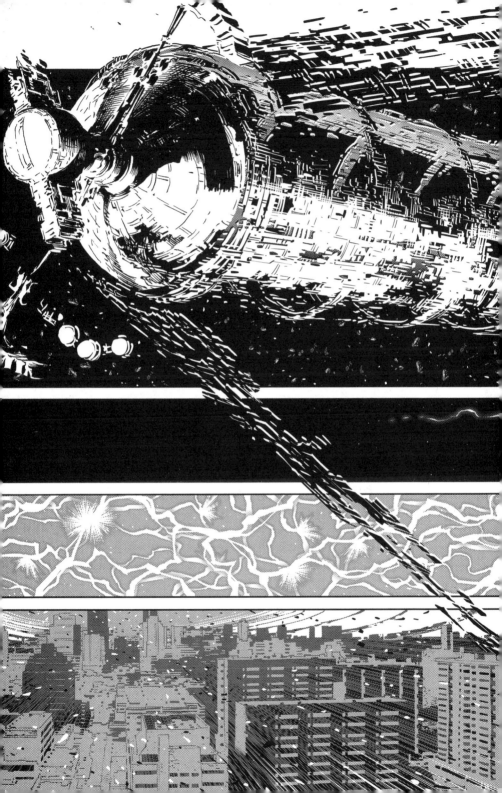

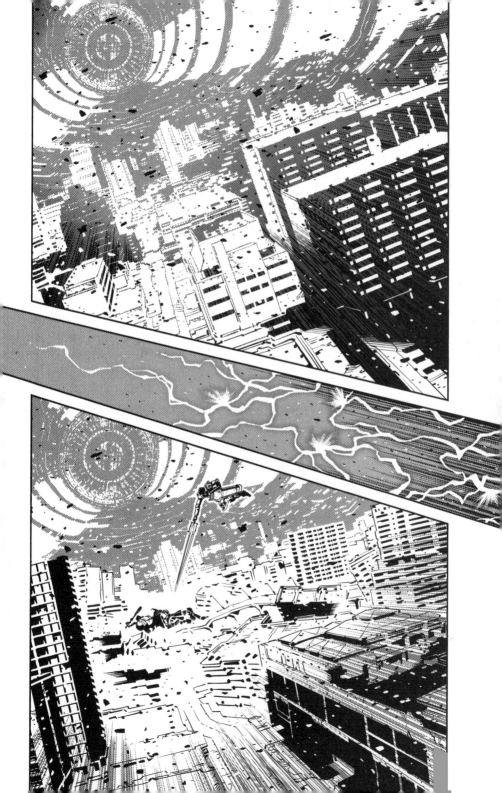

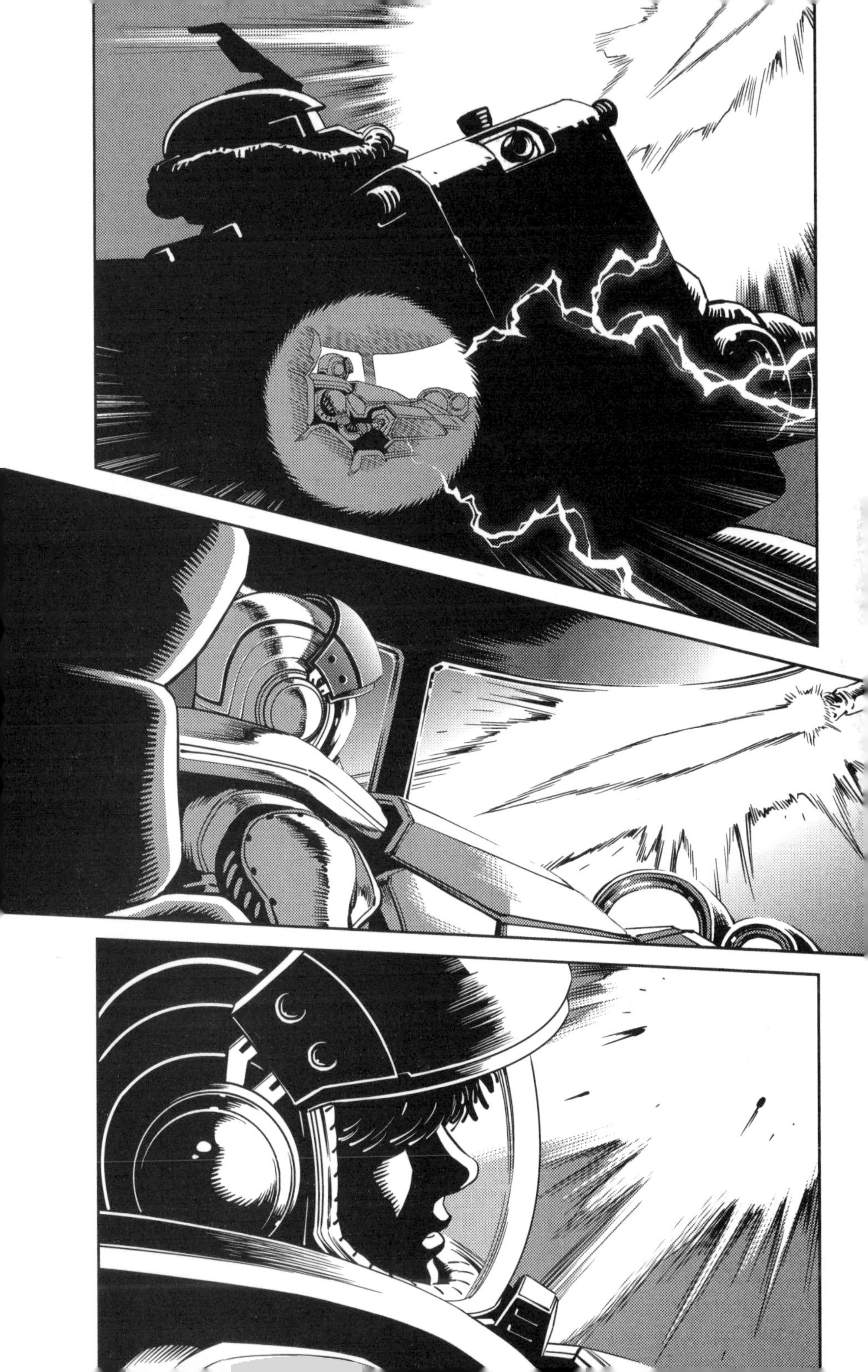

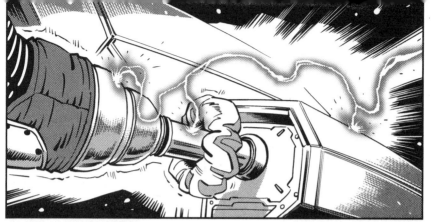

FIRE

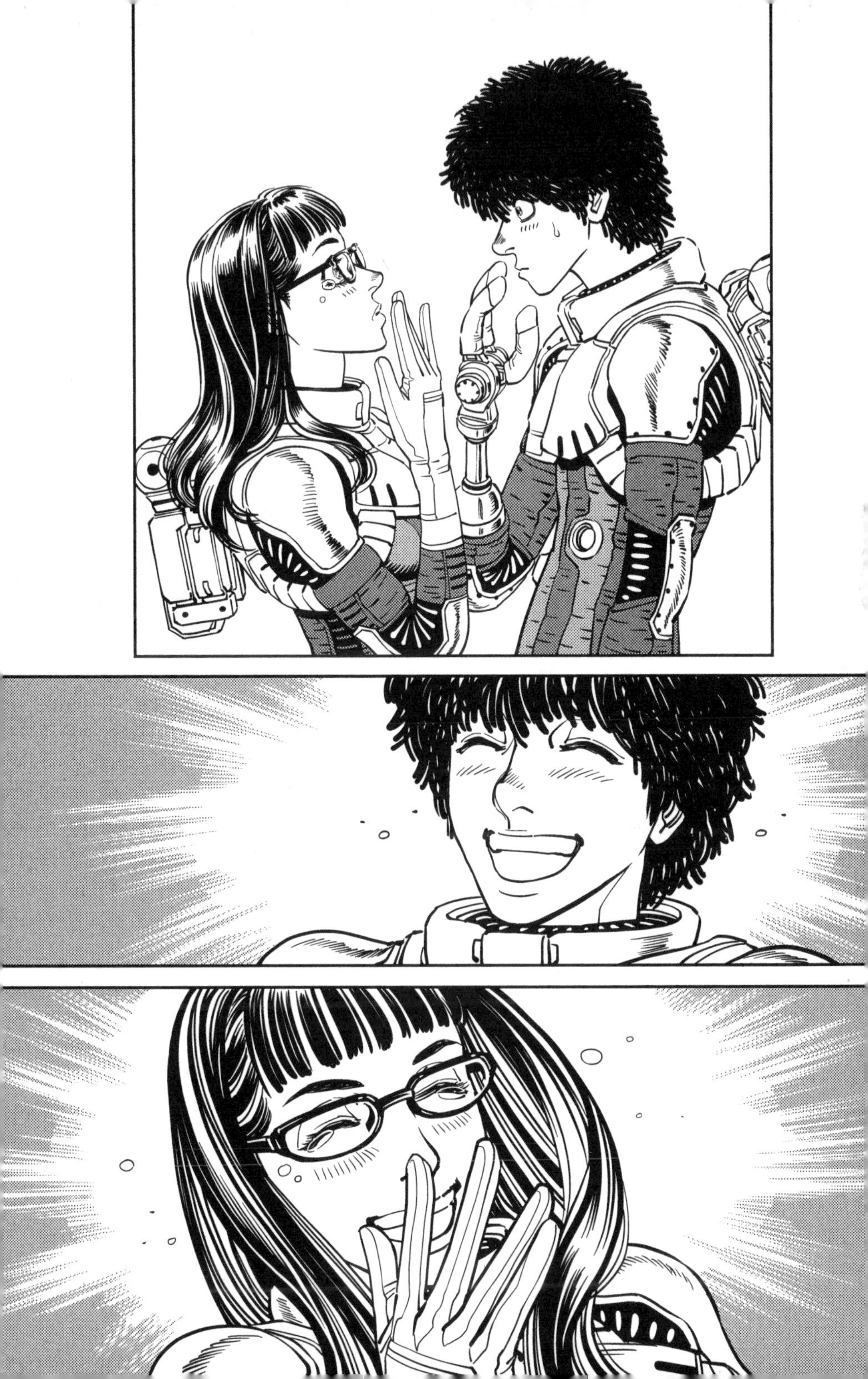

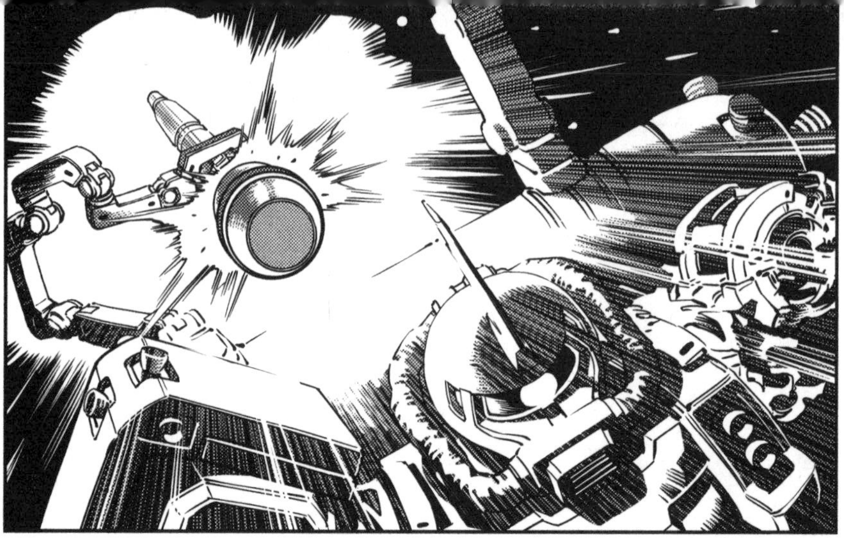
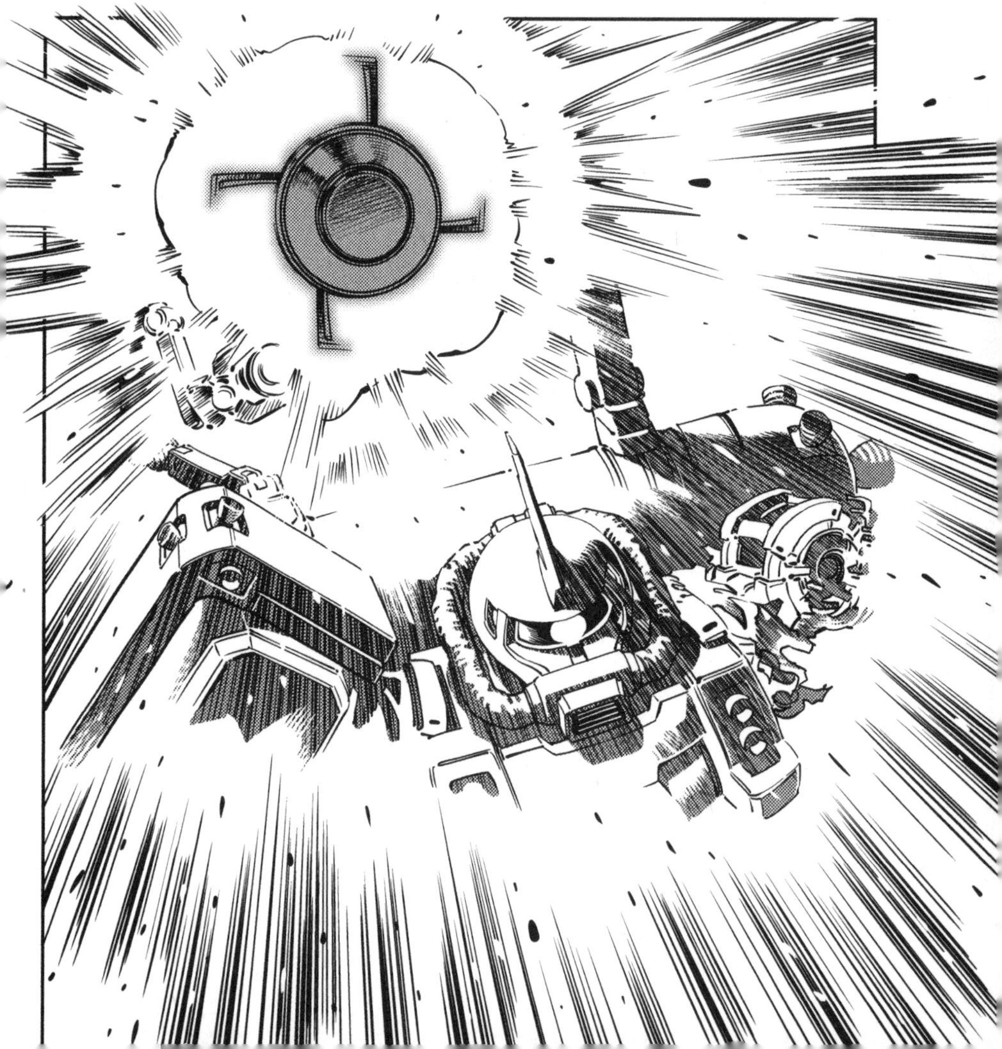

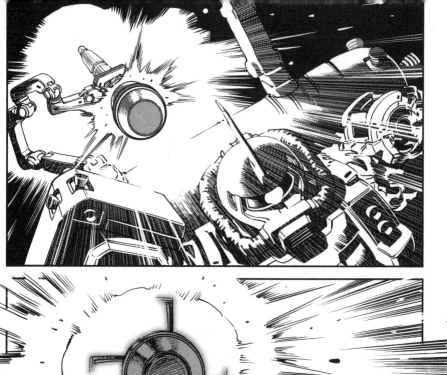

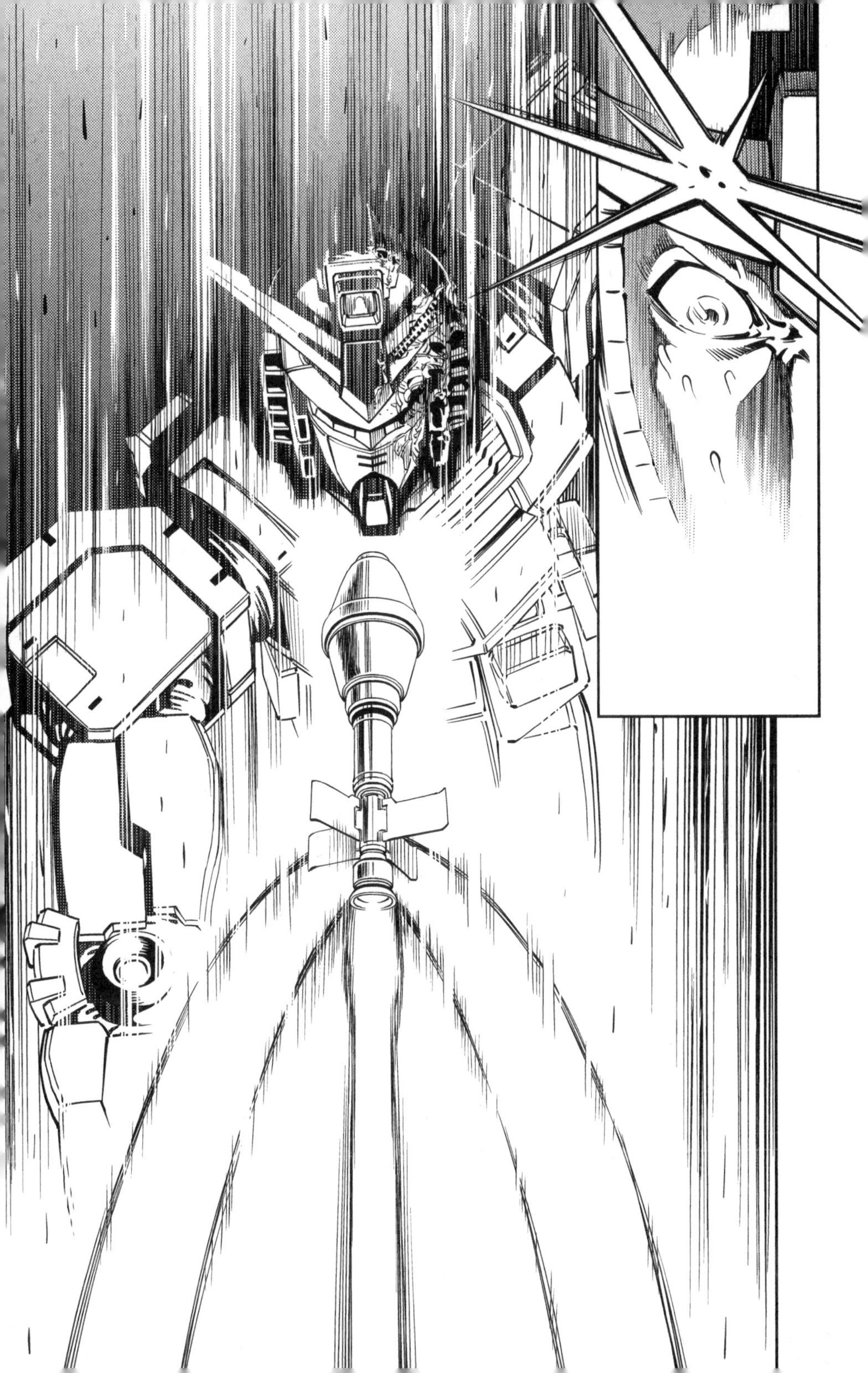

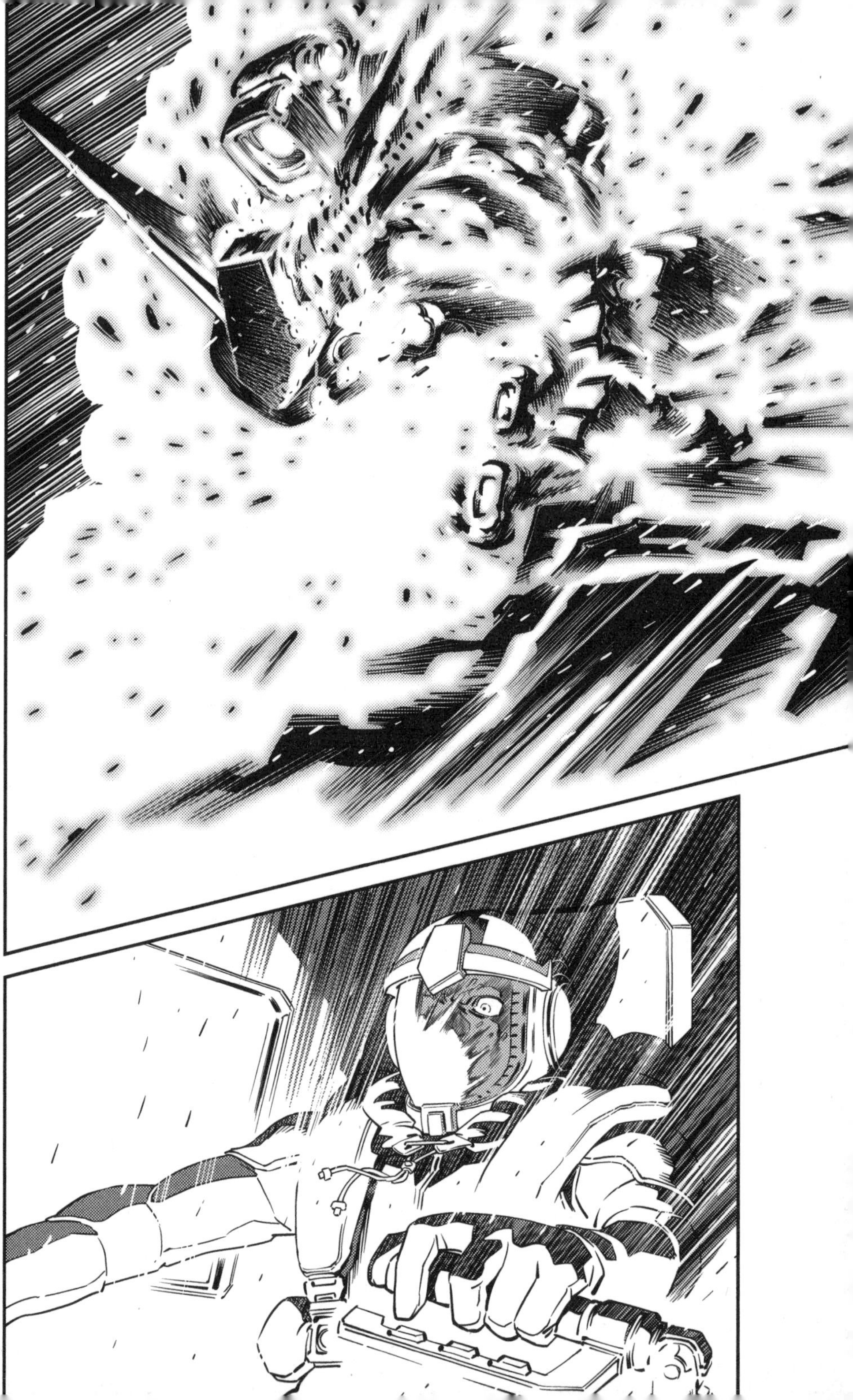

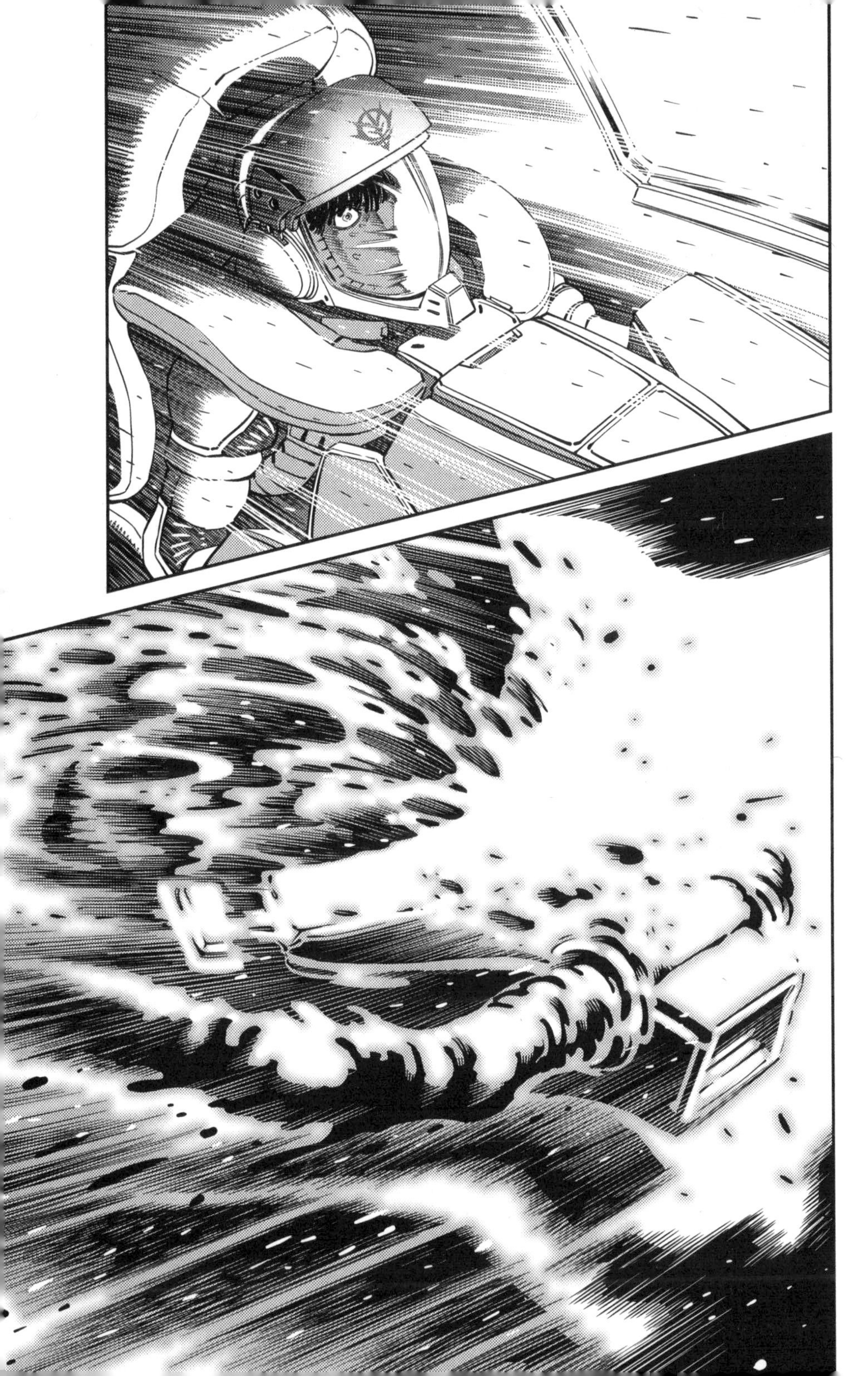

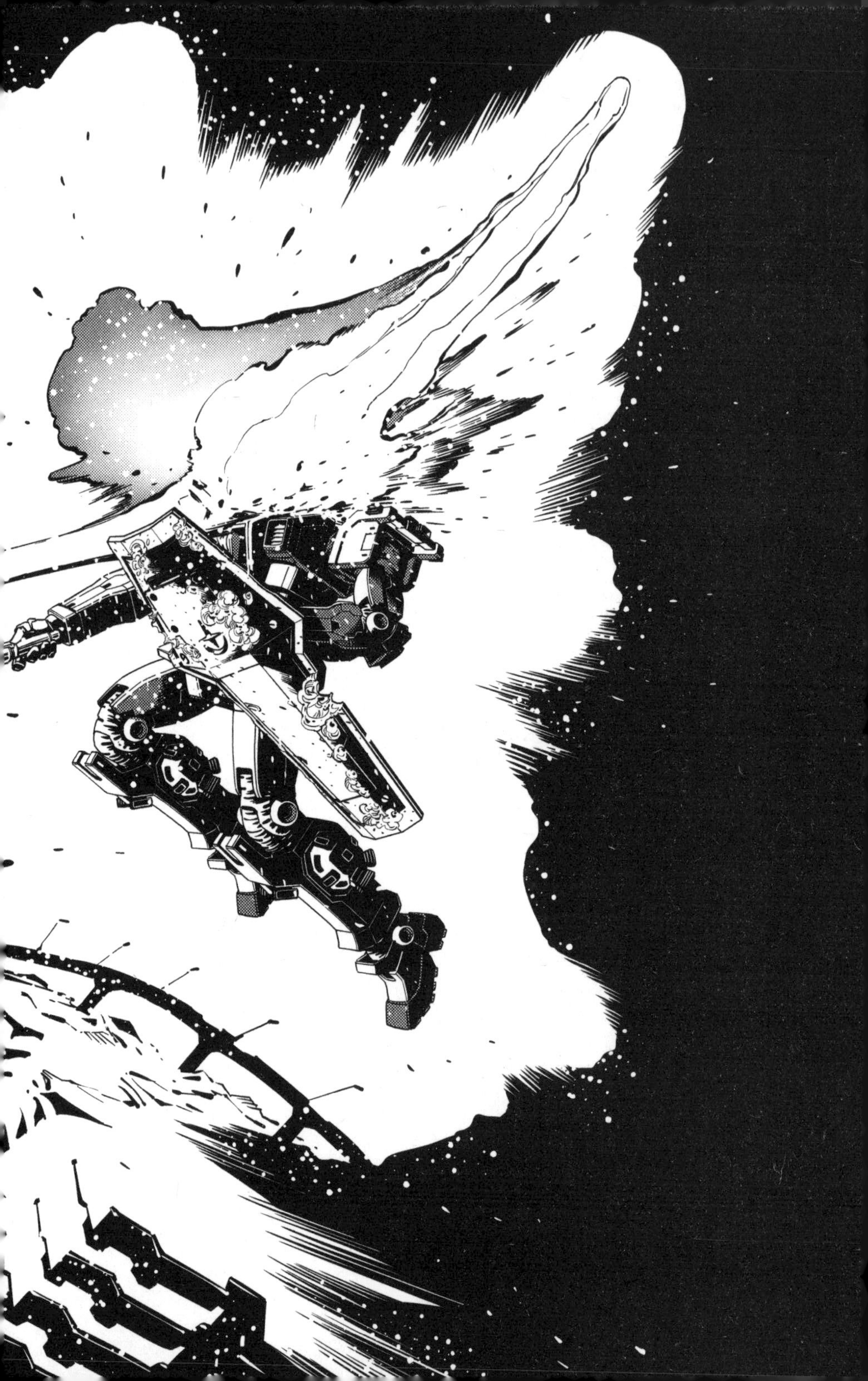

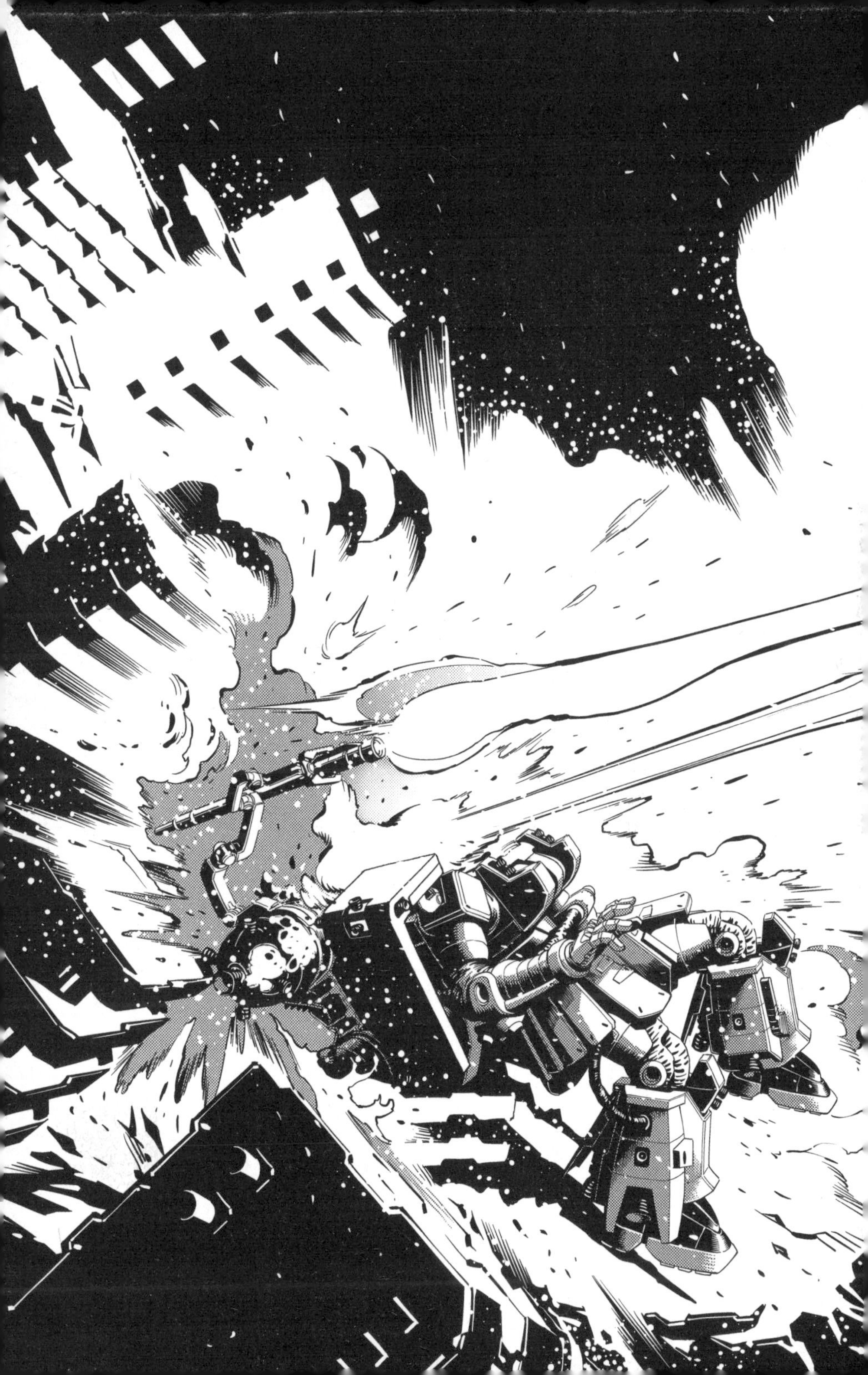

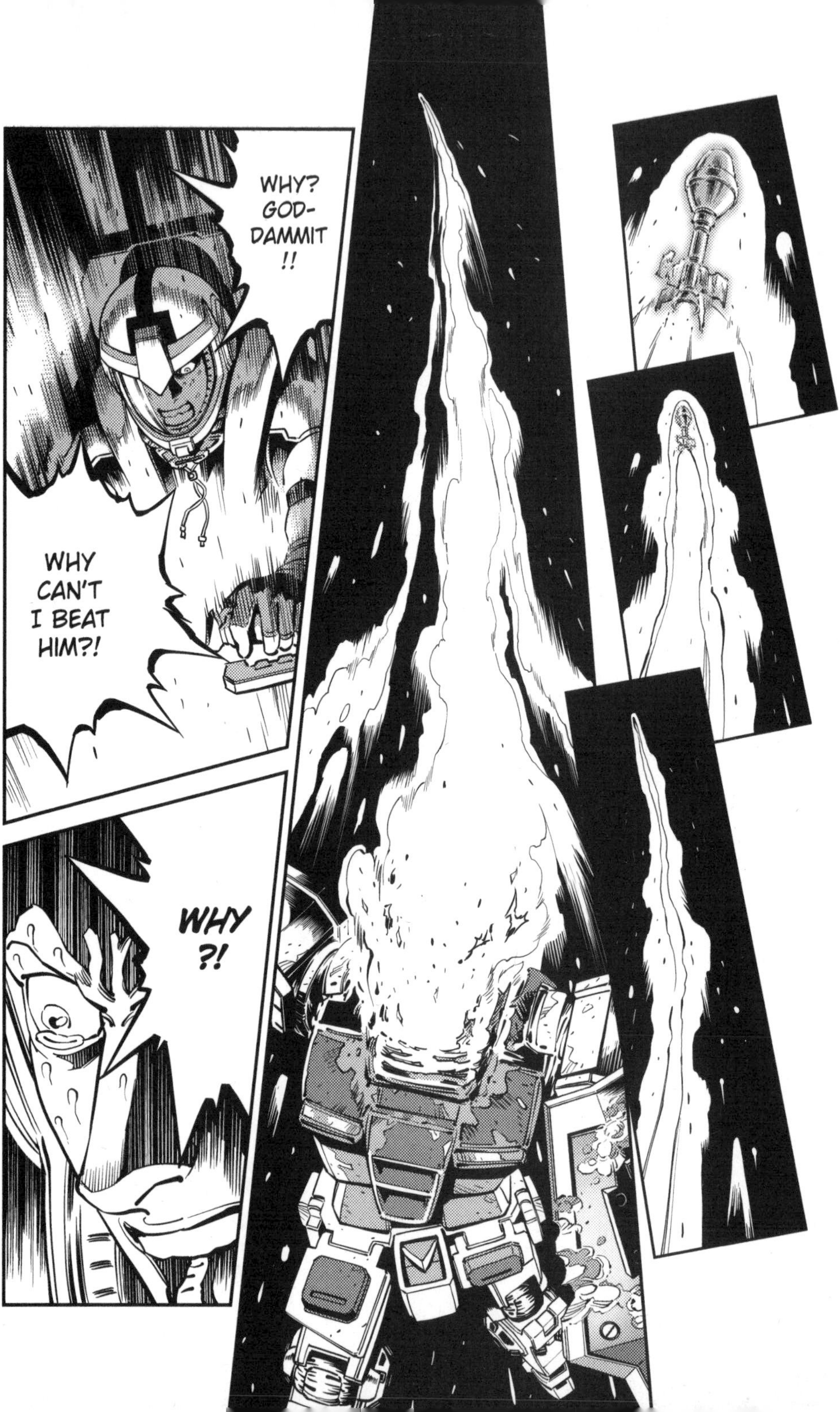
WHY? GOD-DAMMIT!!
WHY CAN'T I BEAT HIM?!
WHY?!

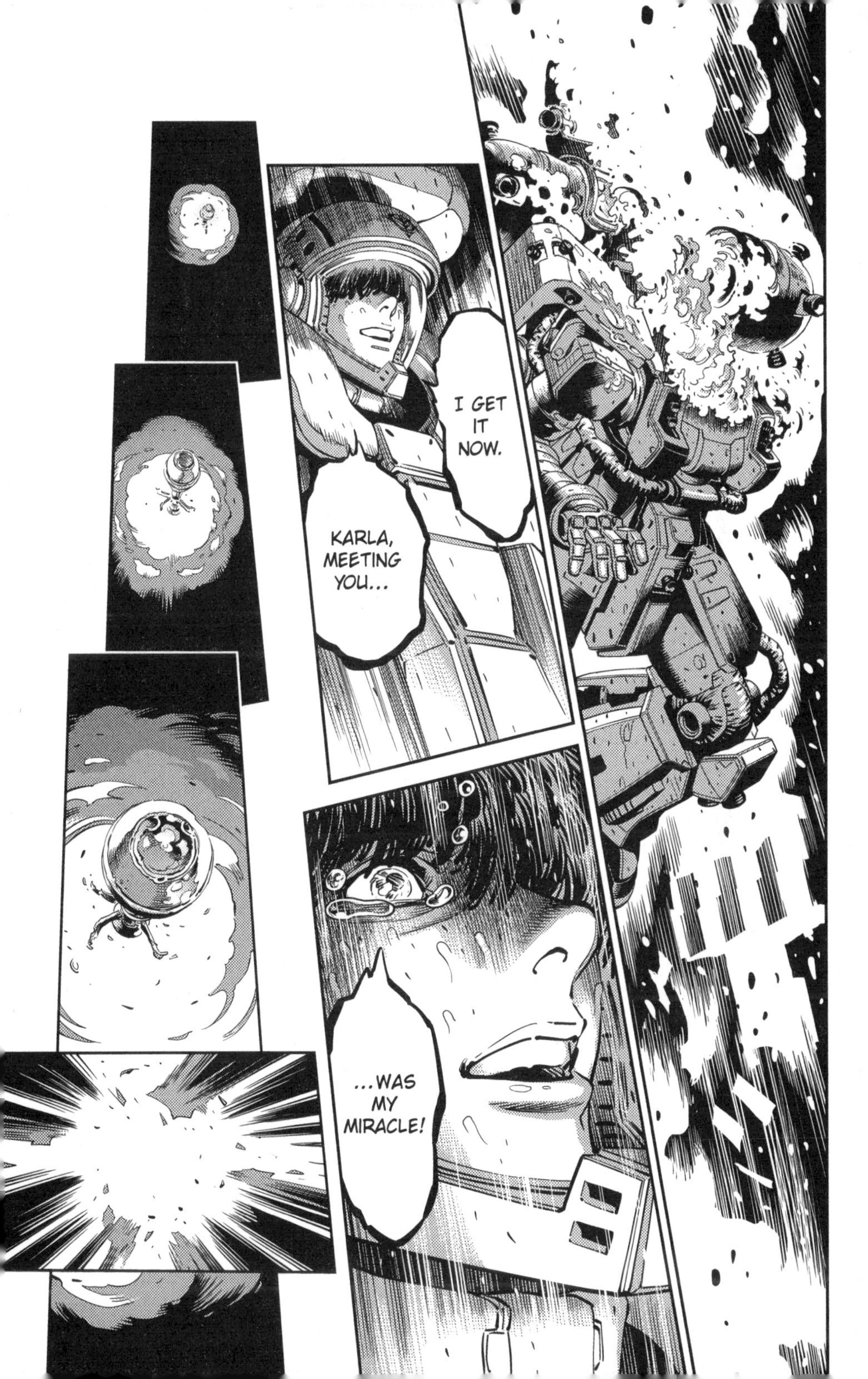
I GET IT NOW.
KARLA, MEETING YOU...
...WAS MY MIRACLE!

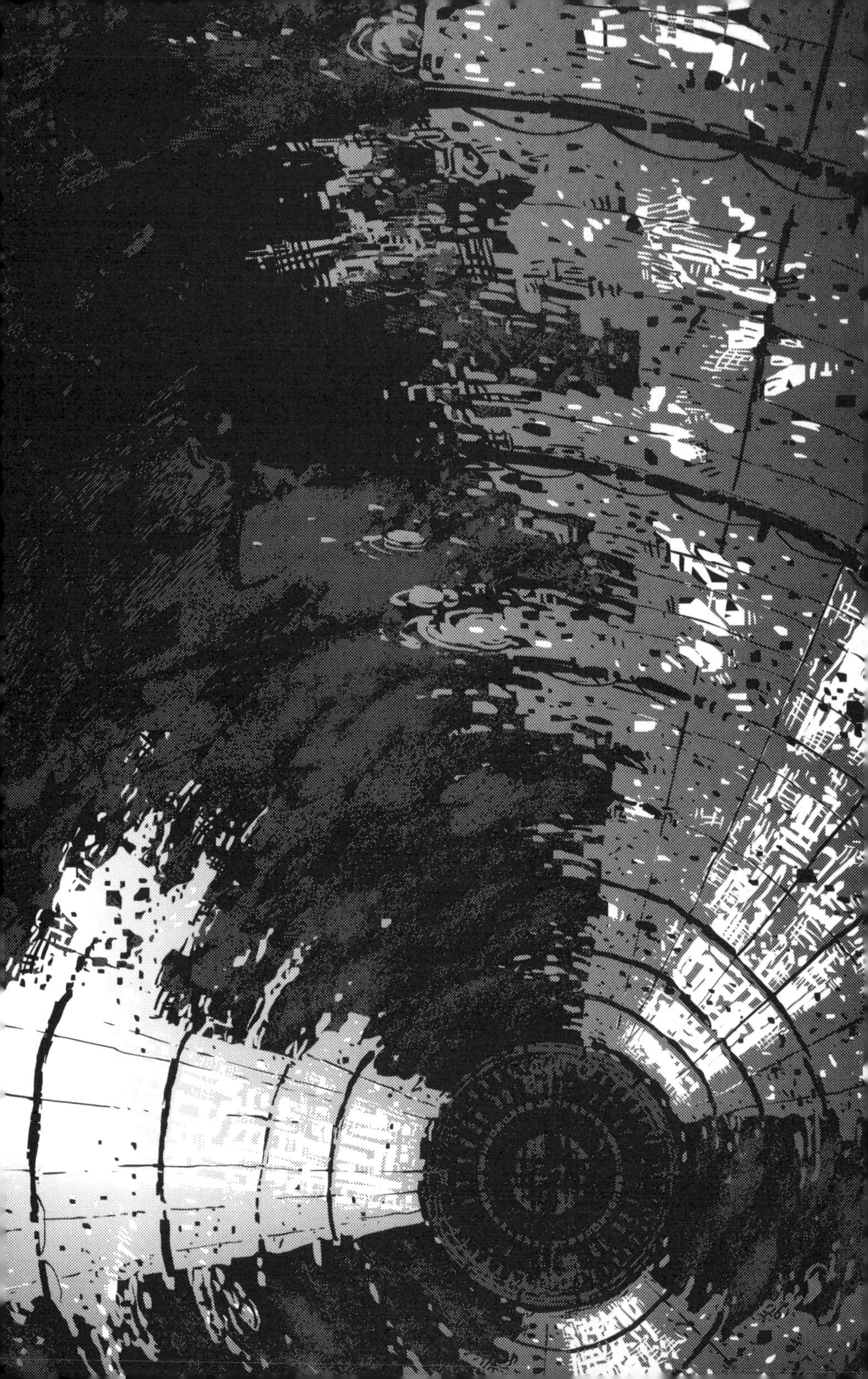

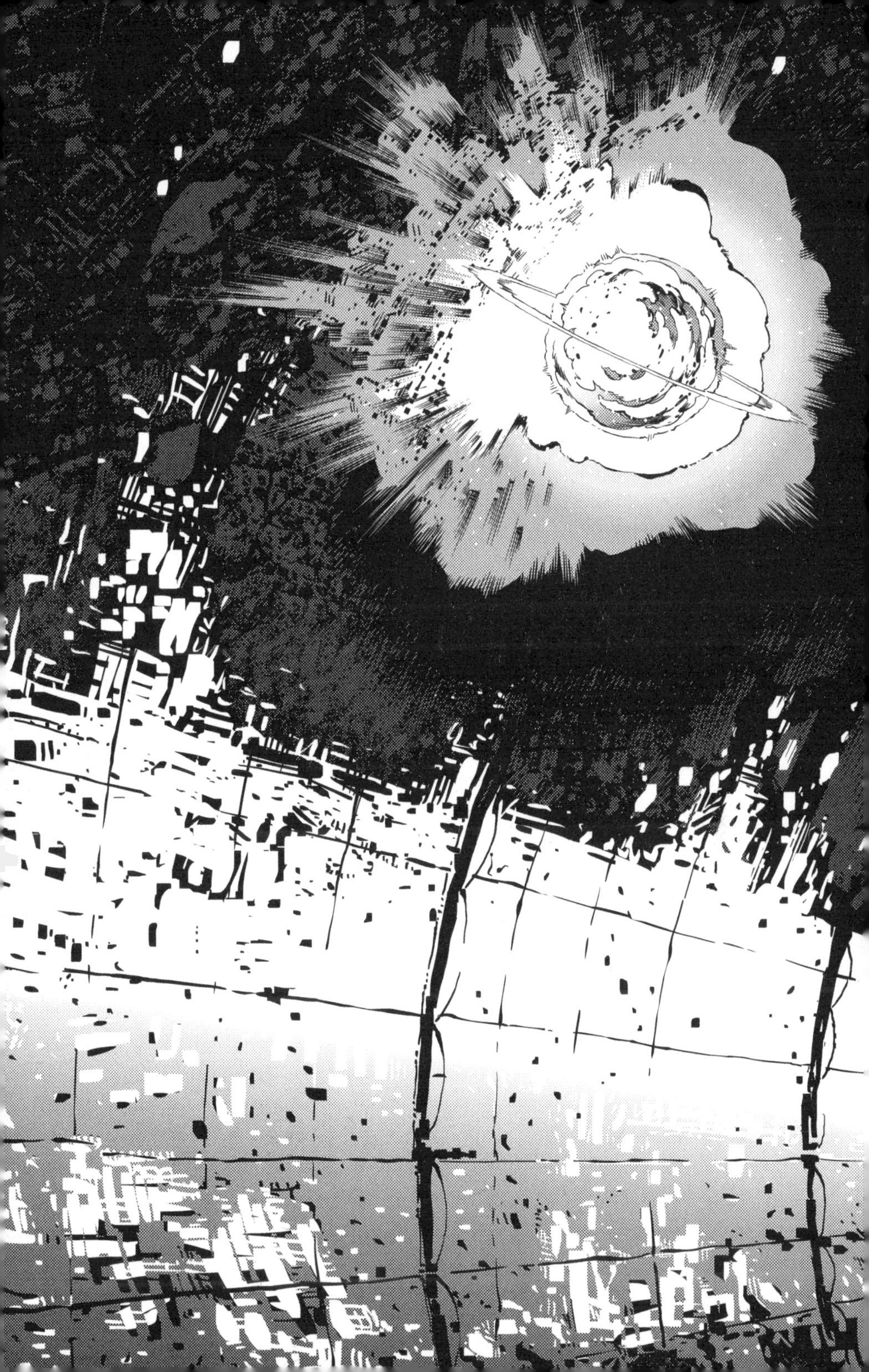

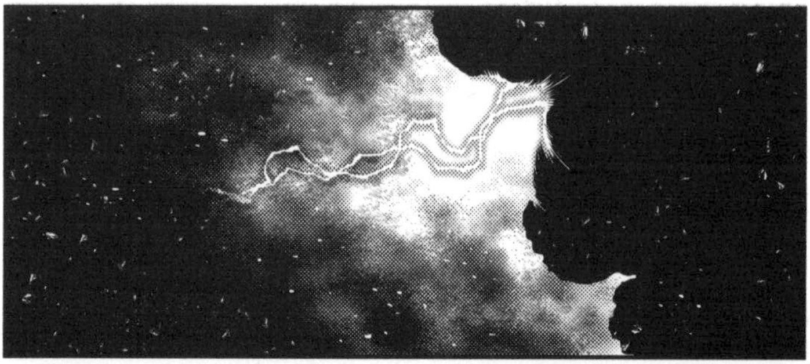
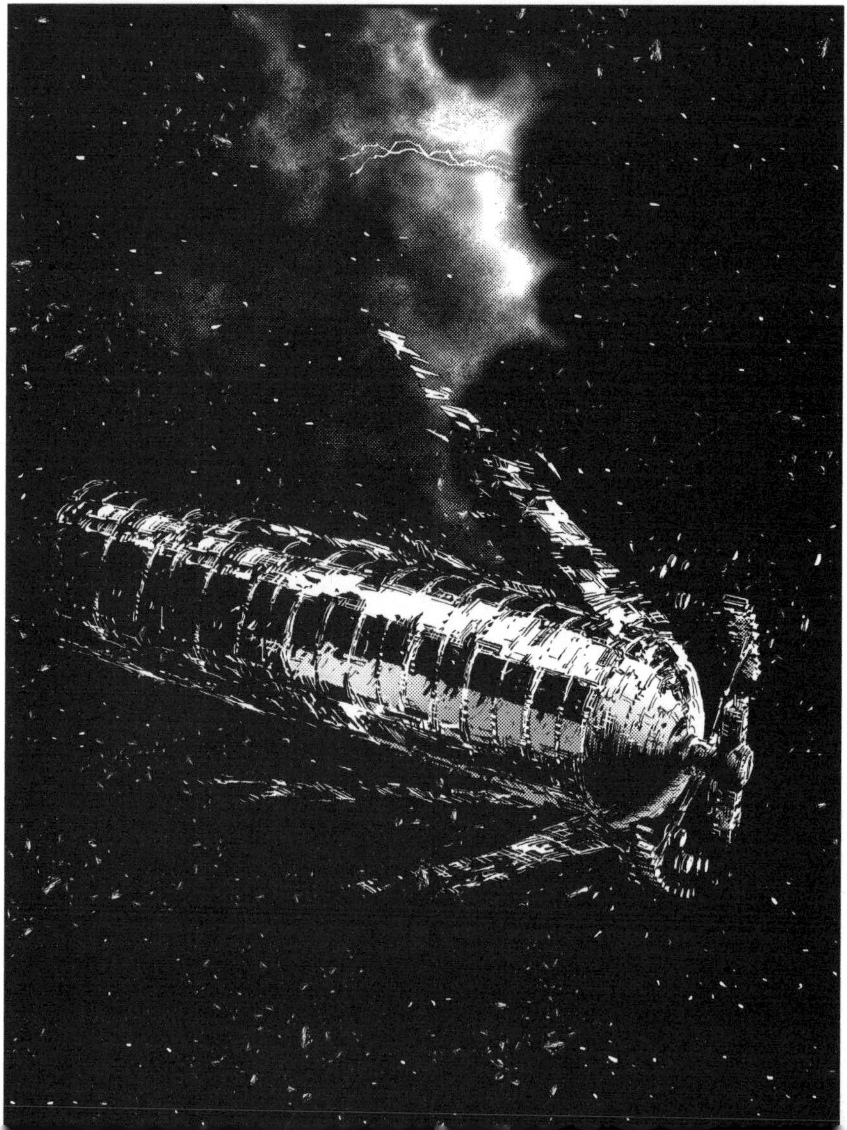

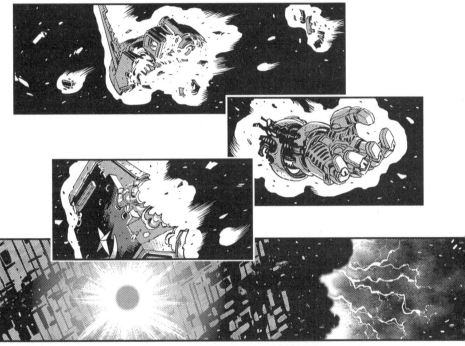

MOBILE SUIT GUNDAM THUNDERBOLT CHAPTER 27

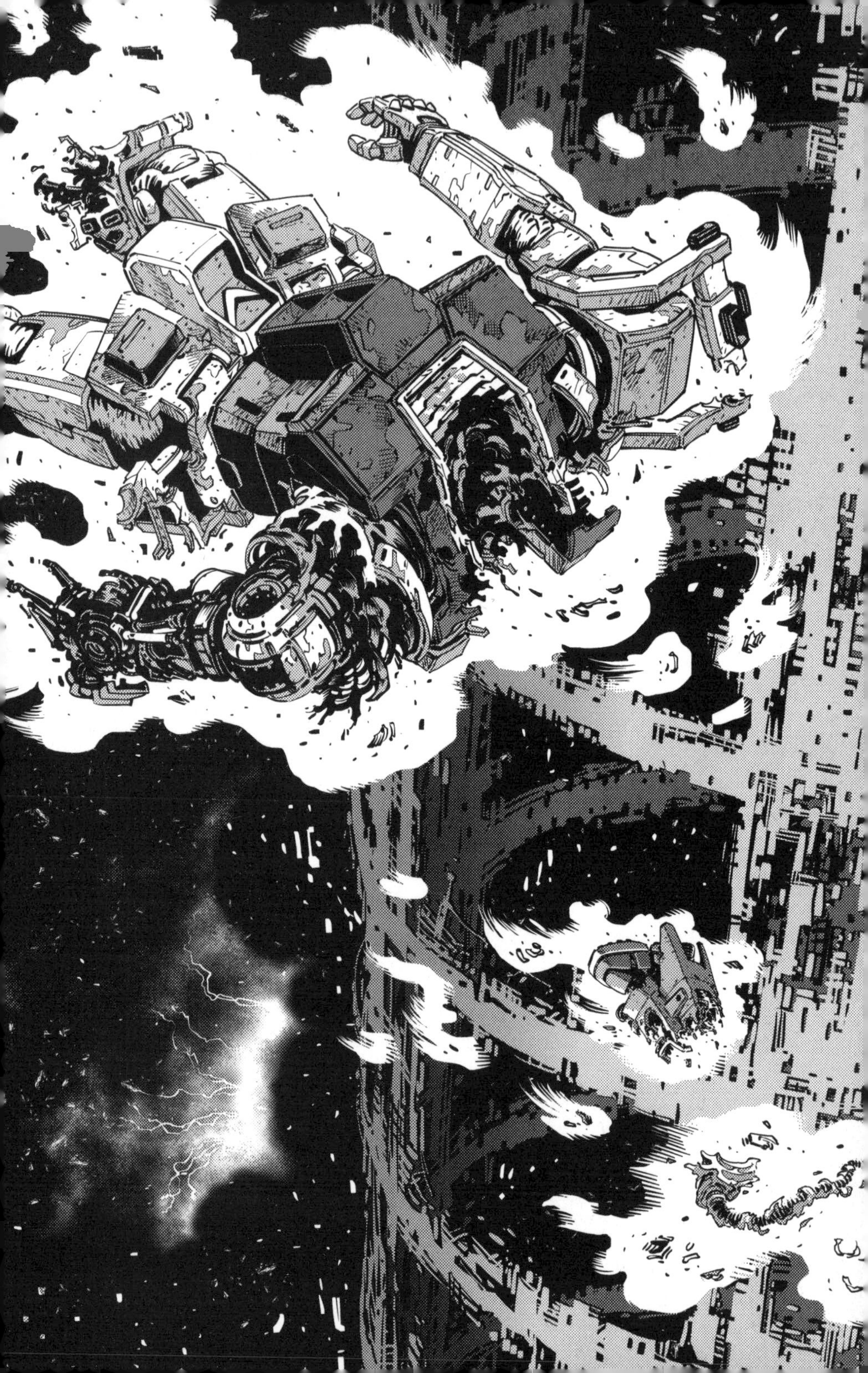

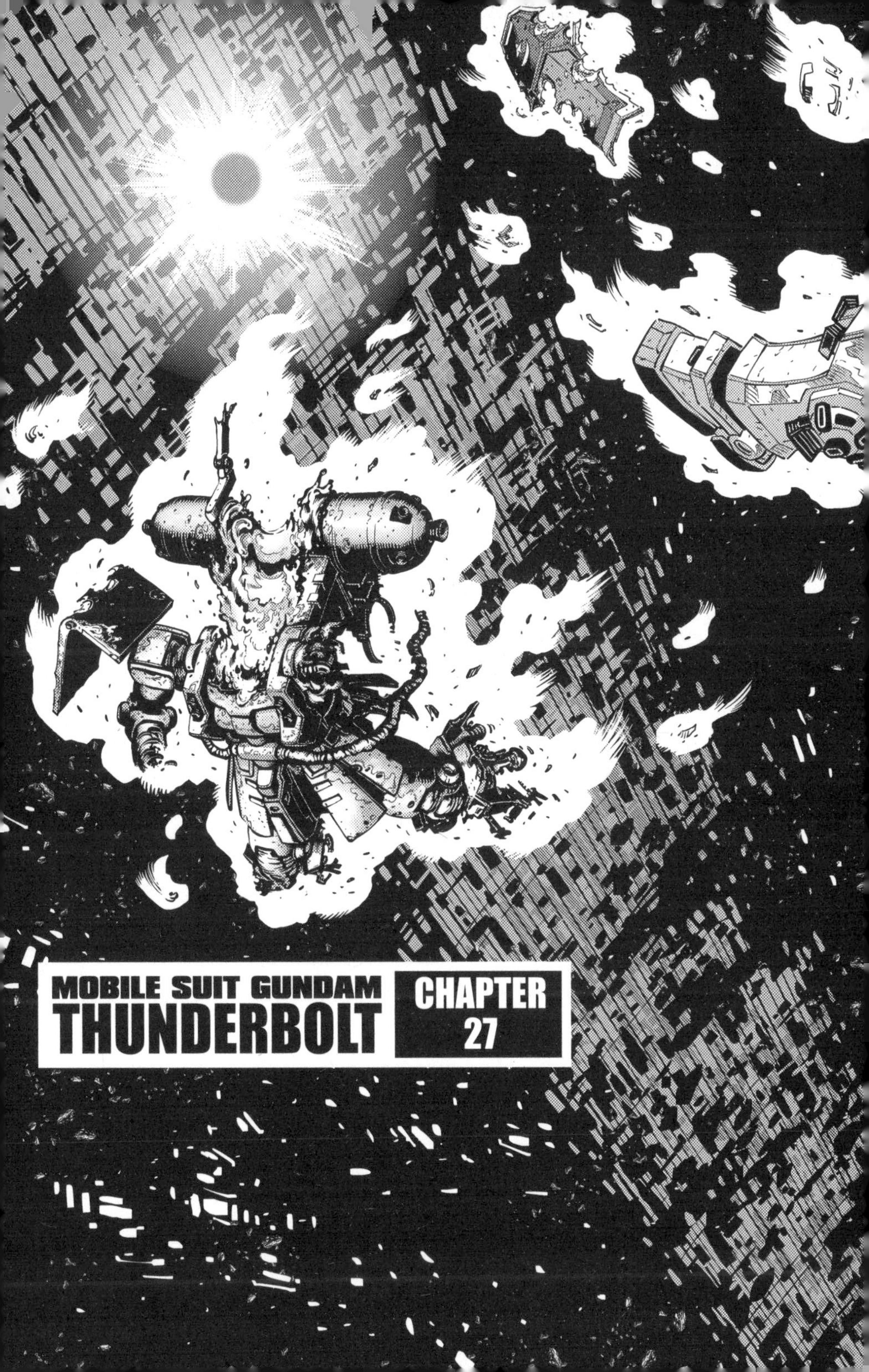
MOBILE SUIT GUNDAM
THUNDERBOLT
CHAPTER
27

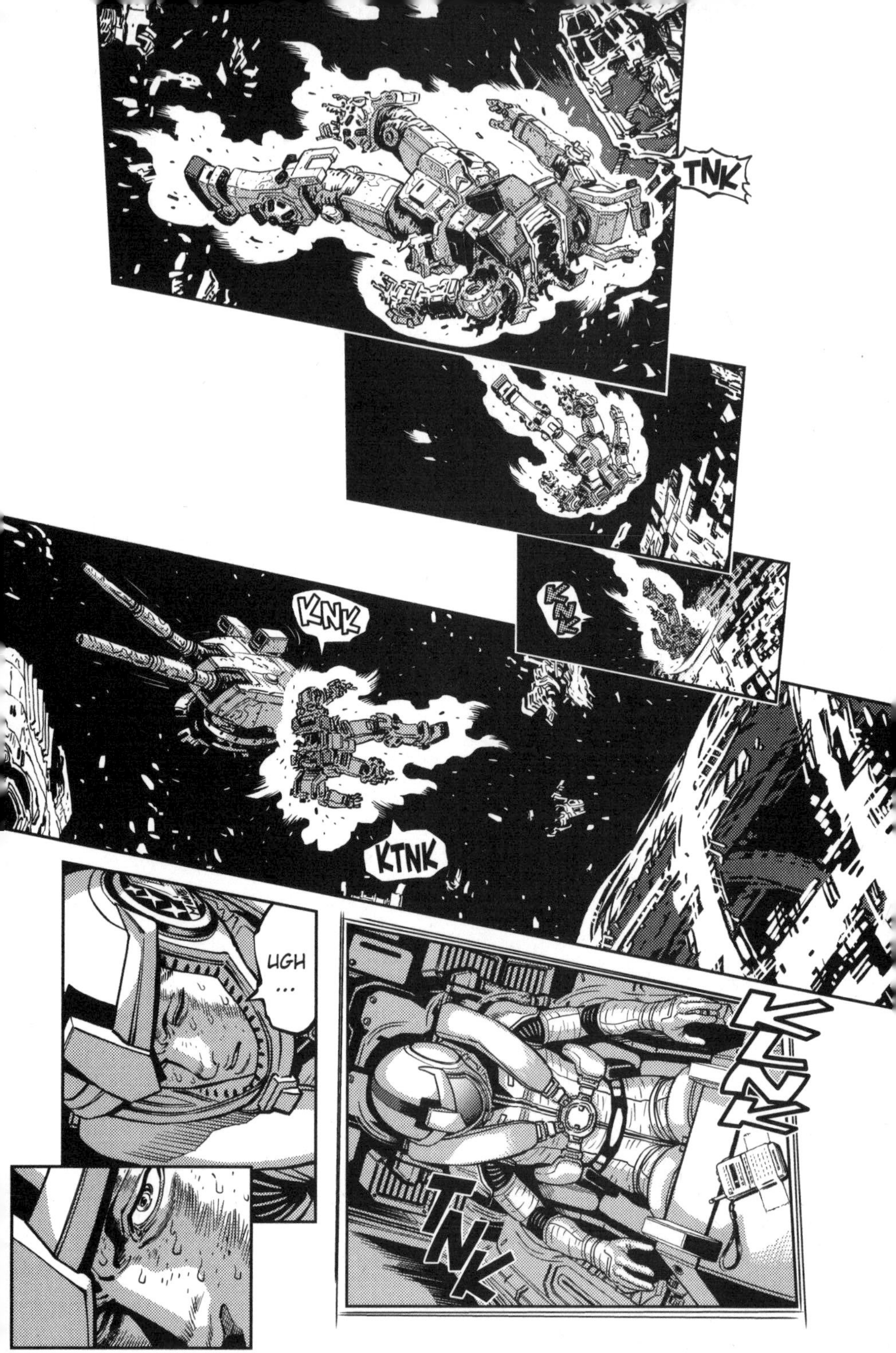
TNK
KNK
K-NK
KTNK
KLNK
TNK
UGH
...

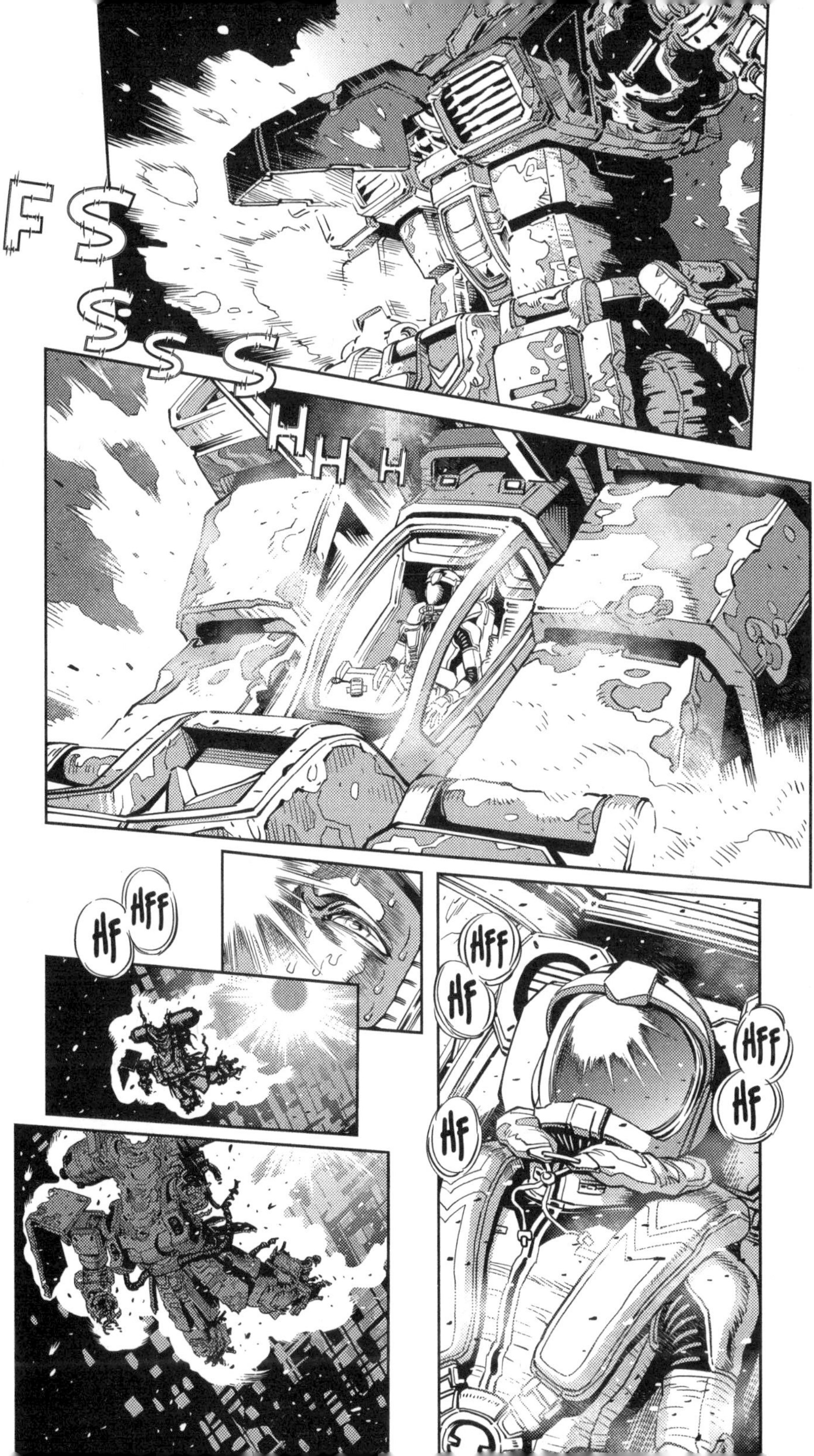
FSSSSHHH
HFF
HF
HFF
HF
HF
HF
HFF

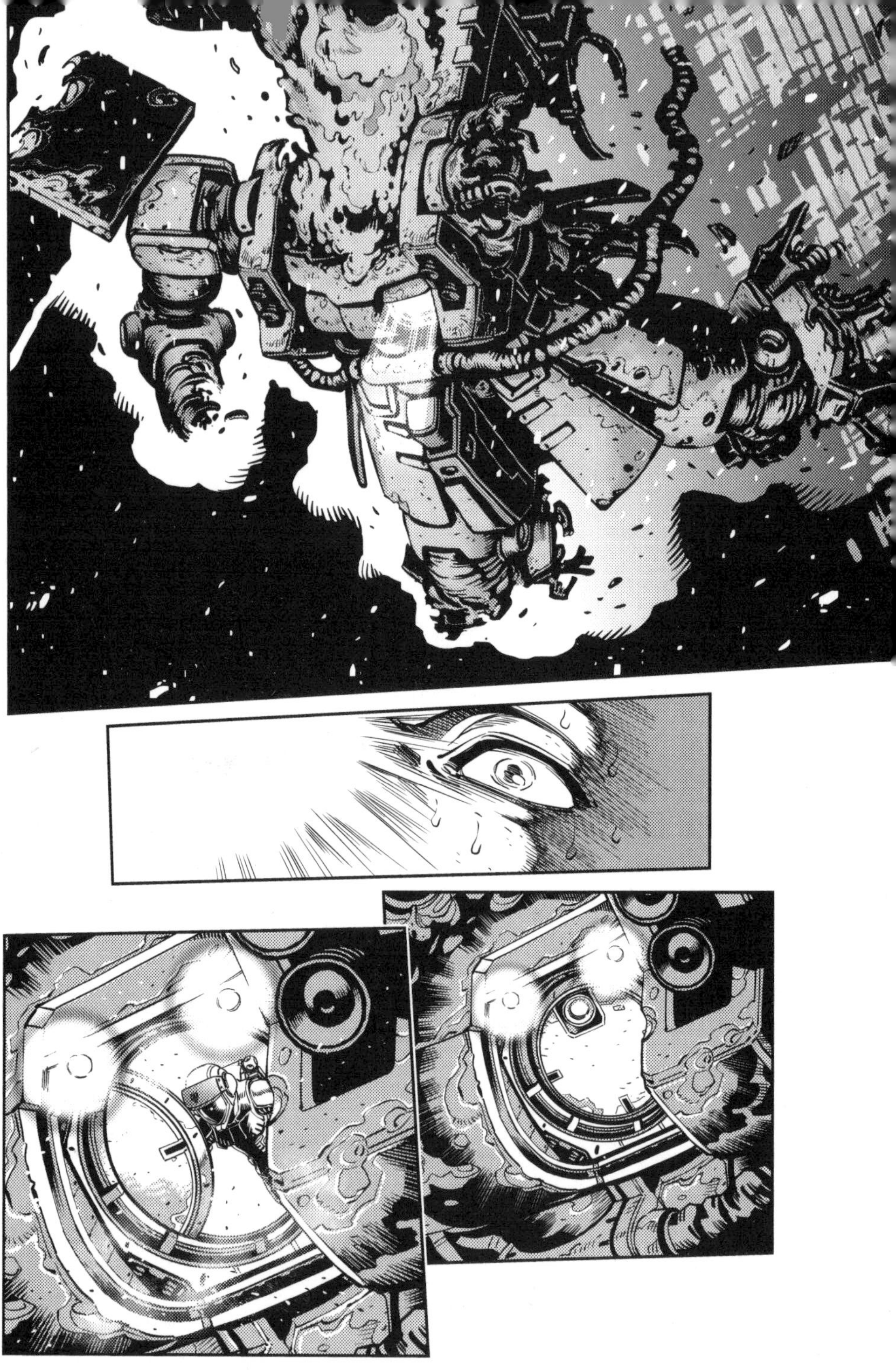

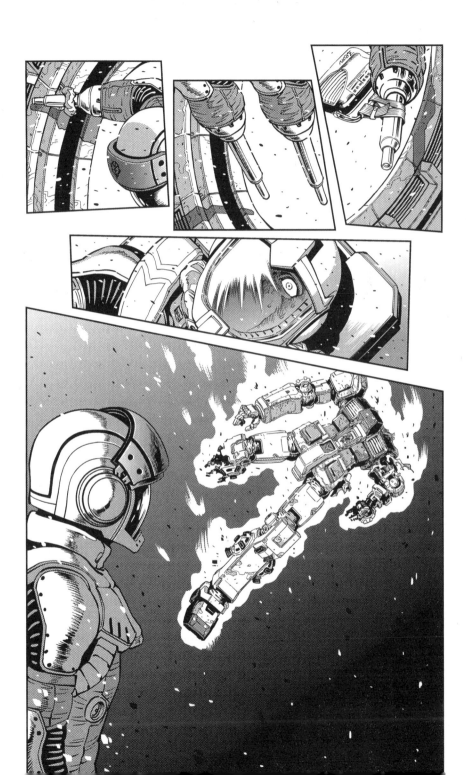

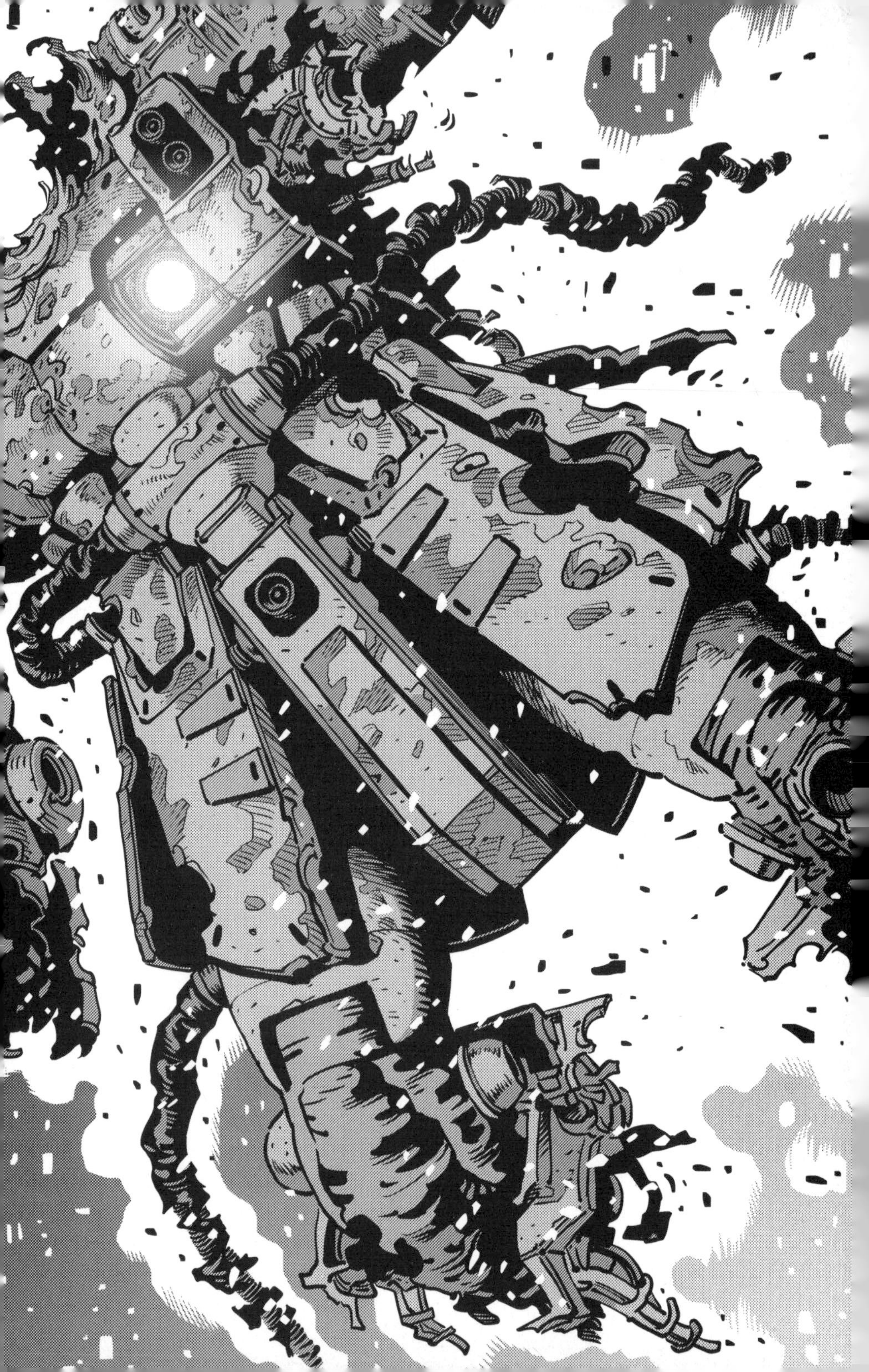

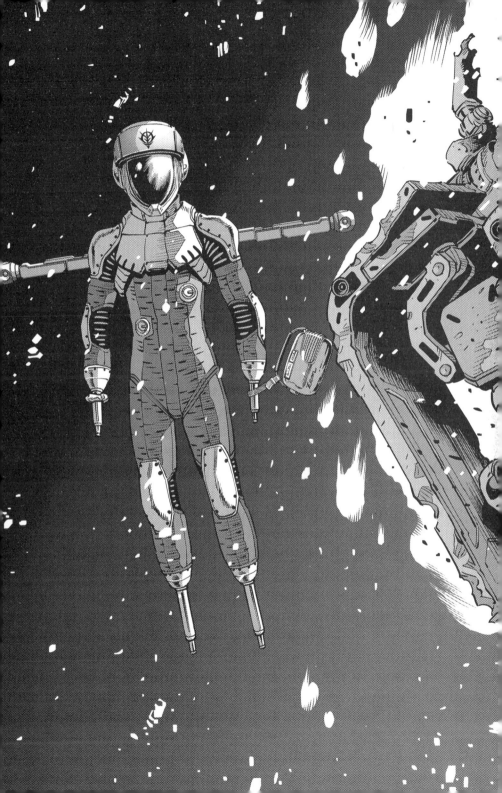

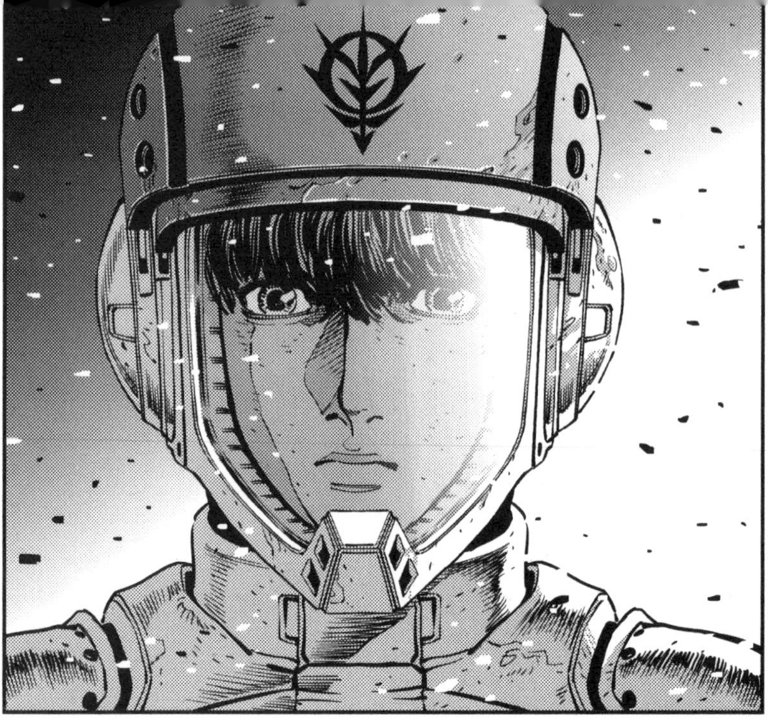

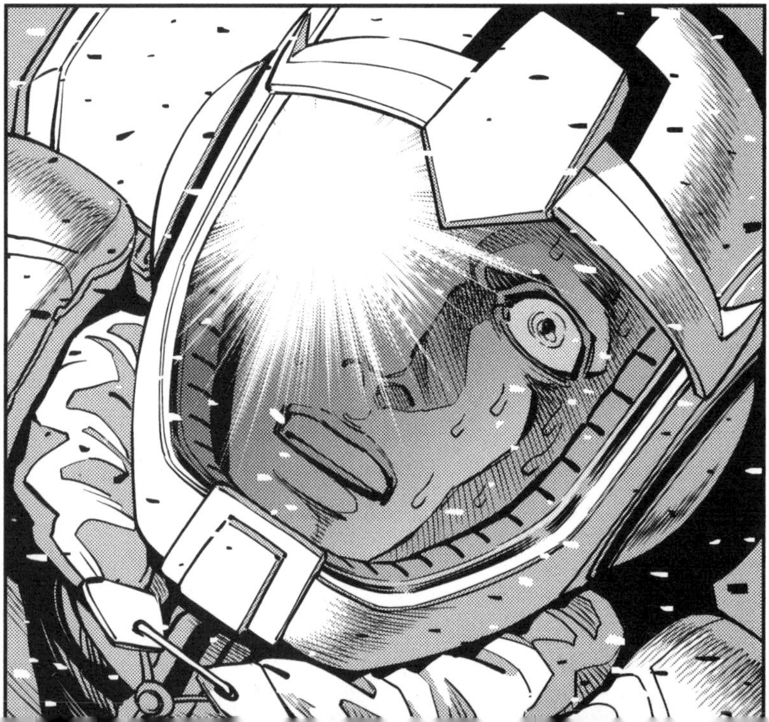

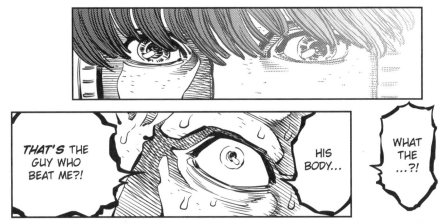

THAT'S THE GUY WHO BEAT ME?!

HIS BODY...

WHAT THE ...?!

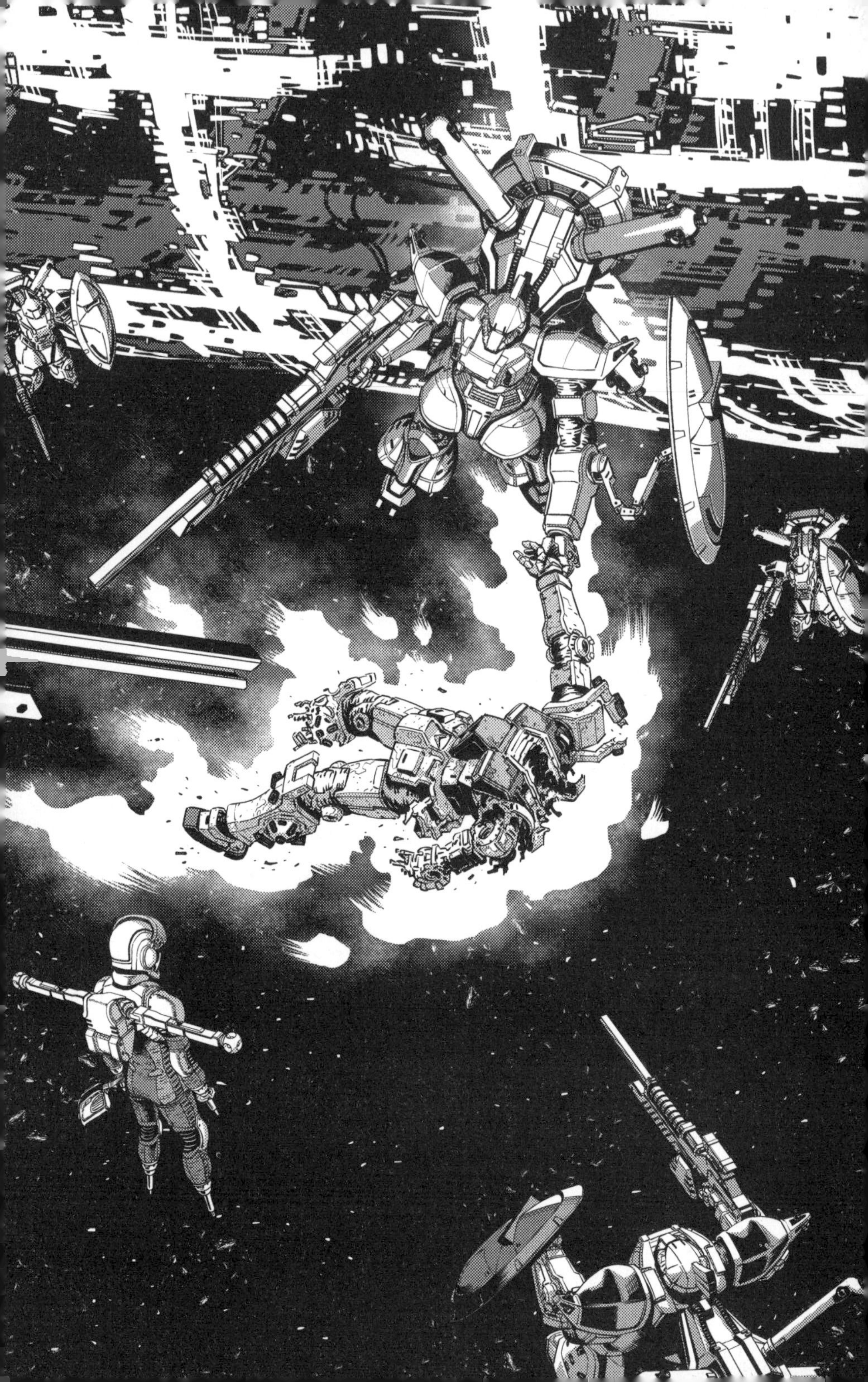

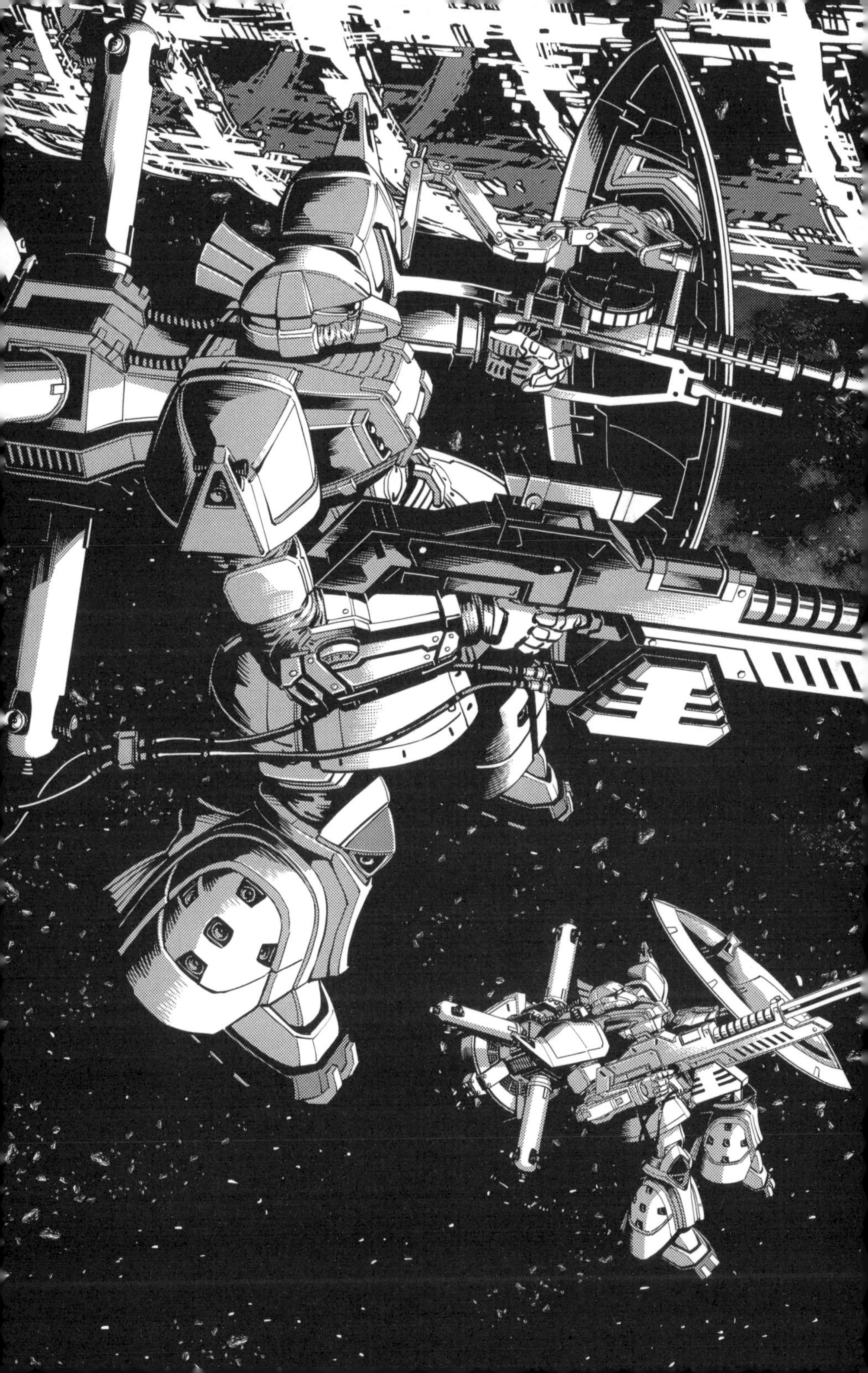

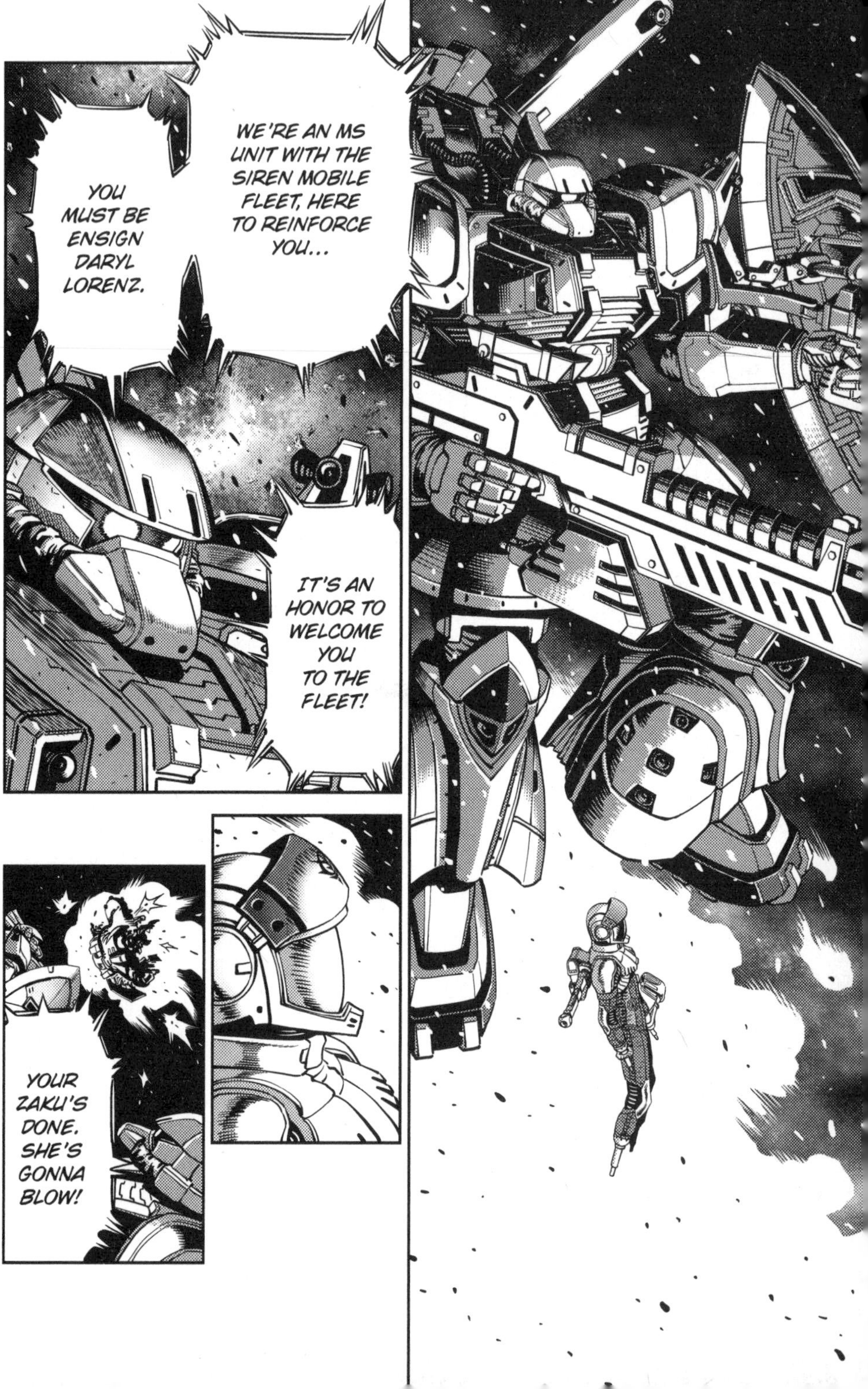
WE'RE AN MS UNIT WITH THE SIREN MOBILE FLEET, HERE TO REINFORCE YOU...
YOU MUST BE ENSIGN DARYL LORENZ.
IT'S AN HONOR TO WELCOME YOU TO THE FLEET!
YOUR ZAKU'S DONE. SHE'S GONNA BLOW!

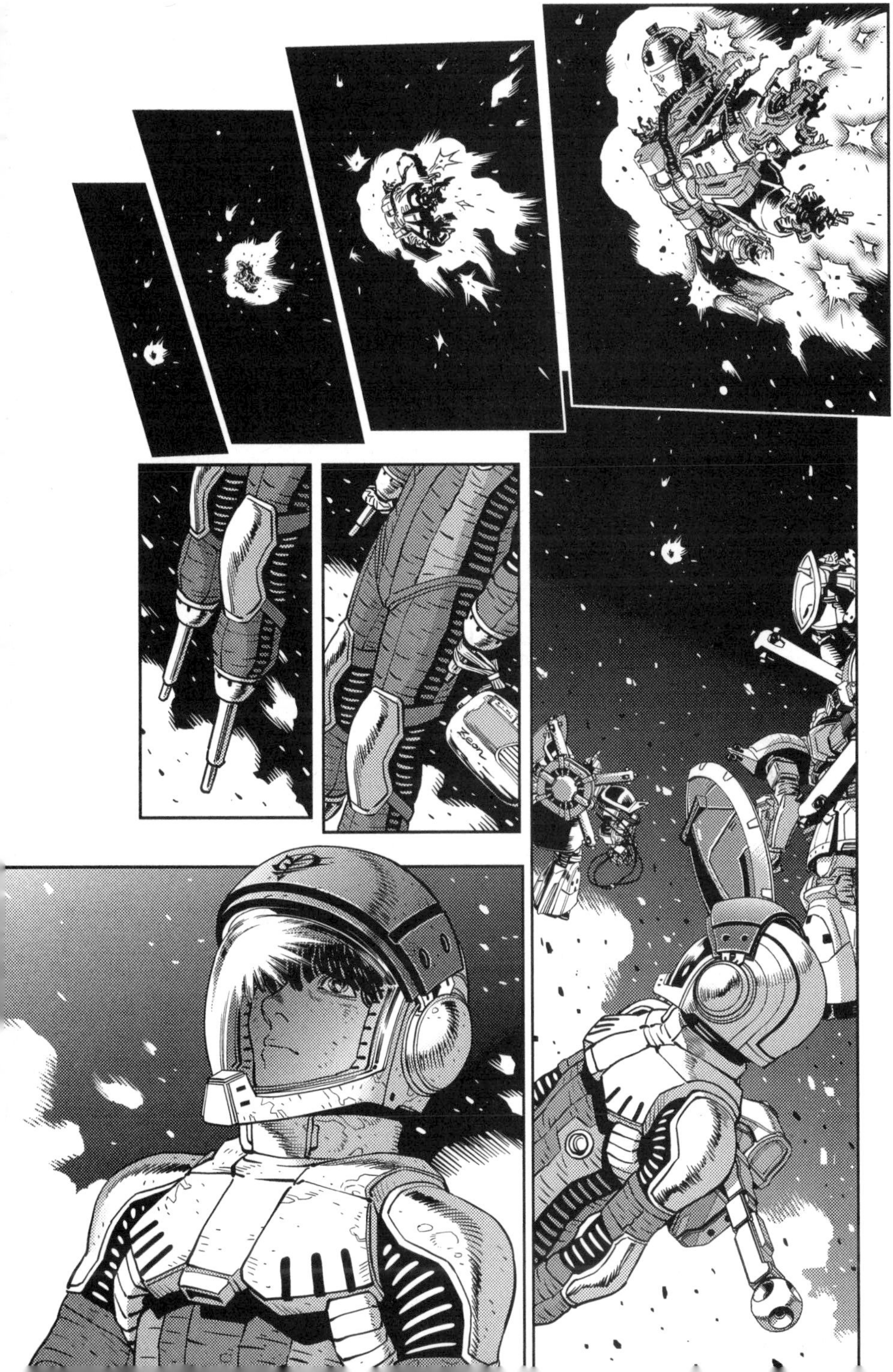
Zeon

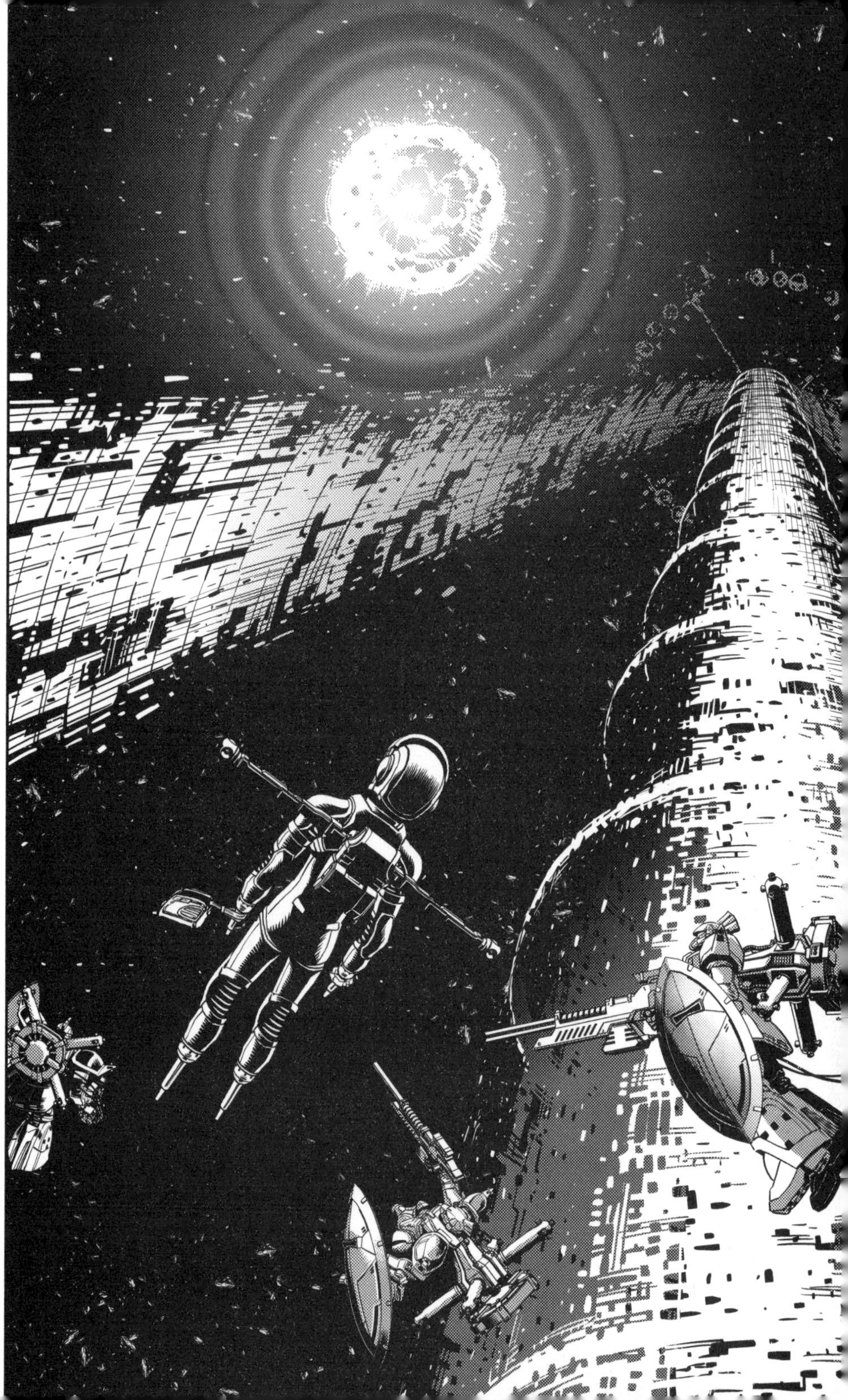

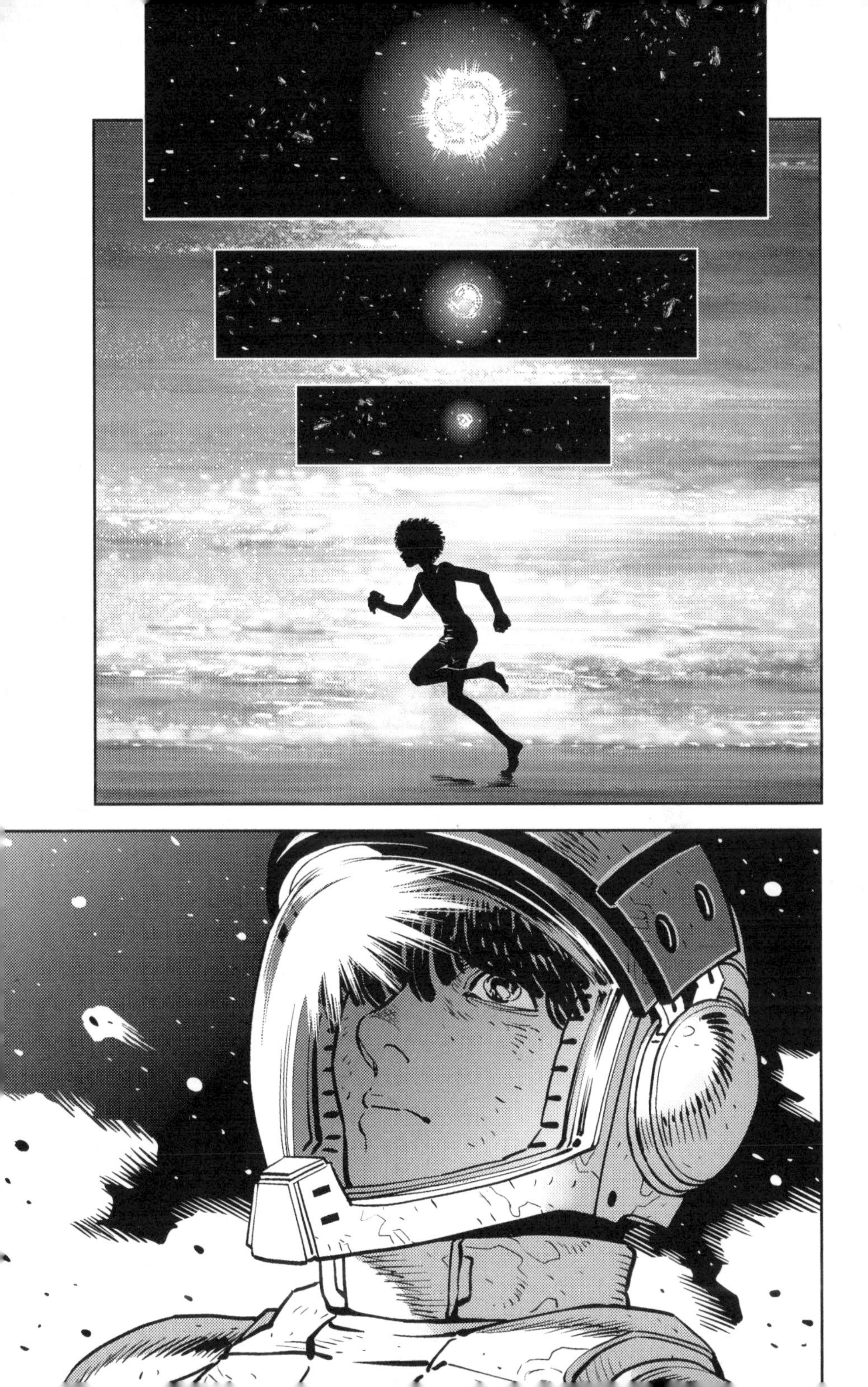

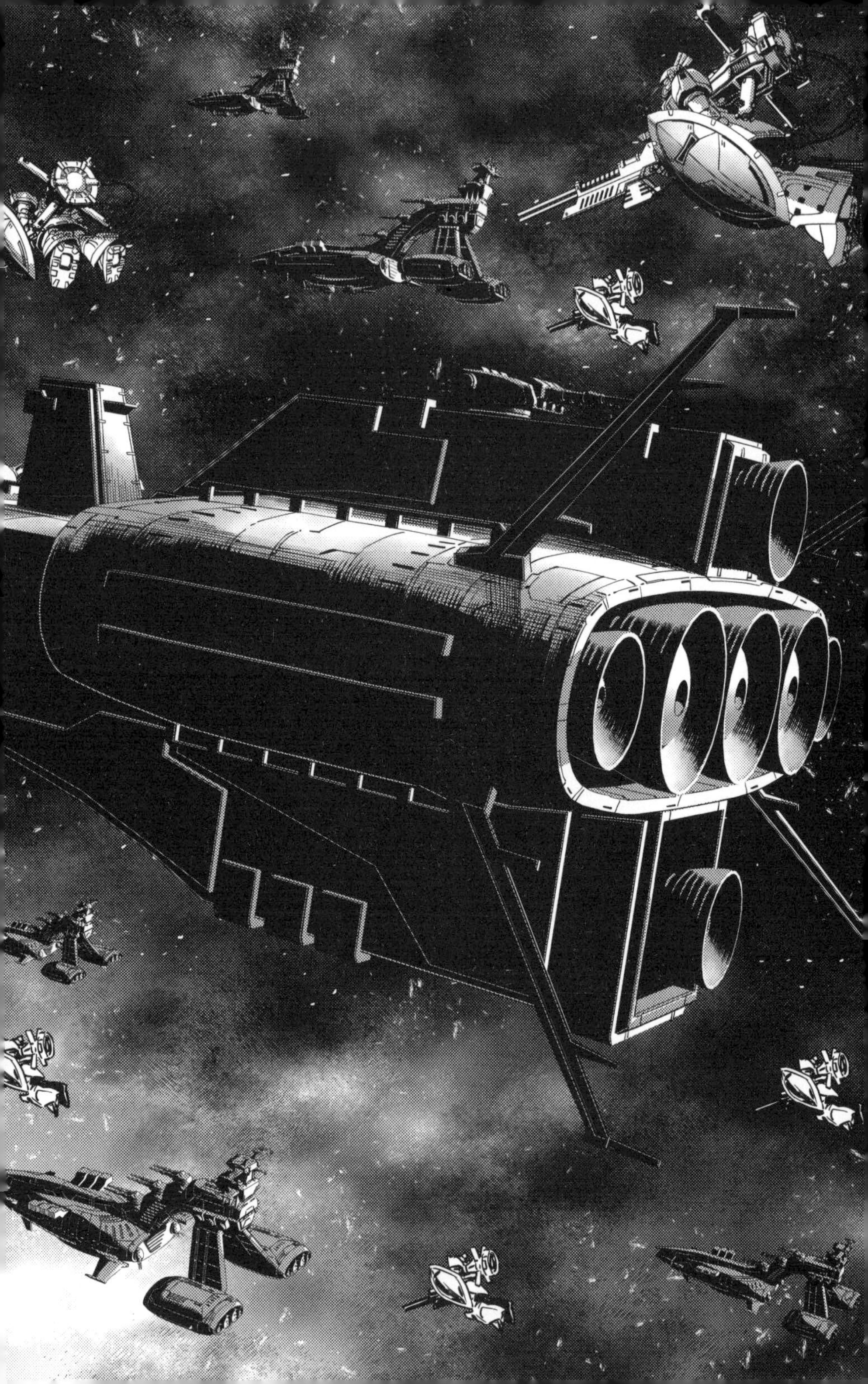

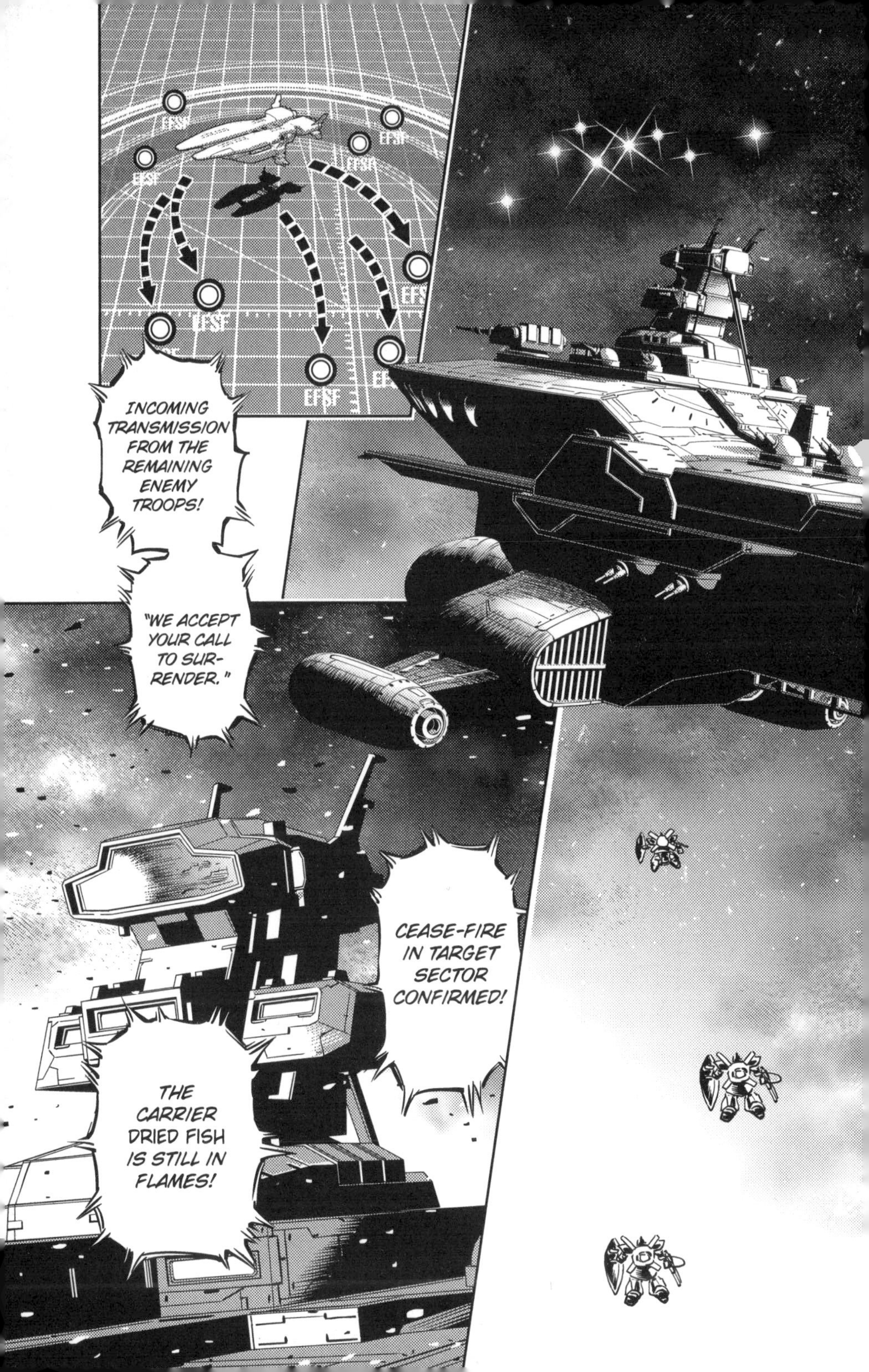
EFSF
INCOMING TRANSMISSION FROM THE REMAINING ENEMY TROOPS!
"WE ACCEPT YOUR CALL TO SUR-RENDER."
CEASE-FIRE IN TARGET SECTOR CONFIRMED!
THE CARRIER DRIED FISH IS STILL IN FLAMES!

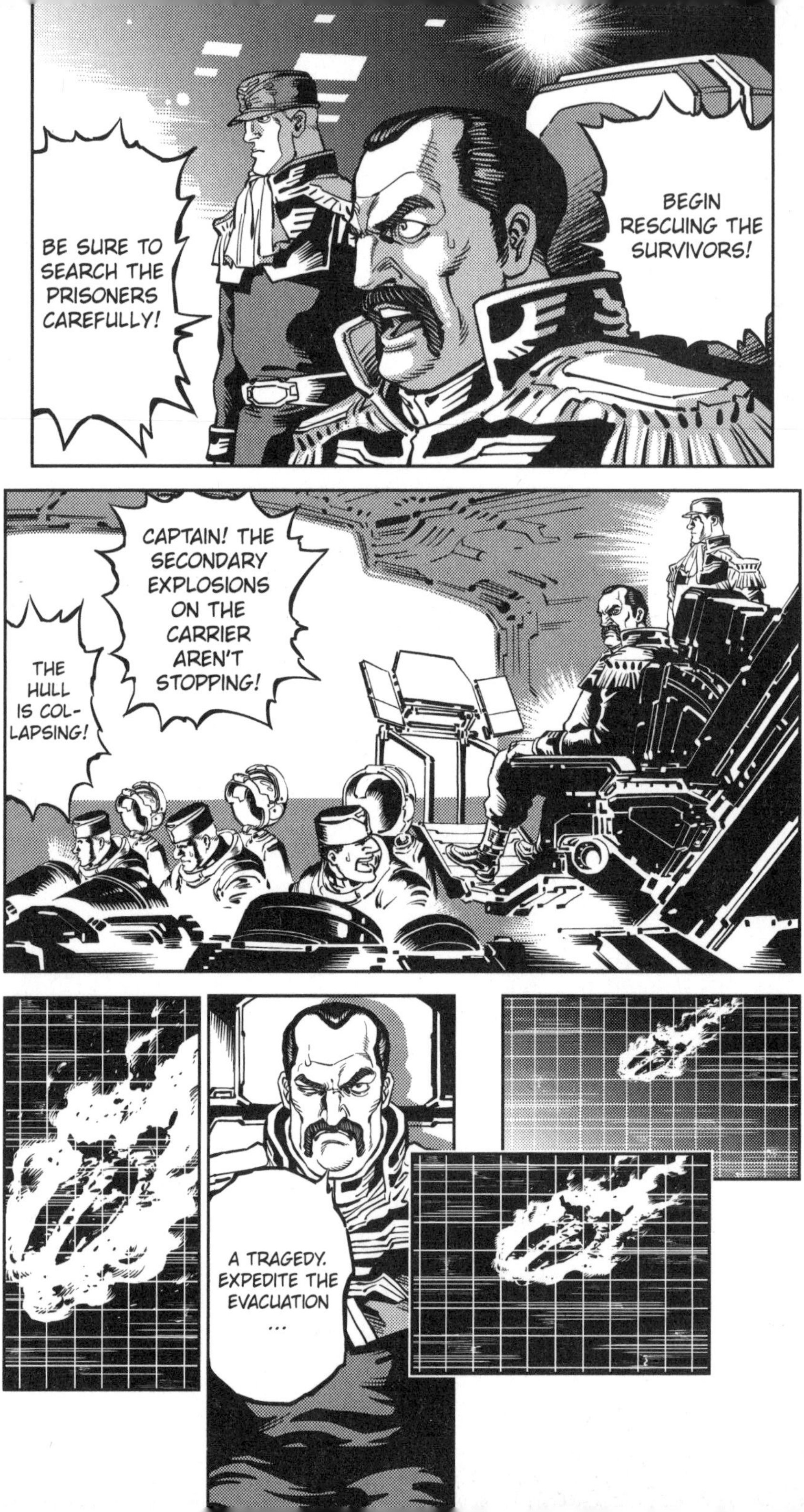
BEGIN RESCUING THE SURVIVORS!
BE SURE TO SEARCH THE PRISONERS CAREFULLY!
CAPTAIN! THE SECONDARY EXPLOSIONS ON THE CARRIER AREN'T STOPPING!
THE HULL IS COL-LAPSING!
A TRAGEDY. EXPEDITE THE EVACUATION ...

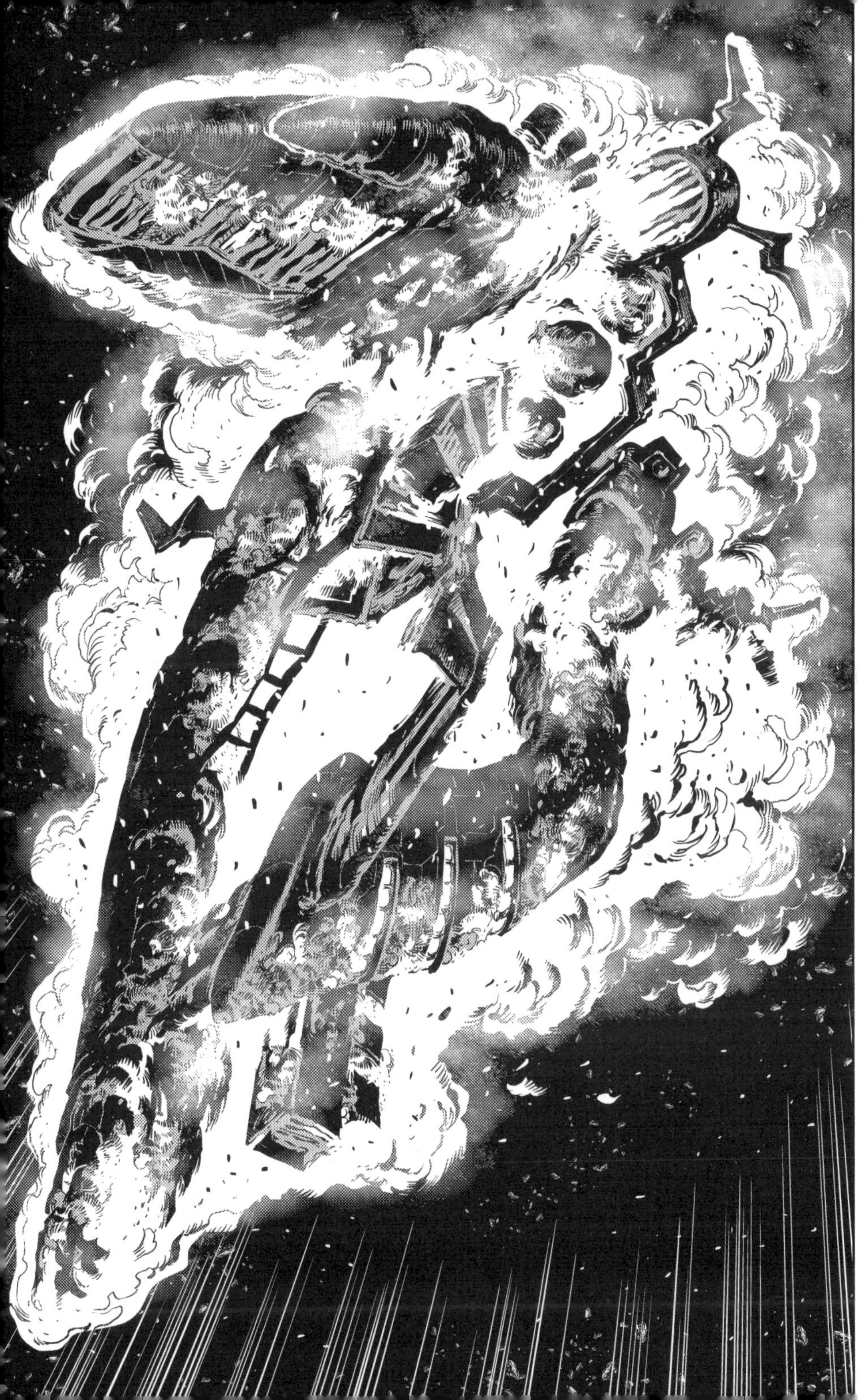

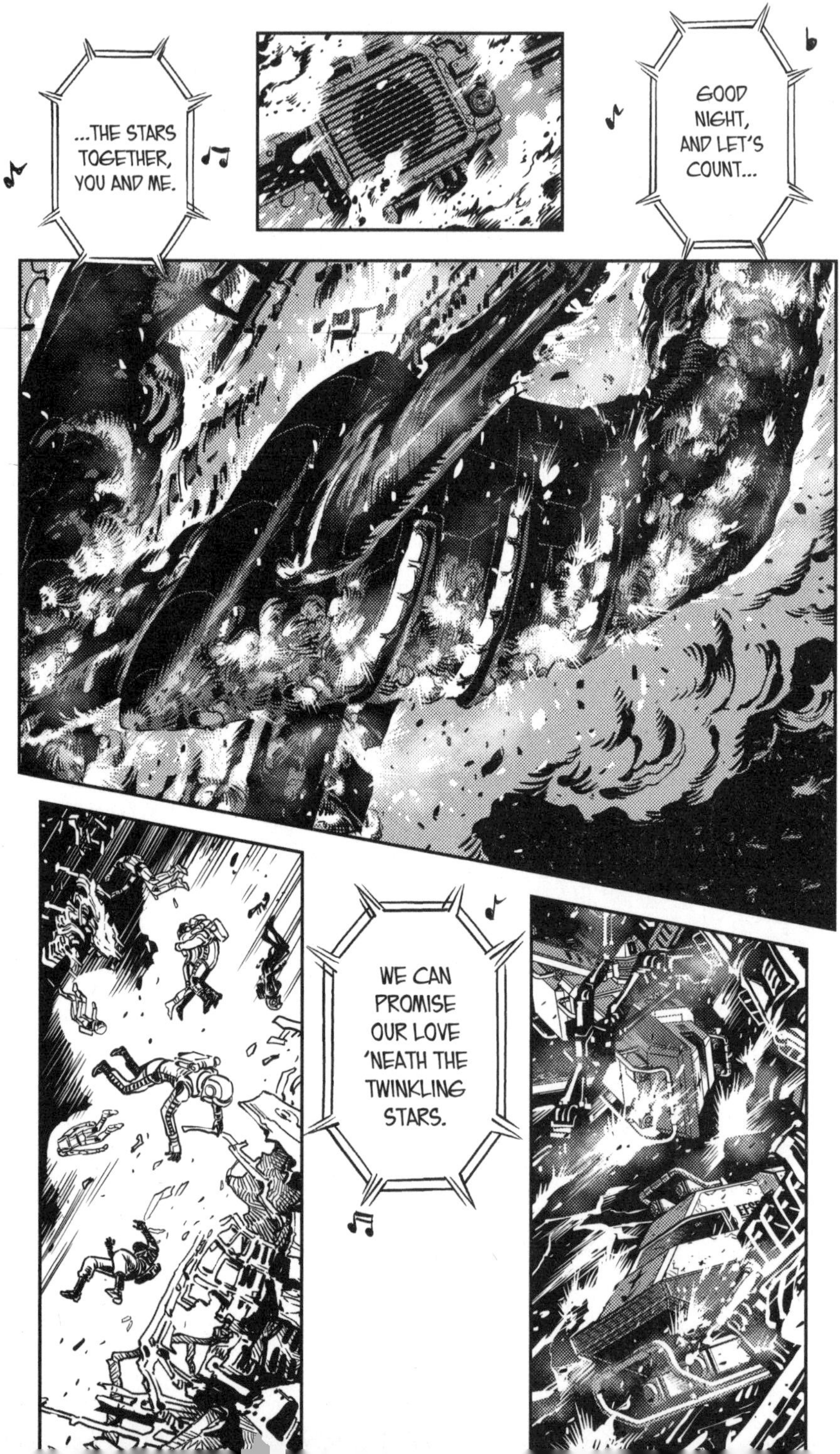
GOOD NIGHT, AND LET'S COUNT...
...THE STARS TOGETHER, YOU AND ME.
WE CAN PROMISE OUR LOVE 'NEATH THE TWINKLING STARS.

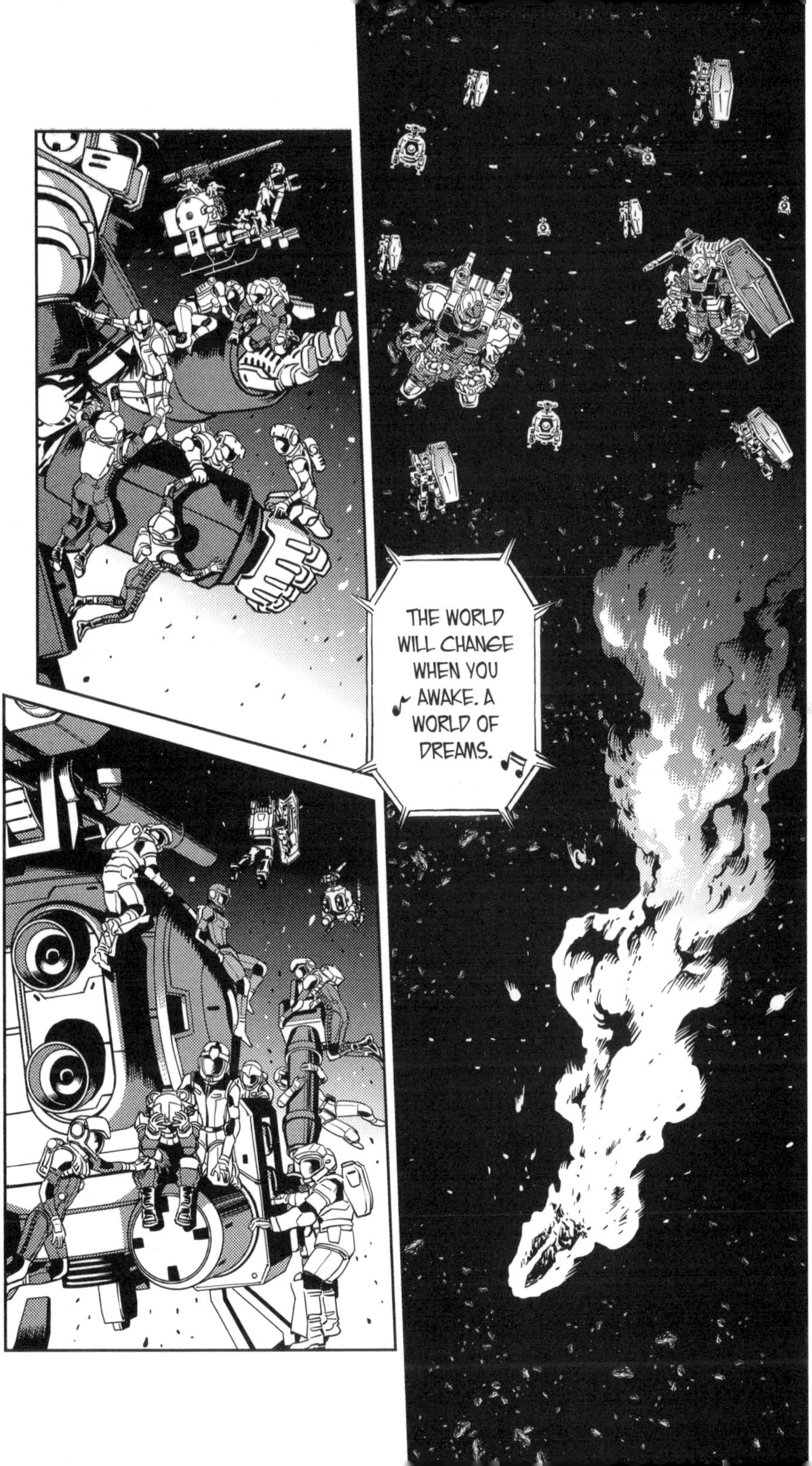
THE WORLD WILL CHANGE WHEN YOU AWAKE. A WORLD OF DREAMS.

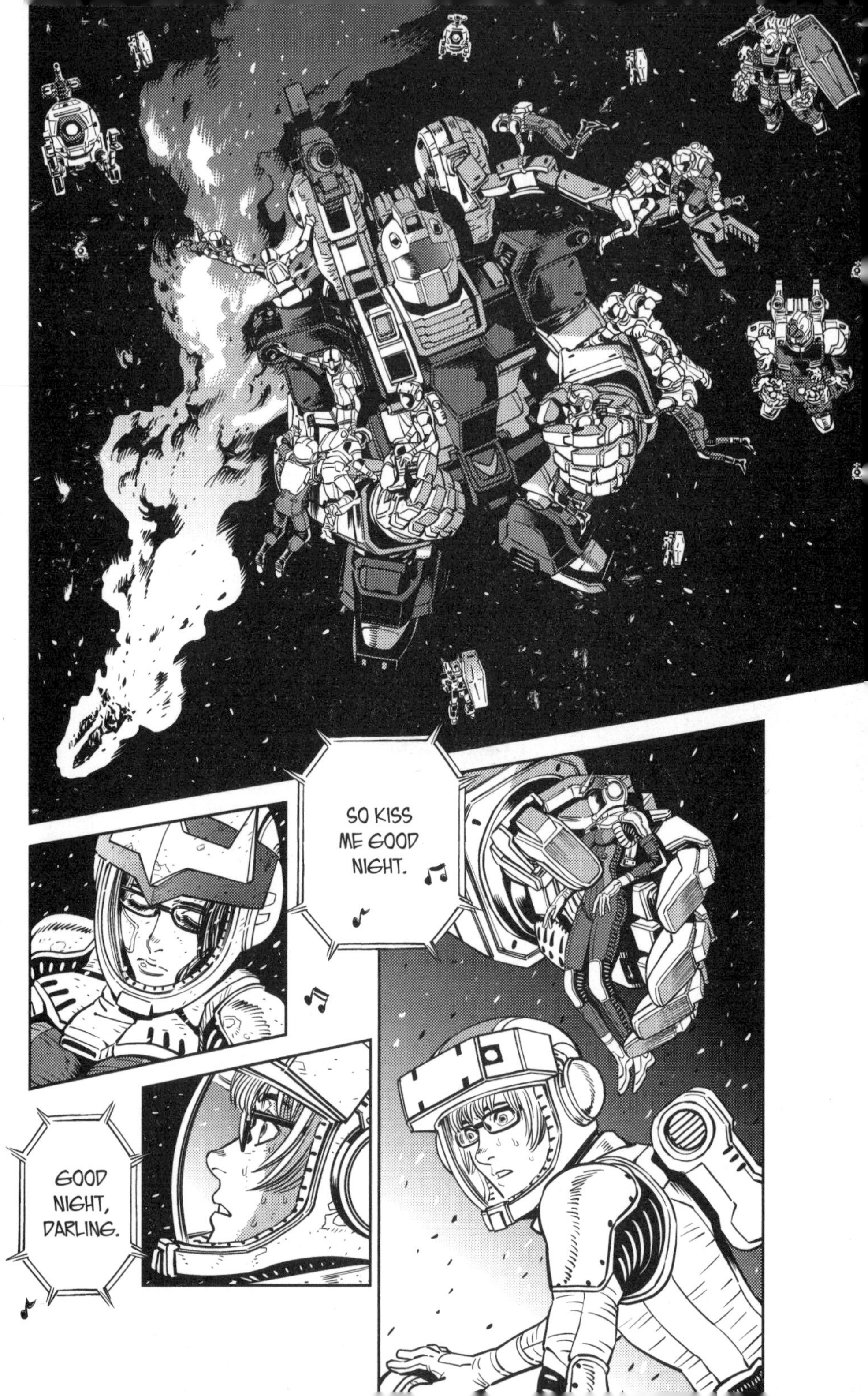
SO KISS ME GOOD NIGHT.
GOOD NIGHT, DARLING.

GOOD NIGHT,
SWEETHEART.
GOOD NIGHT...

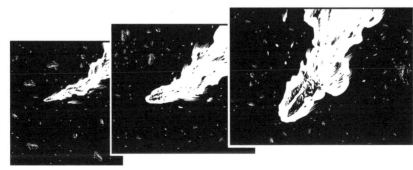

♫ GOOD NIGHT... ♪

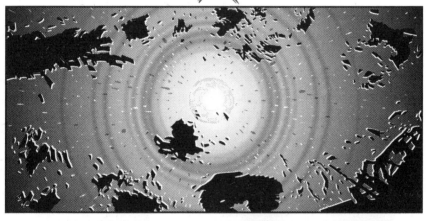

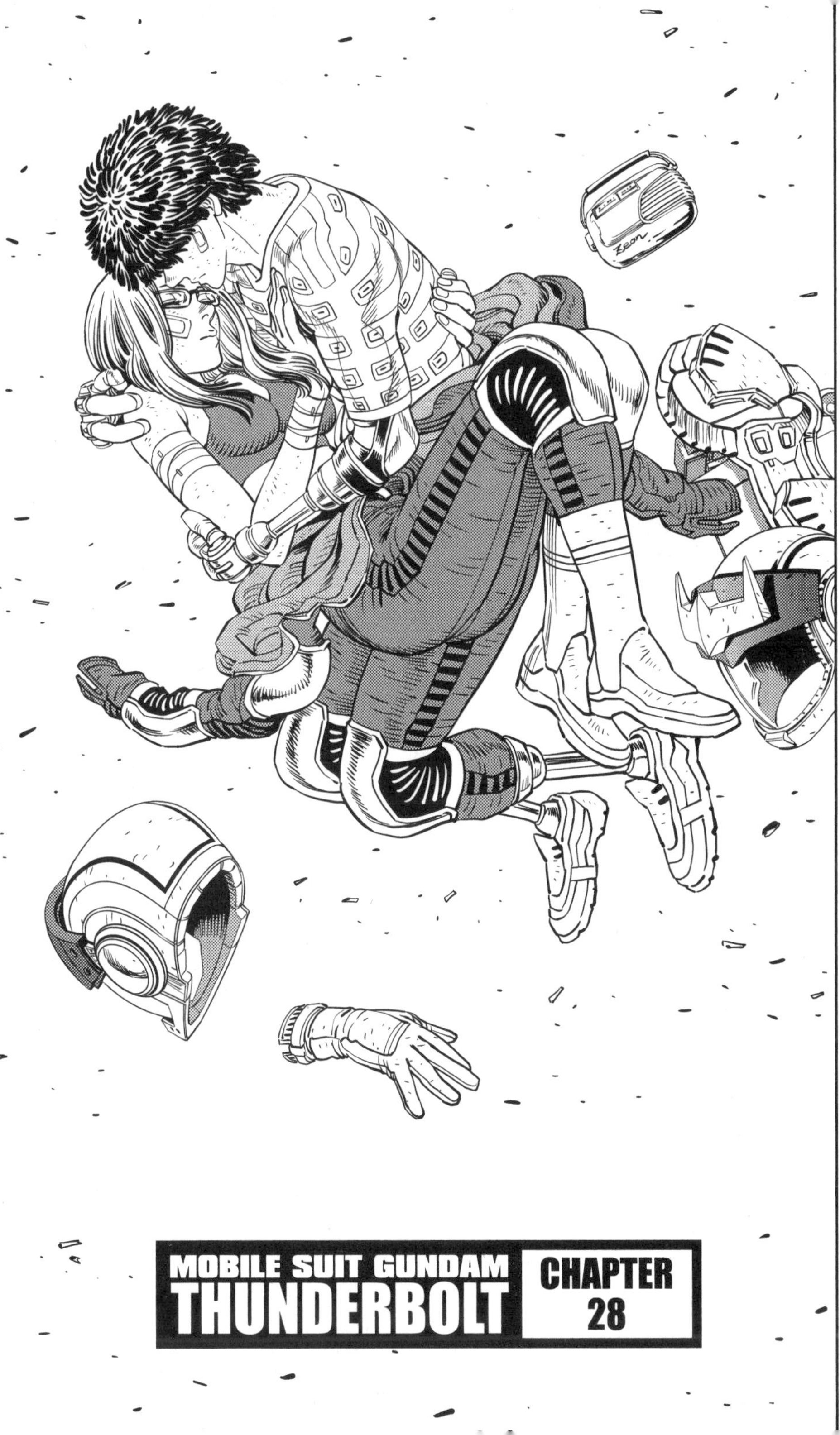
Zeon

MOBILE SUIT GUNDAM THUNDERBOLT

CHAPTER 28

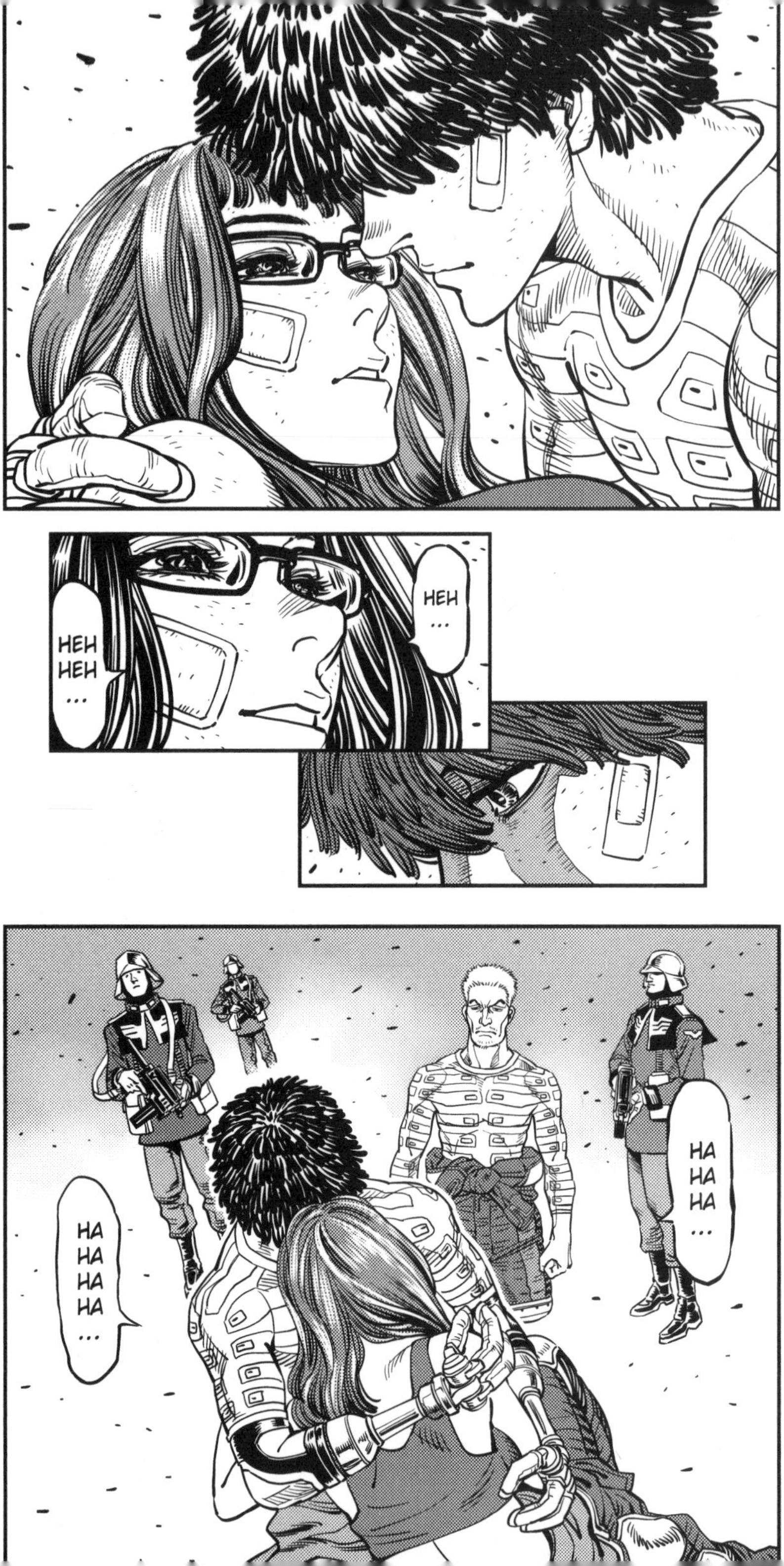
HEH ...
HEH HEH ...
HA HA HA ...
HA HA HA HA ...

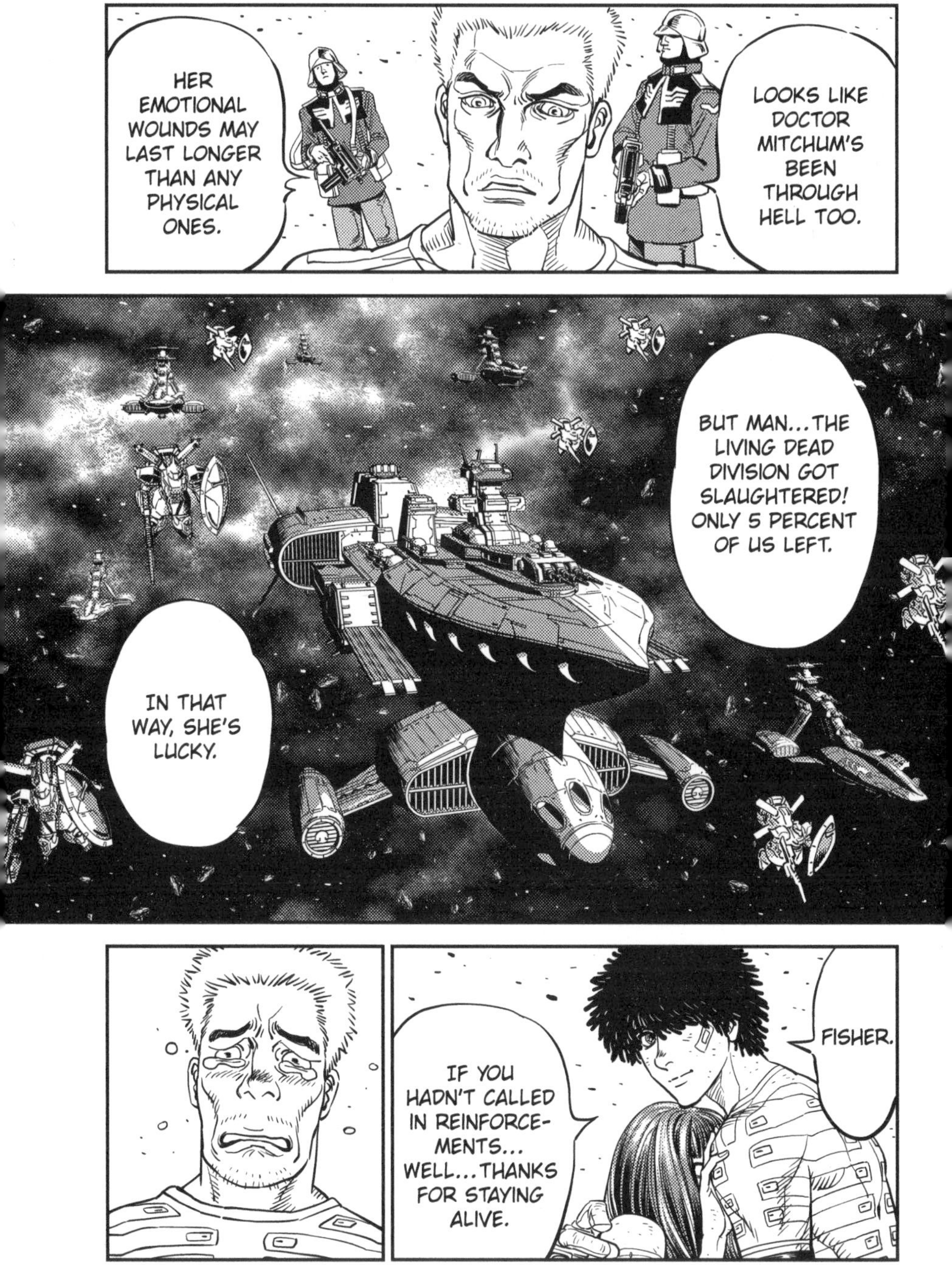
LOOKS LIKE DOCTOR MITCHUM'S BEEN THROUGH HELL TOO.
HER EMOTIONAL WOUNDS MAY LAST LONGER THAN ANY PHYSICAL ONES.
BUT MAN...THE LIVING DEAD DIVISION GOT SLAUGHTERED! ONLY 5 PERCENT OF US LEFT.
IN THAT WAY, SHE'S LUCKY.
FISHER.
IF YOU HADN'T CALLED IN REINFORCE-MENTS... WELL...THANKS FOR STAYING ALIVE.

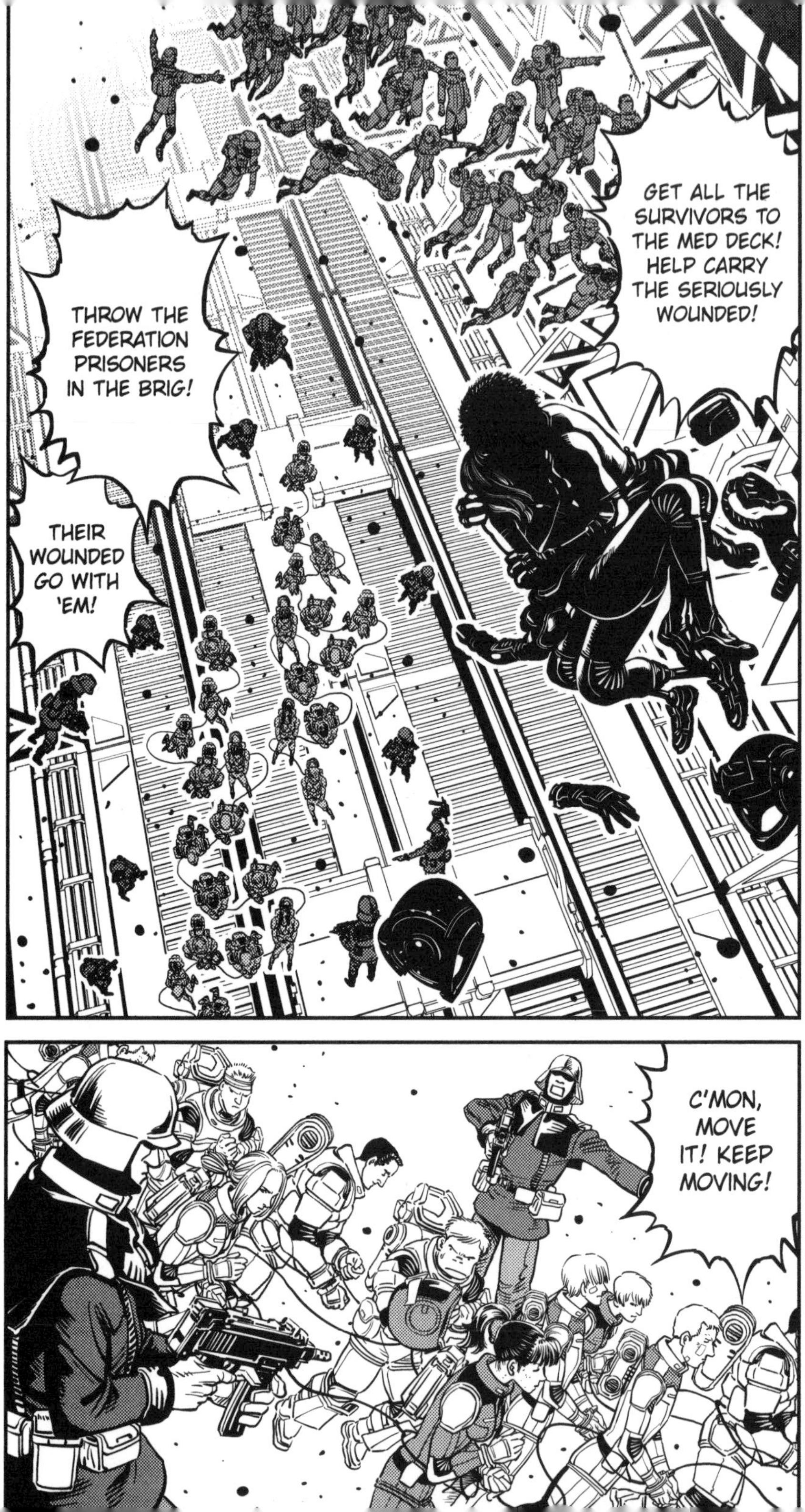
GET ALL THE SURVIVORS TO THE MED DECK! HELP CARRY THE SERIOUSLY WOUNDED!
THROW THE FEDERATION PRISONERS IN THE BRIG!
THEIR WOUNDED GO WITH 'EM!
C'MON, MOVE IT! KEEP MOVING!

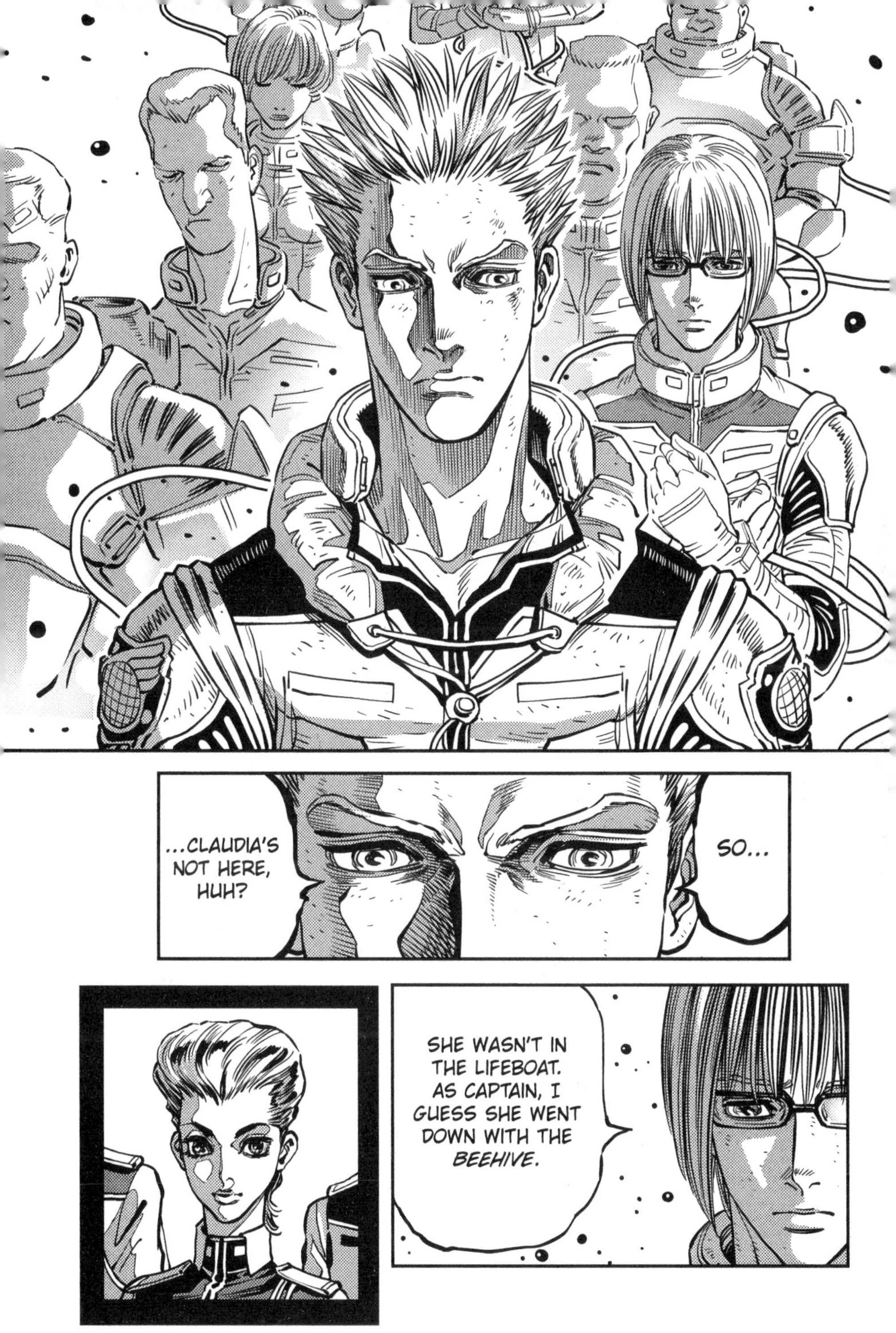
SO...
...CLAUDIA'S NOT HERE, HUH?
SHE WASN'T IN THE LIFEBOAT. AS CAPTAIN, I GUESS SHE WENT DOWN WITH THE *BEEHIVE*.

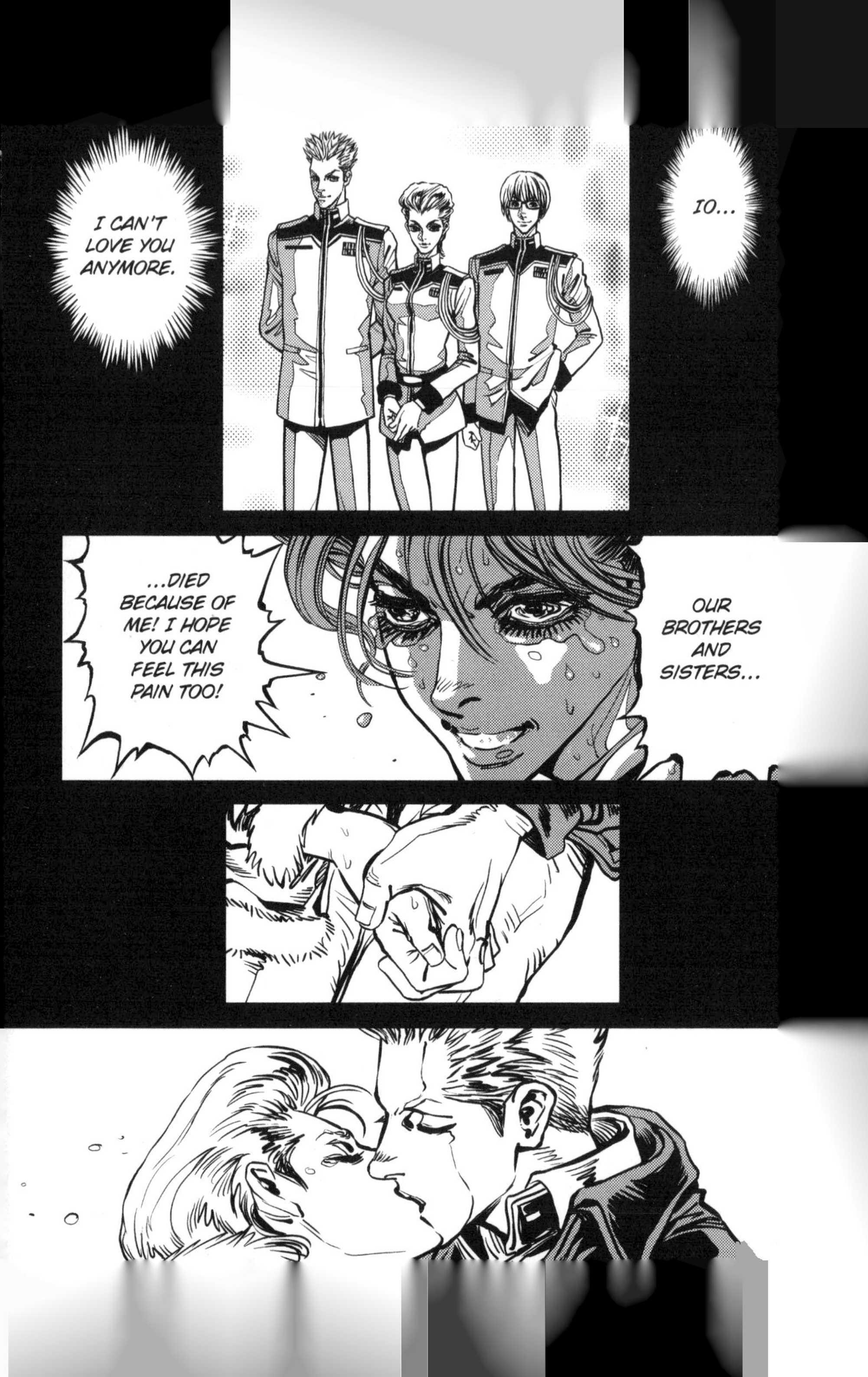
IO...
I CAN'T LOVE YOU ANYMORE.
OUR BROTHERS AND SISTERS...
...DIED BECAUSE OF ME! I HOPE YOU CAN FEEL THIS PAIN TOO!

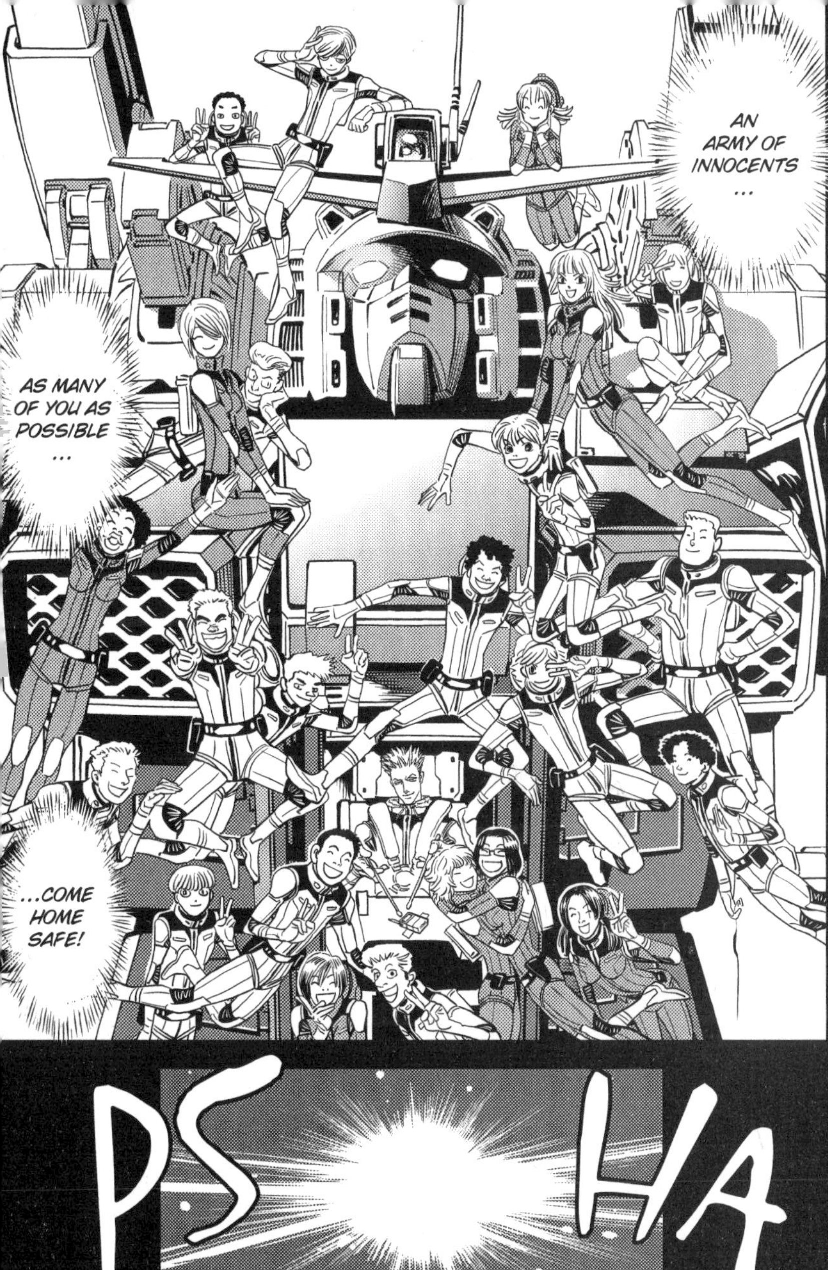
AN ARMY OF INNOCENTS ...
AS MANY OF YOU AS POSSIBLE ...
...COME HOME SAFE!
PSHA

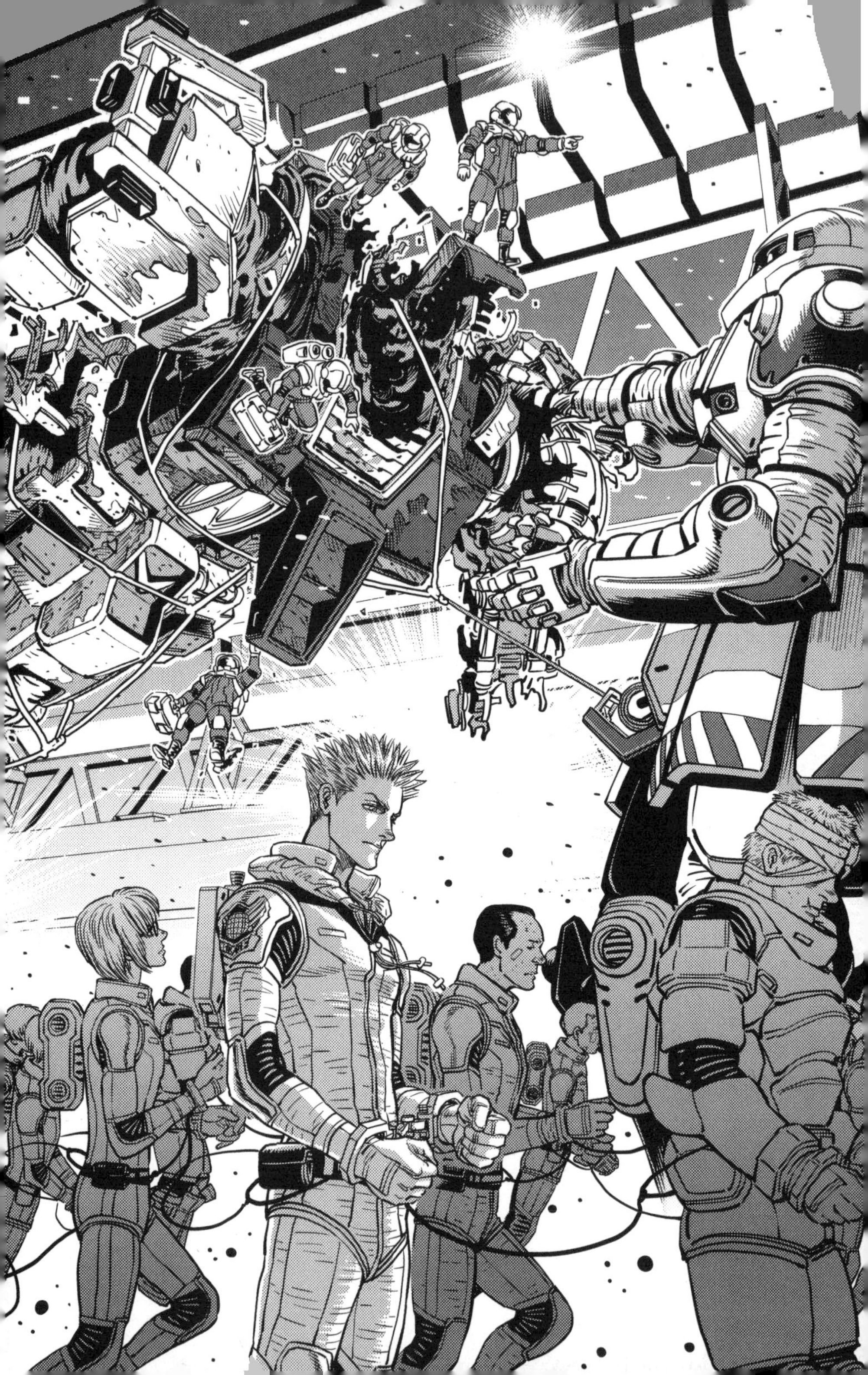

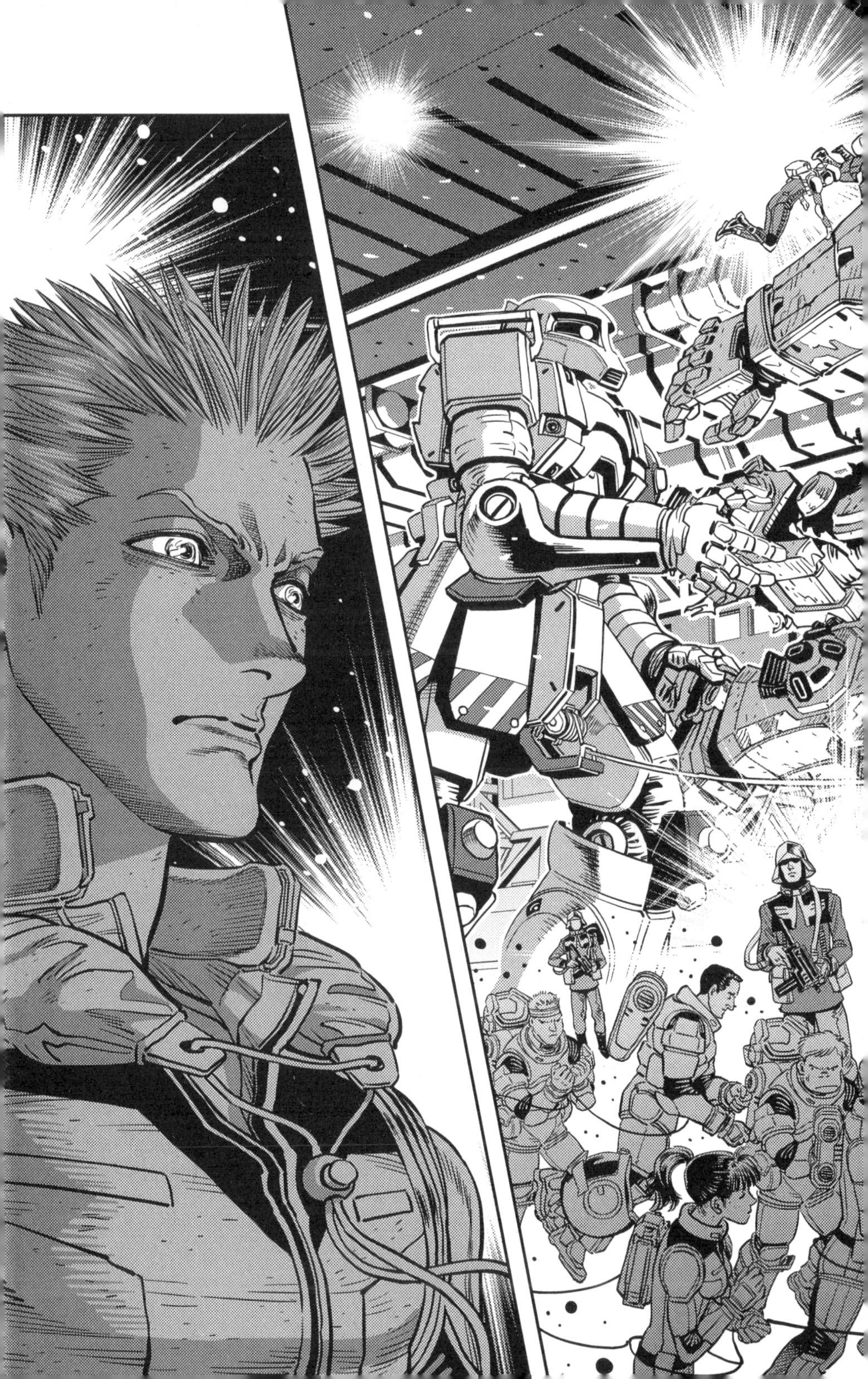

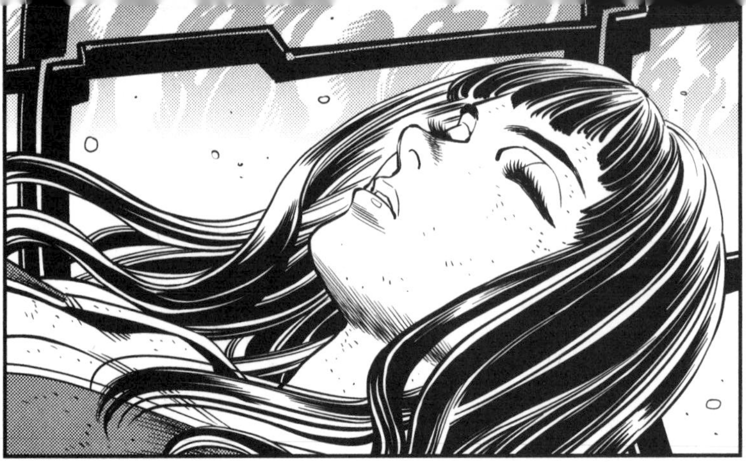
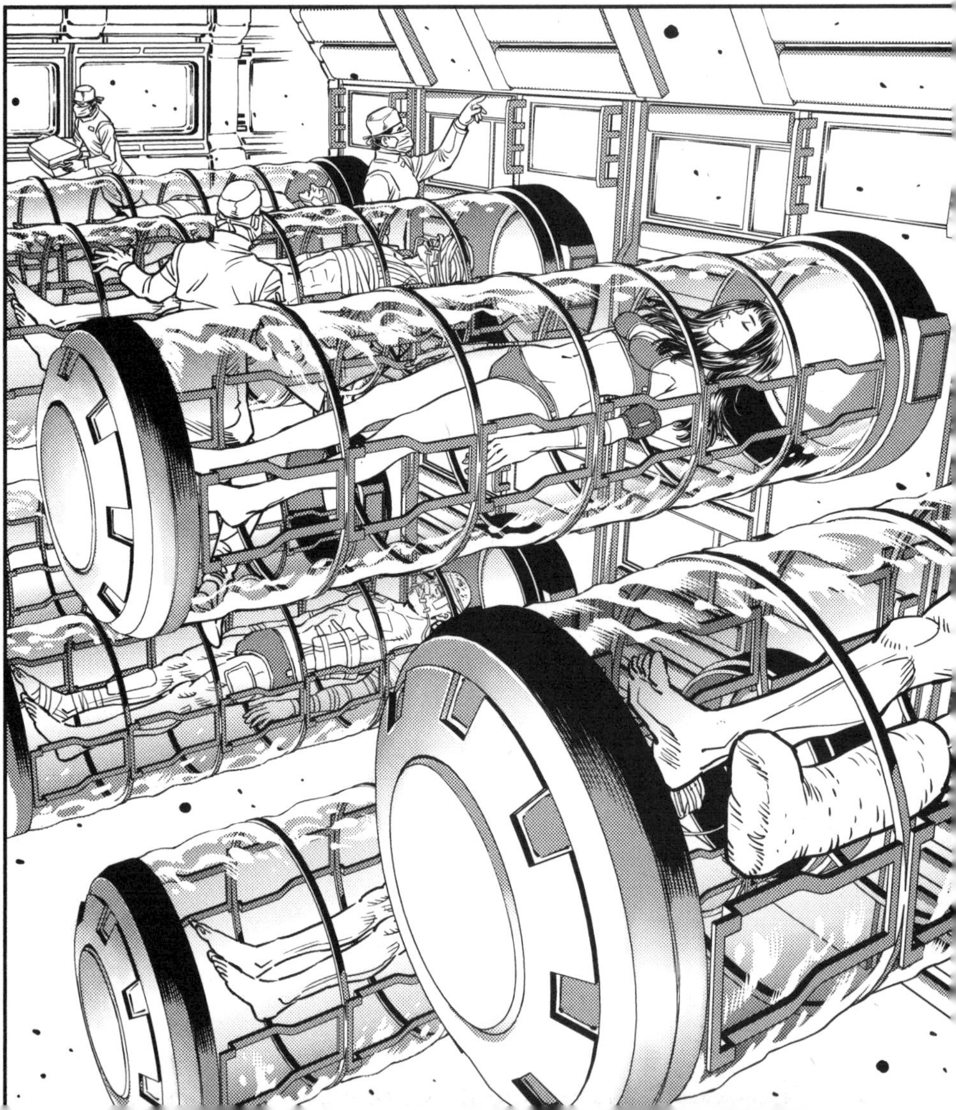

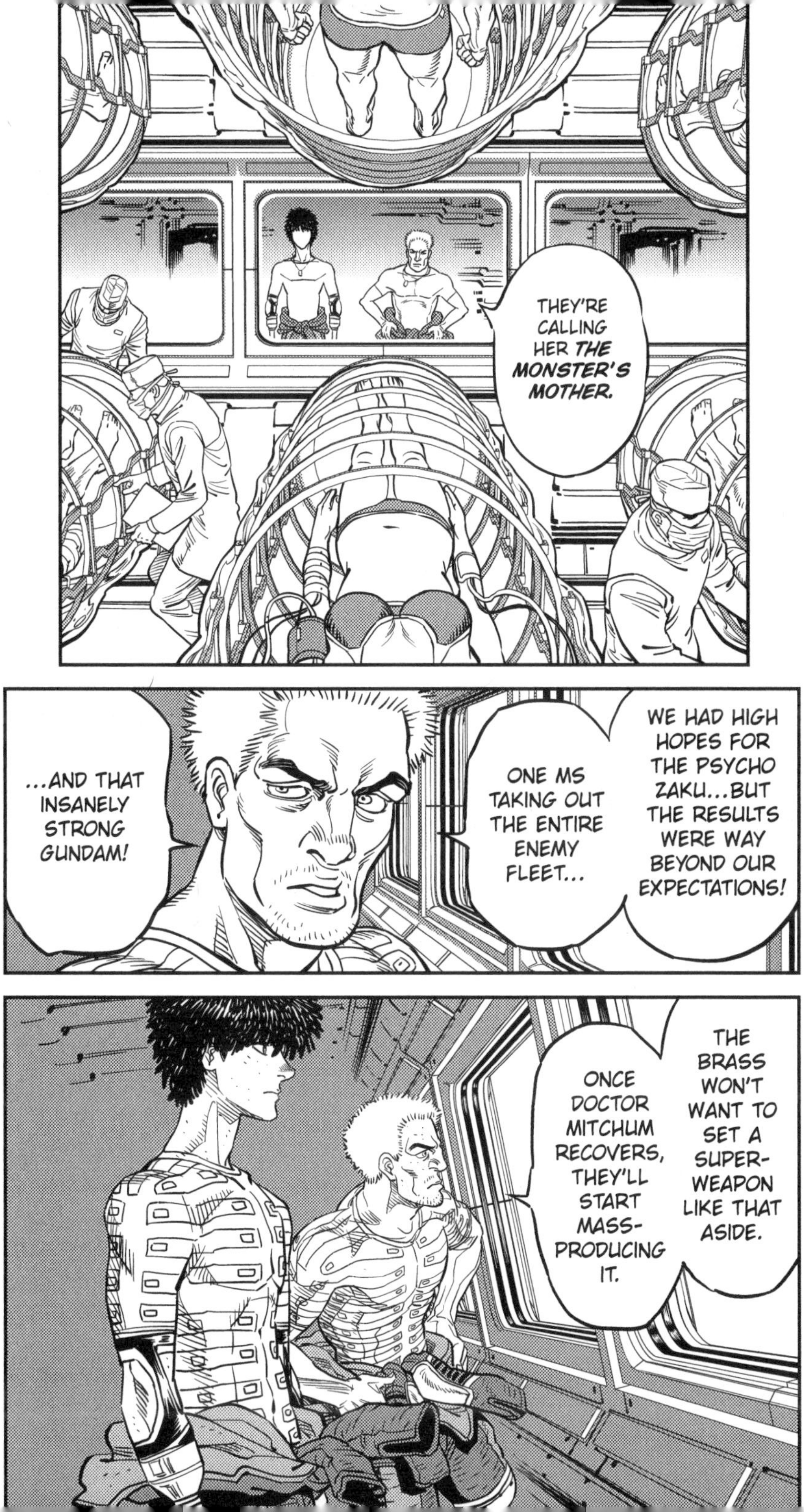
THEY'RE CALLING HER THE MONSTER'S MOTHER.
WE HAD HIGH HOPES FOR THE PSYCHO ZAKU...BUT THE RESULTS WERE WAY BEYOND OUR EXPECTATIONS!
ONE MS TAKING OUT THE ENTIRE ENEMY FLEET...
...AND THAT INSANELY STRONG GUNDAM!
THE BRASS WON'T WANT TO SET A SUPER-WEAPON LIKE THAT ASIDE.
ONCE DOCTOR MITCHUM RECOVERS, THEY'LL START MASS-PRODUCING IT.

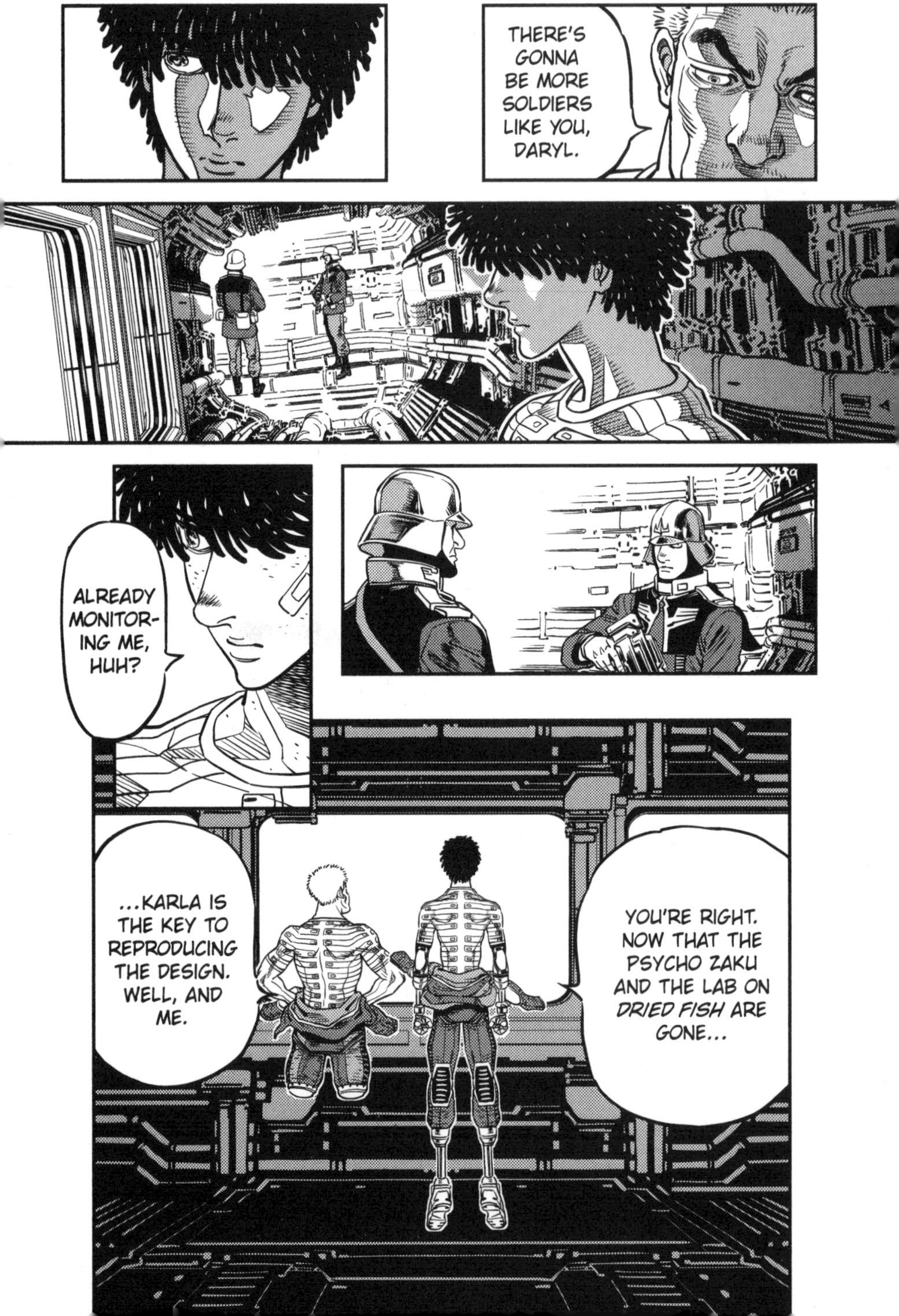
THERE'S GONNA BE MORE SOLDIERS LIKE YOU, DARYL.
ALREADY MONITORING-ING ME, HUH?
YOU'RE RIGHT. NOW THAT THE PSYCHO ZAKU AND THE LAB ON *DRIED FISH* ARE GONE...
...KARLA IS THE KEY TO REPRODUCING THE DESIGN. WELL, AND ME.

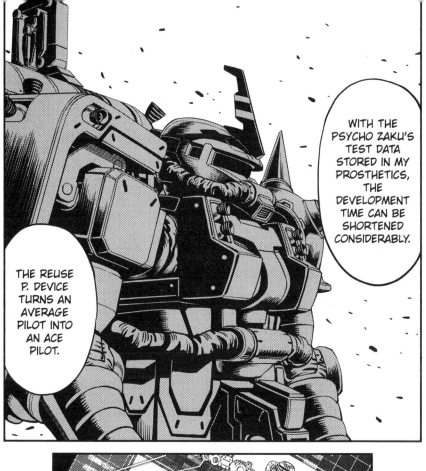

WITH THE PSYCHO ZAKU'S TEST DATA STORED IN MY PROSTHETICS, THE DEVELOPMENT TIME CAN BE SHORTENED CONSIDERABLY.
THE REUSE P. DEVICE TURNS AN AVERAGE PILOT INTO AN ACE PILOT.
XO-70923
7ACR
BUT ONLY IF THEY AMPUTATE ...
...THEIR LIMBS... LIKE ME.

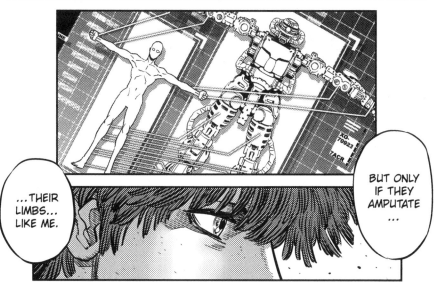

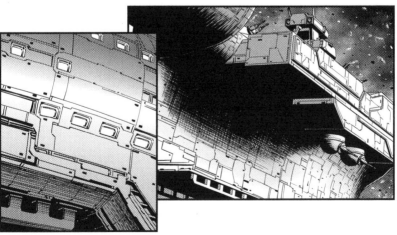

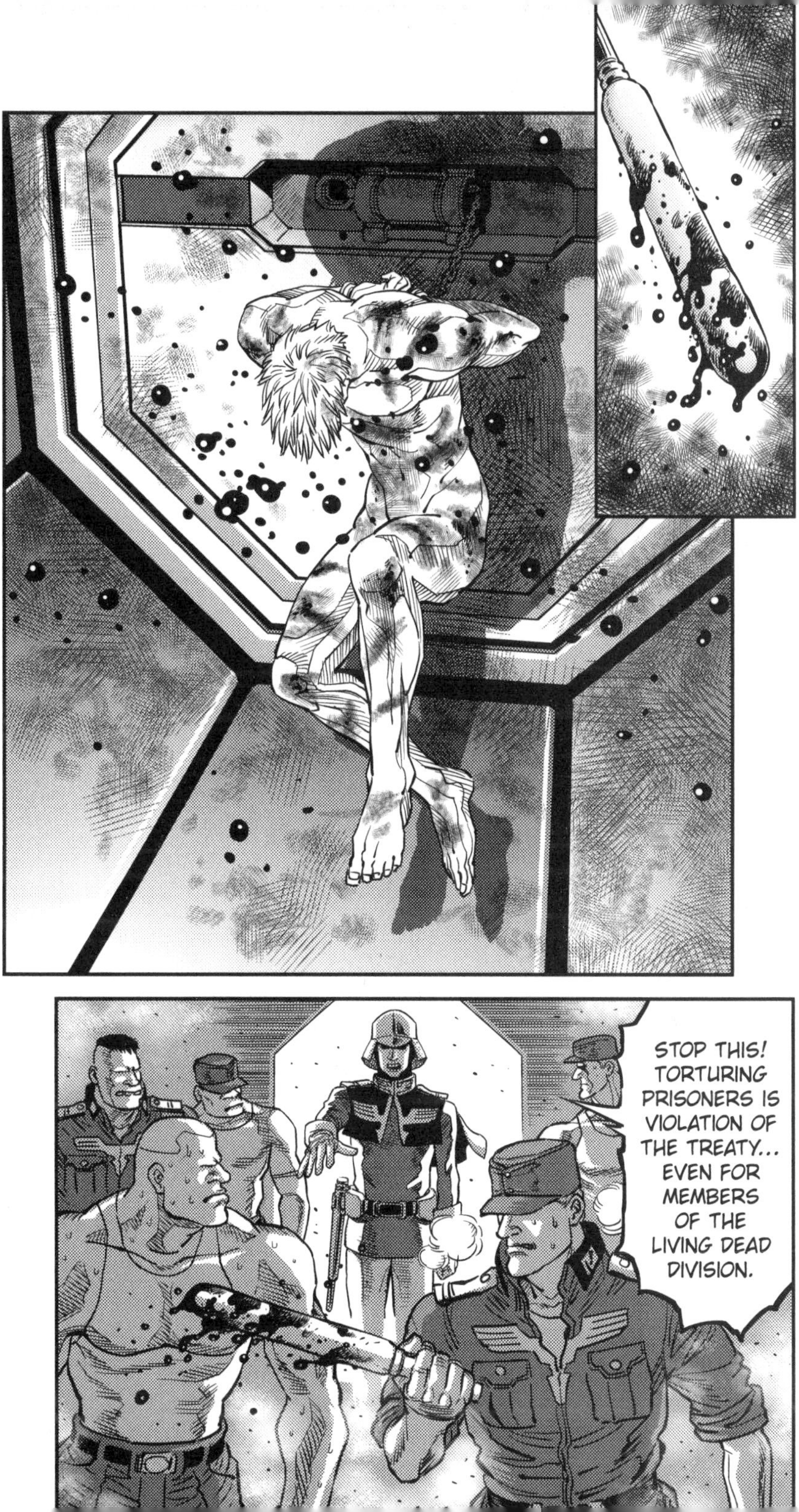
STOP THIS! TORTURING PRISONERS IS VIOLATION OF THE TREATY... EVEN FOR MEMBERS OF THE LIVING DEAD DIVISION.

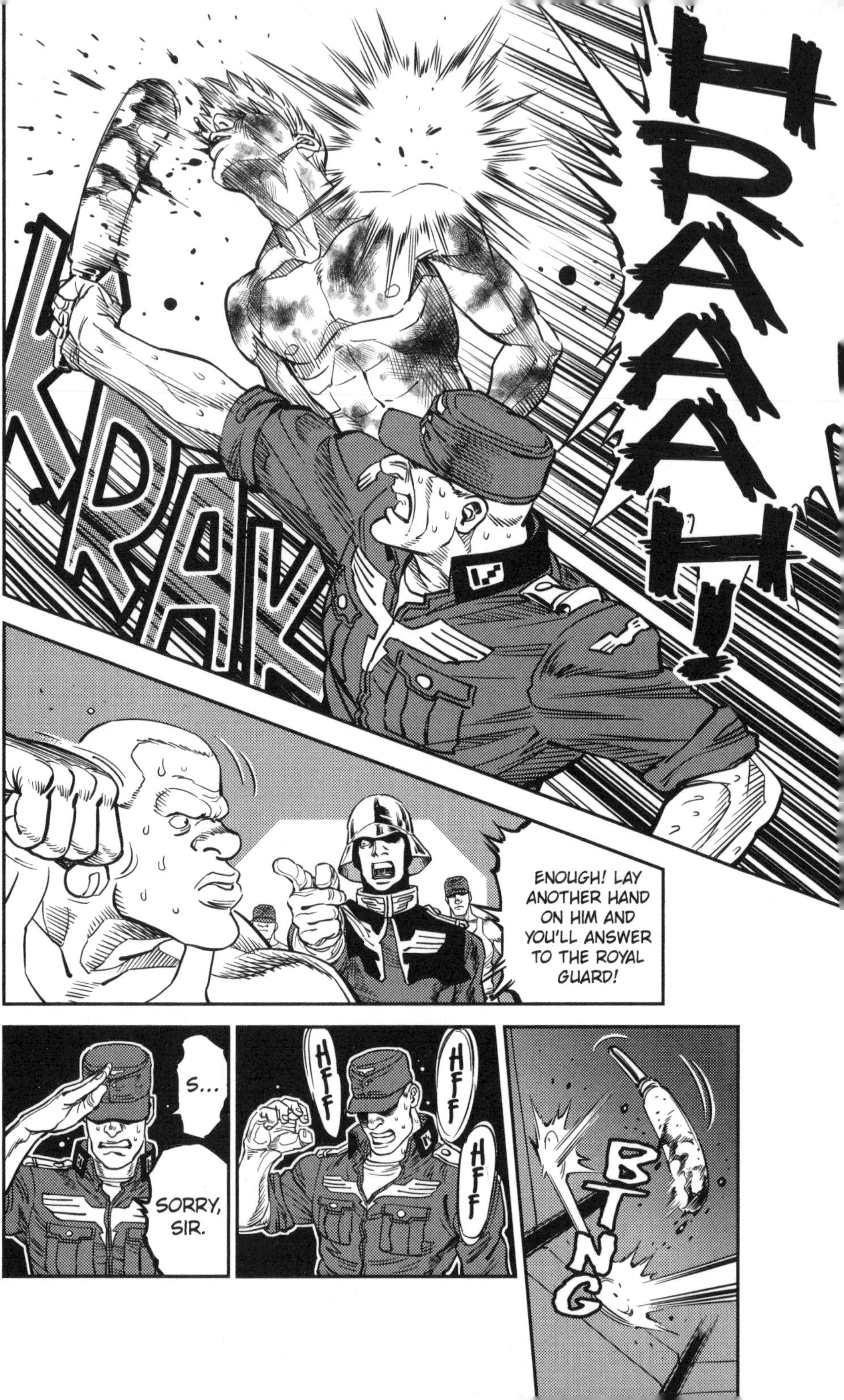
HRAAAH!
KRAK
ENOUGH! LAY ANOTHER HAND ON HIM AND YOU'LL ANSWER TO THE ROYAL GUARD!
BTNG
HFF
HFF
HFF
S...
SORRY, SIR.

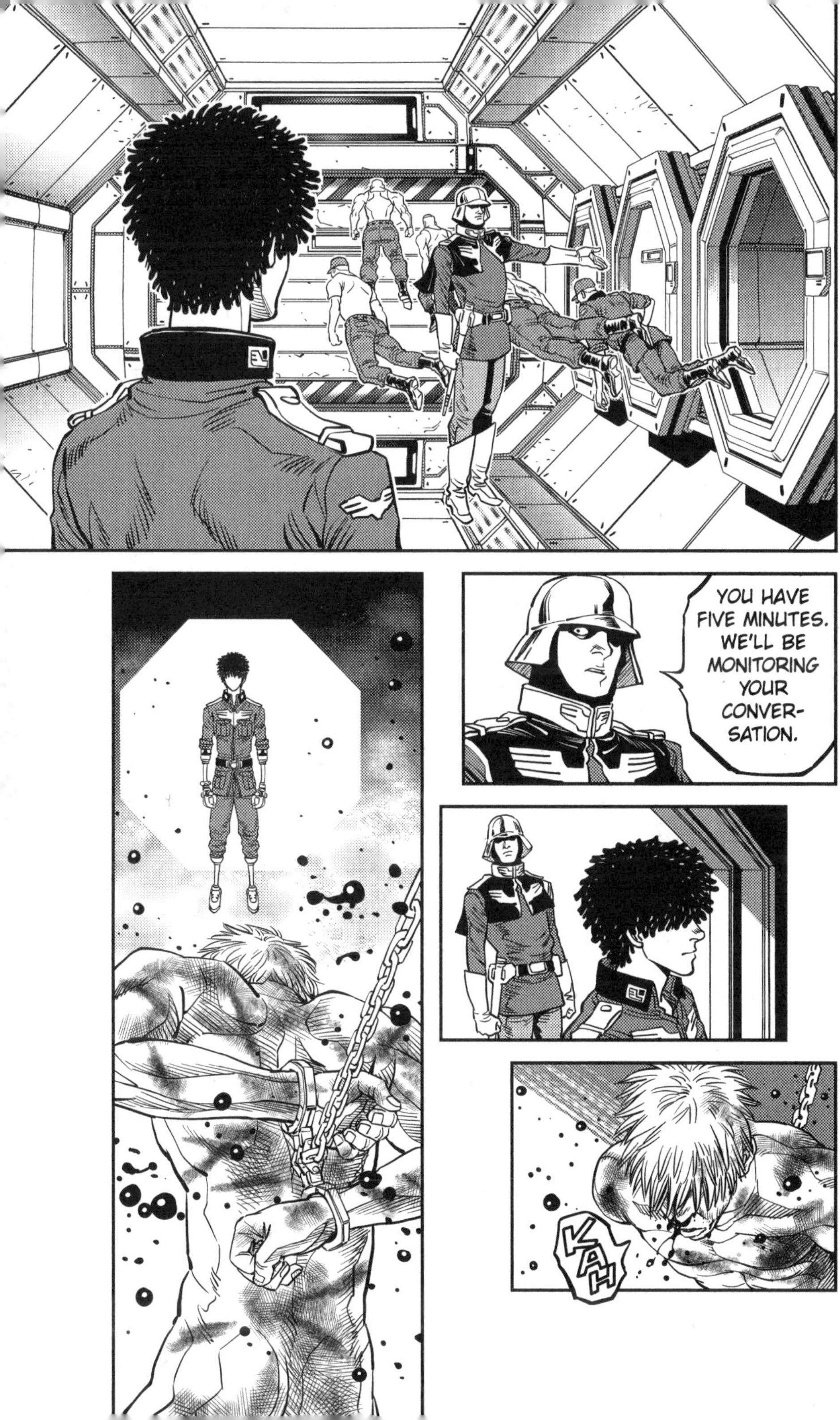
YOU HAVE FIVE MINUTES. WE'LL BE MONITORING YOUR CONVER-SATION.
KAH

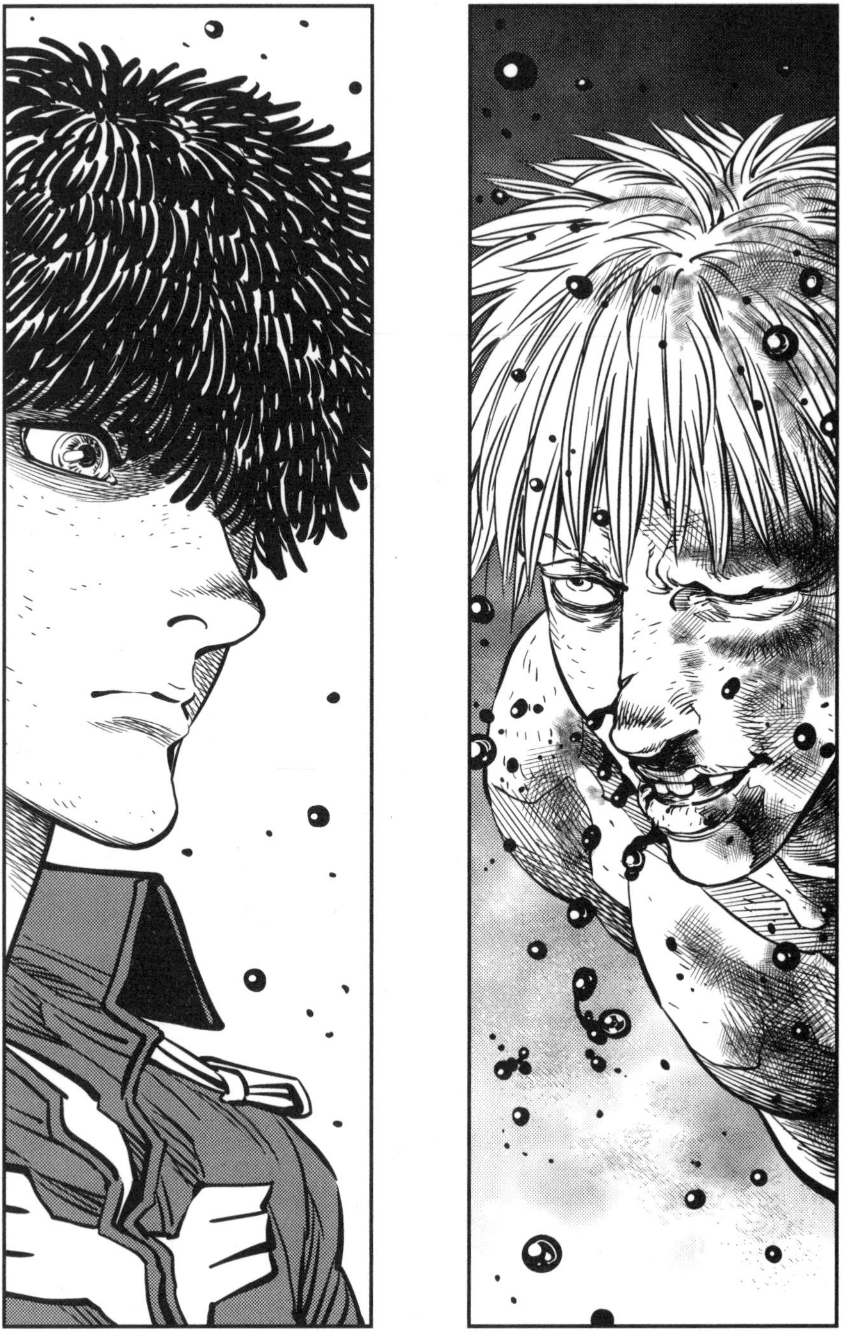

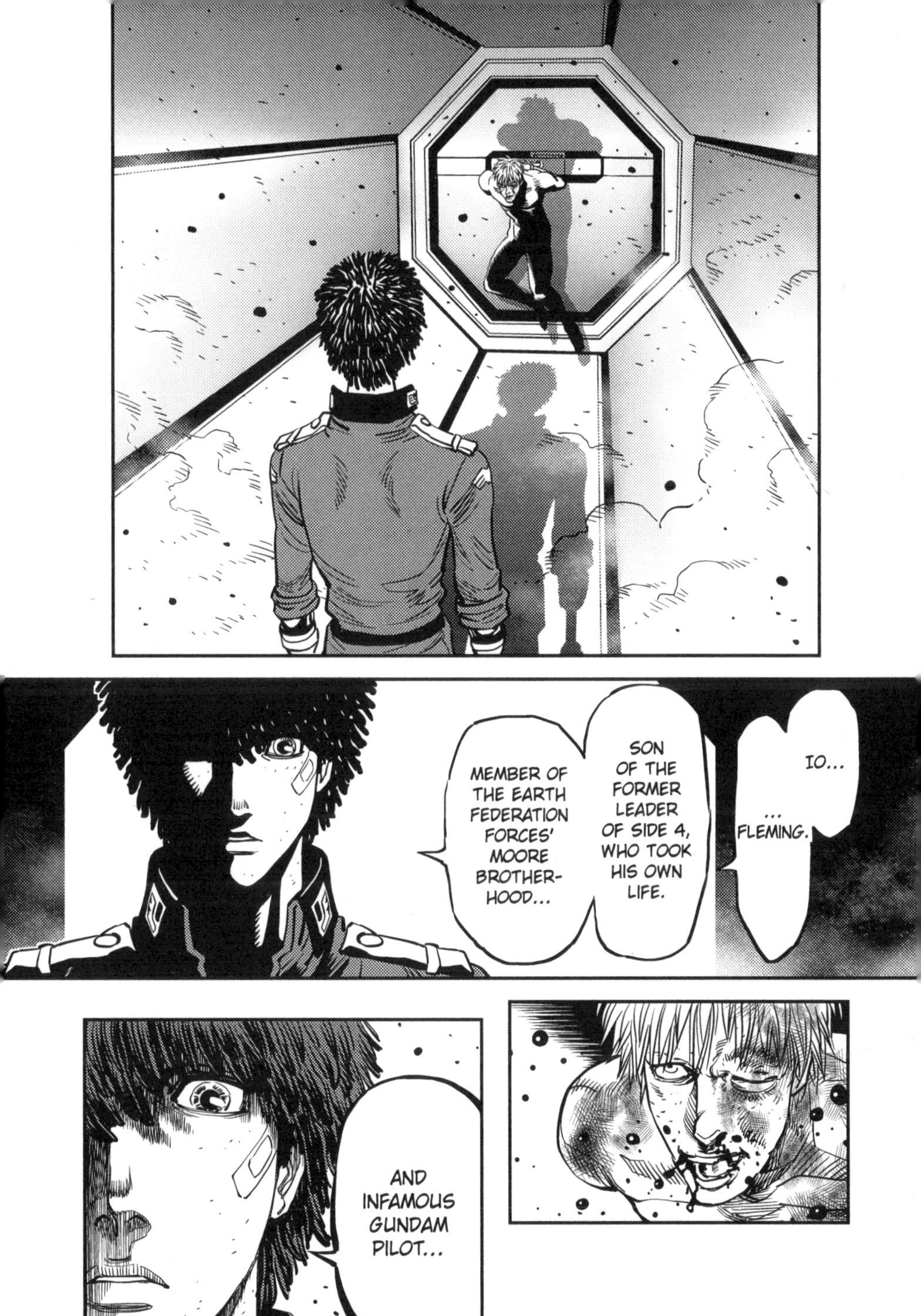
IO... ...FLEMING.
SON OF THE FORMER LEADER OF SIDE 4, WHO TOOK HIS OWN LIFE.
MEMBER OF THE EARTH FEDERATION FORCES' MOORE BROTHERHOOD...
AND INFAMOUS GUNDAM PILOT...

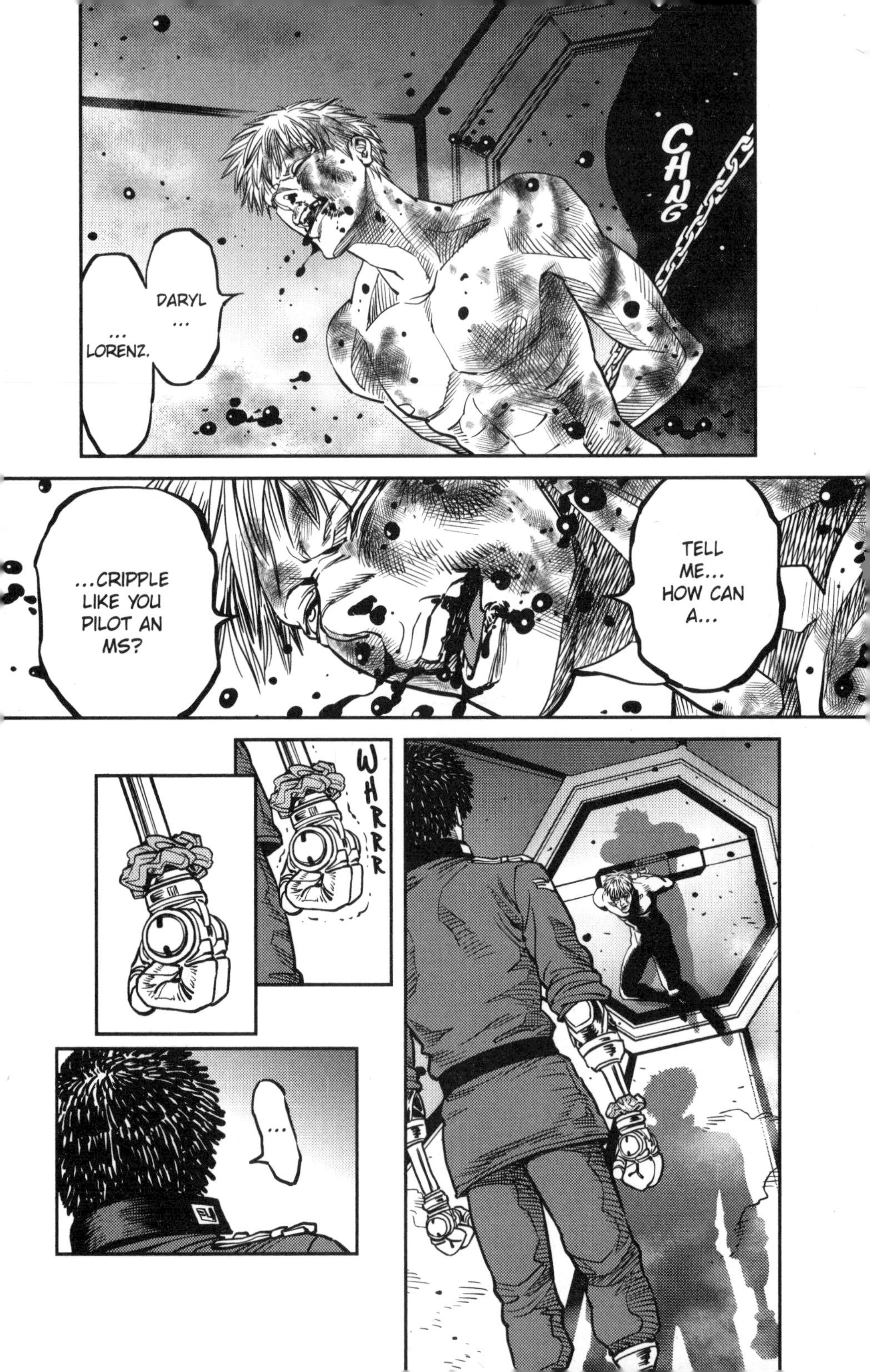
CHUNG
DARYL ... ... LORENZ.
TELL ME... HOW CAN A...
...CRIPPLE LIKE YOU PILOT AN MS?
WHRRRR
...

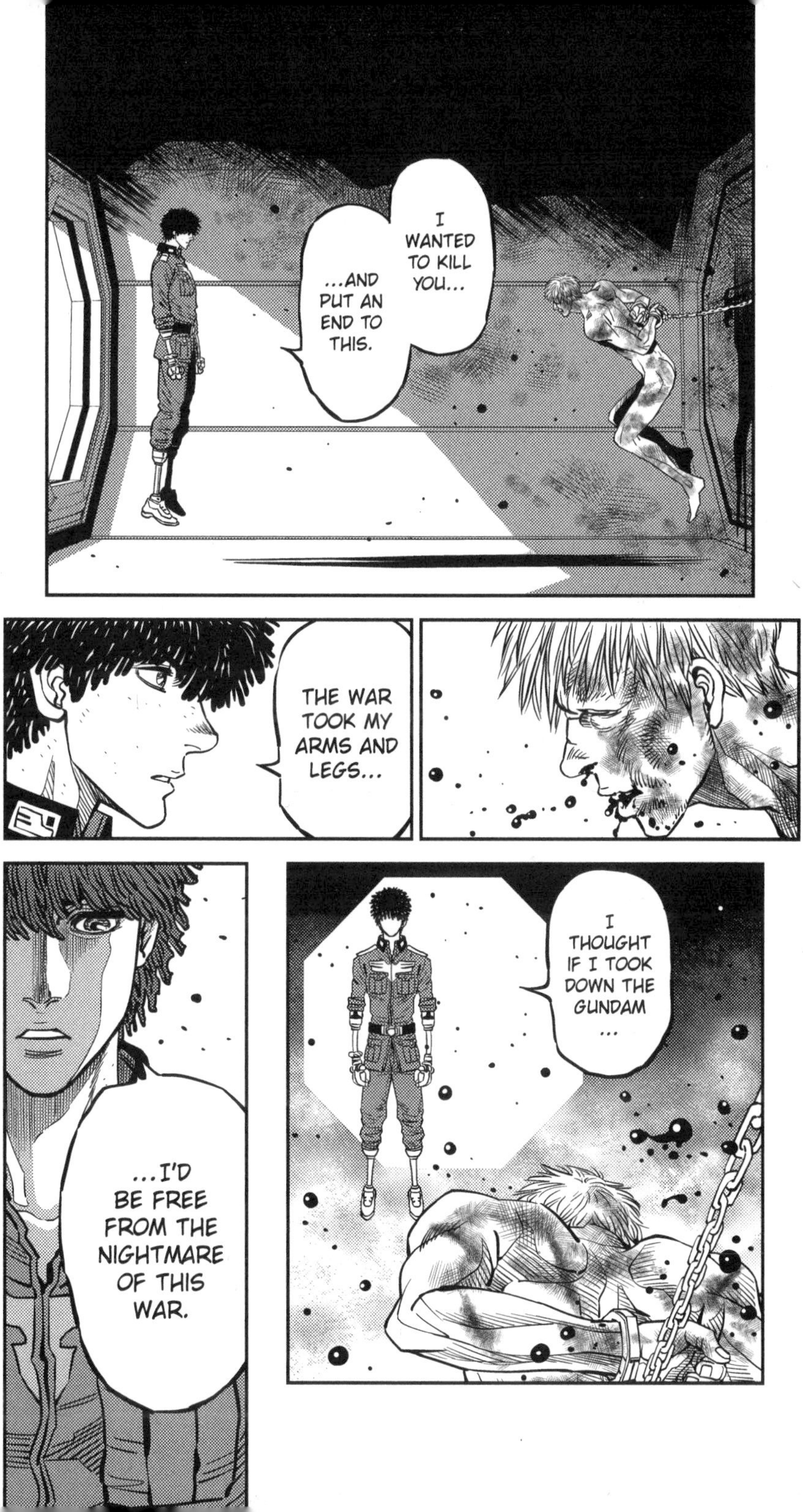
I WANTED TO KILL YOU...
...AND PUT AN END TO THIS.
THE WAR TOOK MY ARMS AND LEGS...
I THOUGHT IF I TOOK DOWN THE GUNDAM ...
...I'D BE FREE FROM THE NIGHTMARE OF THIS WAR.

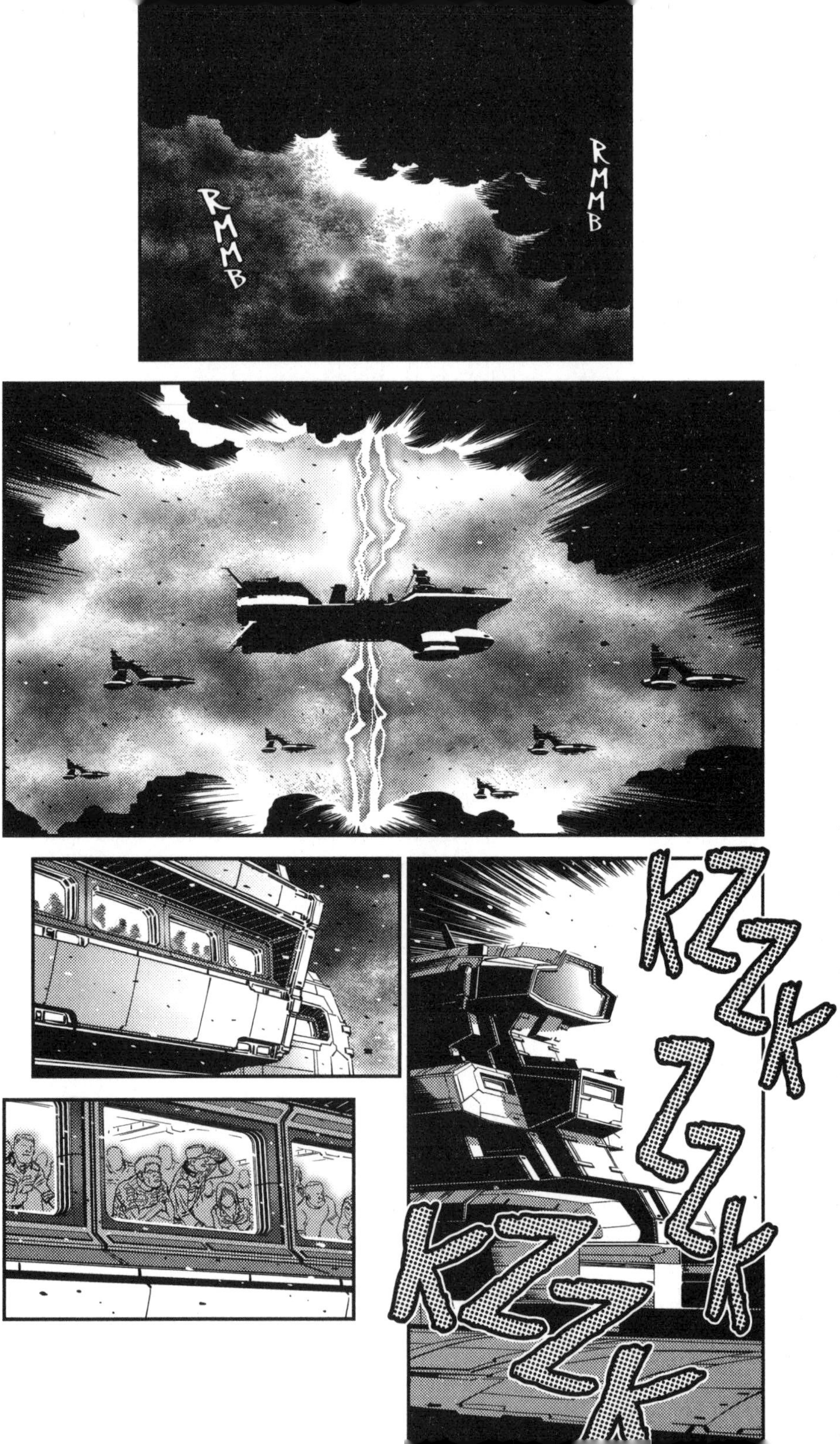
RMMB
RMMB
KZZK
ZZK
KZZZK

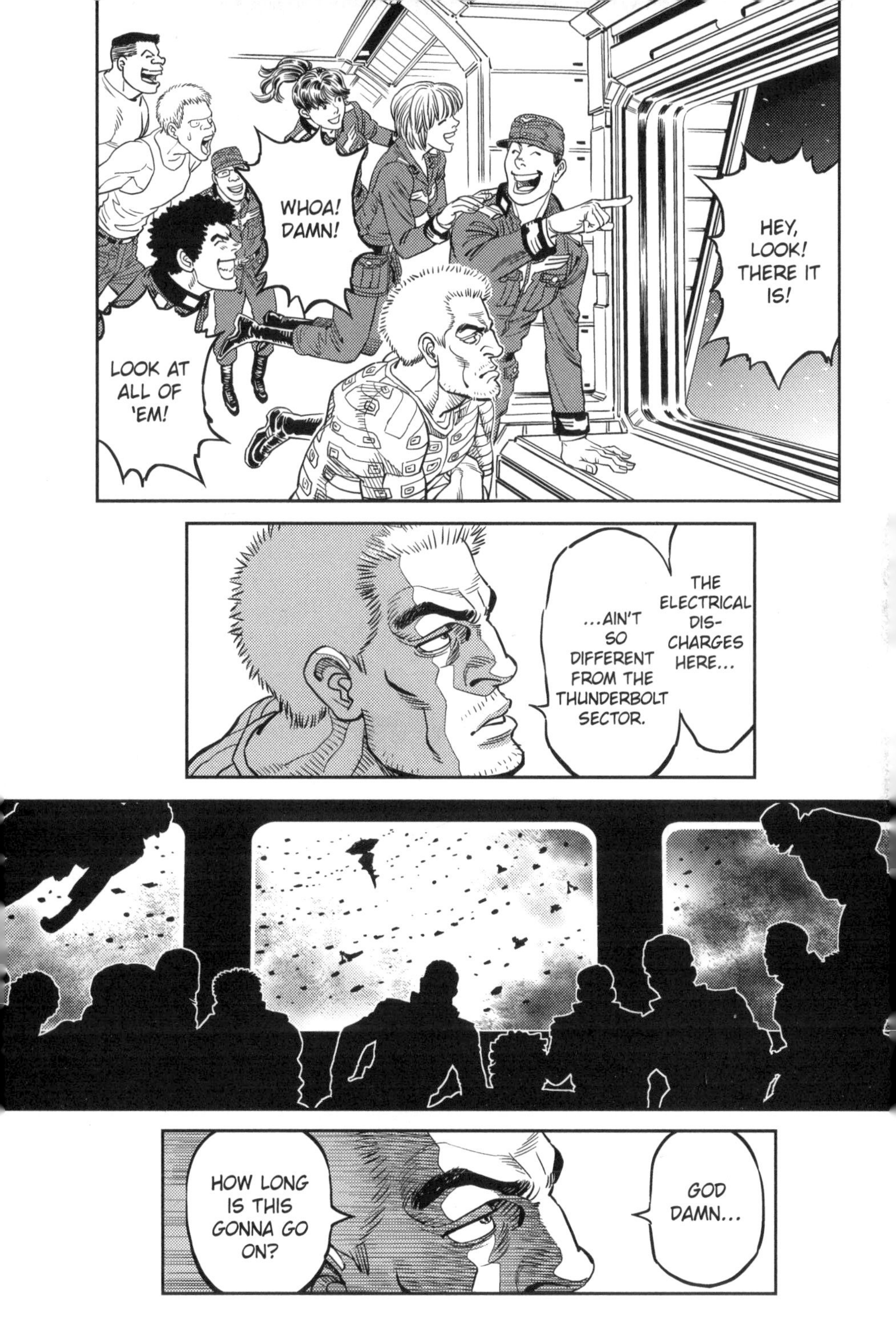
HEY, LOOK! THERE IT IS!
WHOA! DAMN!
LOOK AT ALL OF 'EM!
THE ELECTRICAL DIS-CHARGES HERE...
...AIN'T SO DIFFERENT FROM THE THUNDERBOLT SECTOR.
GOD DAMN...
HOW LONG IS THIS GONNA GO ON?

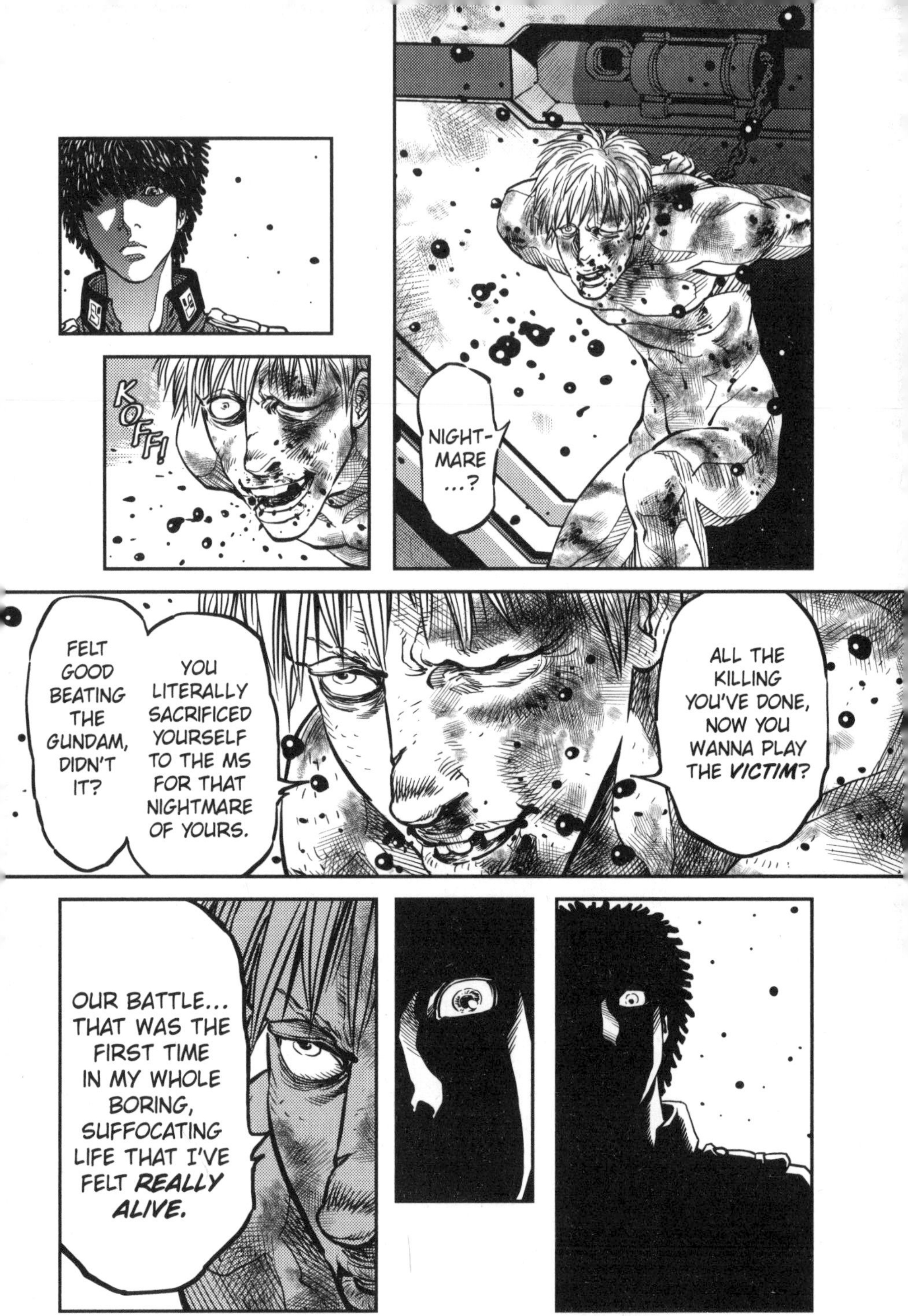
NIGHT-MARE ...?
KOFF!
ALL THE KILLING YOU'VE DONE, NOW YOU WANNA PLAY THE *VICTIM*?
YOU LITERALLY SACRIFICED YOURSELF TO THE MS FOR THAT NIGHTMARE OF YOURS.
FELT GOOD BEATING THE GUNDAM, DIDN'T IT?
OUR BATTLE... THAT WAS THE FIRST TIME IN MY WHOLE BORING, SUFFOCATING LIFE THAT I'VE FELT *REALLY ALIVE.*

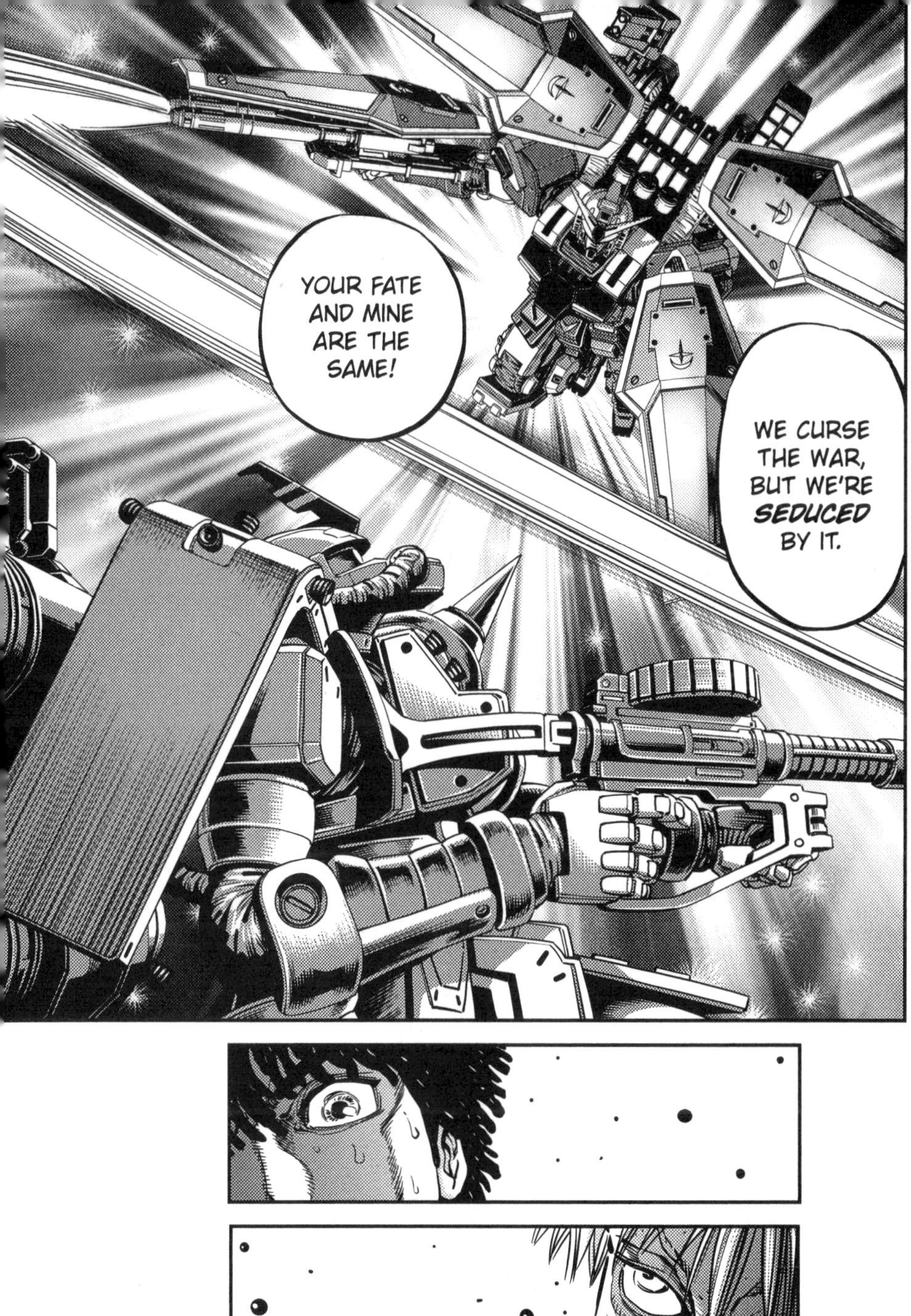
WE CURSE THE WAR, BUT WE'RE SEDUCED BY IT.
YOUR FATE AND MINE ARE THE SAME!

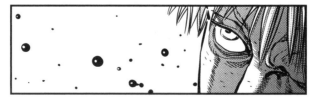

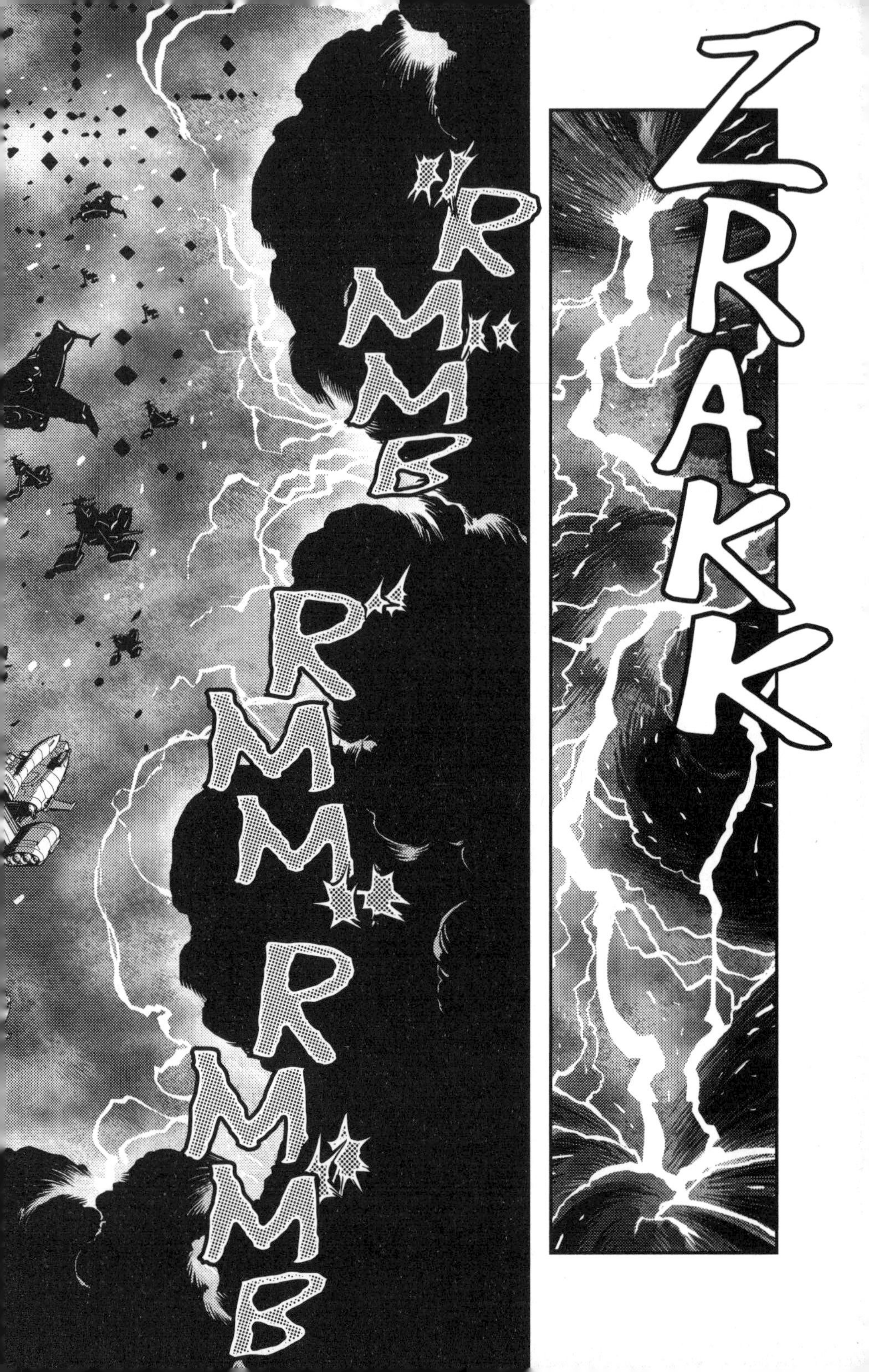
ZRAKK
RMMB
RMMRMMB

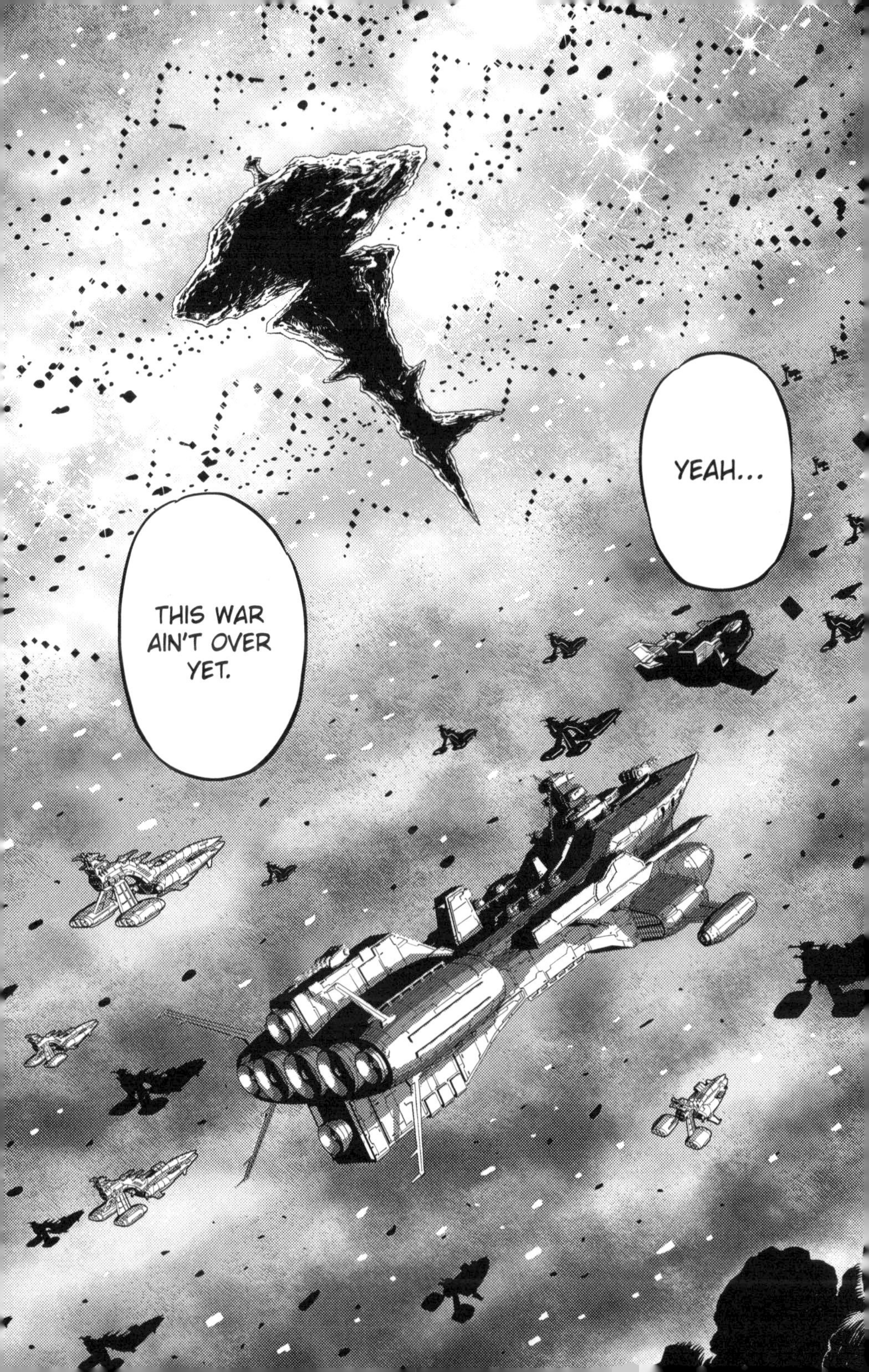
YEAH...
THIS WAR AIN'T OVER YET.

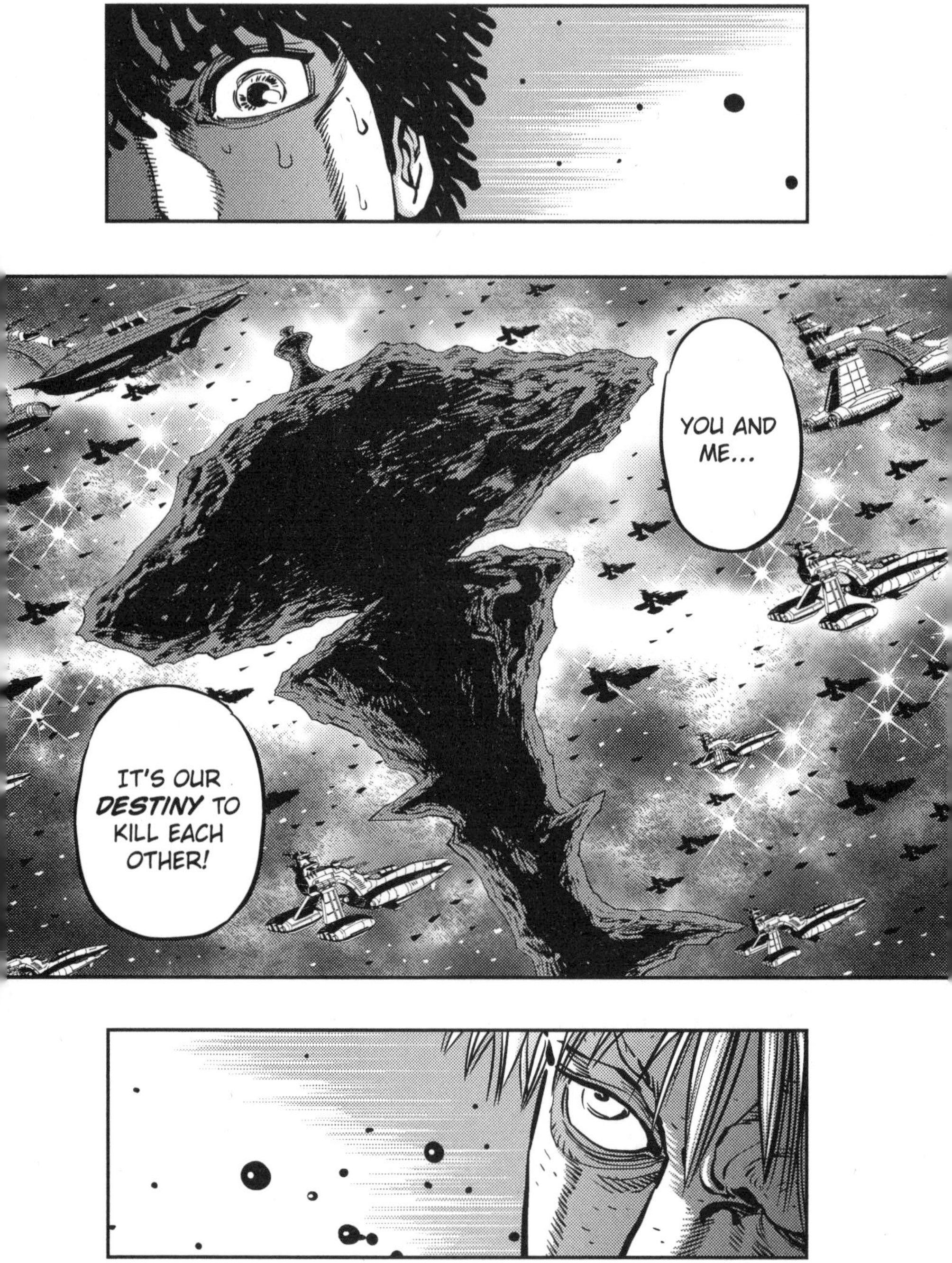
YOU AND ME...
IT'S OUR DESTINY TO KILL EACH OTHER!

MOBILE SUIT GUNDAM - THUNDERBOLT - VOL. 3 - END

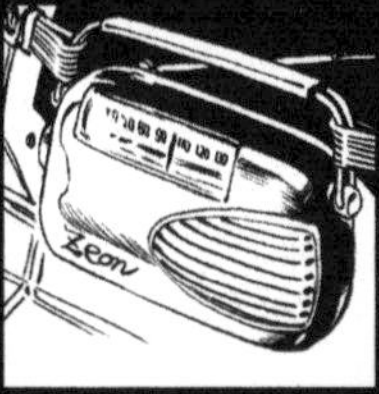
Zeon

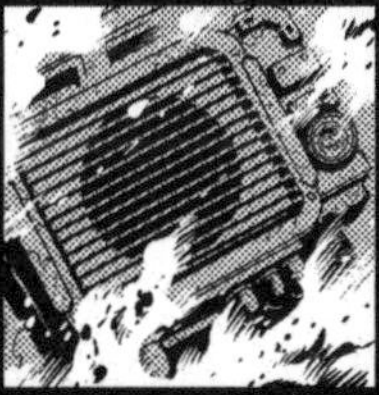

TO BE CONTINUED

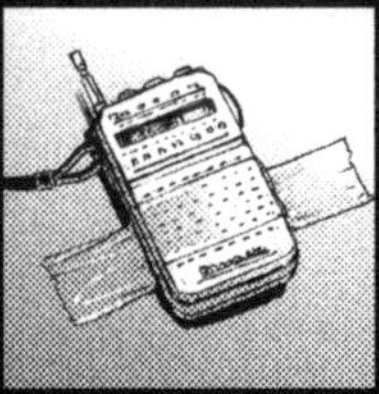

MOBILE SUIT GUNDAM
THUNDERBOLT 3

VIZ Signature Edition

STORY AND ART **YASUO OHTAGAKI**
Original Concept by **HAJIME YATATE** and **YOSHIYUKI TOMINO**

Translation **JOE YAMAZAKI**
English Adaptation **STAN!**
Touch-up Art & Lettering **EVAN WALDINGER**
Cover & Design **SHAWN CARRICO**
Editor **MIKE MONTESA**

MOBILE SUIT GUNDAM THUNDERBOLT Vol. 3 by Yasuo OHTAGAKI
Original Concept by Hajime YATATE, Yoshiyuki TOMINO
© 2012 Yasuo OHTAGAKI
© SOTSU·SUNRISE
All rights reserved.
Original Japanese edition published by SHOGAKUKAN.
English translation rights in the United States of America,
Canada, the United Kingdom, Ireland, Australia and New Zealand
arranged with SHOGAKUKAN.

ORIGINAL COVER DESIGN / Yoshiyuki SEKI for VOLARE inc.

Printed in the U.S.A.

Published by VIZ Media, LLC
P.O. Box 77010
San Francisco, CA 94107

10 9 8 7 6 5 4 3 2 1
First printing, May 2017

VIZ SIGNATURE

www.viz.com

Hey! You're Reading in the Wrong Direction!

This is the _end_ of this graphic novel!

To properly enjoy this VIZ graphic novel, please turn it around and begin reading from **right to left.** Unlike English, Japanese is read right to left, so Japanese comics are read in reverse order from the way English comics are typically read.

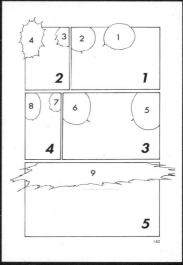

Follow the action this way

This book has been printed in the original Japanese format in order to preserve the orientation of the original artwork. Have fun with it!